Native Peoples
of the Southwest

Native Peoples of the Southwest

NEGOTIATING LAND, WATER, AND ETHNICITIES

Edited by Laurie Weinstein

Native Peoples of the Americas
Laurie Weinstein, General Editor

Bergin & Garvey
Westport, Connecticut • London

Library of Congress Cataloging-in-Publication Data

Native peoples of the Southwest : negotiating land, water, and ethnicities / edited by
Laurie Weinstein.
    p. cm.—(Native peoples of the Americas, ISSN 1521–5091)
   Includes bibliographical references and index.
   ISBN 0–89789–674–2 (alk. paper)—ISBN 0–89789–904–0 (pbk.)
   1. Indians of North America—Land tenure—Southwest, New. 2. Indians of North
America—Southwest, New—Ethnic identity. 3. Indians of North America—Southwest,
New—Government relations. 4. Land tenure—Government policy—Southwest, New. 5.
Water rights—Southwest, New. 6. Southwest, New—Environmental conditions. 7.
Southwest, New—Social conditions. I. Weinstein, Laurie Lee—II. Series.
E78.S7N38   2001
305.897—dc21   00–051924

British Library Cataloguing in Publication Data is available.

Library of Congress Catalog Card Number: 00–051924
ISBN: 0–89789–904–0 (pbk.)

First published in 2001

Bergin & Garvey, 88 Post Road West, Westport, CT 06881
An imprint of Greenwood Publishing Group, Inc.
www.greenwood.com

Printed in the United States of America

The paper used in this book complies with the
Permanent Paper Standard issued by the National
Information Standards Organization (Z39.48–1984).

10 9 8 7 6 5 4 3 2 1

O'odham Dances

'E-atkǐ 'ep 'ai mat o 'e-keihi g o'odham
o 'e-keihi kut hab masma ab o 'i ha-miabǐ g ju:kǐ
'apt ge cuhug oidk o ka:d mat hab o kaijjid:

  "'oig 'o, 'oig 'o
  'at hahawa o ma:si
  'oig 'o, 'oig 'o
  'am o aṣkia wi'is g ñeñe'i
  'oig 'o, 'oig 'o
  'at hahawa o 'i-ceṣ g taṣ
  'oig 'o, 'oig 'o
  'am o aṣkia wi'is g s-cuhug
  'oig 'o, 'oig 'o."

It is the time for the ritual.
To dance, to sing so that rain may come,
so that the earth may be fixed one more time.
Throughout the night,
a night too short for such important work,
the people converge energies.
They call upon the night.
They call upon the stars in the darkness.
They call upon the hot breezes.
They call upon the heat coming off the earth.
They implore all animals.
The ones that fly in the sky.
The ones that crawl upon the earth.
The ones that walk.
The ones that swim in the water and
the ones that move in between water, sky, and earth.
They implore them to focus on the moisture.
All are dependent.
From the dark dryness of the desert,
on that one night the call of the people is heard,

It is heard by the oceans, winds, and clouds.
All respond sympathetically.
Throughout the night you hear the one who is assigned yelling:

    "'oig 'o, 'oig 'o
    before it becomes light
    'oig 'o, 'oig 'o
    there are still songs to be sung
    'oig 'o, 'oig 'o
    before the sun comes up
    'oig 'o, 'oig 'o
    there is still a little bit of night left.

With the dawn we face the sunrise.
We face it with all our humility.
We are mere beings.
All we can do is extend our hands toward the first light.
In our hands we capture the first light.
We take it and cleanse ourselves.
We touch our eyes with it.
We touch our faces with it.
We touch our hair with it.
We touch our limbs.
We rub our hands together, we want to keep this light with us.
We are complete with this light.
This is the way we begin and end things.

Ofelia Zepeda

Contents

Part II Views from the Pueblos and Beyond

**Part III The Melting Pot: Water, Land, and Conflict in
Historical Perspective**

Illustrations

FIGURES

PHOTOGRAPHS

TABLES

Series Foreword

Native Peoples of the Southwest: Negotiating Land, Water, and Ethnicities represents another book in the series, *Native Peoples of the Americas*. It is difficult for the general editor of the series to write an introduction to a book that she has also edited, given her intellectual and emotional commitment to this project for over three years.

The *Native Peoples of the Southwest* examines the history of land and water relations in the region. Each contributor provides a glimpse into the complex nexus of relationships that have shaped the American Southwest over the past 12,000 years. The book begins with a lengthy overview of the history of the native peoples in the region. I include the Hispano populations as native, as well as the local Indian tribes, since the Hispano presence in the Southwest goes back to, at least, the sixteenth century. The first section of the book discusses the prehistory of the region with a focus on innovative Native American farming and water conservation practices. Many of the local Indian tribes, in fact, still use the practices of their ancestors. In the second section of the book, native peoples describe their own history and the sacredness of their resources to their own identities. The last section details some of the common contemporary problems with natural resources: current litigation, misinterpretation of Mexican land grants, land disputes between Indian tribes, and the interplay between ethnicity, power, and resources in both ritual and practice.

As I point out in the preface to the book, where this anthology falls short is in trying to accomplish too much. The book only covers portions of the American Southwest, primarily Arizona and New Mexico. Many issues are raised, such as the history of water litigation, the history of Indian, Hispano, and Anglo relations, inter-Indian relationships, and ideations of landscape and meaning to all populations. At the very least, I hope, readers will appreciate the enormous complexity of the problems that provide both the backdrop of and the future to the Southwest.

Native Peoples of the Americas covers indigenous people in North, Middle, and South America. Each volume explores the history and cultural survival of native peoples by telling their unique stories. Some volumes focus on competing ethnicities and the struggle for resources; other volumes illuminate the archaeology and ethnohistory of particular regions; and still others explore gender relations, warfare, and native cosmologies and ethnobotanies. Yet, despite the particular foci or theoretical frameworks of the editor and the contributors, all volumes reveal the rich cultural tapestry of the American continents. Together they chronicle common historical themes: despite the invasion of foreign explorers, traders, militia, missionaries, and colonists beginning in the late sixteenth century; despite rapid native depopulation because of disease and overt Anglo policies of ethnocide; despite the penetration of a capitalist market system into tribal economies, native peoples have survived.

Laurie Weinstein
General Editor
Native Peoples of the Americas

Preface

Ironically, as I sit here at my desk in New England, we are experiencing the worst drought in 70 years. Even here, too, in the rolling green hills crosscut by meandering streams and rivers, water is an issue. But unlike the experience in the Southwest, water diversion, irrigation, and entrapment did not figure significantly in either the prehistoric or the historic periods of settlement. While New England Indian and then, later, Anglo settlements, were defined by river drainages, water was important for transportation, communication, fishing and industry, and not for irrigation. The rain clouds furnished the waters for the crops. No katchinas danced in the plazas to ensure the spring arrival of the rains. Yet, water in New England, was just as elemental and just as sacred to all its peoples as water in the Southwest.

For all peoples, on all continents, and for all times, water has been the blood of life. It is fitting then, that this book about the peoples of the Southwest be dedicated to an examination of water in a land that has historically been dry. Land rights and ethnicity also played key parts in shaping the history of this region. The Southwest became an important frontier for Spanish and then Anglo explorers and colonizers who battled with the native occupants for strategic locations: choice lands next to water. Each one of these groups who eventually made the Southwest their home was ethnically quite different. They represented diverse histories and cultures and yet, despite their differing nationalities, classes, religions, and world views, they all called the Southwest home. Just like New England, the Southwest became a frontier of possibilities with each new group that arrived.

The Southwest region includes modern day Arizona, New Mexico, southern

Utah, Nevada, and Colorado, and northern Mexico. Ideally, this book would include articles about land, water, and ethnicity from each of these areas. Instead, this book focuses primarily upon one part of the region: Arizona and New Mexico. Despite this limitation in coverage, the book spans prehistoric through contemporary times and touches upon some of the unique ways in which all settlers—Indians, Hispanos, and Anglos—have struggled to access both sufficient water and land, as well as how they have negotiated each other's identities. My goal is to demonstrate the enormous complexity of these issues against the backdrop of time and place.

Acknowledgments

I am indebted to many people who helped make this dream of writing a book on the Southwest a reality. First, and foremost, I wish to thank Dr. Marianne Stoller. I took my very first anthropology class at Colorado College with her, and I've been hooked ever since. She's been a great friend and a mentor throughout my career as an anthropologist. She met with me on several occasions to help me plan this book, and she also suggested contributors.

I also wish to thank my second mentor from graduate school at Southern Methodist University, Dr. Anne Woosley. She was the Chair of my dissertation committee back when I was writing about the Wampanoag of New England. (Somehow, I think I had it backward—I should have started in the Southwest with both Marianne and Anne and then moved east.) Dr. Woosley was also kind enough to read through portions of this manuscript and make suggestions.

I send a very heartfelt thank you to the wonderful people at the University of Arizona. Dr. Hartman Lomawaima, the Associate Director of Arizona State Museum, invited me to spend my sabbatical at the museum in the spring of 1997 and then invited me back in 1998 to complete my research. He has been absolutely wonderful to me and introduced me to many fine people at Arizona State Museum who helped me with this book in one way or another. I also want to thank the directors of the museum for making Hartman's offer official: Dr. Ray Thompson and Dr. George Gumerman.

The staff at the museum library, especially Ms. Madelyn Cook and Ms. Mary Stephenson, were extremely helpful and provided me with space and a great deal of assistance. I knew that if I ever needed a resource, I could go to Madelyn, and she would find it, and even send it to me, once I returned to Connecticut.

Ms. Karen Lominac assisted me with all my computer needs and was always cheerful, no matter when I knocked on the door. Various faculty at the museum and in the Department of Anthropology at the University of Arizona were kind enough to meet with me to share their expertise: Drs. Suzanne and Paul Fish, Dr. Thomas Sheridan, Dr. Robert Adams, Dr. Nancy Parezo, Dr. Lynn Teague, Dr. Emory Sekaquaptewa, and Dr. Thomas McQuire.

Dr. Joseph Wilder, editor of the *Journal on the Southwest*, met with me to discuss my work and make recommendations, and his office kindly provided journal copies when I was missing needed readings for my research.

Dr. Ofelia Zepeda (Languages) and Dr. Michael Meyer (History) took a great deal of their time to discuss my project and to make recommendations. Dr. Jerold Levy (History) was kind enough to send me materials about the Hopi-Navajo land contest.

A very special thank you to Ms. Shoshana Green (Hebrew Languages), along with Fudge and Harris, who housed and fed me on both trips to the Southwest. Shoshana helped me navigate Tucson and the university, and she became a good friend as well.

People outside the university who were also instrumental in my work included Dr. Jose Rivera (University of New Mexico), his brother Lloyd Rivera, Dr. Tim Baugh (Rio Grande Foundation for Communities and Cultural Landscapes), Ms. Loretta Jackson (Hualapai Tribe), Mr. Roland Manakaja (Havasupai Tribe), Ms. Maxine Seletstewa (Hopi Tribe), Dr. Rina Swentzell (Santa Clara Pueblo), and Jonathon Mabry (Desert Archaeology). They either reviewed manuscripts, discussed contributor chapters, sent me materials, or made recommendations.

I was very privileged to work with outstanding scholars in the preparation of this work. Each one of the contributors offered advice and came through with articles, books, recommendations, etc. I could not have completed this book without their much-appreciated expertise: Drs. Suzanne and Paul Fish, Dr. Kurt Anschuetz, Mr. Angelo Joaquin, Mr. Nathan Allen, Mr. Roger Anyon, Mr. T. J. Ferguson, Dr. Frances Levine, Dr. Marianne Stoller, Ms. Maria Varela, Mr. David Brugge, Dr. Sylvia Rodriquez and Dr. Adrian Bustamante. I especially wish to thank Kurt—we met one afternoon and discussed landscape in the southwestern sense; he made a lot of copies of pertinent readings and then continued to e-mail his answers to my unending questions.

Bergin and Garvey Press, the publisher of this book and my series, has been exceedingly helpful and supportive throughout my publishing career with them. Of special mention is my friend and advisor there, Jane Garry. I would also like to thank Lynn Taylor and Lynda Harris. All have helped me bring this and the other volumes to fruition.

On the Connecticut homefront, I send a very special thank you to my wonderful neighbors, Rachel, Harriett, and Glen Lebetkin who took care of my pets while I was away. They nursed Marvin Harris, the bunny, back to health from his deathbed. They drove him to the vet in a blinding snowstorm in the middle of the night. When Marvin died this fall they were there to comfort me through my grief.

Denise Wilkinson, Epson Computers, enabled me to finish my manuscript at home by replacing my old printer with a new one. I am eternally grateful!

I thank my colleagues and friends at Western Connecticut State University for affording me the opportunity to go out west. Many of them also gave me needed reassurance: Dr. James Roach, Dr. Gene Buccini, Mr. Jerry Bannister, Dr. Ros Kopfstein, Ms. Cathie Mahoney, Dr. Susan Maskel, Dr. Paul Simon, Dr. Rolf Johnson, Ms. Beverly Dumonski, Ms. Barb Hall, Dr. Katy Wiss, Mr. Dennis McCarty, and especially Deseree and Scott Heme.

Lastly I wish to thank my own family of people and partners. My parents have always been there to support me, even when I said I wanted to become an anthropologist. My brother, Dr. David Weinstein and his wife, Dr. Gale Sigal, have been good sounding boards for my academic journey. Then, of course, there are the four-pawed beings with whom I share my house: my long time companion Kroeber, along with Darwin, Franz, Rufus Leakey, Jane "Goodie" Goodall, Pete, Marvin, Mary Douglas, and Max Weber (the bunny who was rescued from a restaurant). In loving memory of my wonderful Aunt Miriam.

Timeline for the Southwest

9,500–6,000 B.C.   Paleo Indian Cultural Time Period. These widespread hunters and gatherers were widely known for hunting now-extinct Pleistocene megafauna.

6,000–200 B.C.   Archaic Cultural Time Period. These more modern hunters and gatherers exploited a whole variety of smaller animals and a rich assortment of plant life that became available after the Pleistocene.

700–1400   Development of three of the great civilizations of the Southwest: Mogollon, Anasazi and Hohokam. These groups eventually evolved into some of the modern day rancheria and pueblo peoples.

1530s   Cabeza de Vaca wanders from southeastern North America to the southwest. He exaggerates the wealth of the southwestern Indians such as their emeralds, great homes, and cities. He therefore helps chart future Spanish exploration in the southwest region.

1540–1542   Coronado expedition. Coronado takes Cibola (Zuni) by force and then conquers the Hopi. He strains Pueblo hospitality. When he returns to New Spain (capitol of Mexico City), his treatment of the natives is investigated.

1573   Royal Orders for New Discoveries is the official document for the conquest of North America by Spain.

1598   Juan de Oñate has a contract from the king of Spain to settle the southwest. He proclaims that all Indians are under Spanish dominion. He calls the first pueblo he sees Santo Domingo. He moves across the Rio Grande and builds San Gabriel, which becomes the first Spanish town in the Southwest. He creates problems at Acoma pueblo and cuts off one foot of each adult male.

1680   Pueblo Revolt against Spanish rule. Led by Pope from San Juan Pueblo.

1692   Reconquest of New Mexico by Don Diego de Vargas. Recompilacion de las Indies (1681) becomes the Spanish law for dealing with the Indians.

1700   San Xavier del Bac established by the Jesuit Father Eusebio Kino just south of Tucson.

1772   Regulations of 1772. Establishes southwest frontier presidios (forts).

1783   Plan de Pitic established. This plan becomes the leading water document for New Spain. When new towns are established, the Spanish must ensure that everyone shares the water.

1790s   Non-Intercourse Acts passed by the nascent U.S. government. Only the federal government has the right to negotiate treaties and land deals with Indian tribes.

1821   Mexican Independence from Spain. Initially led by the priest Hidalgo. The infamous Santa Ana becomes one of the foremost emperors of the Mexican state.

1824   The U.S. Indian Bureau is established in the War Department.

1835   Texas declares itself a republic, independent of the Mexican state. Santa Ana moves to suppress the rebellion. The Alamo becomes the rallying point for Texas independence. Eventually, Santa Ana relinquishes Texas.

1844   Manifest Destiny is the leading charter for U.S. expansion in the west and southwest. U.S. President Polk favors a war with Mexico so he can annex Texas.

1846   United States and Mexico go to war.

1848   Treaty of Guadalupe Hildalgo. The United States gains New Mexico, Nevada, Arizona, California, and Texas. California Gold Rush. Streams of settlers move into the southwest and west and take over Indian lands.

1849   The Bureau of Indian Affairs is transferred to the Department of the Interior from the War Department.

1850   The territory of New Mexico is organized.

1853   Gadsden Purchase. Southern Arizona is ceded to the United States from Mexico. Tucson is included in this cession.

1863   The Territory of Arizona is created.

1887	Dawes Severalty Act passed by U.S. Congress. Authorizes Indian lands to be carved into individual allotments so that Indians will use lands like Anglos. Act leads to extreme Indian poverty and desperation. Many Indian lands end up in Anglo hands.
1890	Ghost Dance. This famous dance represented indigenous attempts to bring back their old way of life. Indians throughout the West started to learn this dance. The most tragic and famous Ghost Dance was held at Wounded Knee, South Dakota, where starving and desperate Sioux Indians were slaughtered by the United States cavalry.
1908	Winters Doctrine. This legislation was passed by the United States Supreme Court and it gave priority to prior use rights of Indians when dealing with water conflicts.
1912	New Mexico becomes a state.
1912	Arizona becomes a state.
1934	The Indian Reorganization Act passed by the U.S. Congress. It stops the allotment of Indian lands and provides for tribal ownership of land and Indian autonomy.
1946	Indian Claims Commission begins to provide compensation for the illegal seizure of Indian lands by states and individuals. Many claims are the result of the failure to abide by the Non-Intercourse Acts of the 1790s.
1966	National Historic Preservation Act passed by the U.S. Congress. This act is established to preserve historic and prehistoric properties that have significance to the nation's history. It was designed to extend and maintain the National Register of Historic Places.
1970	Blue Lake, the sacred lake to Taos Pueblo, is returned to the tribe.
1974	Navajo-Hopi Land Settlement Act attempts to resolve the long-standing dispute over boundaries between the two tribes. This dispute continues into the 21st century.
1978	Indian Freedom of Religion Act protects native rituals, practices and sacred lands.
1992	Native American Graves and Repatriation Act passed by the U.S. Congress. It is designed to restore human remains, funerary items, sacred objects and materials of cultural patrimony to Indian tribes. Every federal agency, and institutions receiving federal monies, must inventory their Native American possessions and return remains and items that fall under this law.

1

Introduction

Laurie Weinstein

On one of my first trips to the Southwest, I was in awe of its beauty. It had a certain pull and mystique that still captures my imagination. I flew over rugged mountains covered with pine trees in the four corners region of Colorado. I saw bare, reddish mountains that surrounded huge reservoirs. These reservoirs were created by monumental dams, like the one at Lake Powell, in southeastern Utah. The waterworks belie one great quest—the search for sustainable water in a land that is unforgiving. Many Spanish explorers died thirsty trying to chart a course across the region when the rivers they were following suddenly disappeared. Even the Anasazi Indians, centuries before, were forced to abandon some settlements because their water also ran dry. I flew over huge canyons, like the Grand Canyon, and I marveled at its color, depth, and prodigious beauty. The landscape became less mountainous, and also much less green, as I flew further south and west. Tall peaks poked out of the barren landscape. Deep, dry river channels and arroyos were cut through the sandy, red soil. Eventually, I crossed the Sonoran desert, where I saw tall saguaros reaching up to the sky. My plane landed in Tucson, and I was blinded by both the sunshine and the intense heat of the desert. "Welcome," my host said. "You have arrived in the Southwest!"

This varied landscape includes many extremes: elevations can go from near sea level in desert areas to over 13,000 feet in the Rocky Mountains (Woodbury 1979: 24–25). Just within the Sonoran Desert alone (that stretches from southern Arizona to northwestern Mexico) there are numerous elevational extremes from mountaintop to floodplain (Fish and Nabhan 1991: 31). Richard Woodbury (1979: 25) divides the Southwest into four physiographic zones which generally follow a north-south gradient, much like my plane ride mentioned above: mountains, plateau, basin and range, and plains. The highest mountains are, of course, the Rocky Mountains, in the northeast section of the Southwest. These pine-covered mountains provide a great deal of spring melt water for the rivers that water the southwest, such as the Colorado, Rio Grande, and Pecos rivers (Woodbury 1979: 25). The Colorado plateaus are characterized by deep canyons and sandstone mesas that are dotted with shrubby trees, pinon and juniper pine (Woodbury 1979: 25). The basin and range areas have stretches of hot, dry desert along with intermittent mountain ranges (the Sonoran Desert would fall within this province). The high plains stretch into northwestern New Mexico. Map 1.1 shows elevational zones and major rivers and features.

One of the most unifying themes of this whole region is the search for water. Water was an issue to the prehistoric Indians. Pueblo Indians developed both a rich mythology and a ceremonial cycle in order to bring rain clouds. Hispanos established acequia communities and codified a whole series of legislation so that they could preserve and protect water rights. Anglos fought Indians and Hispanos over water by using their own legal traditions; litigation still continues unabated today. Who owns the water? Who has the right to use it?

PREHISTORY

Archaeologists trace the prehistory of the Southwest back more than 12,000 years. The earliest recognized stage is the Paleo Indian stage which lasted from 9,500 to 6,000 B.C. (Plog 1997: 37). The Southwest environment was comprised of "complex localized mosaics of many different types of plants" (Plog 1997: 37) which were appealing to a wide variety of big and small game. Paleo Indians are often referred to as big game hunters, and, indeed, many of them hunted huge, now extinct large animals, like mammoths and giant sloth, that once thrived at the end of the Pleistocene Ice Age when Paleo Indians developed highly mobile hunting and gathering subsistence strategies. Some groups of Paleo Indians, especially those to the north and west of the American Southwest region, were more dependent on the smaller game and plants available in their environments than on big game (Plog 1997: 38).

The Paleo Indians were followed by the Archaic culture period hunters and gatherers (6000 to 200 B.C.), who took advantage of the ameliorating climatic conditions. They gathered the increasing variety of wild plant foods that became available with the early Holocene environments. These Archaic Indians were characterized by new technologies, including a variety of projectile point styles and ground stone tools, like manos and metates, used for processing new vegetal foods. By the end of the Archaic period, groups were starting to work more intensively with local plants, settle down a bit more, and begin a way of life that would gradually lead to farming and village life.

Did Archaic cultures gradually evolve into the Southwestern farmers of the Early Agricultural period? Archaeological and linguistic evidence links agricul-

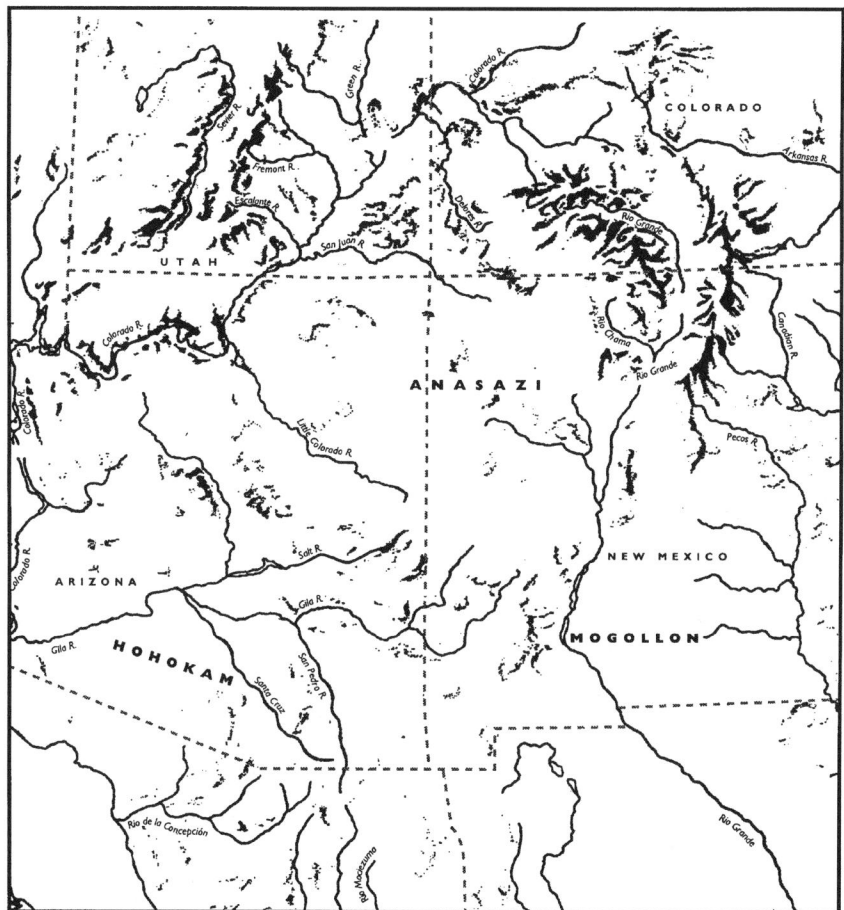

Map 1.1 Archaeological areas

ture with the spread of the Uto-Aztecan language family (includes the Hopi, Piman, and Tohono O'odham). One possibility is that after 3,500 B.C., "Uto Aztecan speakers moved into the southern Southwest from . . . the uplands of northern Mexico; later, agriculture and other Mesoamerican traits like pottery, figurines, and bell-shaped pits diffused rapidly across a linguistic and cultural continuum" (Mabry 1999: 6). Some of the earliest evidence for farming now comes from the Tucson, Arizona, area where the cultural resource management firm of Desert Archaeology has uncovered irrigation networks that precede Hohokam (see Fish and Fish, chapter 2 in this volume). Desert's work suggests that farming settlements were established on the floodplains of the Santa Cruz river between 800 B.C. and A.D. 150 (Mabry 1997:1). These early settlements, which included house groups with communal structures, plazas, storehouses, and cemeteries (Mabry 1997: 1), foreshadowed the birth of large scale agricultural settlements that became distinctive to the Southwest.

The earliest cultigens of corn, beans, and squash originated in Mesoamerica between 6,000 to 8,000 years ago. Corn and squashes were domesticated first and were followed by beans. All were originally wild weeds, but with experimentation, were turned into food crops that increasingly comprised native diets throughout most of North America (see Woodbury and Zubrow 1979; Weinstein 1983). The cultigens gradually diffused north into the Southwest (Plog 1997: 52). Maize, beans, squash, and possibly tobacco and cotton, may have been adopted together as a crop complex (Mabry 1997: 1).

Between A.D. 200 and A.D. 500 the three major southwestern archaeological traditions began to develop. The Hohokam, Mogollon and Anasazi traditions were identified by archaeologists on the basis of unique settlement patterns, architecture, ceramic styles, art work, trade goods, and other artifacts (Gumerman and Gell-Mann 1994: 17–18). While not exclusive, these groups spawned many local variations. See Map 1.1, which shows these archaeological groups.

The Hohokam principally occupied the Salt and Gila river drainages from northern Mexico to north central Arizona. They built extensive irrigation networks, ball courts, and platform mounds and lived in wattle and daub housing (Plog 1997: 73). Their artifacts (such as copper bells and macaw feathers) and settlement patterns (with the platform mound and ball courts) suggest a probable link to the great civilizations to the south in Mesoamerica (Gumerman and Gell-Mann 1994: 19–21). The Hohokam were superb agriculturists and made extensive use of desert plants of the Sonoran environment (Fish and Fish, chapter 2 this volume). The Hohokam developed increasingly complex irrigation communities alongside the canals (Gregory 1991: 170–171). Irrigation, along with dry and floodwater farming techniques enabled the Hohokam to harvest an abundance of resources from a variety of environmental zones, especially when compared to their neighbors, the Mogollon and the Anasazi.

The Mogollon lived in southeastern Arizona and southwestern New Mexico. They, along with the Anasazi to the north, lived in apartment style villages known as "pueblos." The pit house was also distinctive to both of these groups, and archaeologists trace the evolution of the pit house from its use as a semi-subterranean apartment house to a "kiva," or ceremonial chamber. Modern day Pueblos still use kivas for their annual round of sacred ceremonies. The Anasazi also built Great Kivas, such as those found in Chaco Canyon in northwestern New Mexico. These huge structures linked Chaco to outlying settlements—via a series of well-worn roads—for religious, economic and sociopolitical activities (see Vivian 1997; see also Crown and Judge 1991). The Anasazi were also linked to Mesoamerica, and they too imported copper bells and macaw feathers (H. Wolcott Toll 1991: 84–85).

Anasazi and Mogollon peoples did not build as extensive irrigation networks as the Hohokam, but they did innovate technologically simple, yet amazingly effective, means to control water. Gravel mulching, check dams, cobble terraces, and redirection of water runoff after rains, were just a few of the many techniques they used to harvest water (See Anschuetz, chapter 3 in this volume). Kurt Anschuetz (this volume) writes that Puebloan farmers were keenly perceptive about their environment. They understood when to plant, what seeds to plant, how to protect the seedlings, how to preserve water, the importance of seed diversity, etc.

Beginning about A.D. 1140 many of the great prehistoric Indian societies underwent a series of major transformations. Many sites were abandoned; the great Chaco road system collapsed; warfare became more endemic, and eventually, a long-standing drought spread over parts of the region (Gumerman and Gell-Mann 1994: 22–23). Popular and academic writers formerly romanticized these problems. The prehistoric groups "disappeared" much like the enigmatic water. Their populations grew too large for the carrying capacity of their lands and then they simply "vanished." Current thought is more enlightened. There are a complex number of overlapping issues that may explain the Southwest abandonments, such as periods of drought and/or insufficient water, along with severe population pressure, deforestation (timber was used for firewood and for building), and an inability of these large scale regional systems to sustain their members (see Crown and Judge 1991: 303–305; Plog 1997: 111–116).

Native people, however, have a different take on their own histories. "The Tribes do not see them [sites] as abandoned but as places imbued with life that are monuments marking their ancestral migrations. Hopi and Zuni maintain none of these sites have been abandoned, but should be considered as having been left by their ancestors with the intent of fulfilling a purpose" (Anyon 2000).

When the large villages could no longer be sustained by traditional farming, prehistoric groups picked up and moved away to found new, smaller settlements that were scattered over the landscape. Many of their new settlements were situated in defensive locations—up high or tightly clustered together (see LeBlanc 1999; Gumerman and Gell-Mann 1994) because internecine violence and death by trauma had become more common.[1] Despite all these problems in the late prehistoric period, members of these groups did survive, and they became the ancestors of contemporary Indian societies. Anthropologists suggest that the Hohokam are related to the Pima and O'odham while the Anasazi and Mogollon are ancestral to the Pueblos. Tribes may have different interpretations, however, of their historic roots. The Hopi and Zuni peoples, for example, see themselves related to Anasazi, Mogollon, and Hohokam (Anyon 2000).

CONTEMPORARY INDIAN SOCIETIES

Modern day Indian groups have distinctive languages and cultures. They are represented by several language families (the Pueblo groups are italicized): Uto-Aztecan (e.g., *Hopi*, Pima, Tohono O'odham), Zuni (*Zuni*), Keresan (e.g.,

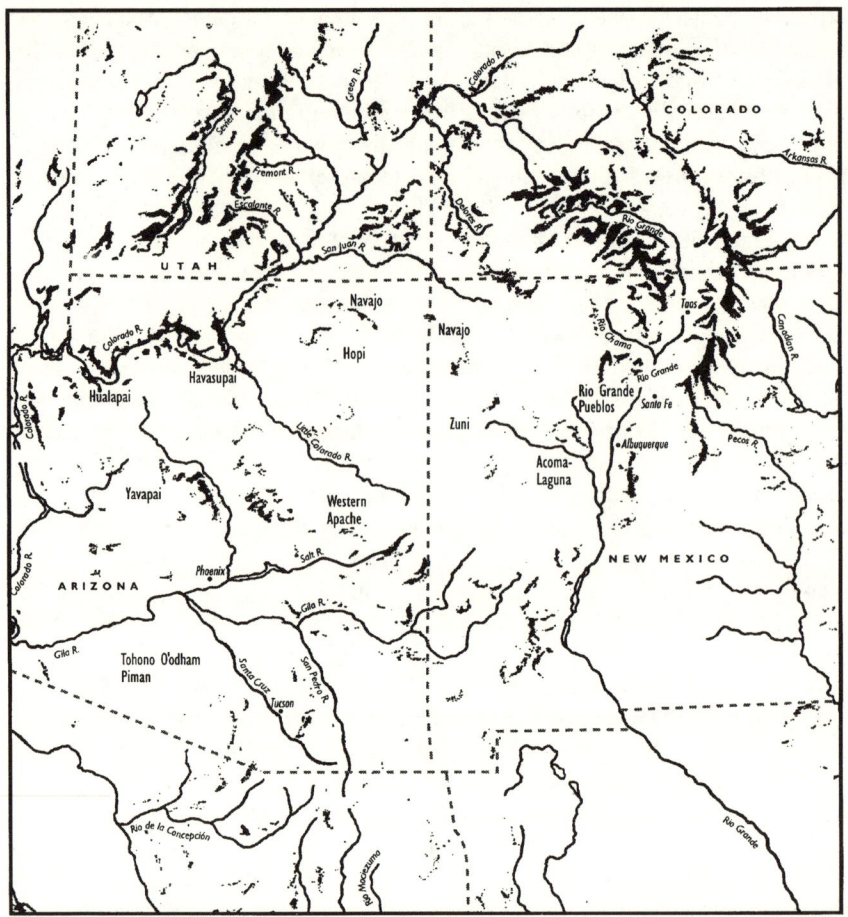

Map 1.2 Modern day Indian groups

Acoma), Tanoan (e.g., *Picuris, Sandia, Isleta, San Juan, Tesuque, Jemez*), Athapaskan (Navajo and Apache), and Yuman (e.g., Havasupai, Walapai, Yavapai,
Maricopa, Mohave, among others) and two broad settlement patterns: the nucleated apartment style pueblos and the dispersed settlement rancherias (Plog
1997: 22–23; Kehoe 1992: 127). Map 1.2 shows the distribution of modern day
groups.

Many of the pueblos consist of tightly packed adobe brick or wattle and daub
houses, some several stories high, surrounding a central plaza and kivas, or
ceremonial chambers. The name, "pueblo," in fact, refers to their apartment style
housing. All Pueblos are farmers, and most of their elaborate ceremonies
throughout the year are devoted to either coaxing precious rain from the sky (or

to help "sustain the movement of water between the natural and supernatural worlds of their cosmos" [Anschuetz, chapter 3 this volume]) or to ensure fertility and abundance. Most of the ceremonies are designed around the agricultural cycle. Ceremonies reflect the Puebloan world view and the beliefs that humans have a reciprocal relationship with nature. By honoring nature with ritual they ensure that nature will in turn honor humans with nourishment (see Ortiz 1972: 135–161). Of no small significance are ceremonies, dances, and even depictions on pottery of thunderbolts, designed to bring/move rain.

Peter Whitely (1998: 192) provides an excellent summary of the sacredness of water to the Hopi Pueblo Indians:

It is hard to imagine anything more sacred—as substance or symbol—than water in Hopi religious thought and practice. . . . Springs, water and rain are focal themes in ritual costumes, kiva iconography, mythological narratives, personal names, and many, many songs, which call cloud chiefs from the varicolored directions to bear their fructifying essence back into the cycle of human, animal, and vegetal life. That essence—as clouds, rain, and other water forms—manifests the spirits of the dead. When people die, in part, they become clouds; songs call to the clouds as ascendant relatives. Arriving clouds are returning ancestors, their rain both communion with, and blessing of, the living. The waters of the earth (where katchina spirits live) are, then, transubstantiated human life.

One of the more conspicuous characteristics of many Western Pueblo societies was the katchina cult. Its beginnings can be traced back to the Anasazi and Mogollon peoples and the development of plazas for the performance of public rituals (Plog 1997: 163; see Adams, 1991). Katchinas are colorful beings associated with the ancestors and with rain. Each January, the children of the Hopi villages look to the sky for rainclouds. When they see the rainclouds they know the katchinas are coming and will spend half the year in the village where they will lead dances in the plaza and bring the much-needed rain to nourish the crops. Then, they will disappear through the sipapu in the San Francisco peaks and return to the underworld (Plog 1997: 160). Zuni katchinas visit throughout the year and return to Kolthu/wala:wa (located at the confluence of the Zuni and Little Colorado rivers) (Anyon 2000).

The rancheria peoples had a different settlement and subsistence pattern than the Pueblos:

Most rancheria groups depended to some extent on farming, but the degree of dependence varied. Those who were mainly farmers resided in riverine areas such as the Colorado, Sonora, or Gila Rivers, inhabiting a single village, or moving between two villages during the course of the year. Other people, such as the Havasupai, consumed wild plants and animals, or like the Navajo, herded flocks of sheep and goats after they were introduced by the Spanish. Such groups were more mobile, often inhabiting primary villages in different ecological zones during the summer and winter, and establishing secondary camps for the collection of different resources or to move herds to new grazing areas.

The hunting and gathering Tohono O'odham moved several times each year as local resources became exhausted, relying on a widespread network of kin to obtain information on the availability of resources in different areas. (Plog 1997: 23)

The Athapaskan speaking Navajo and Apache Indians moved into the Southwest from the north approximately five hundred years ago (the 1500s). When they first moved into the Southwest they were hunters and gatherers. The horse, however, radically changed these groups. The Apache became mounted warriors whose raids were greatly feared by Pueblos and Spanish in later centuries. Horses and other livestock were introduced into the Southwest by the Spanish in the mid-sixteenth century, and these animals quickly revolutionized many Indian societies from the Plains to the Southwest. The Navajo adopted horses, and sheep, and sheep herding became the foundation of their culture. Nancy Parezo (1996: 14–23) notes the cultural significance of sheep to the Navajo when she says that these animals became security both psychologically and materially. Navajo ate mutton, they wove beautiful blankets from wool, and sheep kept the extended families together.

The Pais, or Upland Yumans, lived in a large diversified territory that includes lands from deserts to mountains (Parezo 1996: 94). The Yavapais lived in the desert and mountain areas; the Hualapais lived in riverine, as well as, canyon lands; and the Havasupais lived part of their year in steep canyon lands (Parezo 1996: 94). All groups were hunters, gatherers, and farmers, and like the Navajo, they too had to fight to keep their lands and culture. Miners and ranchers took their lands, leading to a series of conflicts called the Hualapai Wars and then eventually to forced relocations on reservations (Parezo 1996: 100–108).

The Pimans and Tohono O'odham (formerly called Papago), represent the last groups I will mention. They were also desert farmers, like many of the Yumans. For centuries, they were able to cultivate their crops by irrigating their fields; indeed, many scholars believe that they are descendants of the Hohokam who were well known for their extensive and intricate irrigation networks. Today, these groups are embroiled in bitter fights over water. These groups harvested a variety of crops from tepary beans to saguaro cactus fruits. Some groups even grew wheat and became so successful that they supplied Anglos with food (see Sheridan 1996: 133–134). Despite their huge agricultural successes, these groups faced severe water shortages, but not because of their own mismanagement of water. Anglos began tapping their waters and effectively cut off supplies of water to the Indians downstream (see Editor's Note in Allen, chapter 5 in this volume). In one of the cruelest pages from history, the Akimel O'odham went from being a very prosperous nation to paupers after their waters were tapped and Anglos dug a huge canal. The U.S. government failed to intervene on their behalf (see Sheridan 1996: 134–135).

THE COMING OF THE SPANISH

When the Spanish began their explorations of the Southwest in the sixteenth century, they were both intrigued and repelled by the native peoples they encountered. The Spanish quickly wore out their welcome among the Pueblos by taxing Indian farmers with continued demands for food and water. In some cases, the Spanish simply took over the pueblos and forced the occupants to move. Cabeza de Vaca (1530s) was one of the first explorers who came in search of emeralds and other riches. Cabeza de Vaca's own story in the Southwest was rather colorful. He landed in Florida in 1528 and wandered across the Southeast. He was enslaved at one point and even shipwrecked, but he survived to meander his way across the Southwest with the help of a Black slave named Esteban. De Vaca learned Indian languages, survived as a noted medicine man and trader among the tribes, and became a champion of the Indian cause (see Weber 1992: 43–45 and White 1991: 5–6).

As a result of de Vaca's great travels, Viceroy Mendoza sent Marcos de Niza, along with Esteban, on a reconnaissance mission north from Mexico in 1538. De Niza reported a huge city (Cibola) and unbelievable riches in this new world (Weber 1992: 45–47; White 1991: 5–6). This new information prompted the Viceroy to send Francisco Vazquez de Coronado north in the 1540s. Coronado commanded one of Spain's greatest expeditions into the Southwest. Coronado was outfitted with cattle, soldiers, Mexican Indians, and priests. Coronado's legacy became the legacy of exploitation. When Pueblos along the Rio Grande could no longer feed Coronado's huge appetite, the Spaniard fought back and burned Indians at the stake (Weber 1992: 24, 46–49).

Juan de Oñate was probably even less well liked than Coronado by the Indians. Imagine his entrance into the pueblo he named "Santa Domingo" in 1598. He brought everyone together and read them a Spanish document that said that they were all now vassals of the Crown and must therefore embrace the King and the Catholic Church (Weber 1992: 77). Although the Pueblos may not have fully understood this new Spaniard's strange document at the time, they quickly began to experience its implications. The Pueblos were expected to feed and house Oñate's huge entourage. The Acoma became tired of extending so much hospitality and rebelled, but not before Oñate could punish the offenders by ordering the amputation of each adult male's right foot. While many Hispanos in the Southwest celebrate the bicentennial of Oñate's great exploration and settlement today, the Pueblos remember the severe punishment meted out to the Acoma (Weber 1992: 77–86).

In 1680 the Pueblos joined together and revolted against the Spanish. It was not until the 1690s that the Spanish could renew their toehold in the Southwest. When they returned, they remembered the lessons of the past. This second conquest was not as exacting, and a new set of laws, known as the *Recopilacion de las Indies*, guided Spanish and Indian relations (Meyer 1996: 111–115; Briggs and Van Ness 1987: 19). Indians and Spanish found common ground.

They began to work together to create irrigation networks, to afford mutual protection against Apache raids, and to meet the demands of a new *conquesitor*—the Anglos.

Despite common interests, their relationship post 1680 was still problematic, especially with regard to water. Hispanos brought thousands of head of cattle with them and established themselves in clustered communities. Both the population concentrations, as well as the enormous needs of cattle for water and forage, put severe pressures on the land (Meyer 1996: 49–50). Cattle, according to Michael Meyer (1996: 50), ate up the grasses faster than the grasses could regrow, leading to desertification with the erosion of the topsoil. Added to these problems were the multiple Hispanic and Indian users who tapped precious rivers for water. Communities upstream tended to divert waters away from communities downstream; water diversion led to a lot of contentious allegations. Meyer (1996: 53–57) chronicles some of the long-standing disputes between Indian and Hispanic communities at Taos, New Mexico, and Tucson, Arizona. The dispute in Tucson has evolved into an urban versus traditional conflict (see Joaquin, chapter 4 in this volume) and because of its long history, it might be instrumental to illuminate its complicated past.

Throughout the late colonial period, there were four competing demands on the limited Tucson water supply: the Pima village of Tucson (on the west bank of the Santa Cruz River); the Royal Presidio [Spanish military base] of San Augustin de Tucson (on the east bank of the Santa Cruz River); the communal mission lands of San Xavier del Bac; and the individual Indian plots of San Xavier . . . Shortly after Father Eusebio Kino founded the Jesuit mission of San Xavier del Bac in 1700, new agricultural fields were opened there. . . . [D]uring dry years irrigation at the mission prejudiced the Pima village of Tucson. . . . Periodically, until the expulsion of the Jesuits in 1767, quarrels over water were recorded. (Meyer 1996: 55)

Meyer (1996: 56–57) goes on to relate how the establishment of the Presidio at Tucson, with its subsequent pull on the Hispanic population to settle there, put new demands on the waters. Local Hispanic friars often championed the Indians' cause but to no avail. "When Tucson passed from Mexican to United States sovereignty with the Gadsden Purchase, the presidio . . . had legal right to half of the water" (Meyer 1996: 57).

A slightly different interpretation of Hispanic settlement is painted by Jose Rivera,[2] as well as Maria Varela (in chapter 9; see also Levine, chapter 7 this volume). Rivera says that Hispanos created an "acequia culture" that was "ecologically based from the outset" (Rivera 1998: 5). The *Recopilacion*, in fact, stipulated the kinds of lands and resources that should be used for planning new towns. Land and water policies became important parts of Hispano settlement. According to Rivera (1998: 9),

In the process of petitioning for lands, settlers had to specify the natural boundaries of the desired community land grant. The governor would then require an inspection to be conducted by the alcalde mayor of the jurisdiction. This official had to ascertain that the land in question was not already settled nor prejudicial to the welfare of an Indian pueblo. Part of his investigation also included an evaluation of the water supply needed for irrigation, for domestic use, and for the watering of livestock. To comply with Spanish land-distribution policies, the alcalde had to partition the land in a manner that would encourage "the tilling of the land and rearing of cattle." If these and other conditions were met, the governor would then confirm the grant and authorize the possession ceremony.

As a result of the aforementioned policies, acequia communities were established alongside rivers and streams throughout New Mexico. Water was diverted from the river; a series of hand-dug ditches carried the water to farmers' fields, and then the water was returned downstream back to the river.

THE COMING OF THE ANGLOS

Anglos had been trickling west for some time, but with the cession of much of the northern areas to Mexico in 1821, more and more Anglos headed west to find their fame and fortune. The Santa Fe trail system opened commerce between Mexicans, Americans, and Indians (see Jenkins and Schroeder 1974: 33–40). Trade, however, became a source of contention. Anglos from the newly created Republic of Texas attempted to divert commerce to them, and in 1846, war was declared between the U.S. and Mexico (Meinig 1971: 20–22). U.S. General Stephen Kearny "peacefully" conquered New Mexico and established Fort Marcy in Santa Fe, thereby establishing Santa Fe as one of the most important new outposts of the United States (Byrkit 1992: 337). Kearny proclaimed to the inhabitants of the newly conquered lands that they were now living in the Territory of the United States. Further, he promised to protect both their civil and property rights (Jenkins and Schroeder 1974: 47). Yet, despite his reassurance, rights were not respected. Section 10 of the Treaty of Guadalupe Hidalgo stipulated "protection of Mexican citizens' properties, customs, culture and religion" (Varela 1999). "This section was illegally stricken by Congress after the treaty was signed by Mexico; it however, remains forever in the hearts of those in the West whose ancestors passed down from generation to generation. . . ." (Varela 1999). Maria Varela (chapter 9 in this volume) writes about the effects of this treaty on native Hispanos and the unending conflicts over water that continue more than 100 years after the Treaty was signed. The Treaty of Guadalupe Hidalgo, followed by the Gadsden Purchase, conferred American status to most of what we now know as the American Southwest.

With the transfer of the region to American hands, Anglos established a regional railroad system that linked the Southwest to the rest of the U.S. The gold rush in California as well as cattle ranching and mining also enticed Anglos westward across the Southwest (Byrkit 1992: 337–338; Meinig 1971: 23, 35, 72–77). The floodgates had been opened and Anglos poured in.

The new Anglo invasion created a plethora of problems for both the Indians and the Hispanos. Spanish land grants which had been honored by the Mexican government were no longer protected under U.S. law. "Instead of attempting to learn how New Mexican authorities dealt with land grants, the U.S. imposed its own view of Spanish and Mexican law on the adjudication process—a view that was colored by the bias of a different legal system" (Briggs and Van Ness 1987: 26). In addition to the land grant confusion, continuing raids were made upon Pueblos and Hispanos by marauding Navaho, Ute, and Apache bands, which seized horses, cattle, and whatever else they could take. The Anglo presence merely provided another target for these Indian raids, and the Anglos fought back, quite often indiscriminately. They retaliated against any Indians, even those who had demonstrated friendship (see White 1991: 99–102).

By the end of the nineteenth century, Indian tribes throughout North America had been conquered in a series of brutal wars and forced evacuations from their homelands. Each Native American group and each Hispano community has a unique story to tell about themselves as their communities were engulfed by the larger Anglo society. Today, the Southwest has become a mecca for retirees, New Agers, holistic healers, and a whole variety of other "seekers" who are looking for a better way of life. As these new populations press into the Southwest, more and more water from the aquifers, the Colorado, Gila, Rio Grande, and Pecos rivers is being tapped, using modern technologies which have all but sucked the waters dry.

Water battles are now common place. Sylvia Rodriquez (1990) and Frances Levine (1990) show how these conflicts are artificially staged in the sense that despite the enormous amount of investigative research, the outcomes are usually clear: the research serves to justify the agendas of state and local governments, together with those of developers. Further, both researchers show that water and land litigation not only maintains the minority, dependent status of Indians and Hispanos relative to Anglos, but it also forces them to compete against each other. Levine (chapter 7 in this volume) details water rights adjudication in New Mexico. She notes "the privatization of rights changes a fundamental principle of traditional water use in which water is a shared resource and carries with it obligations for shared labor and wise-use responsibilities." Water has become a commodity, much like all other resources which can be bought and sold in a capitalistic economy.

SACRED GEOGRAPHIES

The Southwest is more than just a region. It is home to numerous sacred geographies about time, space, and place. For Indians and Hispanos, the landscape of the Southwest tells many stories. The stories provide a window into each group's past and from this window we can see how the different spaces in the Southwest become sacred places. The Hopi kachinas emerge into this world from the sipapu in the San Francisco peaks. Every direction is sacred in the Pueblo world. The Indians of Rio Grande "identify Sandia Mountain as the sacred peak of the south in their ideational landscapes. . . . [Sandia Pueblo] recently successfully reclaimed the west face of the mountain range for their community" (Anschuetz 1999). Taos Pueblo battled for Blue Lake because it was all-important to the practice of their private religious rituals—non-Indian intruders had undermined the Indians' use of the lake. The Navajo are battling the logging of their lands on Chuska Mountains. These lands are home to revered medicinal plants; they are also where people go to "make sacred offerings of white shell, turquoise, abalone and jet" (Rudner and Yellowtail 1994: 3). The expansion of the ski resort near Santa Fe threatens shrines of the Tesuque Indians (Anschuetz 1999). Even ancient pueblos are inhabited by the ancestors and no Anglo dare tread in areas of those remains that are deemed "too sacred."

Mount Taylor in the San Mateo Mountains of northwestern New Mexico is claimed as a sacred place by at least four different Indian tribes: Acoma, Laguna, Zuni, and Navajo (Blake 1999). Kevin Blake (1999) writes that these groups make sacred pilgrimages to the mountain, gather resources needed for their rituals, and even have mythologies concerning events that took place on the mountain in the past. "The Acoma believe the Rainmaker of the North lives on the mountain, the Laguna believe the mountaintop holds the secrets of rain, and during a drought the Zuni make a pilgrimage to a hole on the peak called Shiwanna Gacheti (Lightning Home)" (Blake 1999: 496). For the Navajo, Mount Taylor is one of the sacred peaks built by First Man and First Woman (Blake 1999: 503). Blake (1999: 503) goes on to say that in "Navajo tradition Mount Taylor is fastened to the earth with a great stone knife and adorned with turquoise, dark mist, deer, beaver, chipmunk, and mountain lion. On the summit the gods placed a turquoise bowl containing two bluebird eggs. The peak is inhabited by the deities Boy Who Carries One Turquoise and Girl who Carries One Grain of Corn."

Hispanos share similar views about their environment's sacredness. For them, the environment contains "religious places," meaning, that various landmarks carry names of individuals and events that are important in the Catholic religion. Hispanos have a tradition of naming landforms after saints, and Mary and God (Varela 1999). "For example, in the Tierra Amarilla land grant, the cliffs which dominate the valley are called the Brazos cliffs, from the original Spanish name 'Los Brazos de Maria' " (Varela 1999). "Similarly, Los Ojos [or the springs] is originally Los Ojos de Dios. . . . Springs are the eyes of God" (Varela 1999). Another Hispano type of sacred place refers to events or something that "happens" or to "an appearance, a tragedy, a death, and even the saving of someone from death" (Varela 1999). Landforms that look like the faces of Christ, Mary, the cross, or other such religious features are also sacred (Varela 1999). Lastly, moradas (where penitents go to worship) are "sacred places that are protected by spirits . . . sometimes in the form of ravens, eagles, coyotes, or other wildlife" (Varela 1999).

Humans are forever creating and recreating the shape of their worlds. They mediate between everyday existence, their historical past, and a future of what they might become (Hirsch 1995). This process also includes reference to "us" versus "them," or "insider" versus "outsider" (Hirsch 1995). For native Indians and Hispanos, their sacred shrines, structures, and directions are a part of a shared past that comprises their ethnicity. Their designated places on the landscape serve as boundary mechanisms which demark them (insiders of particular cultures) from outsiders. It is no wonder that water conflicts pit insiders against outsiders, especially when one group sees water as a sacred gift from the creator and the other group sees water as a divisible commodity.

As a cultural process, landscape is forever changing, evolving, moving, as societies continually layer on meaning and metaphor. "Places gather things in their midst—where 'things' connote various animate and inanimate entities. Places also gather experiences and histories, even languages and thoughts" (Casey 1996: 24). This arrangement of "gathering" is not haphazard, rather, it is a structured arrangement adhering to each group's own peculiar cultural values. When Hispanos discuss the various types of sacred places, they are providing outsiders with an emic view of the landscape that is much different than the Anglo or Indian views. Likewise, the special places that have gathered meaning for Indian peoples is peculiar to their identities. For the people of the Southwest, its rivers, mesas, rock formations, mountains, animals, and plants are all a part of the ongoing, timeless landscape.

ORGANIZATION OF THIS BOOK

This book will examine how the peoples of the Southwest negotiated land, water, and ethnicity. The first part, "The Process of Becoming," includes articles about the prehistory of the region. The chapters address agricultural technologies, especially those concerned with the conservation of water in the Sonoran Desert of Arizona and the Upper Rio Grande of New Mexico. The first chapter, written by Suzanne and Paul Fish, examines prehistoric farming in southern Arizona. They begin their work with a discussion of the Sonoran desert environment before going on to detail the ways in which the Hohokam varied their farming techniques (irrigation canals, planting in alluvial fans, diverting water, cobble fields, etc.) to meet the diverse challenges of that environment. Variation enabled the Hohokam to create "anthropogenic plant communities" that also served as important resources in times of need. Further, Hohokam used practices that conserved scarce resources, like wood and, of course, water. The authors close with a discussion about the dynamism of Hohokam culture: farming fit in with an integrated social system of "population, settlement and landuse" and enabled the Hohokam to tame more of the desert for agriculture than succeeding farmers were able to do in the Historic period.

The next chapter, written by Kurt Anschuetz, examines the innovative farming techniques of the Northern Rio Grande native peoples. Like Suzanne and Paul, Kurt also illuminates the sophisticated knowledge the Indian peoples had about their environment. Anschuetz uses contemporary Puebloan ideas about farming to understand archaeological features, such as cobble fields, terraces, pits, stone bordered plots, etc. He shows how agriculture fit in with a Puebloan worldview about nature and water. Agriculture is a part of an important cycle, and it is not just a seasonal occupation. "To Pueblo people, large harvests of corn and other cultivars throughout the summer and fall stand as irrefutable evidence that the movement of life energy, as it flows between the natural and supernatural worlds of their cosmos, is unimpeded." Farming helps to move this energy just as it helps to move the all-important life force of the universe, water. The people, he concludes, "transformed their landscapes through their physical labors, and the cultural histories that they passed on from one generation to the next that gave meaning to the places they inhabited."

The second part, Views from the Pueblos and Beyond, is a collection of works that address both the pragmatic and sacred nature of land and water to the people themselves and/or to institutions that have power over the people. Two of these chapters are written by native people (Nathan Allen and Angelo Joaquin). The third chapter is written by T. J. Ferguson and Roger Anyon who have had to negotiate land and water issues between the native peoples and the state and federal governments in their capacity as resource managers and consultants.

The late Nathan Allen, an Akimel O'odham, interweaves his autobiography with the story of his people. He begins his narrative with a discussion of the time long ago when Hohokam irrigated their crops of corn, beans, and squash and harvested a variety of desert foods, like saguaro fruits and cholla buds, to supplement their diets. He says that knowing his history gives him answers for living in the present. He has learned about his past from his father and from the teachings of the "Old Ones" who inhabit sacred sites. Allen chronicles the coming of the Spanish, the coming of the Anglos, and the misuse of the waters, including the construction of the ill-fated Coolidge Dam. He compares these modern day blunders with the ways in which water was carefully managed by the community in the past. The Akimel O'odham have recently reclaimed their water—they began construction on a new irrigation system that they will manage. Allen says that all eyes are on these people as they get back to their roots.

T. J. Ferguson and Roger Anyon look at the three "diverse scales of Hopi and Zuni cultural landscapes": ancestral, historic, and recent. Each scale is appropriate for different resource issues and pertinent to the implementation of federal laws, like NAGPRA (Native American Graves Protection and Repatriation Act), and land litigation. The ancestral scale refers to all land used and occupied by Hopi and Zuni ancestors. The historic scale refers to lands used after the arrival of the Anglos. The recent scale concerns the arbitrary boundaries imposed by the federal government.

One of the major problems between the tribes and the federal government concerns the interpretation of history and landscape. For the Hopi and Zuni, according to Ferguson and Anyon, cultural landscape is "memory"—it invokes special meanings and the identification of ancestral beings and their movements in time and space. The authors add, cultural landscapes "are a template in the process of constructing and transmitting tradition that is an essential part of how memories are formed." Ferguson and Anyon point out that regrettably, when the U.S. government negotiated land claims with the tribes, tribal ancestral lands (including the all-important clan migration areas) did not figure into the negotiations; rather, the government examined aboriginal areas of the tribes only as far back as when the U.S. assumed sovereignty over the Southwest. The diverse scales of cultural landscape therefore conflict because each side, Indian and Anglo, interprets them so radically differently.

The last part of the book is entitled "The Melting Pot: Water, Land and Conflicts in Historical Perspective." It brings together a number of scholars who write about a variety of complex issues: water litigation, land grants and land disputes, native ecologies, racism, and the demonstration of identity vis-á-vis ritual and *casta* systems. Fran Levine writes the first chapter, "Traditional Use in a Changing Landscape." She looks at the Northern Rio Grande cultures—pueblo, Spanish and Mexican land grant communities, and the new sun belt communities of retirees and others—and their history of water litigation. *Beneficial use and priority of appropriation* are key court issues in the fight for water. Because Levine has been an expert witness in a number of cases, she has a keen perspective about process and outcome. Oral traditions, she says, have not been given their due weight as evidence. Indian and Hispano communities have rich oral traditions that not only speak to how water was conserved and shared, but they also attest to the people's historic claims to the resource (*priority*). Contemporary water litigation is filled with all sorts of legal devices to divide the pueblo and Hispano communities and ensure that individuals and institutions with money/power win a favorable decision.

The next chapter by Marianne Stoller concerns the Baca land grants in the San Luis Valley of Colorado. She examines the connection between myth and history and the legendary figure Luis María Cabeza de Baca himself. The contemporary battles over who owns the water of the Valley and how that water will be used go back to the early Spanish land grants and the Baca heirs. Her detailed analysis illuminates the complexity.

Maria Varela of The Rural Resources Group writes about water policy and environmentalism in the New West. In her chapter, "Collaborative Conservatism" she says that the traditional agriculturalists' concerns have often been neglected as thousands of new migrants pour into the region. Neglect of native peoples, especially the local Hispanos, is part of the history of the West. Stephen Kearny promised to respect and uphold the rights of the Mexican citizens in the United States. His legacy is perpetuated in the New West where water board commissions and other government agencies make empty promises to protect native concerns.

Varela also examines how local Hispanos historically made use of the land and its resources, and early on, she notes, they understood the importance of good environmental science. One case in point is the development of local businesses, like Ganados del Valle, that promote locally grown meat, produce, arts and crafts. Despite Ganados' success, it became mired in a legal battle with environmentalists. She describes this long battle and provides a lengthy interpretation of these new problems in the New West. Her work points to the myriad problems, and their historical roots, that are currently shaping the New West.

The chapter on the Navajo-Hopi land dispute is written by David Brugge and is based upon his book, *The Navajo-Hopi Land Dispute: An American Tragedy* (1994). Brugge is well known for his archaeological work, particularly at Chaco Canyon, and his many articles about the Navajo people. In his contribution to this book, he fastidiously details the complicated and entwined history of the Navajo and Hopi Indians and the many attempts that were made to adjudicate their historic land conflicts which predate the assignment of reservation lands to both tribes in the 1880s. He writes from a decidedly pro-Navajo perspective as he chronicles the negative impact this long-standing dispute has had on the Navajo people and why relocation of Navajo families out of Hopi land (HPL or Hopi Partition Lands) has been so destructive to these people. He says many of the people were moved to off-reservation urban areas where they did not know the language and found themselves in debt to creditors; worse, he says, they lost their traditional hogans and ranching way of life. Brugge includes a time-line that provides a good reference for putting the land conflict in historic perspective.

The Hopi Indians have a different perspective on these land conflicts than the one presented by Brugge. When I asked several members of the tribe for their views, I was told that the Hopi believe that "the truth will out." The Hopi Tribe Cultural Preservation Office sent me several reports ("A Brief History of the 1882 Hopi-Navajo Land Problem"; "The Taking of Hopi Land: A Hopi Perspective") that reflect a part of that Hopi "truth." According to these reports, the Navajo had been raiding Hopi villages and squatting on Hopi land since their arrival in the Southwest. The Executive Order which established the Hopi reservation in 1882 did not include a lot of Hopi land nor their village of Moenkopi. Further, many Navajo were already living on the newly created Hopi reservation. For the next hundred years, the problems of Navajo on Hopi lands continued with the eventual decision, in 1974, to partition the lands and relocate members of the tribes that were on the wrong side of the boundaries. Relocation has proven to be just as problematical as all other solutions to the land dispute. According to the Hopi, the Navajo rejected an agreement that would have facilitated the enactment of the 1974 Public Law—Navajo have refused to relocate and those who have stayed have refused to acknowledge a lease agreement which recognizes that the leased land does, indeed, belong to the Hopi.[3] The Hopi watched as their once extensive land base dwindled to a fraction of their former holdings; court settlements that were supposed to restore and/or honor Hopi lands ended up rewarding Navajo for "squatting" on Hopi lands.

Adrian Bustamante's contribution is the chapter from his classic article on the casta system in colonial New Mexico (Bustamente 1991). Not much is known about the settlers and explorers who came with and followed on the heels of Juan de Oñate in 1598. Early Spanish documents about the ethnic composition of these people were burned in the Pueblo Revolt in 1680. With the return of the Spanish in the 1690s came a glimpse into the emic categories they used to describe ethnicity in the succeeding century. The inhabitants were divided into castas or ethnic categorizations in New Mexico: *Español* was the highest casta and referred to Spaniards; *mestizo*, parents of mixed marriages; *coyote*, mix of Spaniard, Indian and Black; *mulato*, mixed Black parentage; *Negroid*; and *indios vecinos*, formerly the Mexican Indians accompanying the Spaniards and, later, the natives of New Mexico. These terms were often used by church officials, census takers, government officers, and so forth to denote ethnicity and to either give or deny rights, even though all Mexican citizens were theoretically entitled to the same rights in 1821.

The closing chapter in this book is Sylvia Rodríguez's (1998) article on the Taos fiesta, reprinted from the *Journal of American Folklore*. The article is the second in the series of articles she is writing about the fiesta. Rodríguez is well known for her many contributions to Southwest studies, and in particular, her work with rituals (e.g., the Matachines Dance) that demonstrate the delicate and complex ways in which Anglos, Indians, and Hispanos negotiate their ethnicity.

Rodríguez grew up in Taos as a watcher and occasional participant of the fiesta. She says that the fiesta is now the only time during the year when local Hispanos are able to reclaim the plaza, which was once the center of their daily lives. The fiesta has become a form of resistance "defined by the very hegemonic process it seeks to undermine." She critically examines the origins of the fiesta as an Anglo attempt to boost tourism. In her previous article (Rodríguez 1997) she describes the history of the two summer fiestas in Taos (only one fiesta is celebrated today; the San Geronimo fiesta was celebrated in the past). The Anglos romanticized a tricultural theme with Indian dances at the neighboring Taos Pueblo and Spanish dancing and Anglo reenactments of the wild Old West (Rodríguez 1997: 37–38). The Taos Indians gradually withdrew from the fiestas, and Hispanos and Anglos began to argue over both the language and the content of the ceremonies. Gradually too, the organization of and participation in the fiestas went from Anglo to Hispano, just as the Plaza and community of Taos went from Hispano to Anglo. She closes chapter 12 by noting that the "power, genius and irony of the fiesta lie in the fact that it simultaneously undermines the status quo [Anglo hegemony and the reign of tourism] it reinforces."

NOTES

1. A lot of recent scholarship has examined violence in prehistoric southwestern societies, especially among the Anasazi Indians. Whereas some sort of violence is indicated

throughout the long chronology of Puebloan settlement, the types of violence differ. According to one controversial interpretation, during the "climax" of the Anasazi tradition, violence (including cannibalism) was intracommunity based as a possible means of social control. By the time Anasazi influence was waning, violence turned outward, possibly toward other Anasazi groups, resulting in new settlement patterns in defensible locations. See Turner and Turner 1999; and LeBlanc 1999 for information.

Another point of view (see Billman, Lambert, and Leonard 2000) posits that violence was the outcome of degrading environmental conditions in the Chaco Canyon region around A.D. 1150. Ethnobotanical evidence, as well as evidence from human coprolite analysis, suggests that plant yield was very low and local populations were dealing with a destructive drought. Events at the Cowboy Wash site were not isolated, but part of a general pattern of environmental degradation where human populations responded with increased cannibalism, as seen by widespread disarticulation of human bones, cut marks, and burning of bone.

2. See Frances Leon Quintana (1990) who also paints of a favorable view of early Indian-Hispano relations. Her work is focused on relationships in northern New Mexico where, she says, both groups learned to work together for their common good. "While not idyllic, Pueblo-Hispanic relations have over centuries built interethnic communication and means for solitary action" (Quintana 1990: 295). See the *Journal of the Southwest* 29, no. 2 (Summer 1987) and 32, no. 3 (Autumn, 1990) for issues related to the historical complexity of water litigation.

3. A good, concise chronology of the land dispute can be found in a publication of the American Friends Service (1992): Much of what remains today of the original 1882 reservation of the Hopi tribe consists of District 6. This and other grazing districts were created by the federal government in 1933. The lands outside of District 6 were still within the Executive Order (1882) reservation of the Hopi. However, because of the large number of Navajo living on these lands, they, in particular, became the subject of long, protracted litigation. In 1958 the Hopi filed against the Navajo in federal court. This case became known as Healing vs. Jones (after the tribal chairmen of each group). The court decision gave both tribes "joint, undivided, and equal interests in and to all of the 1882 reservation lying outside the boundaries of land management District 6. . . ." The Hopis went back to court to force the issue of partition. Public Law 93–531, the Navajo-Hopi Land Settlement Act, was signed in 1974 and became the basis for relocation.

REFERENCES

Adams, Charles. 1991. *The Origin and Development of the Pueblo Katsina Cult*. Tucson: University of Arizona Press.

Anschuetz, Kurt. 1999. Personal communication.

———. 1995. Two Sides of a Coin: Early Pueblo Indian Farming Practices in the Rio Arriba and the Rio Abajo of the Northern Rio Grande Region. Paper presented at the symposium on Native American Agricultural Systems of North America. Society for American Archaeology annual meeting.

Anschuetz, Kurt, and Glenna Dean. 1994. North American Desert People. In *Deserts: The Illustrated Library of the Earth*, ed. Mary Seely, pp. 122–127. Sydney: Weldon Owen.

Anschuetz, Kurt, and Cherie Scheick. 1998. Unveiling Archaeological tierra Incognita: Evaluating Time, Place-Making and Tradition Through a Cultural Landscape Paradigm. Paper presented at the Society for American Archaeology annual meeting.

Anyon, Roger. 2000. Personal communication.

Billman, Brian, P. Lambert, and Banks L. Leonard. 2000. Cannibalism, Warfare and Drought in the Mesa Verde Region During the 12th Century, A.D. *American Antiquity* 65(1): 145–178.

Blake, Kevin. 1999. Sacred and Secular Landscape Symbolism at Mount Taylor, New Mexico. *Journal of the Southwest* 41(4): 487–509.

Briggs, Charles and John Van Ness. 1987. *Land, Water and Culture: New Perspectives on Hispanic Land Grants*. Albuquerque: University of New Mexico Press.

Brugge, David M. 1994. *The Navajo-Hopi Land Dispute: An American Tragedy*. Albuquerque: University of New Mexico Press.

Bustamante, Adrian. 1991. "The Matter was Never Resolved": The Casta System in Colonial New Mexico, 1693–1823. *New Mexico Historical Review* 66(2): 143–164.

Byrkit, James. 1992. Land, Sky and People: Southwest Defined. *Journal of the Southwest*. 34(3): 256–387.

Casey, Edward. 1996. How to Get From Space to Place in a Fairly Short Stretch of Time: Phenomenological Prolegomena. In *Senses of Place*, edited by Steven Feld and Keith Basso, pp. 13–52. Santa Fe: School of American Research.

Crown, Patricia and W. James Judge. 1991. Introduction. In *Chaco and Hohokam: Prehistoric Regional Systems in the American Southwest*, edited by P. Crown and W. James Judge, pp. 1–10. Santa Fe: School of American Research.

Ebright, Malcolm. 1987. New Mexican Land Grants: The Legal Background. In *New Perspectives on Hispanic Land Grants*, edited by Briggs and Van Ness, pp. 15–64. Albuquerque: University of New Mexico Press.

Feld, Stephen and Keith Basso, editors. 1996. *Senses of Place*. Santa Fe: School of American Research.

Fish, Suzanne and Gary Nabhan. 1991. Desert as Context: The Hohokam Environment. In *Exploring the Hohokam: Prehistoric Desert Peoples of the American Southwest*, edited by George Gumerman, pp. 29–59. Dragoon: Amerindian Foundation and Albuquerque: University of New Mexico Press.

Gregory, David. 1991. Form and Variation in Hohokam Settlement Patterns. In *Chaco and Hohokam*, edited by P. Crown and W. J. Judge, pp. 159–194. Santa Fe: School of American Research.

Gumerman, George and Murray Gell-Mann. 1994. Cultural Evolution in the Prehistoric Southwest. In *Themes in Southwest Prehistory*, edited by George Gumerman, pp. 11–31. Santa Fe: School of American Research.

Hirsch, Eric. 1995. Introduction: Landscape Between Place and Space. In *The Anthropology of Landscape: Perspectives on Place and Space*, edited by Eric Hirsch and Michael O'Hanlon. Oxford: Clarendon Press.

Hobson, Arline, Karl Karlstrom, Juan Pascoe, and Allyn Spence. 1992. *Hopis and Navajos: Understanding Their Land Disputes*. Pamphlet prepared on behalf of the Arizona Area Program Committee of the American Friends Service.

Jenkins, Myra and Albert Schroeder. 1974. *A Brief History of New Mexico*. Cultural Properties Review Committee of State of New Mexico. Albuquerque: University of New Mexico Press.

Journal of the Southwest 29, no. 2 (Summer 1987).

———. 32, no. 3 (Autumn 1990).

Kehoe, Alice. 1992. *North American Indians: A Comprehensive Account*. Englewood Cliffs: Prentice Hall.

LeBlanc, Steven. 1999. Southwestern Warfare: Reality and Consequences. *Archaeology Southwest* 13(2): 1–7.

Levine, Frances. 1990. Dividing the Water: The Impact of Water Rights Adjudication on New Mexican Communities. *Journal of the Southwest* 32(3): 268–287.

Mabry, Jonathan. 1997. Rewriting Prehistory: Recent Discoveries at Cienega Phase Sites in the Santa Cruz Floodplain. *Archaeology in Tucson* 11(3): 1.

———. 1999. The Transition to Agriculture and Sedentism in Southern Arizona. Paper presented at the symposium Current Research on the Late Archaic Along the U.S.-Mexican Borderlands. Society for American Archaeology annual meeting.

Meinig, D. W. 1971. *Southwest: Three Peoples in Geographical Change, 1600–1970*. New York: Oxford University Press.

Meyer, Michael. 1996. *Water in the Hispanic Southwest: A Social and Legal History, 1550–1850*. Tucson: University of Arizona Press.

Ortiz, Alfonso. 1972. Ritual Drama and the Pueblo World View. In *New Perpectives on the Pueblos*, edited by Alfonso Ortiz, pp. 135–162. Albuquerque: University of New Mexico Press.

Parezo, Nancy. 1996. The Diné (Navajos): Sheep is Life. In *Paths of Life: American Indians of the Southwest and Northern Mexico*, edited by Thomas Sheridan and Nancy Parezo, pp. 14–23. Tucson: University of Arizona Press.

———. 1996. The Havasupais, Hualapais and Yavapais: The Great Creator Has Given Us this Country. *In Paths of Life: American Indians of the Southwest and Northern Mexico*, edited by Thomas Sheridan and Nancy Parezo, pp. 91–114. Tucson: University of Arizona Press.

Plog, Stephen. 1997. *Ancient Peoples of the American Southwest*. London: Thames and Hudson.

Quintana, Frances. 1990. Land, Water and Pueblo-Hispanic Relations in Northern New Mexico. *Journal of the Southwest* 32(3): 288–299.

Rivera, Jose. 1998. *Acequia Culture: Land, Water and Community in the Southwest*. Albuquerque: University of New Mexico Press.

Rodríguez, Sylvia. 1990. Applied Research on Land and Water in New Mexico: A Critique. *Journal of the Southwest* 32(3): 300–315.

———. 1997. The Taos Fiesta: Invented Tradition and Infrapolitics of Symbolic Reclamation. *Journal of the Southwest* 39: 33–57.

———. 1991. The Matachines Dance at Taos Pueblo. *American Ethnologist* 18(2): 234–256.

———. 1996. *The Matachines Dance: Ritual Symbolism and Interethnic Relations in Upper Rio Grande Valley*. Albuquerque: University of New Mexico.

———. 1998. Fiesta Time and Plaza Space: Resistance and Accommodation in a Tourist Town. *Journal of American Folklore* 111(439): 39–56.

Rudner, Ruth and Bill Yellowtail. 1994. Sacred Geographies. *Wilderness* 58(206): 10–28.

Sheridan, Thomas. 1996. The O'odham (Pima and Papagos) The World Would Burn Without Rain. In *Paths of Life*, edited by Thomas Sheridan and Nancy Parezo, pp. 114–140. Tucson: University of Arizona Press.

Sheridan, Thomas and Nancy Parezo. 1996. *Paths of Life: American Indians of the Southwest and Northern Mexico*. Tucson: University of Arizona Press.

Toll, H. Wolcott. 1991. Material Distributions and Exchange in the Chaco System. In *Chaco and Hohokam*, edited by P. Crown and W. James Judge, pp. 77–108. Santa Fe: School of American Research.

Turner, C. G. II, and J. A. Turner. 1999. *Man Corn: Cannibalism and Violence in the Prehistoric American Southwest*. Salt Lake City: University of Utah Press.

Varela, Maria. 1999. Personal communication.

————. 1998. The Ghost of General Stephen Watts Kearny. Western Water Policy Advisory Committee Report, Sept. 15. The Rural Resources Group.

Vivian, Gwinn. 1997. Chaco Roads: Morphology. *Kiva* 63(1): 7–33.

————. 1997. Chaco Roads: Function. *Kiva* 63(1): 34–67.

Weber, David. 1992. *Spanish Frontier in North America*. New Haven: Yale University Press.

Weinstein, Laurie. 1983. Indian vs. Colonist: The Competition for Land in 17th Century Plymouth Colony. Unpublished Ph.D. dissertation, Department of Anthropology, Southern Methodist University, Dallas.

White, Richard. 1991. *It's Your Misfortune and None of My Own. A History of the American West*. Norman: University of Oklahoma.

Whitely, Peter. 1998. *Rethinking Hopi Ethnography*. Washington: Smithsonian Institution Press.

Willey, Gordon. 1966. *An Introduction to American Archaeology*. Vol. 1, *North and Middle America*. Englewood Cliffs: Prentice Hall.

Woodbury, Richard. 1979. Prehistory: Introduction. In *Southwest*, edited by Alfonso Ortiz, pp. 22–30. Vol. 9 of *Handbook of North American Indians*, William Sturtevant, gen. editor. Washington: Smithsonian Institution Press.

Woodbury, Richard and Ezra Zubrow. 1979. Agricultural Beginnings 2000 BC–AD 500. In *Southwest*, edited by Alfonso Ortiz, pp. 43–60. Vol. 9 of *Handbook of North American Indians*, William Sturtevant, gen. editor. Washington: Smithsonian Institution Press.

I

THE PROCESS OF BECOMING

2

Prehistoric Environment and Agriculture in the Hohokam of Southern Arizona

Suzanne K. Fish and Paul Fish

INTRODUCTION

The environmental relationships and legacies of past societies are central inquiries in the archaeology of the Southwest. Agriculture was the medium through which southwestern farming societies transformed their natural environment, and in turn, were shaped by the opportunities and constraints inherent in it. Direct impacts of cultivation included the removal and replacement of natural vegetation, manipulation of topography and soil, and, in this arid region, the diversion and concentration of supplemental water. Other intentional and unintentional activities of farmers created anthropogenic landscapes profoundly shaped by primary and secondary effects. Additional far-reaching consequences resulted from the capacity of agriculture to support relatively large populations in the same location over time.

The following discussion examines the environmental role of the Hohokam who inhabited the southern deserts of the southwestern United States (Map 2.1). Members of this archaeologically defined cultural tradition were not the first agriculturalists in the low elevation basins of southern Arizona. Preceramic cultivators and early pottery-making populations preceded the Hohokam by more than 1,000 years. Newly emerging information reveals that these initial farmers already occupied villages for prolonged intervals and possessed a range of agricultural technologies that included moderate-sized canals (e.g., Huckell 1996; Mabry 1998, personal communication). From the third to the fifteenth centuries A.D., however, the Hohokam far surpassed their predecessors by constructing more massive irrigation networks than any built by the high cultures of Me-

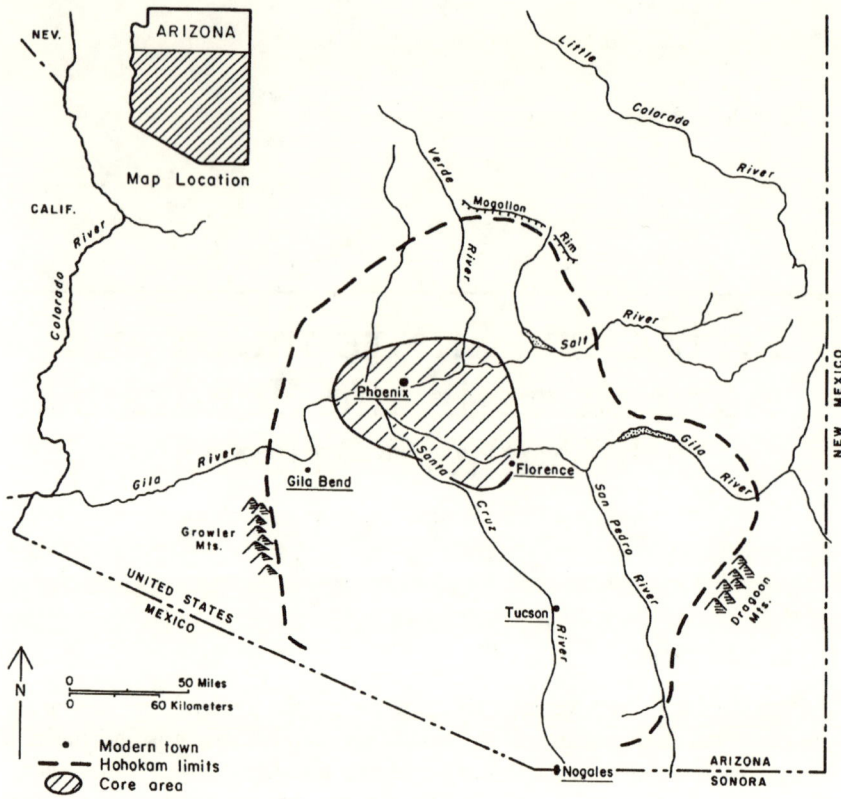

Map 2.1 Hohokam territory in southern Arizona

soamerica and by extending agricultural landscapes well beyond settlements and well-watered fields.

Hohokam productivity supported a developmental trajectory that attained uppermost levels of southwestern social complexity within the maximally hot, dry confines of the northeastern Sonoran Desert. More than those of other southwestern cultures, Hohokam occupations must have tested the delicate balance between fragile arid ecosystems and the impingements of sustained agriculture. Even within the desert setting, the manner and magnitude of impact by Hohokam societies cannot be characterized in a singular way. An understanding of Hohokam impacts rests on the accurate reconstruction of relevant cultural practices, their scale, and their consequences within the environmental variation of their Sonoran Desert homeland.

SONORAN DESERT ENVIRONMENT OF THE HOHOKAM

The Sonoran Desert encompasses almost 120,000 sq mi (310,000 sq km) of desertscrub and enclaves of upland vegetation types within Arizona, Sonora, southeastern California, and Baja California (McGinnies 1981: 41). Within the Hohokam range in southern Arizona, two vegetational subdivisions of the Sonoran Desert biome predominate. The Arizona Upland on the northeast edge includes more large and diverse desert species, while the western-lying Lower Colorado Valley is restricted to shrubs (Brown 1982, 1994). At higher elevations (above 3,500 ft/1,200 m), semidesert grassland, interior chaparral or madrean, and evergreen woodlands occur, all but the latter within 60 mi (100 km) of any Hohokam settlement. Within a 120 mi (200 km) reach of any Hohokam village, and usually much closer, Rocky Mountain subalpine conifer forest above 6,000 ft (1,900 m) is a vegetation type that the Hohokam visited to obtain large structural timbers (P. Fish et al. 1992; Dean et al. 1996; Wilcox and Shenk 1977).

A bimodal distribution of rainfall in the Hohokam area contrasts with winter dominant rainfall to the west and summer dominant rainfall to the east. Although total annual precipitation is low, this seasonal balance of rainfall in the Sonoran Desert has been associated both with the greater structural diversity of the Sonoran Desert vegetation and with the arborescent character of many of its perennials, compared to the greater predominance of shrubs in the neighboring Chihuahuan, Great Basin, and Mohave deserts (Brown 1982: 182). As a result of the vegetational advantages of rainfall in two yearly seasons rather than one, gatherable resources are particularly abundant. Distinctively large Sonoran Desert species, including such important economic plants as the leguminous mesquite, paloverde, and ironwood trees, furnished edible beans and relatively large cacti, such as cholla, prickly pear, hedgehog, and saguaro, furnished edible fruit, buds, and pads. Higher precipitation in a broad arc to the north, east, and south of the Phoenix Basin in the center of Hohokam territory is correlated with increased density and diversity in these important food species. Wildlife densities and diversities also increase along this gradient of decreasing aridity (Vander Wall and MacMahan 1984).

In the sense that they circumscribe the distribution of distinctive Hohokam styles within southern Arizona, two factors can be considered key environmental correlates of Hohokam culture. These are location within the northeast boundaries of the Sonoran Desert and, with few exceptions, an elevational range below 3,500 ft (1,065 m). Residence and subsistence activity was concentrated on the floors and slopes of basins and frequently extended onto the adjacent lower slopes of moderate-sized desert mountains. Even where larger mountain masses occur, as in the Santa Catalinas near Tucson, utilization of higher elevation slopes and valleys was minor when compared with upland residence and farming by other southwestern cultures (Fish and Nabhan 1991: 30).

AN OVERVIEW OF HOHOKAM CULTURE AND
AGRICULTURE

The prehistoric Hohokam constructed the most massive irrigation system north of Peru (Doolittle 1990: 79). Hohokam inhabitants of the Phoenix Basin extended over 500 kilometers of main trunk lines from the perennial Salt and Gila rivers. In other narrower surrounding basins, Hohokam farmers irrigated from intermittent rivers and used a variety of additional techniques tapping ephemeral watercourses and surface runoff. These combined methods greatly expanded the productive boundaries and cultural imprint of Hohokam occupations.

The Hohokam endured as an archaeologically recognizable entity for more than a millennium, from approximately A.D. 200 until 1450 or later. Members of this cultural tradition inhabited 45,000 sq mi (120,000 sq km) of generally linear basins separated by moderate-sized mountain ranges (P. Fish 1989). Densities of regional population reflected the greater productive capacities of irrigated land along the perennially-flowing rivers. Nevertheless, stylistic and organizational trends progressed in tandem throughout the Hohokam domain.

The Hohokam were masterful agriculturalists in the Sonoran Desert. Studies of subsistence remains throughout Hohokam territory reveal a consistently strong component of crop domesticates, indigenous species that were tended or cultivated, and a broad array of wild resources (Bohrer 1991; S. Fish and Nabhan 1991; Gasser and Kwiatkowski 1991). Remains of Hohokam settlements, water management devices, and fields cover substantially greater areas than were inhabited by succeeding historic farmers of Indian and Hispanic heritage, who employed many of the same techniques. The ecological parameters of prehistoric subsistence were irreversibly altered in the early contact era; a similarly direct extractive and productive orientation, without domesticated animals as intermediaries, exists nowhere today.

During pre-Classic times before A.D. 1150, pithouses were the common domestic structures and earthen-banked ballcourts the predominant form of Hohokam public architecture. Thereafter, in the Classic period, both free-standing and contiguous adobe rooms were built and often enclosed by a surrounding wall to form residential compounds. Platform mounds, which supported adobe buildings on their summits and were also enclosed by thick adobe walls, became the foremost public edifices in increasingly formal layouts at larger Classic sites (Gregory 1987; P. Fish and Fish 1991).

For most of the Hohokam cultural sequence, the primary units of territory and concentrated landuse were clusters of villages and interspersed land that archaeologists term "communities." Hohokam communities consist of a central site and an outlying set of related and usually smaller settlements. Ballcourts mark the centers of the earliest communities. By A.D. 1000, these territorial entities integrating multiple sites can be widely defined in Hohokam settlement patterns (Wilcox and Sternberg 1983). During the ensuing Classic period, centers of communities were distinguished by the presence of platform mounds for community-wide observances. Community organization in the Phoenix Basin has been interpreted as providing a framework for allocating water among settlements along a shared canal system and for mobilizing and coordinating the labor for canal construction and maintenance (Crown 1987; Doyel 1976, 1980; Gregory and Nials 1985). Community organization was also pervasive, however, in other parts of the Hohokam domain where mixed agricultural technologies were the rule. In the densely packed occupied sites corresponding to large-scale riverine irrigation, communities were virtually continuous; in other areas they were separated by intervening expanses without residential settlements (S. Fish 1996).

REGIONAL VARIABILITY IN HOHOKAM AGRICULTURE

Water sources, topography, and other variables critical to agriculture were not uniform across the desert country inhabited by the Hohokam. This environmental variability resulted in differing deployments of a common repertoire of farming technologies. Where hydrological opportunity was more circumscribed, individuals, households, and villages tended to be more dependent on multiple techniques. Methods of water acquisition and topographic settings were distinctive for each class of techniques. The environmental and cultural consequences of these agricultural practices must also be considered as distinctive outcomes.

Converging just southwest of modern Phoenix, the Salt and Gila rivers flow through the Phoenix Basin topography that is among the lowest, hottest, and driest in Hohokam country (Map 2.1). Annual precipitation is 7.5 in (180 mm) and temperatures above 50° C (100° F) occur on 90 or more days (Sellers et al. 1985). These two perennial rivers, fed by vast upland watersheds outside the desert, in conjunction with the broadest expanse of irrigable basin floor, more than compensated for the otherwise harsh conditions of the Phoenix Basin. This area of 750 sq mi (2000 sq km), often termed the Hohokam core, supported the densest populations and largest settlements. Almost all estimates for Phoenix peak population are higher than 25,000 and range up to 100,000–150,000 persons (Haury 1976: 356; Schroeder 1960: 20; Doyel 1991: 265–266; P. Fish and Fish 1991: 155–157).

Although always less than 15 in (385 mm), annual precipitation increases with elevation in areas of Hohokam occupation to the north, east, and south of the Phoenix Basin, where maximum temperatures also are slightly moderated. In these regional sectors, intermittently flowing rivers originate primarily in watersheds within the desert rather than in external highlands. Valley and floodplain morphologies also restrict the width of irrigable land in those locations where riverine canals could be filled. Inhabitants of the vast remainder of the Hohokam tradition outside the Phoenix Basin practiced a smaller scale of irrigation and depended heavily on techniques for capturing the floodwaters of ephemeral drainages and overland runoff.

Whether based on riverine irrigation or runoff technologies, the sustainability of Hohokam agriculture appears not to have been significantly inhibited by soil exhaustion or the buildup of salinity. Occupations of large sites in the Phoenix Basin often span hundreds of years, while irrigation networks were present in the earliest ceramic phases and developed toward a maximum extent in late prehistoric times (Masse 1981; Nicholas and Feinman 1989; Howard 1993). Two analyses (Ackerly et al. 1987; Nials et al. 1989) of overall system capacity in the Phoenix Basin concur in a total for irrigated acreage ranging between 30,000 and 60,000 acres (12,100 and 24,200 ha). Multiple excavated examples of canal interruption, abandonment, and rebuilding have increased appreciation of the dynamic and labor-intensive nature of these systems.

Zones of active soil deposition from ephemeral drainages likewise witnessed longterm continuity in settlement, although occupations of individual small sites within these zones were often of lesser duration. Drainages crossing basin slopes carry water rich with suspended sediment following seasonal storms. This sediment is deposited when slopes begin to flatten, forming fertile, well-watered alluvial fans. Floodwater farmers of alluvial fans on lower basin slopes, broader arroyo bottoms, and upper basin pediments watered their crops by diverting storm flows onto fields at the sides of shallow drainages. As active channels shifted across the surfaces of alluvial fans and new fans became hydrologically active, Hohokam settlements likewise shifted within the topographically defined zones of depositional enrichment.

Another broad category of Hohokam agricultural techniques obtained water from overland runoff rather than from channelized flow in drainages. A variety of simple constructions were designed to intercept and concentrate storm runoff from sheet flows and shallow rills on broad surfaces. Archaeological remains associated with these techniques are widely scattered across the slopes of Hohokam basins, but the scale and implications of this form of cultivation are only now beginning to be recognized. The most extensive arrays of cobble features supplied by surface runoff are termed "rockpile fields," after planting facilities consisting of rounded heaps or piles, but diversionary walls, contour terraces, hillside terraces, grids, and other cobble constructions were also employed to direct and retain surface flow.

OCCUPATIONAL AND AGRICULTURAL SUSTAINABILITY

The nature of agricultural water use by the Hohokam was central to their achievement of longterm population and settlement continuity. In restricted, high elevation locales of the northern Southwest where rainfall alone was sufficient for farming or where clear mountain streams furnished supplemental water, eventual soil exhaustion may have induced progressive clearing of short-term fields, prolonged fallowing, and the sequential abandonment of arable locales (cf. Kohler and Matthews 1988). The Hohokam were not similarly subject to such processes. Although water sources are highly localized in the low southern deserts, those supplying Hohokam cultivation renewed soil fertility with each wetting.

Canals carried suspended sediment from the undammed flow of the Salt and Gila rivers to the perimeters of irrigated cultivation, up to 6 mi (10 km) inland from the river channel and for linear distances up to 20 mi (30 km). Some of this rich soil and detritus was delivered directly to fields through irrigation and some appears to have been spread beyond the banks of canals in the course of periodic channel cleanings. Ribbons of distinctive soil types of waterborne origin still mark the paths of both Hohokam canals tapping perennial rivers and those filled from intermittently flowing watercourses (Dart 1986).

On alluvial fans of lower basin slopes, broader arroyo bottoms, and upper basin pediments, farmers simultaneously watered and fertilized their crops by diverting storm flows in shallow drainages. Organic debris concentrated in these waters by rapid runoff following seasonal rains offset a major deficiency of desert soils (Bryan 1929; Nabhan 1979, 1986). Farmers could even improve the coarse texture of soil in new fields by diverting flows to deposit fine-grained sediments prior to field use (S. Fish et al. 1992).

Highly localized sources of domestic and agricultural water in Hohokam basins must have created a strong impetus for extractive practices that conserved the longterm productive potential of the environment. Limited situations for water diversion or canal headings and investment in the construction of canals and runoff features added to locational constraints. Movement to new locations was not a simple alternative if the local environment became depleted or degraded, and mobility options further decreased as populations grew.

Several natural and cultural patterns contributed to the Hohokam ability to maintain stable occupations and an adequate reserve of natural resources in their fragile environment. Pit-ovens, or hornos, were fuel-efficient cooking facilities of Hohokam villages. Food was placed in these pits along with coals and heated stones, then covered and left to cook slowly over long periods. Shared horno usage by several households was a typical pattern (Sires 1987: 180) that would have further minimized fuel consumption. Ceramics were fired at relatively low temperatures. Pithouse, wattle and daub, and adobe architectural styles utilized a minimum of structural wood. Materials from alternative species of desert plants such as the ribs of saguaro cactus and ocotillo (*Fouquieria*) were frequently substituted.

Compared to prehistoric groups of the northern Southwest, the Hohokam had a much lower need of fuel for heating homes, with long months of hot weather and average annual temperatures between 10 and 15° C (50 to 64° F) (Sellars et al. 1985). Destruction of leguminous trees, the most common desert species, was likely minimized in deference to the dietary importance of their abundant and nutritious beans. Among historic Piman groups, the geographic successors and probable descendants of the Hohokam, desirable trees such as mesquite were often left standing in fields and grew densely in hedgerows benefiting from agricultural water (Rea 1981; Castetter and Bell 1942). Charred seeds and wood al from lengthy prehistoric occupations attest to the consistent availability of such trees, if not always in the same proportions. Wide ranging sources of additional fuels included riparian trees, driftwood, and woody desert shrubs.

ANTHROPOGENIC CHANGE

The Hohokam created distinctively anthropogenic settings about their settlements with culturally altered distributions of plants and animals. Agricultural activity would have produced a variety of vegetational effects (Bohrer 1970; Gasser 1982; S. Fish 1984, 1985; Miksicek 1984, 1988). Farming on floodplains in the environs of drainages probably created the least divergence from surrounding plant communities of naturally distributed riparian habitats. Even in these situations, manipulation through such documented aboriginal practices as selective removal of unwanted species, reseeding and tending of utilized ones, or introduction of nonlocal taxa could have altered distributions toward advantageous ends.

In large part, insight into Hohokam creation and management of anthropogenic vegetation derives from ethnographic studies of plant use by Piman-speaking groups who intensively harvest wild plants as well as crops in field, ditch, hedgerow, abandoned field, and dooryard garden microhabitats (Rea 1981, 1983; Crosswhite 1981; Nabhan et al. 1983). Such practices serve as analogues for the Hohokam capacity for transporting, transplanting, watering, or otherwise managing wild plants for their desirable products. The presence of particular weedy or semi-cultivated species in the archaeobotanical record is not definitive evidence for origin in anthropogenic plant communities, but patterns of quantitative contrast and contextual correspondence have been increasingly identified in recent studies. These provide the basis for reconstructing environmental alterations that included both intentional manipulation and unintentional enhancement of species other than cultigens.

Supplemental water in fields must have increased biomass production over surrounding vegetation. Pollen samples from prehistoric agricultural contexts differ from natural vegetation in the distribution of weedy taxa. They reveal a rich weedy flora alongside crops responding to agriculturally enhanced conditions (S. Fish 1984, 1985). The Hohokam likely followed ethnographic southwestern practices of permitting desirable weeds to remain in fields and sometimes even scattering seeds to insure a sufficient supply (Whiting 1939; Crosswhite 1981; Bye 1979). Among weedy plants of Hohokam fields were species such as chenopods, amaranths, and spiderling (*Boerhaavia*) that furnish edible seeds and greens. In seasons when water was inadequate to mature cultigens, these secondary resources of fields may have constituted a lesser but welcome harvest.

Modified environments created by the Hohokam also featured transplanted desert species receiving more directed attention. The agave or century plant is now recognized as a mainstay of Hohokam cultivation. Less conclusive evidence suggests additional candidates for this cultivated category that include cholla, prickly pear, and little barley (Bohrer 1991; Fish and Nabhan 1991). Such plantings in poorer fields, field borders, and fallow ground may have supplemented the production of natural stands near longterm residence. A continuum of active intervention involving a variety of plants is probable. Proposed species included mesquite, hedgehog cactus, wolfberry (*Lycium spp.*), hog potato (*Hoffmanseggia densiflora*), amaranth (*Amaranthus*), chenopods (*Chenopodium berlandieri, C. murale, Monolepis nutalliana, Atriplex wrightii*), tobacco (*Nicotiana trigonophylla*) and spiderling (Fish and Nabhan 1991).

A major proportion of animals hunted by the Hohokam also conforms to the culturally modified environs of their settlements (e.g., Szuter and Bayham 1989; Szuter and Gillespie 1994). Bones of large animals such as deer are infrequent compared to quantities for small species. Rabbits and rodents, characteristic of agricultural habitats, were key components of Hohokam cuisine. Animals attracted to the vegetation and water in fields could be conveniently trapped or hunted during agricultural tasks. At sites occupied for long intervals, trends in consumption reflect increasing percentages of species that prefer environmental situations corresponding to anthropogenic vegetation. In multiple instances, an earlier predominance of cottontail was superseded by greater reliance on jackrabbit.

Numerous combinations of happenstance and design are embodied by the array of noncultigens now thought to have been productively enhanced or concentrated in anthropogenic vegetation by the Hohokam. Among this group are plants such as mesquite that may have been differentially spared in field clearing, become dense in hedgerows, thrived on canal seepage, or been tended and selectively harvested in adjacent natural settings. Species such as cholla may have been transplanted to dooryard gardens or fields as a crop, to out-of-the-way spots among habitations and fields, or employed as residential fencing. Chenopods and spiderling are representative of weedy herbaceous plants that may have received focused attention or none at all in fields and other culturally disturbed habitats (Fish and Nabhan 1991).

NEW INSIGHTS INTO LAND-EXTENSIVE CULTIVATION

The scale of runoff-dependent techniques is one of the surprising outcomes of ongoing Hohokam research. Although not replicating the extent of Hohokam systems, historic canals of the Pima Indians furnish a means for visualizing former irrigation. Likewise, the vestigial floodwater farming of recent times by Piman cultivators and traditional farmers of northern Mexico serves as a guide to prehistoric methods. The ethnographic record is mute, however, with regard to more land-extensive farming practices of the Hohokam. Archaeological studies provide the only insights into the areally diffuse Hohokam techniques that disappeared in the postcontact era.

Cobble features are the key to comprehending an agriculturally engineered landscape in southern Arizona that extended well beyond the confines of habitations, irrigation, floodwater fields, and other cultivated land that depended on channelized sources of water. Subsumed under the general term of rockpile fields or complexes, these features consist of rounded heaps and linear arrangements of unshaped rock. In most parts of the Hohokam domain, distributions of such features have been shown to fill appreciable segments of what otherwise would be considered voids in settlement pattern. In place of empty or natural areas with solely extractive potential, rockpile distributions demonstrate a significant modification of land surfaces and managed productivity.

Archaeological studies and replicative experiments in recent years have revealed much about the agricultural functions of rockpiles (S. Fish et al. 1985, 1992). Rockpiles enhance the growth environment for crops planted in them. Excavated cross sections reveal that cobbles often cap mounds of soil beneath. The uneven, porous texture of piled rocks permits greater penetration of rainfall than does the surrounding hard-packed and impermeable ground surface, and also increases the interception of rapid, transitory surface runoff. The rocks then act as a mulch, slowing evaporation of soil moisture by blocking capillary action and preserving higher moisture levels beneath. Gauged experiments show higher levels of moisture in rockpiles than in surrounding soil for days to weeks following rainfalls of varying size. Suspended nutrients in overland runoff and accumulations of windblown soil appear to have been sufficient to maintain fertility (S. Fish et al. 1992).

Fields consist of contiguous sets of these agricultural features (Map 2.2). The rockpiles rarely exceed 1.5 meters in diameter and 75 centimeters in height. Contour terraces and checkdams of one to several cobble courses are often interspersed in small fields and are always present in large complexes. Field sizes range from clusters of as few as 10 rockpiles to arrays of rockpiles and linear features covering many hectares.

Roasting pits are present in most rockpile fields, ranging from 3 to more than 30 meters in diameter. The typically large pits of extensive fields have the shape of broad, shallow basins and a complicated stratigraphy chronicling the intrusions and accretions of seasonal reuse over many years. Pits are filled with ash, charcoal, fire-cracked rock, and occasional artifacts. Flotation of charred plant material preserved in fill has identified agave, a desert succulent, as the crop in many fields. Cooking up to 48 hours in sealed pits converted carbohydrates stored in the base of the agave into a sugary, nutritious food. Stone tools on field surfaces include knife-like implements resembling tools used ethnographically to sever agave leaves during harvest of the plants. Other specialized tools for removing leaf pulp to extract fiber for nets, baskets, sandals, and textiles, the second product of the agave, are recovered in associated habitation sites (S. Fish et al. 1992).

The cultivation of drought resistant agave in rockpile fields permitted expanded cropping on large expanses of otherwise marginal slopes in Hohokam

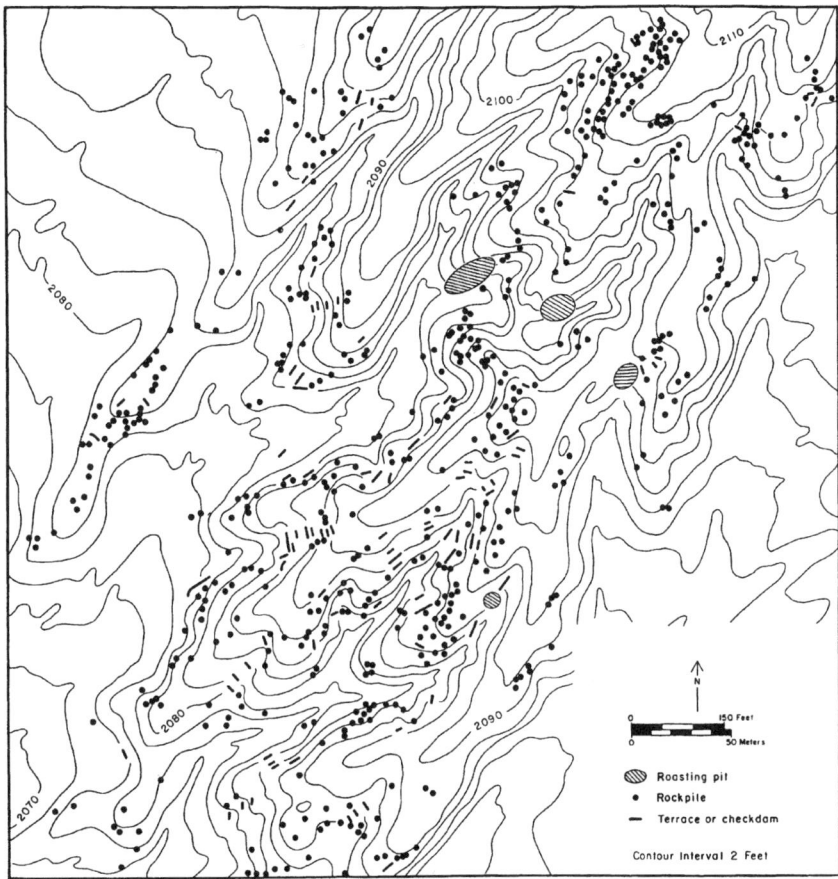

Map 2.2 Mapped segment of a typical distribution of rockpiles, checkdams, contour terraces, and roasting pits in a southern Arizona field

basins. The moisture-enhanced microhabitats of rockpiles, terraces, and checkdams benefited these succulents that were cultivated at somewhat hotter and lower elevations than natural populations. Modern experimental plantings also indicate that rockpiles significantly inhibit rodent predation, which is preferentially focused on the bases and roots and is accomplished by digging beneath the plant (S. Fish et al. 1992).

THE REGIONAL SCALE OF ROCKPILE TECHNIQUES

Recognition of the form and function of dispersed agricultural features such as rockpiles is not a sufficient basis for assessing environmental or economic impact without a means for evaluating areal extent. Estimates are difficult at a regional scale because archaeologists have only sporadically noted these relatively unobtrusive remains. The failure to systematically record such agricultural traces is undoubtedly related to the lack of an ethnographic framework for understanding their significance.

Entries in the Arizona State Museum site files—the largest and most complete repository for archaeological records in Arizona—furnish data for examining scale. A criterion of at least 10 cobble features minimizes the inclusion of non-agricultural activities that might create one or a few heaps of rock. In spite of sporadic recording, 556 locations fitting the minimal criterion have been reported since the early 1950's. The 556 sites represent about 2 percent of the 25,000 entries in the Arizona State Museum files (S. Fish and Fish, in press).

The regional distribution of fields is a significant pattern that emerges despite the incomplete nature of available records. In general, the distribution of rockpile fields parallels the outline of Hohokam and culturally-related occupations of the Classic period (A.D. 1150–1450). A gap coinciding with urban Phoenix reflects modern land disturbance as well as the competing prehistoric alternative of largescale irrigation. Stone agricultural features of various sorts were constructed throughout other parts of Arizona and the Southwest, but the Hohokam domain coincides with a generally well-delimited and continuous distribution of fields in which rounded heaps or rockpiles are a predominant form.

In light of pervasive inconsistencies in the manner of quantifying and bounding rockpile occurrences, areal magnitude must be approached cautiously. The total area reported for all 556 locations is 20,600 acres (8,350 hectares) or about 30 square miles. Average size of fields is not a meaningful figure when individual complexes range from tens of square meters to over 247 acres (100 hectares), and the extremes are unquestionably biased by highly divergent recording procedures. Rockpiles are concentrated in an area between Phoenix and Tucson. In the area surrounding Phoenix, they tend to become more common toward the outer edges of the massively irrigated core. They occur widely in conjunction with Classic period communities along the Santa Cruz, San Pedro, and Gila rivers (S. Fish and Fish, in press).

EXPANDING CONCEPTS OF AGRICULTURAL LANDUSE

Multiple lines of evidence identify agave as the primary crop in a majority of intensively investigated fields. Pollen of corn, cotton, and cucurbits from some fields indicates other, and possibly intercropped, cultigens in a minority of situations that often afford access to sources of supplemental water in addition to surface runoff. The typical location of rockpile fields on dry basin slopes and the location of almost every large complex in such situations, however, is commensurate with drought-resistant agave as the main crop. In the manner of the small leguminous trees and large cacti that distinguish Sonoran Desert vegetation, but unlike annual crops, agaves can make cumulative use of the region's seasonally bimodal rainfall, divided between summer and winter months.

Environmental modifications in rockpile fields take several forms. Pollen assemblages show a proliferation of weedy species in response to soil disturbance and the manipulation of surface runoff. Surficial characteristics of the land were altered by the gathering and piling of rocks. Porous rockpiles and linear features along contours and across small channels intercepted transitory runoff that otherwise would have been rapidly lost from desert hydrological systems. Nevertheless, it is unlikely that runoff captured by rockpile constructions significantly reduced amounts available downslope for other methods of farming.

The ultimate impact of rockpile farming was its contribution to the support of relatively large Hohokam populations in persistent settlements and a correspondingly heightened pressure on the plant and animal resources of their arid surroundings. It enabled cropping on vast stretches of marginal land without other sources of supplemental water. At the same time, localized crop plants in dispersed rock features would have presented no serious conflict with the continued presence of useful wild species within and around rockpile fields.

The cultivation of agave augmented overall Hohokam subsistence by (1) providing an additional, relatively low-maintenance crop; (2) avoiding seasonal bottlenecks in agricultural labor through an alternative schedule for tending, harvesting and processing; (3) permitting "field storage" of harvestable, semi-mature plants that could temporarily counteract catastrophic shortages of annual crops; and (3) insuring a low-level, productive stability on large expanses of land because entire crops of these desert succulents were not lost in seasons of poor precipitation. These land-extensive practices can be seen as an arid land version of agricultural intensification, particularly when fields at a distance from habitations necessitated increased travel.

Dispersed agricultural features serve as a reminder that much of the natural setting of prehistoric settlements was in fact a socially structured landscape that is only partially demarcated by durable remains. Occasional fieldhouses and upright stones resembling ethnographic field boundary markers occur within rockpile complexes. These suggest systems of individual and collective tenure.

Another clue to the socially structured nature of these expansive segments of agricultural landscape comes from regularities in the ratios of communal roasting pits to cultivated area in large fields (S. Fish and Fish, in press). Ratios were calculated for sets of fields in three widely separated Hohokam communities in the Tucson region. Average amount of cultivated land per huge roasting pit in each case fell into a restricted range between 32–42 acres (13 and 17 hectares). This modal tendency strongly suggests commonly held concepts about the organization of land and tenure in rockpile fields and the proper size of groups roasting their harvests in shared pits. Communal harvesting and roasting also enabled efficient expenditure of scarce desert fuels that were already taxed by longterm residence.

Rockpile complexes are difficult to date on the basis of highly diffuse surface scatters of mostly undecorated ceramics. Only a minority of well-studied fields can be assigned an age with reasonable certainty. Hohokam rockpile technology appears to have been employed as early as A.D. 600 (S. Fish et al. 1992). Relatively small rockpile fields occur widely in conjunction with habitation sites clearly dating between A.D. 750 and 1150. However, very large rockpile fields that substantially expanded the agricultural landscape at a distance from villages appear to be a hallmark of the Classic period after A.D. 1150 and to coincide with dense, aggregated populations.

Where systematically recorded, rockpile features disclose a previously unsuspected scale of land-extensive agriculture as a routine component of settlement systems. Recognition significantly expands the scale of culturally-altered Hohokam landscapes. In view of the prominent role of earthen and brush constructions in the ethnographic agriculture of the Sonoran Desert, rockpile technology may well represent the most durable and archaeologically visible remains among a broader but related set of runoff techniques.

Zonal Landuse in a Hohokam Community of the Tucson Basin

The overall impact of Hohokam agriculture can best be judged in the framework of the territorial organization of multi-site communities. It was within these entities that individuals and groups of farmers determined the layout of landuse and the proportional emphasis on different techniques. A comprehensively investigated study area in the northern Tucson Basin near Marana, Arizona, exemplifies the typical duration of Hohokam settlement, varied components of the subsistence base, community development, and responses to increasing population (S. Fish et al. 1992). The Marana Community, reaching maximum size in the early Classic period (ca. A.D. 1150 to 1300), integrated topographic zones presenting reciprocal annual threats to agriculture in the Southwest: floodplains of the primary drainages flooded destructively with too much rain, and upper basin slopes yielded poorly with too little (cf. Lightfoot and Plog 1984; Abruzzi 1989). The greatest degree of productive specialization and exchange within this Marana community, coinciding with highest population levels of the prehistoric sequence, would have served to diffuse localized effects of low and unpredictable precipitation.

Developments in the Classic period illustrate the flexibility of community organization in integrating larger and denser populations. At this time, two earlier communities coalesced into a single larger one incorporating 56 sq mi (146 sq km). A platform mound was constructed in a new central site at the juncture of the two pre-Classic axes of settlement. Additional sites appeared in the previously intervening area, and substantial population growth is apparent. The Classic Marana Community encompassed all environmental diversity in a territory transecting the Tucson Basin from edge to edge. Within the enlarged Classic community boundaries, six topographic zones can be defined on the basis of residence patterns, productive activities, and environmental variables. Environmental opportunities and limitations were different in each of these zones, as were methods and consequences of Hohokam landuse (Map 2.3 and Figure 2.1).

Zone 5

The floodplain and terraces of the Santa Cruz River constitute Zone 5. The densest populations were concentrated along the stretches of high water table. Irrigation would have made this zone the foremost producer of annual crops, such as corn, with high moisture requirements. Due to alluvial deposition on the Santa Cruz floodplain, canals have been identified only through excavation, and the precise extent of irrigation networks is unknown. Where canals could be filled from high water tables along the river, relatively minor investment is apparent in other methods of farming. From a point where canals leave the active floodplain, their paths can be traced for more than 6 mi (10 km) north to the community center. Such canals would have extended fields with crops and dense stands of weedy annuals into the habitat of shrubby creosote bush and bursage associations.

Zone 1

In Zone 1 at the lower edge of the basin slope above the river floodplain, the gradients of tributary streams decrease and the deposition of suspended soil forms alluvial fans. Shallow channels were easily tapped by the ditches and short canals of floodwater farmers. Ethnographic data suggest that better flood-water fields yielded as bountifully as irrigated ones (Doelle 1980: 67–75), although at greater risk from spotty rainfall. Village locations over time correspond with depositionally active fans, but no permanent water occurs in Zone 1. Pre-Classic settlement was within daily travel distances for domestic water from the river. At the beginning of the Classic period, a new canal permitted sites farther from the Santa Cruz.

Zone 2

Permanent water is even more distant from Zone 2, and large drainages are too entrenched for diversion onto fields. This zone was utilized primarily for hunting and gathering prior to the Classic period. Increasing Zone 1 populations at that time transformed large segments of these dry slopes into fields for agave, a dual source of food and fiber. Rockpile field locations, up to 124 acres (50 ha) in extent, covered a total of 1,200 acres (485 ha) in Zone 2. Crop identity is confirmed by charred remains in roasting pits for fieldside processing. In large fields, pits up to 30 m in diameter cooked the communal harvests of groups of farmers (S. Fish et al. 1985, 1992).

Although a few smaller rockpile fields for agave are of pre-Classic age, Classic populations expanded this cultivation onto broad tracts of previously uncultivated and agriculturally marginal land. Zone 2 fields are the most striking evidence for response to the heightened subsistence requirements of Classic community inhabitants. Fields of the largest size were constructed uphill from

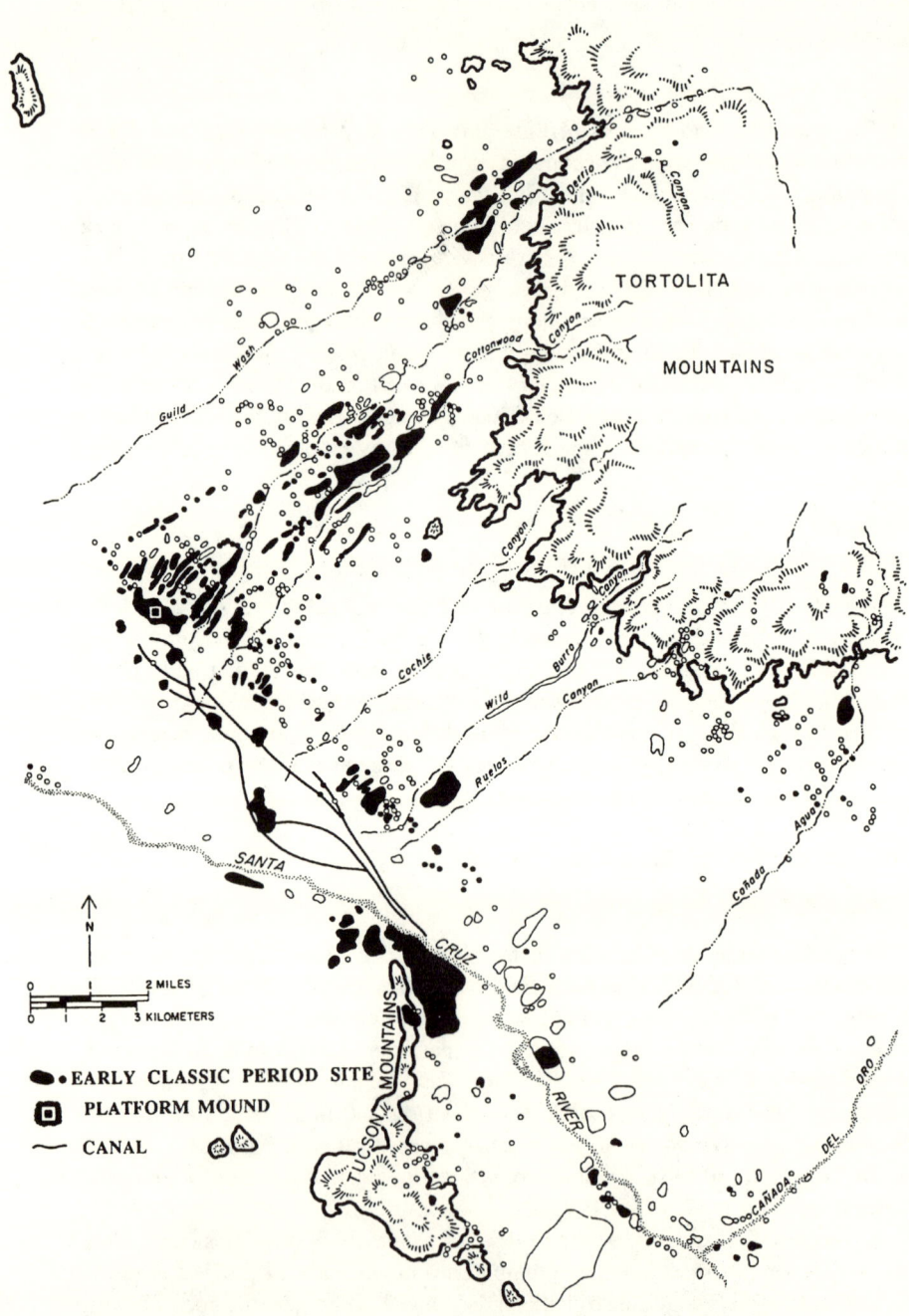

TORTOLITA

MOUNTAINS

EARLY CLASSIC PERIOD SITE

PLATFORM MOUND

CANAL

Map 2.3 The early Classic Period Marana community

40

Figure 2.1
Zonal land use in the Marana Community

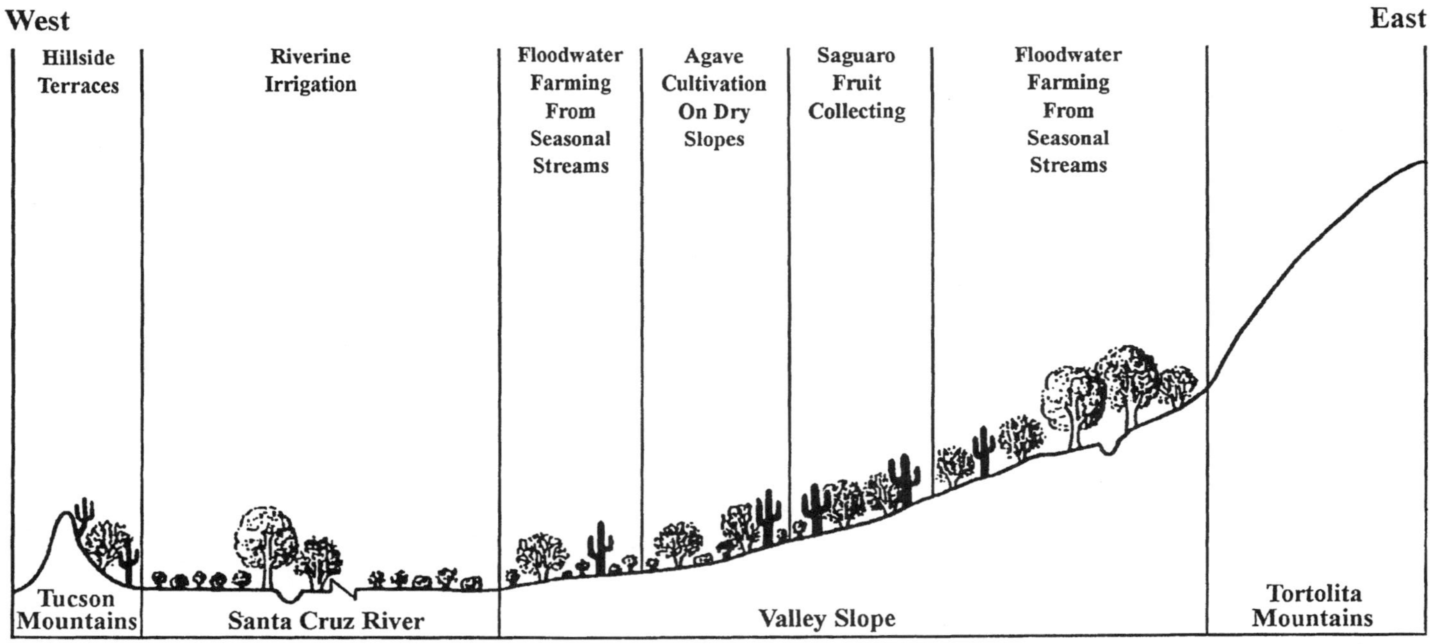

West — East

Hillside Terraces | Riverine Irrigation | Floodwater Farming From Seasonal Streams | Agave Cultivation On Dry Slopes | Saguaro Fruit Collecting | Floodwater Farming From Seasonal Streams

Tucson Mountains | Santa Cruz River | Valley Slope | Tortolita Mountains

41

a densely settled segment of Zone 1 where residents had relatively poor access to land for irrigated or floodwater farming.

Zone 3

Domestic and agricultural water is also absent in Zone 3. Residential sites are lacking. The common site type consists of huge scatters of broken pottery and few other artifacts. Like Piman groups of later times, community members appear to have returned to the same camps near dense stands of saguaro cactus year after year, harvesting the fruits for a few weeks in the early summer. Vessels for camp water supplies and for boiling the fruit to make saguaro syrup were broken, and the debris accumulated over time.

Zone 4

Shallow bedrock on the mountain flanks insures high water tables in Zone 4 drainages. The three largest streams originating in the mountains had floodplains of sufficient width for floodwater farming on bottomland and are correlated with clustered sites of all periods on surrounding ridges. Smaller drainages and surface runoff were also utilized, with low terraces and checkdams at scattered locations. Sets of rockpiles and contour terraces for agave are present in Zone 4, but do not compare in size or number with fields in Zone 2 below.

Zone 6

The compressed basin slope west of the Santa Cruz forms Zone 6. Small alluvial fans supported only minor floodwater farming. In the adjacent Tucson Mountains, rock-walled terraces that supported dwellings and small gardens were constructed on hillsides. Volcanic soils in this low range are high in clay and are moisture retentive. Above the elevation affected by cold air drainage and winter freezes on the basin floor, small spring crops or terraces could precede major summer harvests. Charred agave and tools related to its cultivation from excavated structures suggest a planting pattern still followed in Mexico, with agaves lining the walls and annual crops on the remainder of the planting surfaces (S. Fish et al. 1984; Downum et al. 1994).

HOHOKAM AGRICULTURE IN LONGTERM PERSPECTIVE

The Hohokam are noted for the most enduring settlements of the prehistoric Southwest. Renewal of fields through waterborne nutrients was fundamental to their achievement of a sustainable agriculture based on a combination of technologies from the most impressive irrigation systems of aboriginal North America to simple diversions of flooding streams. Domesticated crops were supplemented by a series of tended and weedy indigenous species of enhanced productivity in agricultural landscapes. The effects of intensive landuse were concentrated in the vicinity of settlements and water sources. Surrounding areas of land-extensive cropping utilized water that otherwise would have escaped from desert ecosystems in rapid downstream runoff. Uninhabited land within and beyond community boundaries offered reserves of wild resources.

The massive canals of the Phoenix Basin, supporting what may well have been the densest populations of the prehistoric Southwest, made lasting imprints on the land. Their paths could still be largely traced across basin floors prior to accelerating land development in the early part of this century. Modern soil maps still delineate bands and swaths of alluvial sediments along the courses of ancient irrigation networks. Canal segments resurrected by Pima successors of the Hohokam in the nineteenth century produced surpluses sold to the United States army, gold rush travelers, and others crossing the Arizona deserts to California. Thereafter, entrepreneurs from the East revamped additional prehistoric canal lines for the beginnings of largescale irrigated agriculture surrounding the present day cities of Phoenix and Florence.

Hohokam struggles with the powerful surges of Sonoran Desert rivers are documented in parallel sets of adjacent canal lines. These attest to the ongoing need to repair, rebuild, and realign. Centuries later, less experienced desert irrigators unwittingly rerouted desert rivers on occasion through their disastrous capacity to redirect scouring floods with unyielding cement dams.

Hohokam floodwater cultivators lived from the bounty of storm-driven floods but were simultaneously subject to the unpredictable consequences of uncontrolled flows. As shallow drainages flooded and shifted across alluvial fans, they often buried the houses of farmers in the same rich sediments that nourished their fields. Reoccupations at successively higher intervals in the accumulating stratigraphy of desert alluvial fans are a reminder that floodwater farmers were the beneficiaries of natural processes beyond their direct control.

Untold thousands of rockpiles still dotting southern Arizona slopes mark the outlying expanses of agricultural landscapes virtually unchanged since the era of Hohokam planting. Rockpiles and contour terraces rest undisturbed on modern surfaces, demonstrating a remarkable geomorphic stability from the time of their construction until the present. Thin layers of waterlaid sand overlie the intact ashy fill of roasting pits that the Hohokam preferentially excavated into the softer soils of tertiary drainages rather than the hard-packed ground to either side. Only the dense halos of modern annual and perennial plants in and around prehistoric cobble features attest to their persisting status as enhanced microhabitats for desert plants.

Neolithic societies of the world's arid regions add a broader perspective for the environmental relationships and impacts of Hohokam agriculturalists. Unlike their counterparts in the Old World, the Hohokam were direct gatherers and consumers of desert vegetation, without domesticated animal herds as highly efficient, but ultimately destructive, intermediaries in harvesting dispersed desert biomass. As a result, fragile Sonoran Desert ground covers were not comprehensively destroyed, nor was damage to perennial woody vegetation as far-reaching.

Hohokam continuity cannot be fully explained, however, by a versatile suite of productive and extractive techniques in desert settings. The integration of the residents of multiple settlements into community organization played a critical role in their ability to meet both short and longterm subsistence challenges. Population in individual communities must have represented a successful balance between adequate and sustainable production under arid conditions and the numbers of farmers necessary to maintain canal networks or to spread agricultural risks over a sufficient number of environmental zones. The constraints of the Sonoran Desert environment did not preclude social and economic innovation by the Hohokam, despite their continued dependence on the same repertoire of farming methods. Changing configurations of population, settlement, and landuse continued to appear as dynamic and evolving societies implemented new combinations and intensities of existing techniques.

REFERENCES

Abruzzi, W. S. 1989. Ecology, resource distribution, and Mormon settlement in northeastern Arizona. *American Anthropologist* 91: 642–655.

Ackerly, Neal, Jerry B. Howard, and Randall H. McGuire. 1987. *La Ciudad Canals: A Study of Hohokam Irrigation Systems at the Community Level*. Arizona State University Anthropological Field Studies No. 17. Tempe: Department of Anthropology, Arizona State University.

Bohrer, Vorsila L. 1970. Paleoecology of Snaketown. *The Kiva* 36: 11–19.

———. 1991. Recently recognized cultivated and encouraged plants among the Hohokam. *The Kiva* 56: 227–236.

Brown, David E., editor. 1982. Biotic communities of the American Southwest: United States and Mexico. *Desert Plants* 4: 1–341.

———. 1994. *Biotic Communities: Southwestern United States and Northwestern Mexico*. Salt Lake City: University of Utah Press.

Bryan, Kirk. 1929. Floodwater farming. *The Geographical Review* 19: 444–456.

Bye, Robert. 1979. Incipient domestication of mustards in northwestern Mexico. *The Kiva* 44: 237–256.

Castetter, E. F. and W. H. Bell. 1942. *Pima and Papago Indian Agriculture*. Albuquerque: University of New Mexico Press.

Crosswhite, Frank. 1981. Desert plants, habitat, and agriculture in relation to the major pattern of cultural differentiation in the O'odham people of southern Arizona. *Desert Plants* 3: 47–76.

Crown, Patricia. 1987. Classic period Hohokam settlement and land use in the Casa Grande ruin area, Arizona. *Journal of Field Archaeology* 14 (2): 147–162.

Dart, Allen. 1986. Sediment accumulation along Hohokam canals. *The Kiva* 51: 63–84.

Dean, Jeffrey S., Mark C. Slaughter, and Dennie O. Bowden. 1996. Desert dendrochronology: tree-ring dating prehistoric sites in the Tucson Basin. *The Kiva* 62: 7–26.

Doelle, William. 1980. *Past Adaptive Patterns in Western Papagueria: An Archaeological Study of Nonriverine Resource Use*. Ph.D. dissertation, Department of Anthropology, University of Arizona, Tucson.

Doolittle, William E. 1990. *Canal Irrigation in Prehistoric Mexico: The Sequence of Technological Change*. Austin: University of Texas Press.

Downum, Christian, Paul Fish, and Suzanne Fish. 1994. Refining the role of the Cerros de Trincheras in southern Arizona settlement. *The Kiva* 59: 271–296.

Doyel, David E. 1976. Classic period Hohokam in the Gila Basin. *The Kiva* 43: 27–38.

———. 1980. Hohokam social organization and the Sedentary to Classic period transition. In *Current Issues in Hohokam Prehistory*, edited by D. Doyel and F. Plog, pp. 23–40. Arizona State University Anthropological Research Paper No. 23. Tempe: Department of Anthropology, Arizona State University.

———. 1991. Hohokam cultural evolution in the Phoenix Basin. In *Exploring the Hohokam: Prehistoric Desert Peoples of the Southwest*, edited by George J. Gumerman, pp. 133–161. Albuquerque: University of New Mexico Press.

Fish, Paul R. 1989. The Hohokam: 1000 years of prehistory in the Sonoran Desert. In *Dynamics of Southwestern Prehistory*, edited by Linda S. Cordell and George J. Gumerman, pp. 19–63. Washington: Smithsonian Institution Press.

Fish, Paul R., and Suzanne K. Fish. 1991. Hohokam political and social organization. In *Exploring the Hohokam: Prehistoric Desert Peoples of the Southwest*, edited by George J. Gumerman, pp. 84–101. Albuquerque: University of New Mexico Press.

Fish, Paul R., Suzanne K. Fish, C. Brennan, D. Gann, and J. Bayman. 1992. Marana: configuration of a Hohokam platform mound site. In *Proceedings of the Second Salado Conference, Glob, Arizona, 1992*, edited by R. Lange and S. Germick, pp. 62–68. Phoenix: Arizona Archaeological Society.

Fish, Suzanne K. 1984. The modified environment of the Salt-Gila Aqueduct Project sites: a palynological perspective. In *Hohokam Archaeology along the Salt-Gila Aqueduct, Central Arizona Project*. Vol. 7, *Environment and Subsistence*, edited by L. Teague and P. Crown, pp. 39–51. Arizona State Museum Archaeological Series No. 150. Tucson: Arizona State Museum, University of Arizona.

———. 1985. Prehistoric disturbance floras of the lower Sonoran Desert and their implications. In *Late Quaternary Vegetation and Climate in the American Southwest*, edited by B. F. Jacobs, P. L. Fall, and O. K. Davis, pp. 77–88. American Association of Stratigraphic Palynologists Contribution Series No. 16. Houston: American Association of Stratigraphic Palynologists.

———. 1996. Dynamics of scale in the southern deserts. In *Interpreting Southwestern Diversity: Underlying Principles and Overarching Patterns*, edited by P. Fish and J. J. Reid, pp. 107–114. Arizona State University Anthropological Research Papers No. 49. Tempe: Department of Anthropology, Arizona State University.

Fish, Suzanne K. and Paul R. Fish. In press. Unsuspected magnitudes: the scale of Hohokam agriculture. In *Human Impact on the Environment: An Archaeological Perspective*, edited by C. L. Redman, S. James, P. Fish, and J. D. Rogers. Washington: Smithsonian Institution Press.

Fish, Suzanne K., Paul R. Fish, and Christian Downum. 1984. Hohokam terraces and agricultural production in the Tucson Basin. In *Prehistoric Agricultural Strategies in the Southwest*, edited by S. Fish and P. Fish, pp. 55–71. Arizona State University Anthropological Research Paper No. 33. Tempe: Department of Anthropology, Arizona State University.

Fish, Suzanne K., Paul R. Fish, and John H. Madsen. 1990. Analyzing regional agriculture: a Hohokam example. In *The Archaeology of Regions: The Case for Full-*

Coverage Survey, edited by S. Fish and S. Kowalewski, pp. 189–218. Washington: Smithsonian Institution Press.

Fish, Suzanne K., Paul R. Fish, and John H. Madsen. 1992. *The Marana Community in the Hohokam World*. Anthropological Papers of the University of Arizona No. 56. Tucson: University of Arizona Press.

Fish, Suzanne K., Paul R. Fish, Charles H. Miksicek, and John H. Madsen. 1985. Prehistoric agave cultivation in southern Arizona. *Desert Plants* 7 (2): 107–112.

Fish, Suzanne K. and Gary P. Nabhan. 1991. Desert as context: the Hohokam environment. In *Exploring the Hohokam: Prehistoric Desert Peoples of the Southwest*, edited by George P. Gumerman, pp. 35–54. Albuquerque: University of New Mexico Press.

Gasser, Robert E. 1982. Hohokam use of desert plant foods. *Desert Plants* 3: 216–234.

Gasser, Robert E., and Scott M. Kwiatkowski. 1991. Food for thought: recognizing patterns in Hohokam subsistence. In *Exploring the Hohokam: Prehistoric Desert Peoples of the American Southwest*, edited by George P. Gumerman, pp. 417–460. Albuquerque: University of New Mexico Press.

Gregory, David A. 1987. The morphology of platform mounds and the structure of Classic Hohokam sites. In *The Hohokam Village: Site Structure and Organization*, edited by David E. Doyel, pp. 183–210. Glenwood Springs, Colorado: Southwestern and Rocky Mountain Division of the American Association for the Advancement of Science.

Gregory, David A. and Fred Nials. 1985. Observations concerning the distribution of Classic period Hohokam platform mounds. In *Proceedings of the 1983 Hohokam Symposium*, edited by A. E. Dittert, Jr., and D. E. Dove, pp. 373–388. Arizona Archaeological Society Occasional Paper No. 2. Phoenix: Arizona Archaeological Society.

Haury, Emil W. 1976. *The Hohokam: Desert Farmers and Craftsmen*. Tucson: University of Arizona Press.

Howard, Jerry B. 1993. A paleohydraulic approach to examining agricultural intensification in Hohokam irrigation systems. In *Economic Aspects of Water Management in the Prehispanic New World*, edited by B. Isaac and V. Scarborough, pp. 263–324. Research in Economic Anthropology Series, Supplement 7. Greenwich, Conn.: JAI Press.

Huckell, Bruce B. 1996. *Of Marshes and Maize: Preceramic Agricultural Settlements in the Cienega Valley*. Anthropological Papers of the University of Arizona No. 59. Tucson: University of Arizona Press.

Kohler, Timothy A. and M. H. Matthews. 1988. Long-term Anasazi land use and forest reduction: a case study from southwest Colorado. *American Antiquity* 53: 537–564.

Lightfoot Kent G. and Fred Plog. 1984. Intensification along the north side of the Mogollon Rim. In *Prehistoric Agricultural Strategies in the Southwest*, edited by S. Fish and P. Fish, pp. 79–95. Arizona State University Anthropological Research Papers No. 33. Tempe: Department of Anthropology, Arizona State University.

Mabry, Jonathan B., editor. 1998. *Archaeological Investigations of Early Village Sites in the Middle Santa Cruz Valley*. Center for Desert Archaeology Anthropological Papers No. 19. Tucson: Center for Desert Archaeology.

Masse, W. Bruce. 1981. Prehistoric irrigation systems in the Salt River Valley, Arizona. *Science* 214: 408–415.

McGinnies, William. 1981. *Discovering the Desert: Legacy of the Carnegie Desert Botanical Laboratory*. Tucson: University of Arizona Press.

Miksicek, Charles. 1984. Historic desertification, prehistoric vegetation change, and Hohokam subsistence in the Salt-Gila Basin. In *Hohokam Archaeology along the Salt-Gila Aqueduct*. Vol. 7, *Environment and Subsistence*, edited by L. Teague and P. Crown, pp. 53–80. Arizona State Museum Archaeological Series No. 150. Tucson: Arizona State Museum, University of Arizona.

———. 1988. Rethinking Hohokam paleoethnobotanical assemblages: a progress report for the Tucson Basin. In *Recent Research on Tucson Basin Prehistory*, edited by W. Doelle and P. Fish, pp. 47–56. Institute for American Research Anthropological Papers 10. Tucson: Institute for American Research.

———. 1995. Temporal trends in the eastern Tonto Basin: an archaeobotanical perspective. In *The Roosevelt Community Development Study*. Vol. 3, Paleobotanical and Osteological Analyses, edited by M. Elson and J. Clark, pp. 43–84. Center for Desert Archaeology Anthropological Papers No. 14. Tucson: Center for Desert Archaeology.

Nabhan, Gary P. 1979. The ecology of floodwater farming in southwestern North America. *Agro-ecosystems* 5:245–255.

———. 1986. Ak-chin "arroyo mouth" and the environmental setting of the Papago Indian fields in the Sonoran Desert. *Applied Geography* 6: 61–75.

Nabhan, Gary P., A. M. Rea, K. L. Reichhardt, E. Melink, and C. F. Hutchinson. 1983. Papago influences on habitat and biotic diversity: Quitovac Oasis ethnoecology. *Journal of Ethnobiology* 2: 124–143.

Nials, Fred, David Gregory, and Donald Graybill. 1989. Salt River streamflow and Hohokam irrigation systems. In *The 1982–1984 Excavations at Las Colinas: The Site and Its Features*, by D. Gregory, W. Deaver, S. Fish, R. Gardiner, R. Layhe, F. Nials, and L. Teague, pp. 275–306. Arizona State Museum Archaeological Series 162. Tucson: Arizona State Museum, University of Arizona.

Nicholas, Linda and Gary M. Feinman. 1989. A regional perspective on Hohokam irrigation in the lower Salt River Valley, Arizona. In *The Socio-political Structure of Prehistoric Southwestern Societies*, edited by Steadman Upham, Kent G. Lightfoot, and Roberta Jewett, pp. 199–236. Boulder: Westview Press.

Rea, Amadeo M. 1979. Hunting lexemic categories of the Pima Indians. *The Kiva* 44: 113–119.

———. 1981. Resource utilization and food taboos of Sonoran Desert peoples. *Journal of Ethnobiology* 1: 69–83.

———. 1983. *Once a River: Bird Life and Habitat Changes on the Middle Gila River*. Tucson: University of Arizona Press.

Schroeder, Albert. 1960. *The Hohokam, Sinagua, and the Hakataya*. Society for American Archaeology Archives of Archaeology 5. Madison: Society for American Archaeology.

Sellers, William D., Richard H. Hill, and M. Sanderson-Rae. 1985. *Arizona Climate: The First Hundred Years*. Tucson: Institute of Atmospheric Physics, University of Arizona.

Sires, Earl W. 1987. Hohokam architectural variability and site structure during the Sedentary-Classic transition. In *The Hohokam Village: Site Structure and Organization*, edited by D. Doyel, pp. 171–182. Glenwood Springs, Colorado:

Southwest and Rocky Mountain Division of the American Association for the Advancement of Science.

Szuter, Christine R. and Frank E. Bayham. 1989. Sedentism and animal procurement among desert horticulturalists in the North American Southwest. In *Farmers as Hunters: The Implications of Sedentism*, edited by S. Kent, pp. 80–95. Cambridge: Cambridge University Press.

Szuter, Christine R. and W. B. Gillispie. 1994. Interpreting use of animal resources at prehistoric American Southwest communities. In *The Ancient Southwest Community*, edited by R. Leonard and W. W. Wills, pp. 67–76. Albuquerque: University of New Mexico Press.

Vander Wall, S. B. and J. A. MacMahan. 1984. Avian distribution patterns along a Sonoran Desert bajada. *Journal of Arid Environments* 7: 59–74.

Whiting, Alfred E. 1939. *The Ethnobotany of the Hopi*. Museum of Northern Arizona Bulletin No. 15. Flagstaff: Museum of Northern Arizona.

Wilcox, David and Lynette Shenk. 1977. *The Architecture of the Casa Grande and its Interpretation*. Arizona State Museum Archaeological Series No. 115. Tucson: Arizona State Museum, University of Arizona.

Wilcox, David and Charles Sternberg. 1983. *Hohokam Ballcourts and Their Interpretation*. Arizona State Museum Archaeological Series No. 160. Tucson: Arizona State Museum, University of Arizona.

3

Soaking It in: Northern Rio Grande Pueblo Lessons of Water Management and Landscape Ecology

Kurt F. Anschuetz

INTRODUCTION

Agriculture in the North American Southwest is not an easy undertaking. Successful farming requires tremendous knowledge of cultivars' needs, climate, soil, physiography, and the natural history of water among the many scattered localities making up the setting's physically vast and diverse landscape. The task of sustaining agricultural prosperity in this region over the long term demands ingenuity and a commitment both to place and to one's cultivars. Perhaps by virtue of their more than 1,500-year-long history of interaction with their landscape as subsistence farmers, the Southwest's Pueblo people developed economic, social, and ideational technologies (after Stone 1993: 78; see also Earle 1980: 4)[1] that allowed resiliency in responding to unpredictable changes in their physical, social, and cultural environments. More than just responding to environmental change, the Pueblos also used their technologies to prepare for anticipated departures from usual everyday living conditions (after Anschuetz 1998a). Even as they coped with disturbances that potentially threatened the welfare of their communities, the Pueblos likely redefined their own conditions for living in the future (after Minnis 1985: 19; see also Watts 1980).

   In making these statements, my purpose is neither to glorify nor romanticize the Pueblos' past. The spatial expanse of the physically inhabited Pueblo world today is greatly circumscribed in comparison to the breadth of the territory occupied by Pueblo people in centuries past (e.g., see Adler 1996). Whatever its causes, the geographic contraction in the Pueblos' range of permanent habitation between the twelfth and early seventeenth centuries and the displacement of people to scattered enclaves around the central Colorado Plateau's periphery must have been a difficult time.

Archaeologists carefully delineate patterns of quantitative change exhibited among old Pueblo material cultural assemblages across the dimensions of space and time. They also ascribe qualitative behavioral meanings to the observed changes in the organization of Pueblo settlement, production, consumption, and social interaction. In building explanations for cultural-historical sequences, investigators characterize patterns of settlement displacement and realignment of social relations as the failure of existing organizations to buffer the stresses that confronted the people participating in—and being served by—the cultural system. Although the economic, social, and ideational technologies that defined certain ancestral Pueblo cultural systems, such as the "Chaco Phenomenon" disappeared long ago, archaeologists never have forwarded the claim that Pueblo culture ceased to exist. For these reasons, we can say that Pueblo culture evolved over time, all the while sustaining a coherent sense of tradition across the generations.[2]

Today, the success of the Pueblos in dampening the many great challenges to their physical and cultural survival over their long history is readily visible. To witness: Hopi, Keresan, Tewa, Tiwa, Towa, and Zuñi peoples persisted in their centuries-old communities as subsistence agriculturalists in the core areas of their traditional homelands through the first part of the twentieth century. The comprehension and effective application of lessons of sustainable water management and landscape ecology that permitted these peoples to sustain their families in place between roughly A.D. 1300 and 1940 unquestionably constitutes a cornerstone of this significant cultural-historical achievement. While many families have members who still garden and farm, none of the 20 living Pueblo communities in Arizona and New Mexico[3] depend primarily on agriculture for their economic sustenance today. Nonetheless, references to a community's agricultural heritage are ubiquitous in each Pueblo's stories, songs, and ceremonies, both public and personal. For each community, its agricultural traditions define the prevailing cultural fabric and inform the people of their past. In this way, valuable lessons learned by people long ago, including those pertaining to sustainable water management and landscape ecology, are embedded within the Pueblos' richly textured cultural-historical narratives. Encoded in metaphor, highly meaningful qualitative information from the past awaits to be drawn upon, as is appropriate, for use by present-day generations as they prepare for the future.

The purpose of my discussion is to examine the major principles of water management and landscape ecology that underlay traditional Pueblo agricultural adaptations in the North American Southwest. Given the long history of the production of domestic cultigens in this region and the great diversity in the structure and organization of Pueblo agriculture across the dimensions of space and time, this review is neither all encompassing nor synthetic. Instead, I focus my comments primarily on findings obtained while participating in studies of late pre-Columbian and early Colonial Tewa, Keresan, Tiwa, and Towa farming adaptations along the Rio Grande Valley in north-central New Mexico (Maxwell and Anschuetz 1992; Anschuetz 1994, 1995, 1998a among others). I supplement these archaeological observations with information compiled while working with ethnographic materials regarding Hopi agriculture and water management (Anschuetz 1976; Ford with Anschuetz 1989). Residents of Tesuque, Santa Clara, San Juan, Picuris, Taos, and Jemez pueblos have shared wisdom about their agricultural traditions through various community publications (e.g., see Santa Clara Pueblo Cultural Preservation Program 1995; Abeyta et al. 1995; Sanchez and Cajete 1997). Community members also have offered insightful comments during slide presentations and archaeological field trips (e.g., see Anschuetz 1998a; see also Anschuetz, Scheick, and Hena 1998). I also have benefited from generous invitations to attend permacultural and environmental workshops at several of these communities.

My present survey necessarily is selective. Nonetheless, I believe that its five topics are broadly relevant to evaluations of Pueblo water management and landscape ecology.

First, I consider seemingly widespread perceptions that subsistence agriculture, such as that practiced traditionally by the Pueblos, necessarily (1) depends on simple technology and (2) is a passive endeavor dependent almost exclusively on natural environmental conditions. To the contrary, I suggest that while the Pueblos' physical tools, indeed, are technologically simple devices, the strategies governing their use and manipulation of all other agricultural resources are dependent on highly evolved systems of cultural knowledge. Through their tactics and strategies, Pueblo people interacted dynamically with their physical, social, and cultural environments to allow the resiliency that they needed to cope with ever-changing conditions.

Second, I examine another common perception that agriculture in temperate climates is a seasonal endeavor defined by the last killing frost in the spring and the first killing frost in the fall. In the semiarid Southwest especially, agriculture depends heavily on technologies to harvest and conserve valuable moisture resources throughout the annual cycle. Among the Pueblos, harvest time simultaneously marks the end of one agricultural cycle and the beginning of another in an ever-renewing process.

Third, I discuss how Pueblo farmers traditionally interacted with their physical environments to enhance the water absorption properties of local watersheds to capture and protect precipitation, runoff and groundwater moisture for their crops. I suggest that the Pueblo populations physically manipulated their agricultural landscapes on a much broader scale than has been recognized by most people familiar only with Anglo-European farming techniques.

Fourth, I consider the appropriateness of the ideas that (1) pre-Colombian Pueblo agricultural field technologies are functionally interchangeable in the production of crops and (2) their economic usefulness is defined by the frost-free season at which time they are directly under cultivation. I suggest the development of agricultural fields, the methods used to harvest crops, and the maintenance of agricultural landscapes over the long term, including fallow cycles, have significant ecological implications for increasing the availability of "wild" plant and animal species.

Finally, I explore possible meanings of a prevalent Pueblo metaphor, "Movement is life," from a cultural-ecological perspective. I conclude that archaeology, history, and ethnography indicate old fieldworks can, under circumstances where sustainable land use practices were sustained for generations, be a material manifestation of a people's commitment to place over a long-term cycle of ecological renewal.

ELEGANT TECHNOLOGIES, SOPHISTICATED UNDERSTANDINGS

Having grown up in northwestern Indiana and southeastern Michigan, I was acculturated into thinking that maize production required John Deere tractors, deep plowing, petrochemical fertilizers, monocropping, Pioneer Hi-Bred International seeds, insecticides, and mechanical harvesters. Driving regularly across the Saginaw bay area to visit family living along Michigan's Lake Huron shore, I was exposed to tilled fields and ditch works, whereby farmers drained excess moisture from their soils to prevent the waterlogging of their crops. Passing through the Midwest's Corn Belt on my journey out to New Mexico to participate in my first archaeological fieldwork as an undergraduate student, I remember thinking of one of twentieth-century America's great agricultural icons, the Jolly Green Giant. Although I was familiar with the sight of maize agriculture, I found the Corn Belt surprising at first sight. With the humanity of individual farmers obscured by their mechanically complex and powerful technologies, the great magnitude of their landscape engineering promoted feelings of awe. It seemed only natural that small prairie towns swallowed up by vast fields densely packed with corn stalks and dwarfed by towering grain elevators led to the idea of using an unworldly anthropomorphic figure to promote this industrial agricultural miracle. I recall contemplating that the Jolly Green Giant symbol implies that the sum of these agricultural transformations and successes, although made possible by our mechanical inventions, is bigger than ourselves. Was it, perhaps, that the scale of these changes is rather monstrous?

Later during that summer, I drove through a number of Pueblo land grants and reservations across the Southwest and saw cornfields growing under what I would have thought were insurmountably arid conditions. I was curious: How did these farmers grow crops in desiccated environments often characterized by barren, sandy soils? Moreover, I wondered: How were the Hopi, Keresan, Tewa, Tiwa, Towa, and Zuñi people able to endure as subsistence agriculturalists in villages that archaeology has shown to have continuous occupational histories extending seven or more centuries back in time?

In pursuing these questions, I have found that archaeology, history, ethnography, and permaculture have offered many useful insights into the structure and organization of the Pueblos' agricultural traditions that evolved over countless generations. I learned that the answer to questions about the Pueblos' ability to sustain agricultural production in fragile, arid environments largely lies in their development of elegant economic, social, and ideational technologies that offered resiliency in the face of ever-changing environments. Through their long history of interacting with often-formidable challenges to their survival, the Pueblos developed dynamic tactics and strategies[4] for structuring their farmwork and organizing their agricultural labor that allowed flexibility in responding to realized or anticipated environmental changes.

We can use a well-known photograph dating to circa 1915 to illustrate this discussion, both for what it shows and for what the camera cannot possibly observe. In this picture, an elderly Hopi man leans over his dibble as he digs a small, deep hole for planting maize seed in the barren, sandy soil of his field (Photo 3.1).

In comparison to the transformation of the Midwest into the Jolly Green Giant's bountiful dominion, we might be tempted to say that the Hopi farmer's digging stick technology is crude, if not downright primitive. We might suggest further that where contemporary industrial agriculture demonstrates a capacity to impose control on nature, the Pueblo farmer's influence over—and impact upon—his physical environment is minor. On the other hand, through its depiction of the dignity, grace, and propriety that this farmer brings to his labor, the scene answers the very question that the Jolly Green Giant's presence seems to ask: Yes, agriculture is a distinctly human enterprise, whereby people interact with—and modify culturally—their environments to produce domesticated cultigens.[5]

Despite its visual power, the photograph offers only a constrained glimpse into traditional Pueblo agricultural technologies. After all, we only see a farmer working with a wood digging stick. We cannot comprehend the cultural context—that rich milieu of economic, societal and ideational information—defining the full range of tactics and strategies governing how the farmer was using the dibble.

For example, the photograph reveals nothing about the sandy soil's ability to harvest and conserve water from both the winter's melting snow and the summer's high intensity, but short-lived, monsoons to recharge the soil's moisture reserves for crop production. We cannot see that the farmer is digging a hole (See photo 3.1) that will measure between (25–40 cm [10–16 in]) in depth for sowing seed corn directly within the soil's greatest moisture reserves for springtime germination and vigorous early summer growth. The picture does not show us that the Pueblos long ago had developed specialized maize varieties whose seedlings possess a specialized organ, the mesocotyl, that can survive the deep planting that would be fatal to Midwestern hybrid corn seed. How can the picture inform us that the farmer's stalks only will grow to a height of just slightly more than one meter (3.3 ft) under usual conditions? How will we ever know

Photo 3.1 Hopi farmer working his field using a wood digging stick, circa 1915. Note the seed bag that the man is holding in his left hand. He will dig a hole between 25 and 40 cm (10–16 in) deep to sow his seeds in moist soil, which can sustain the plants through the dry spring until the arrival of the summer rains. The farmer will place as many as a dozen seeds in the hole with the expectation that four to six healthy corn plants will survive to produce ears of corn. (Courtesy Museum of New Mexico, Neg. No. 21606)

that the stunted-appearing plants are neither weak nor damaged but effectively conserve moisture and energy for the production of an ear measuring 30 cm (12 in) in length?

The photograph does not indicate that the planting of multiple seeds in a hill allows the stalk's outer leaves to absorb the brunt of damage from abrasive spring sands and dry summer heat to protect the plant's delicate reproductive parts. We cannot tell that the farmer will place the corn hills sufficiently far apart (usually three to four paces) to ensure that the lateral root systems of plants among neighboring hills will not compete with one another for valuable moisture. The scene does not instruct us about the refined systems of botanical and soil classification, hydrological engineering, solar observation, color symbolism, social relationship, and ceremonialism that inform the Pueblos' elaborate decision-making processes governing when, where, and what to plant. Lastly, the picture offers no information about varying cornfield productivity across space and over time, calendrical community ritual, or the need for families to maintain a two- or three-year supply of corn for food and seed in their storehouses.[6]

The digging stick visible in this picture is a technologically simple instrument. Yet, the dibble was one of the principal implements in the Pueblos' agricultural tool kit for many hundreds of years. Moreover, despite the digging stick's unexceptional material form, it is wholly incorrect to characterize traditional Pueblo agriculture systems as having been based on a singular or crude technology. A complex interplay of physical, social, and cultural environmental variables defines the Pueblos' world and imposes critical limits on subsistence-level agricultural production. Constrained by the physical limitations of the people's labor but empowered by their astute knowledge of the world, the tactics and strategies of Pueblo agricultural production include sophisticated social and ideational components that complement the people's comparatively limited physical implements. Together, their economic, social, and ideational technologies helped minimize the likelihood that the Pueblo people's energies—and precious seed stock and water resources—would be wasted.

Of course, crop failures are an ever-present risk in agricultural practice, regardless of technology. Consequently, farmers never have a guarantee that they always will enjoy a bountiful harvest in return for their investments.

In the face of the Southwest's often difficult climatic conditions, the Pueblos periodically did suffer crop losses because of frost, hail, prolonged drought (unless ample irrigation water was available), flooding, infectious disease, insect infestation, and raiding. Given the vagaries of the region's environment, some farmers suffered crop failures any given year, although most others enjoyed average yields (see Ford 1972a). During exceptionally difficult climatic downturns spanning more than two or three years in duration, productive shortfalls periodically afflicted regional areas. Farming families that experienced immediate duress undoubtedly would have relied on their storehouses, increased hunting and gathering, and exchange or, possibly, short-term residence with kin and partners whose fortunes might not have been so dire. As conditions hostile to farming persisted over time and subsumed ever-wider geographic areas, pueblo groups would have needed to rely upon other, more costly tactics and strategies to cope with their agricultural losses. Such mechanisms likely included long-term settlement shifts, among others.

To sustain their communities year after year, the Pueblos had to incorporate ways to buffer the stresses that arose from recurrent seasonal and interannual cycles of crop failure. Although without writing and formal academic training, the Pueblos developed considerable practical knowledge in astronomy, biology, climatology, hydrology, pedology, and ecology. The Pueblos also used oral history based on metaphor to trace the intricate culture history of their people across the generations to remember how their ancestors acted when confronted with exceptional environmental states (e.g., see Whiteley 1989). Together, cultural mechanisms that facilitated both the empirical observation of contemporary worldly phenomena and the remembrance of learned experiences from time beyond the seven generations of living memory provided guidelines for the people in developing strategies of action.

Importantly, the Pueblos did not simply wait passively for some environmental perturbation to damage their crops. Through their ability to anticipate short-term future conditions, the Pueblos' long history of cultural survival indicates that they were successful, more often than not, in developing appropriate strategies for mobilizing resources to dampen perceived—and anticipated—risks.

We need to return once more to the illustration of the Pueblo farmer working in his field. By acknowledging the evolved and sophisticated cultural system of understanding that informed the man how to use his digging stick, we at last can grasp the reality that his putatively simple technology actually is highly refined. In contrast, the technological marvel of industrial agriculture seldom is feasible in the Southwest without huge (and often prohibitively expensive) quantities of water for canal, drip, or spray irrigation. The Pueblos' enduring history of sustainable subsistence farming that works interactively with, rather than attempts to forcibly impose upon the environment, then, allows us to characterize the digging stick as an elegant tool by virtue of its effective simplicity.

AGRICULTURE AS AN EVER-RENEWING PROCESS

In writing about the life cycle of maize, agronomists characteristically focus on temperature as the controlling variable in plant maturation (e.g., see Arnon 1975; Shaw 1988; Tivy 1990; Ritchie et al. 1992; Muenchrath and Salvador 1995: 311). To operationalize temperature studies, however, investigators necessarily assume that there will be adequate moisture over the span of the frost-free season.

Of course, it is easy to comprehend that freezing temperatures, as manifest physically in the form of plant frost damage, pose absolute limits to most agricultural production. In temperate climates, the last springtime frost marks the final time that too little temperature can threaten plant mortality until the fall.

Moreover, inadequate temperature early in the life cycle of a plant hinders its development over the rest of its existence, thereby adversely affecting its yield at harvest time (Muenchrath and Salvador 1995).

Although these concerns are significant, temperature management is an extremely difficult undertaking. Comprehensive ethnographic study of Hopi agriculture provides a clear example of these difficulties. Hopi farmers use a variety of techniques to modify the thermal environments of their plants. These practices include monitoring field soil temperatures, situating fields in places where either south and west exposures increase solar gain or nearby landforms radiate absorbed heat in the evenings, and constructing low stone or brush borders that affect ground level wind flow (see Forde 1931; Whiting 1939; Page 1940; Stewart 1940; Hack 1942; Stewart and Donnelly 1943; Bradfield 1971; Anschuetz 1976; Koshear 1987). These efforts still cannot completely erase the risk of crop loss during hard freezes, however. In this sense, late spring or early fall frosts undoubtedly defined the limits of the growing season in some Pueblo fields in any given year.

This said, it also is easy to comprehend that water availability clearly is the single most limiting factor in crop production once maize plants enter the summer season until the fall. Nonetheless, the prevalence of the concern over springtime temperature tempts us to downplay the importance of over-winter moisture in semi-arid environments.

As several soil scientists working with pre-Columbian Pueblo fields have observed recently, "Water is the most important single factor controlling all facets of life in arid and semiarid regions" (White et al. 1998: 252). Water— either in the form of extreme seasonal paucity or as a periodically excessive abundance—characteristically stands as the single most limiting variable to crop production over which people can exercise effective influence. To return to ethnography for insights, we see that Hopi farmers cogently recognize late winter snows as having a decisive influence on the following season's harvest (Bradfield 1971: 6). Winter precipitation, after all, recharges the moisture content of parable soils for successful seed germination and vigorous early plant growth in the spring. As agronomic studies have shown, vigorous growth early in the life of the plant results in growth of greater leaf area (Muenchrath and Salvador 1995). Enhanced leaf development rates promote heightened photosynthetic capacity, which, in turn, favors the production of economically useful leaf, fruit, vegetable, seed, or fiber in the summer and fall. Hopi farmers also comprehend the need to capture summer monsoon moisture to ensure the maturation of their crops by the time of the first fall frost (see Forde 1931; Whiting 1939; Page 1940; Stewart 1940; Hack 1942; Stewart and Donnelly 1943; Bradfield 1971; Anschuetz 1976; Koshear 1987). Through their practical application of hydrological principles in locating, preparing, and maintaining fields, much of the Hopi farmers' agricultural work is dedicated to harvesting and conserving water throughout the year, not just the frost-free season (after Anschuetz 1995, 1998a; see also below).

This concern is manifest materially among the Pueblos' agricultural tool kits and constructed field devices. Moreover ethnographic observations show that, despite wide cross-cultural diversity in form, Pueblo people understand the substance of corn, the souls of humans, and the life force of the supernatural beings who inhabit the underworld of their cosmos as being composed of the same essence: *water* (Anschuetz and Dean 1994: 122).

Anthropologists traditionally have identified rainmaking as the principal referent of Pueblo ritual and religious belief (e.g., Beaglehole 1937: 45). Given the great many references to rain documented in Pueblo ceremonies, this perspective is not wrong per se. Nonetheless, I suggest that the common consequential assertion that the purpose of Pueblo ritual is to make rain is inappropriate. Cross culturally, Pueblo religion rests on a coherent system of belief about how water mediates between the natural and supernatural worlds of the cosmos through a constantly repeating cycle of transformations in form and power (e.g., see Anschuetz 1992, 1998a). In this metaphorical ebb and flow of energies, water is not simply a material product and time is not a linear sequence. Rather, they are components in a continual process of becoming, based on the renewal of supernatural associations (e.g., see Ortiz 1969).

Concepts of renewal and process similarly underlie the Pueblos' understandings of agriculture. That is to say, water in its various material and ethereal forms unifies the contrasting seasons of the annual cycle and reaffirms the interdependency of people and their cultigens, especially maize. To Pueblo people, large harvests of corn and other cultivars throughout the summer and fall stand as irrefutable evidence that the movement of life energy, as it flows between the natural and supernatural worlds of their cosmos, is unimpeded (after Anschuetz and Dean 1994: 124). In this sense, agricultural work, given that it embodies both physical and mental energies, stands as the day-to-day practice of Pueblo religion.

A harvest, therefore, denotes neither simply the end of a task nor the achievement of material gain. Instead, a harvest is a time of transformation and recommitment to a continuing process, whereby people renew their obligations to help sustain the movement of water between the natural and supernatural realms of the cosmos. Physically and metaphysically, actions during the harvesting of a crop also simultaneously represent steps to prepare the earth to absorb winter moisture for the next growing season. In this sense, agriculture is a year-round activity.

THE LAND AS A SPONGE

Through the framework of meaning structured by their world view, the Pueblos understood that they could not sit back passively and assume that there would be adequate moisture for crop production (Anschuetz 1995, 1998a). After all, from the perspective of contemporary agronomic experts, the average monsoonal season in many parts of the Southwest used for large-scale farming today is inadequate for successful agriculture practice without irrigating fields with water from rivers, streams, or aquifers.[7] Based on their considered observation of the natural history of water in their environment, the Pueblos recognized that they could ill afford to overlook winter precipitation in devising their tactics and strategies of agricultural water management. They knew that if they were able to enhance the absorption and retention of snow melt into the soil when such ample moisture was available in the spring, more rapid seedling development would occur than otherwise would be possible. The Pueblos also knew that they had to capture and to conserve water received during the summer's often high-intensity but brief monsoons to ensure their cultigens would have sufficient moisture to mature fully. They had to prevent natural runoff from robbing valuable water from their fields. Oftentimes, the Pueblos diverted runoff from its natural drainage channels into their planting areas to bring fresh, fertile sediment as well as additional water to their crops. Incorporating their comprehension of the moral principle for crop production along with their understanding of the material need, the Pueblos mastered techniques responsive to their southwestern ecological setting for enhancing the ground's capacity to absorb both winter and summer precipitation in ways quite unlike the Anglo-European agricultural experience.

Given the available ethnographic literature (see note 5) and an ever-expanding body of archaeological findings (e.g., see Anschuetz 1995, 1998a; Fish and Fish 1984; Lightfoot 1990, 1993; Lightfoot and Eddy 1995; Maxwell 1997; Maxwell and Anschuetz 1992; Toll 1995; Vivian 1974, among others), we see that the Pueblos relied upon integrated systems of technologically diverse farming tactics and strategies to harvest and conserve water for agricultural production. Together, ethnographic and archaeological information show that the Pueblos traditionally manipulated all four principle moisture resources available in their natural settings: direct precipitation, intermittent runoff, ground water, and permanently flowing river, spring, and seep water (after Anschuetz 1995, 1998a: 139–151). Archaeologically, we find that Pueblo farmers deployed morphologically similar features in a variety of contexts for managing valuable moisture resources.

One of the best known field technologies visible in the northern Rio Grande archaeological record—gravel-mulched plots (Photo 3.2) with and without formal cobble borders—densely cover low mesas and terrace escarpments overlooking the best-watered alluvial bottomlands in settings with average elevations of more than 1,830 m (6,000 ft) (see Anschuetz 1994, 1995; Anschuetz et al. 1985; Lightfoot 1990, 1993; Lightfoot and Eddy 1995; Maxwell and Anschuetz 1992). Typically raised in profile relative to their surrounding ground surfaces, these gravel-mulched plots seemingly depend entirely upon direct snow and rainfall for their moisture (Anschuetz 1994, 1998a). Because their massive stone construction renders them impermeable to runoff, some fields placed at slope bases work to trap and redirect runoff to nearby terraces, pits, or other technologically distinct field features (described after the following). Data obtained

Photo 3.2 A small portion of an extensive system of cobble-bordered and gravel-mulched fields near the old Tewa pueblo of Hupobi in the Ojo Caliente Valley near the present-day Hispano village of Ojo Caliente. These squares average just 60 cm (24 in) on a side. Pollen samples collected from nearby grids in this field complex yielded pre-Columbian corn and cotton pollen. (Photograph by Kurt F. Anschuetz, 1991)

during excavations of late fourteenth- and middle fifteenth-century gravel-mulched fields show Pueblo farmers literally built many of these features from the ground up (Anschuetz 1998a; Maxwell and Anschuetz 1992; White 1986; C. S. White et al. 1995). The Pueblos piled fill consisting of a heterogeneous mixture of stone and alluvial sand on the natural ground surface in areas where caliche underlies a sand layer. The resulting modified root zone commonly measures 20 to 40 cm (8 to 16 in) deep.

The sand content of sediments within gravel-mulched plots is greater and more consistent than in soils outside the features (C. S. White 1986). Even though the sandy soil has a lower water holding capacity relative to a true loamy soil, the sediment yields a higher proportion of its moisture to plants. In addition, the underlying impermeable caliche layer serves to hold moisture within the root zone. The surface gravel possesses significant thermal conservation properties that apparently warmed soil temperatures, protected seedlings from late spring frost damage, and possibly even captured additional small quantities of moisture by enhancing dew formation.[8]

Loosely clustered complexes of rock-bordered grids and cobble step terraces occur on high mesas with thin sandy mantles, moderate gradients, and broad washes that lead to the heads of mesa-side arroyos (Anschuetz 1994, 1995, 1998a). Because surface sediments in these settings saturate rapidly during downpours, runoff flows characteristically along the drainages toward the rock structures, which trap and hold water (Maps 3.1 and 3.2). In this way, the Pueblo farmers prevent the loss of runoff and enhance the potential that short-term surface moisture surpluses percolate into the ground where they might benefit plants.

Stone-lined ditches that channel water from gravel-mulched plots to stone terraces occasionally occur (Anschuetz 1995, 1998a). Circular depressions, usually measuring three to eight meters (10 to 26 ft) in diameter and originally excavated to obtain cobbles, pebbles, and sandy alluvium needed for the construction of nearby gravel-mulched and stone-bordered plots, also are present. Once dug, the depressions form moisture traps that farmers apparently used as planting beds. In one setting, a series of 15 depressions apparently received moisture from mesa-side seeps (Anschuetz 1994, 1995, 1998a). In other localities, multitiered lines of pits capture runoff. Interestingly, F. W. Hodge reports that at the beginning of the twentieth century, the Pueblos still remembered their ancestors irrigating pits by filling these small round depressions "in winter by rolling into them immense snowballs" (Hodge 1971: 621).[9]

Areas of deep sand associated with low-density distributions of small, expediently worked cobble tools on some flat mesa tops represent a different type of snow- and rainfall-fed field (Anschuetz 1994, 1995, 1998a; Neely 1995). The thick, sandy mantle likely functioned as a natural mulch, facilitating the downward percolation of snow melt and rainwater, as well as prevented the loss of soil moisture to the atmosphere through evaporation. While some sharpened implements are easily recognizable as axes used to cut trees and shrubs (Photo

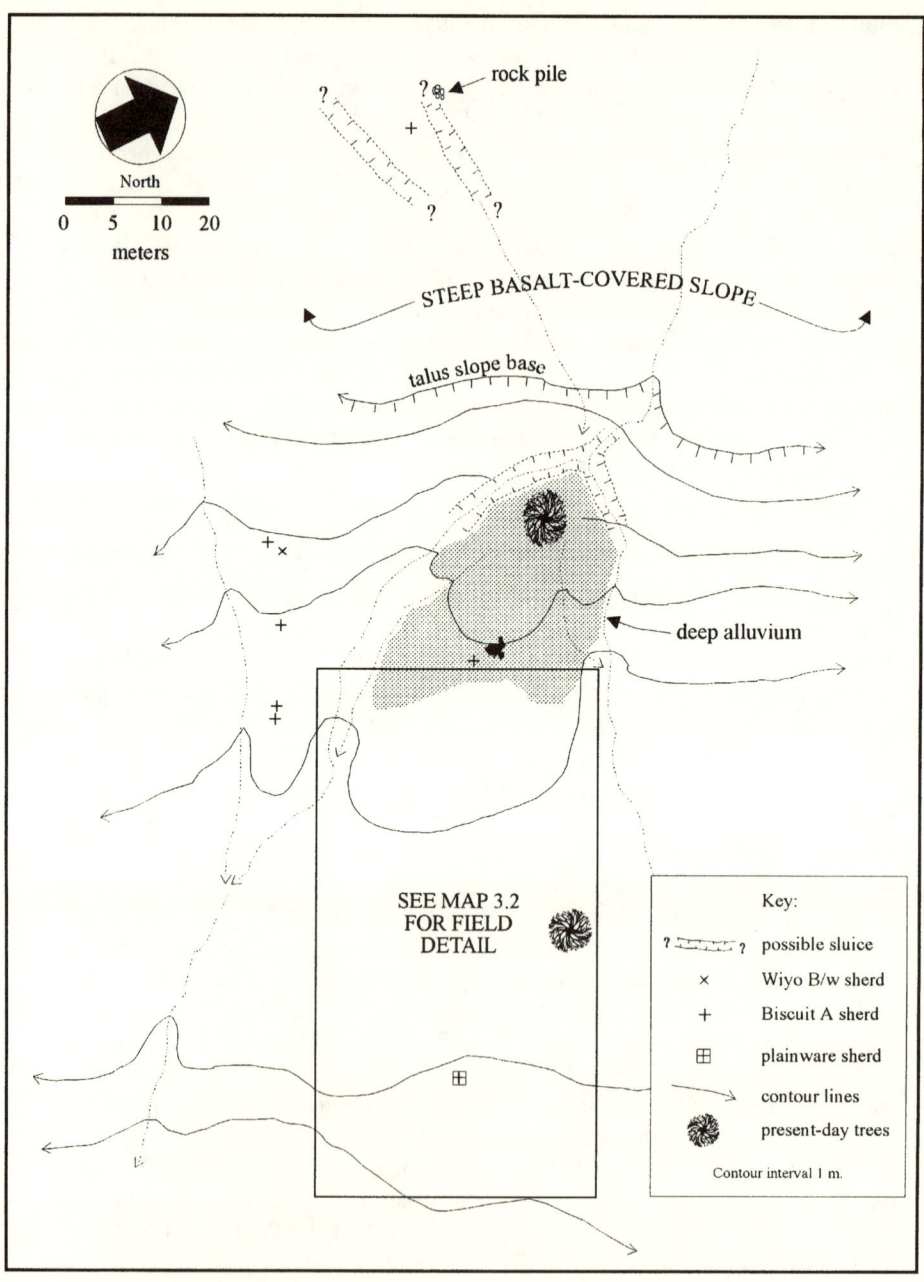

Map 3.1 Physical setting of a fifteenth-century archaeological cobble terrace field complex in the Rio del Oso Valley (LA90817)

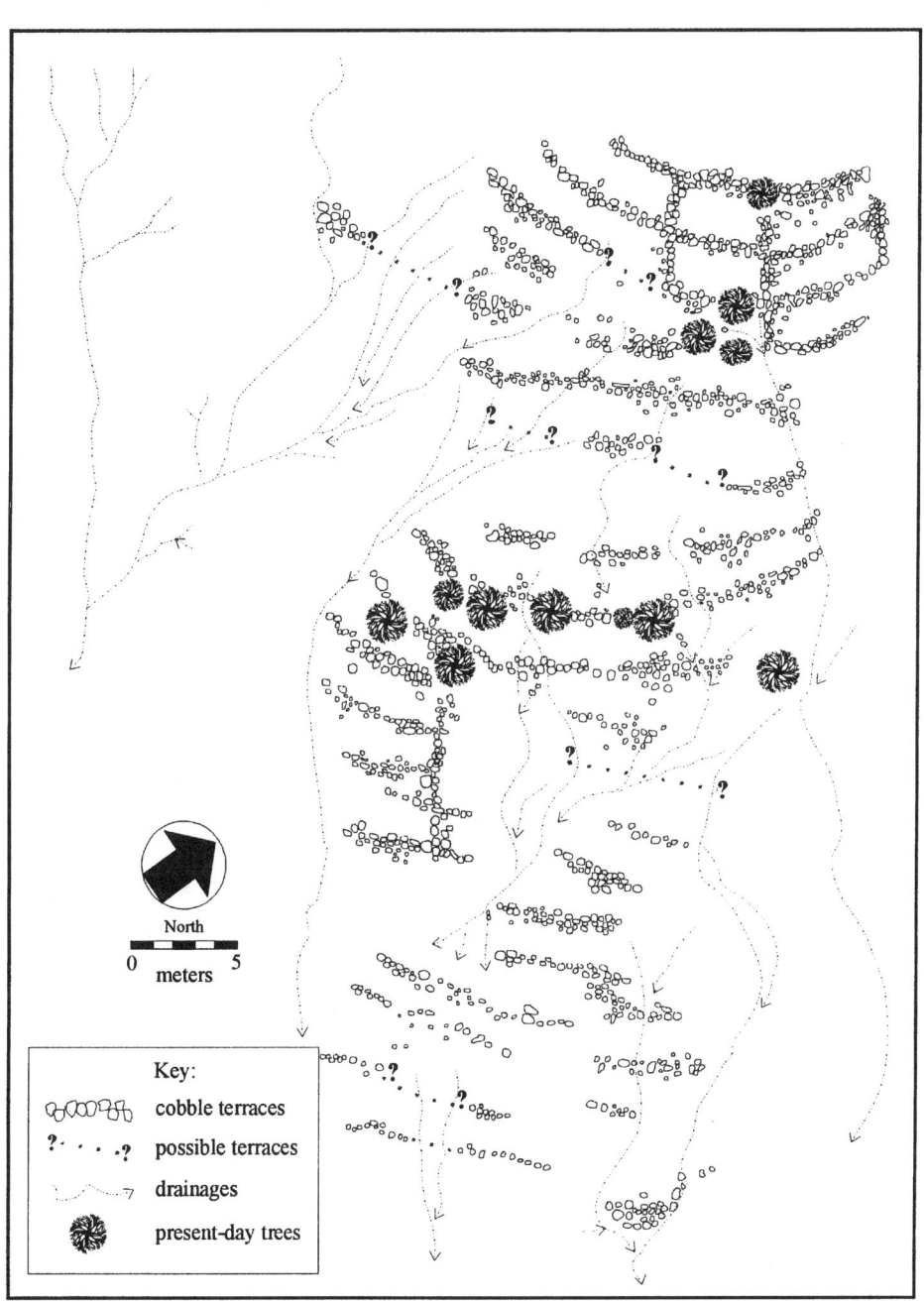

Map 3.2 Detail of gridded cobble terrace field complex with present-day water flows noted (LA90817)

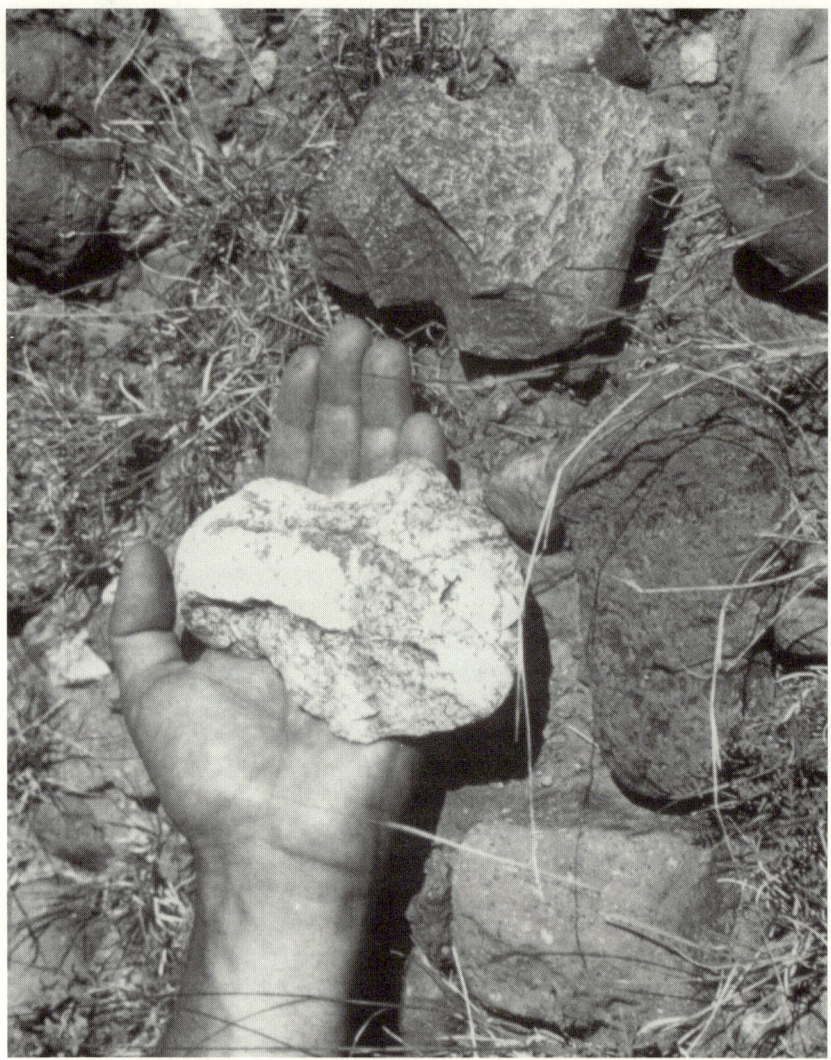

Photo 3.3 Two axes found next to a mesa-side pit and associated gravel-mulched plot. These tools are among the nearly 100 field tools documented during an archaeological survey in the Rio del Oso Valley. (Photograph by Kurt F. Anschuetz, 1993)

3.3) tools found in areas of deep, soft sand characteristically are unmodified except for bifacially flaked lateral notches. Because their waterworn cortex often remains intact without evidence of battering, the simply notched tools probably are hoe bits and/or hand trowels.

Diverse complexes of short terraces, cobble alignments constructed across washes to slow runoff, and stone spreaders that divert water from natural drainage channels to sandy planting areas are other common field structures. These features usually occur in direct association with more visible field technologies, such as the gravel-mulched plots and cobble-bordered grids (Anschuetz 1994, 1995, 1998a). Basalt boulders with distinctive ground slicks along mesa and bench escarpments next to—or overlooking—archaeologically visible fields also occur. Because the basic morphology of these boulders excludes their use as bedrock metates, these features might be, in part, the product of Pueblo farmers sharpening their axes to clear planting areas (Anschuetz 1994, 1995, 1998a). The scattered distribution of ground slicks on talus slopes above agricultural field complexes further implies that farmers cleared microwatersheds to enhance the quantity of runoff flowing downslope toward crop areas.

The evolution of Pueblo agricultural landscape engineering depended on more than just the hydrological integration of disparate technologies and planting strategies. In the face of marked increases in regional Pueblo population densities between the thirteenth and fifteenth centuries, farmers actively managed both quantitatively and qualitatively different sources of moisture for crop production. Archaeological evidence suggests that late pre-Columbian Pueblos continually added to their earlier field complexes over time. Moreover, they even began harvesting seepage moisture, runoff flowing down larger watersheds, and deep sand deposits, which function as natural mulches, on mesa tops that they previously had not used.

Through the construction and hydrological integration of pits, low earthen or stone terraces, check and diversion dams, earthen and stone grids, gravel-mulched plots, and ditches across expansive land tracts, the Pueblos effectively increased the water absorption properties of their farmlands. The expansive fields dependent upon direct precipitation that Pueblo farmers built on the tops of terraces and mesas worked along with dedicated water diversion techniques, reduced the overall quantity, and modified the timing of surface water flow into riparian habitats (e.g., see Periman 1996).

Pueblo environmentalists now studying the field works of their ancestors are beginning to raise compelling questions how the old technologies' direct precipitation and runoff water harvesting properties might positively have influenced ground water stores feeding riparian communities, as well as supplying springs and seeps (Louis Hena, Picuris Pueblo Environmental Department, personal communication 1999). Louis Hena argues that the fieldworks have more than just agro-ecological functions: The water harvesting and conservation properties of the Pueblos' agricultural technologies might contribute in important ways to the historical ecology of the localities they occupy by enhancing ground water resources for the benefit of all flora and fauna.

The reader might question why I have neglected discussion of irrigation technologies dependent on river and spring waters in this review of traditional northern Rio Grande Pueblo farming practices. It certainly is not my intent to disclaim the Pueblo's use of irrigation in this region before Columbian contact.

Irrigation, quite simply, is the diversion of surface water from the path of its natural drainage course. Importantly, this definition does not restrict the act of irrigation to the diversion of just river or spring water resources. In considering the Pueblos traditionally treated the land as a sponge, it is quite safe to say that the northern Rio Grande's indigenous people irrigated extensively by diverting runoff moisture derived from snow melt and heavy rainfall episodes. Although by no means widespread, there are archaeological (Anschuetz 1998a) and ethnohistorical data (Martin de Pedrosa, in Hammond and Rey 1966: 118; Antonio de Espejo, in Hammond and Rey 1966: 220, 221; Gaspar Castaño de Sosa, in Hammond and Rey 1966: 282, 283; Don Francisco de Valverde y Mercado; in Hammond and Rey 1953: 626; see also Anschuetz 1998a: 164–170) indicating the Pueblos, in fact, did divert river and spring water in certain locales before European contact. While the Pueblo's use of irrigation is beyond refute, I do question whether indigenous northern Rio Grande farmers deployed river and spring water irrigation technologies on a sufficiently large-scale from year-to-year to form *the* principle foundation of their subsistence economies. Rather, river and spring irrigation practices were technological components of a much broader system of water management engineering.

A FIELD IS NOT A JUST FIELD

The tremendous morphological and organizational variability observed among the northern Rio Grande Pueblos' agricultural technologies immediately challenge the idea that individual fields necessarily are interchangeable with one another. While sharing a common theme of water harvesting and conservation, the diversity exhibited among archaeologically documented agricultural features implies that Pueblo farmers adapted their technologies to interact with highly localized climatological, physiographic, sedimentological, and hydrological conditions across the dimensions of space and time. Once we consider the ecological dynamics confronting Pueblo farmers, we recognize there is no singular archetype for defining a Pueblo field or even a field complex comprising technological diverse features. Moreover, there is no persuasive material basis for suggesting that irrigation canals, gravel mulches, or gravel mulch and pit complexes necessarily were *the* technologies of choice across the region at particular points in time.[10] I think that such a generalization stands in stark contradiction of the Pueblos' cogent recognition of their need to maintain a wide range of material and organizational tactics and strategies in their agricultural tool kits. This maintenance of technological diversity allowed the Pueblos the behavioral flexibility that they needed to cope with shifts in the frequency and magnitude of the ecological variables defining the absolute parameters of their agricultural production.

If we acknowledge the tactical and strategic diversity in farming technologies but steadfastly hold onto the idea that every planting bed simply represents a place of domestic cultigen production, we still miss an essential principle of Pueblo subsistence agricultural practice: A field is not just a field. Rather, each field is a culturally constructed component of a dynamic ecological system. We only now are beginning to comprehend how the Pueblos' indigenous agricultural technologies harvested and conserved moisture over the span of the annual cycle. We similarly might build an understanding of how fields provided economically, socially, and culturally useful products throughout the year if we look beyond the constraints imposed by the exclusive association of field productivity with the frost-free season and the farmer's manipulation of domestic cultigens.

Ethnography teaches us that Pueblo farmers traditionally polycropped their fields with a mixture of domesticated and various wild plant taxa for edible greens and seeds, tools, twine, dyes, pot herbs, medicines, and ceremonial uses (e.g., see Ford 1968; Nabhan 1989). Archaeological study of sediment collected from old fields suggests indigenous populations actively cultivated a variety of wild plant taxa, including little barley grass, panic grass, grain amaranth, sunflower, tobacco, and devil's claw (Bohrer 1991; Fish 1984; Ford 1985; among others). After documenting great prickly pear pollen concentrations in Pueblo fields in north-central New Mexico, Smith (1998: 84) remarked that farmers might have also tended this plant taxon in their fields.

Although they harvested their domestic cultigens, such as corn, beans, squash, and cotton, through the late summer and fall, the Pueblos traditionally did not leave their fields barren of useful ground cover. Quite to the contrary: The farmers did not follow the common sense Iberian practice of plowing their fields under following the harvest. Noting the "messy" condition of Pueblo fields, early Spanish chroniclers condemned the Pueblo farmers for their "sterile . . . labor and cultivation" (Dominguez 1956: 126). Others expressed amazement that the people harvested "very good crops from the stubble of the year before, without having given it any other working than a little [stream] irrigating" (Benavides 1916: 36). The Europeans mistakenly concluded that the Rio Grande Valley was naturally a Garden of Eden "so fertile that they [the Pueblos] do not have to break up the ground year round, but only have to sow the seed" (Winship 1990: 146 [1904]).

By acknowledging ethnohistoric and ethnographic evidence that the Pueblos' fields characteristically were still full of stubble and wild plants after harvest, we can begin to evaluate the possibility that Pueblo people supplied themselves with plant products, such as edible prickly pear pads (*nopales*), whose availability is not determined by the frost-free season. This field use pattern has other significant ecological implications: A rich admixture of plants might serve to maintain the kind of biodiversity that sustains the soil's fertility. Some species might repel insect predators and diseases, while others might attract the kinds of beneficial insects, birds, and animals needed for successful pollination. In addition, fields left full of plants over the fall and winter might attract game bird and mammal species that the people can harvest for food (Richard Ford, University of Michigan Museum of Anthropology, personal communication 1998).

If we extend this ecological logic further, we also can begin to grasp the idea that fields left fallow in both the short and long term can also be productive in the sense that their disturbed habitats can produce plants directly useful to people, attractive to game birds or animals, or needed to restore the soil's fertility.

MOVEMENT IS LIFE

Linda Cordell, in her recently published study of Rowe Pueblo, described a thirteenth- and fourteenth-century village in the Upper Pecos Valley. She writes,

Aggregated settlements did not last for centuries. Their inhabitants seemed to come and go, the settlements themselves changing both size and configuration in response to social forces we barely understand. In my mind, the shifting locations of population and the modification of community layout that suggest the incorporation and dispersal of groups of people are signs of a social landscape with far fewer constraints than any we know in the region today. They are mirrored in the fluidity and lack of formality that seem to characterize the patterns of exchange in ceramics. They seem to be part of a larger but much more open social world in which the notion of abandoning a dwelling or a site may have been of minimal importance, perhaps something to have been embraced rather than resisted. (Cordell 1998: 64)

The task now remaining at hand is to contextualize and evaluate these widespread archaeologically observed patterns of residential instability and movement. As outsiders looking back upon the Pueblos' past from a putatively objective scientific perspective, we can view these repeated cycles of people's movement in and out of the big villages as productive and organizational strategies for sustaining their populations through perpetual change. Moreover, we can characterize such movement as the people's responses to natural environmental vagaries, changing agricultural productivity because of soil depletion, and/or patterns of intergroup conflict.

While the ethnographic present should not be projected uncritically onto the past, the cultural landscape constructions and understanding held by contemporary Pueblo people provide useful ideas and perspectives for evaluating movement in terms of historical ecological processes. For example, Pueblo oral traditions commonly employ the concepts of rest and renewal when referring to population movement, houses, agricultural land, and foraging and collecting areas. As stated by Pueblo authors in a variety of documentary contexts, "[M]ovement is the revered element of life" (Naranjo and Swentzell 1989: 261). Another Pueblo author adds, "Movement, clouds, wind and rain are one. Movement must be emulated by the people" (Naranjo 1995:248). Such concepts of rest and renewal coincide nicely with the idea of fallow cycles for hunting and gathering territories, as well as for agricultural land.

Listening to traditional community histories and viewing archaeological patterns among the old fields these many years has taught me that Pueblo farmers characteristically did not develop lands for agricultural production only to abandon them easily, or without further regard, after a few years or even a few generations of use. The idea that the Pueblos would not farm a locality to allow it to "rest and renew" (its fertility) carries the implication that the people would return to this location at some time in the future. Moreover, the ideas of abandonment and the people's permanent dispossession of their traditional land holdings are antithetical to this system of landscape belief.

The likelihood that a sizable portion of the northern Rio Grande Pueblo population traditionally cycled across their cultural landscape in a series of settlement shifts over the course of their lives as a formal long-term strategy for sustainable agricultural production in intriguing. Importantly, this strategy was not limited to the pre-Columbian past: A new body of archaeological and ethnohistorical evidence indicates that Pueblo people periodically reoccupied some of their old home and agricultural field sites in the Rio Chama and Rio Santa Cruz watersheds into the early eighteenth century. For example, Tewa groups reused houses and fields in the Chama district on a small-scale basis during the seventeenth and early eighteenth centuries (e.g., Harrington 1916; Hammond and Rey 1966 [Enrico Martínez Map of 1602]; Schroeder 1979; Ford and Anschuetz 1995; Anschuetz 1998a, 1998b; Ramenofsky 1998; Naranjo 1998).

One the one hand, these new findings challenge still-prevalent cultural-historical constructions positing that the northern Rio Grande Pueblos relinquished their physical occupation to major portions of their traditional homelands, including the Rio Chama and Rio Santa Cruz watersheds, during the century preceding Spanish colonization. While the economic values of these early Historic period reoccupation cycles likely were greatly reduced compared to pre-Columbian times, the reuse episodes were socially and politically crucial for maintaining the Pueblos' traditional land-use ties. Accompanying the Pueblos' continued use of the land for agricultural production, of course, is their system of water management tactics and strategies. The task awaiting investigators is to learn to identify and interpret how Pueblo populations occupied the land and modified it for their own purposes in ways that depart substantively from our current interpretive frameworks.

CONCLUDING COMMENTS

Identifiable Tewa, Tiwa, Towa, and Keresan Pueblo communities have sustained their occupation of New Mexico's northern Rio Grande Valley between Albuquerque in the south to Taos in the north since the thirteenth century. Ancestral Pueblo communities whose cultural affiliations are unknown (at least to archaeologists, anyway) date back to the seventh century. Earlier still, for the better part of a millennium Archaic hunters and gatherers tended domestic cultigens and began building the knowledge—and lifeways—needed to sustain both their plants and their communities as the people became ever more dependent on cultigens for their livelihood.

The surviving material traces of the Pueblo's landscape engineering and management accomplishments are often subtle in appearance and have required the patient efforts by many different individuals to discern. A diverse consortium of researchers, including hydrologists, biologists, soil scientists, archaeologists, and Indian peoples, increasingly are working together to build an understanding of Pueblo water harvesting and conservation tactics and strategies dating to the pre-Columbian and early Spanish Colonial periods.

Equally important, based on lessons that the Pueblos have shared with anthropologists over more than a century, it is clear that the Pueblos are inseparable from the cereal staple—maize (*Zea mays*)—that they traditionally produced for sustaining both their physical well-being and the cultural fabric of their communities (e.g., see Anschuetz 1992; Anschuetz and Dean 1994). Judging from recent archaeological findings (Anschuetz 1998a), it is reasonable to suggest that the Pueblos' physical and ideological associations of themselves with maize occurred long ago in their history of becoming. In domesticating themselves to an agricultural lifeway, the Pueblos transformed their landscapes through their physical labors and the cultural histories that they passed on from one generation to the next that gave meaning to the places they inhabited. In so doing, the Pueblo people became an inseparable part of the land and its waters. Just as the water their ancestors worked so hard to harvest and conserve, the present-day Pueblos' history, their culture, and their cosmological understandings of their very being, are soaked deeply into the land that their families have occupied since time immemorial.

NOTES

1. People characteristically associate "technology" with a physical tool or an applied science that leads to the development of refined or new tools. The idea that technology also refers to mechanisms underlying how people organize their productive behaviors is much less familiar. As G. D. Stone (1993) notes, however, all production requires "technology, including what we might call social technology—conventions for mobilizing human resources" (Stone 1993: 78; citing Earle 1980: 4). When social technologies facilitate a production strategy, we can say that they lower the cost of the strategy. Moreover, the efficiency of a given productive strategy, such as agricultural intensification, can vary given the interplay of various cultural factors other than tool use, all other factors held equal. Consequently, Stone argues that research needs "to consider social [or informational or even ideational] technology that affects costs and benefits" (Stone 1993: 78).

2. I define "culture" as a uniquely human cognitive and behavioral system for producing, storing and transmitting information (e.g., see Anschuetz 1998a: 31–80, after Tylor 1871; L. A. White 1949; Hall 1959, 1969; Ford 1977; Rappaport 1979; Kirch 1980; Trigger 1991; among others). "Traditions," on the other hand, generally relate to peoples' understandings of "how they became who they are" (Peckham 1990: 2) and provide a set of unifying principles that help guide how the members of a cultural community ideally should conduct their lives (e.g., see Anschuetz 1998a:44–58). As such, subscription to tradition potentially can structure behavior in significantly patterned ways.

S. Peckham (1990: 2–5) recognizes that even though traditions are mutable, they allow for persistence and continuity in culture.

Given this background, students must use caution not to think of Pueblo people and their culture in either narrow or static senses. The term "Pueblo" derives from sixteenth-century Spanish conquistadors' generalized characterizations of culturally diverse peoples who commonly farmed large quantities of corn and congregated, at least seasonally, in quadrangular, multistoried villages. With the Spanish colonization of the New Mexican territory in 1598, secular governmental and ecclesiastical policies wrought huge changes in Pueblo economy, society, and culture by effectively limiting the indigenous people's access to major portions of their traditional homelands, introducing new productive technologies, imposing new political organizations upon communities, and demanding the adoption of Christianity. Loss of population because of disease, slavery, and out-marriage, especially of Pueblo women to Hispanic men, further fueled significant changes in Pueblo lifeways. Anthropologists' earliest descriptions of Pueblo people and their culture, in turn, date to the late nineteenth century, nearly three centuries after the imposition of Spanish colonial governance and settlement. Investigators now are focusing greater attention on the many sources of variability in the structure and organization of Pueblo material culture assemblages across the dimensions of space and time in an increasingly systematic effort to document and understand the many-layered complexities embedded within Pueblo adaptations.

3. The Pueblo occupation of the Rio Grande is the most culturally diverse and extends from just south of Albuquerque to Taos near the New Mexico-Colorado state line. The pueblos of Cochiti, San Felipe, Santa Ana, Santo Domingo, and Zia are Keresan-speaking communities. Nambe, Pojoaque, San Ildefonso, San Juan, Santa Clara, and Tesuque are Tewa pueblos. While the pueblos of Isleta and Sandia represent southern Tiwa linguistic communities, Picuris and Taos are northern Tiwa pueblos. Jemez Pueblo, located at the southwestern end of the Jemez Mountains, is the last surviving Towa-speaking community. Four other Pueblo communities are west of the Rio Grande Valley. Two Keresan communities, Acoma and Laguna, are in the Rio San Jose watershed west of Albuquerque. The Zuñis occupy west-central New Mexico, while the Hopis live in northeastern Arizona. These last two communities represent distinct linguistic groups.

4. In talking about Pueblo agriculture, I use "tactics" to refer to implements (such as tools, planting bed mulches, watering, harvesting, and conserving features, and seeds) and techniques (such as permanent water irrigation, runoff irrigation, precipitation-dependent farming, and ground-water farming) (see Anschuetz 1998a: 139–151). In this sense, we can talk about the structure of a technological assemblage. "Strategies" are decision-making frameworks, both social and ideational, for motivating and organizing the use of productive techniques. Following Stone's (1993: 78) lead, we can say that people use a variety of nonmaterial techniques to manage the costs and benefits of production.

5. I follow Wills (1988: 2) to define agriculture simply as the cultivation of domesticated plants by people. In this sense, agriculture is, in large measure, "the evolution of behavioral patterns" (Rosenberg 1990: 405). This definition, however, does not assume any particular kind of technological structure or labor organization other than people interacting with domesticated cultivars in "a behaviorally based biological symbiosis" (Rosenberg 1990: 405). Of equal importance is the recognition that the cultivation of domesticated cultigens does not preclude, or even necessarily assume, predominance over peoples' relationships with wild plant species. As I note later in my discussion of Pueblo agricultural landscape ecology, the people traditionally managed a great variety of non-

domesticated flora in their day-to-day lives to complement their agricultural tactics and strategies. They gathered and even tended wild plants, deliberately introduced native species into their agricultural plots, and even tolerated field invaders if they were useful to the people in some way.

6. The body of ethnographic literature documenting Pueblo agricultural tactics and strategies is far too vast to identify and to annotate fully. For readers interested in learning more about this encompassing topic, I recommend the following references for the Hopi and Zuñi as a convenient starting point for developing an understanding of the diverse physical technologies commonly used by the Pueblos to harvest and conserve water for producing crops: Cushing (1920), Forde (1931), Page (1940), Stewart (1940), Hack (1942), Stewart and Donnelly (1943), Bradfield (1971), Anschuetz (1976), and Koshear (1987). The literature addressing the physical mechanics of the traditional eastern Pueblo is less extensive and often is included as sections within more encompassing ethnographic studies. Stevenson (1894), Lange (1959) and Hill (1982). Ellis (1970) and Anschuetz (1998a) offer useful summary accounts, however.

Muenchrath and Salvador (1995) provide practical information about maize biology and agroecology that complements the ethnographic literature and offers insights into the sophistication and efficacy of the Pueblo's botanical and agronomic techniques. Ford (1968, 1972a, 1972b, 1977, 1980, 1987, 1994) develops and illustrates an important cultural-ecological framework for how to include social and ideational technologies in evaluations of agricultural productive tactics and strategies. With this background in hand, Stephen (1936), Beaglehole (1937), Titiev (1938, 1944), Parsons (1939), Whiting (1939), Ortiz (1969, 1972, 1994), Anschuetz (1976, 1992, 1998a), Black (1984), Anschuetz and Dean (1994), and Bohrer (1995) illustrate some of the many kinds of cultural contextual information that helps inform Pueblo agricultural decision-making processes.

7. For example, Shaw (1988) reports agronomists generally consider 150 mm (6 in) of growing season rainfall as the lower limit for maize production without irrigation.

8. Researchers (Anschuetz et al. 1985; Ellis and Dodge 1983–1987; Lightfoot 1990, 1993; Maxwell and Anschuetz 1992; Moore 1990, 1992; Ware and Mensel 1992; C. S. White et al. 1995) investigating the northern Rio Grande Pueblo Indian gravel mulch agricultural technologies have compiled a substantive body of ethnohistorical and modern agronomic literature that quantifies the moisture and thermal retention characteristics of different types of mulches and measures their effects on plant growth.

9. Because the Pueblos were removing the snow from its natural watershed through their labors, Hodge (1971: 621) correctly characterizes this activity as a kind of hand irrigation.

10. For example, reporting the seemingly ubiquitous distribution of cobble-bordered and gravel-mulched fields in many locales, investigators initially suggested that these features might have constituted the technology of choice and necessity for coping with periodic drought and unpredictable frost in cool upland settings during the fourteenth and fifteenth centuries (e.g., Anschuetz et al. 1985; Lightfoot 1990; Maxwell and Anschuetz 1992).

REFERENCES

Abeyta, C., L. Meade, V. Ochoa, and J. Yepa, compilers. 1995. Corn for the Community: Our Summer Americorps Agricultural Experience, Santa Clara Pueblo. Santa Clara Pueblo, NM: Americorps Program.

Adler, M. A. 1996. Land Tenure, Archaeology, and Ancestral Pueblo Social Landscape. *Journal of Anthropological Archaeology* 15:337–371.

Anschuetz, K. F. 1976. The Hopi and their Maize: An Ethnobotanical Perspective. Senior Honors Thesis, Department of Anthropology, University of Michigan.

———. 1992. Corn in the Flow of Life: Further Consideration of Hopi Concepts of Zea Mays. Paper presented at the Fifteenth Annual Conference of the Society of Ethnobiology, National Museum of Natural History, Smithsonian Institution, Washington, DC.

———. 1994. Earning a Living in the Cool, High Desert: Transformations of the Northern Rio Grande Landscape by Anasazi Farmers to Harvest and Conserve Water. Paper presented at the 5th Southwest Symposium, Arizona State University, Tempe.

———. 1995. Two Sides of a Coin: Early Pueblo Indian Farming Practices in the Rio Arriba and the Rio Abajo of the Northern Rio Grande Region. Paper presented at the 60th Annual Meeting, Society for American Archaeology, Minneapolis.

———. 1998a. Not Waiting for the Rain: Integrated Systems of Water Management for Intensive Agricultural Production in North-Central New Mexico. Ph.D. dissertation, Department of Anthropology, University of Michigan.

———. 1998b. Summary and Conclusions. In Pre-Columbian Pueblo Agricultural Plots (AR-03–02–02–0460 [LA114161]) within the Proposed Las Clinicas del Norte Special-Use Permit Parcel, El Rito Ranger District, Carson National Forest, Rio Arriba County, New Mexico, edited by K. F. Anschuetz, 121–123. *Community and Cultural Landscape Contribution* 2. Santa Fe: Rio Grande Foundation for Communities and Cultural Landscapes.

Anschuetz, K. F., and G. Dean. 1994. North American Desert People. In *Deserts: The Illustrated Library of the Earth*, edited by M. Seeley, pp. 122–127. Sydney, Australia: Weldon Owen.

Anschuetz, K. F., T. D. Maxwell, and J. A. Ware. 1985. Testing Report and Research Design for the Medanales North Project, Rio Arriba County, New Mexico, note 347. Santa Fe: Laboratory of Anthropology, Museum of New Mexico.

Anschuetz, K. F., C. L. Scheick, and L. Hena. 1998. Early Pueblo Agricultural Traditions and Landscape Project. Unpublished MS, Rio Grande Foundation for Communities and Cultural Landscapes, Santa Fe.

Arnon, I. 1975. Physiological Principals of Dryland Crop Production. In *Physiological Aspects of Dryland Farming*, edited by U. S. Gupta, pp. 5–145. New Delhi: Oxford and IBH Publishing Company.

Beaglehole, E. 1937. Notes on Hopi Economic Life. *Publications in Anthropology* 15. New Haven: Yale University.

Benavides, F. A. de. 1916. *The Memorial of Fray Alonso de Benavides, 1630*. Translated by Mrs. E. E. Ayer and annotated by F. W. Hodge and C. F. Lummis. Chicago: Privately printed.

Black, M. E. 1984. Maidens and Mothers: An Analysis of Hopi Corn Metaphors, *Ethnology* 23:297–288.

Bohrer, V. L. 1960. Zuni Agriculture. *El Palacio* 67:181–202.

———. 1991. Recently Recognized Cultivated and Encouraged Plants among the Hohokam. *Kiva* 56:227–235.

———. 1995. The Where, When, and Why of Corn Guardians. In *Soil, Water, Biology, and Belief in Prehistoric and Traditional Southwestern Agriculture*, edited by

H. W. Toll, pp. 361–368. Special Publication 2. Albuquerque: New Mexico Archaeological Council.

Bradfield, M. 1971. The Changing Pattern of Hopi Agriculture. *Occasional Paper* 30. London: Royal Institute of Great Britain and Ireland.

Cordell, L. S. 1998. Before Pecos: Settlement Aggregation at Rowe, New Mexico. *Anthropological Papers* 6. Albuquerque: Maxwell Museum of Anthropology, University of New Mexico.

Cushing, F. H. 1920. Zuñi Breadstuff. *Indian Notes and Monographs* 8. New York: Museum of the American Indian, Heye Foundation.

Domínguez, F. F. A. 1956. *The Missions of New Mexico, 1776: A Description by Fray Francisco Atanasio Domínguez, with Other Contemporary Documents*, translated and annotated by E. B. Adams and F. A. Chavez. Albuquerque: University of New Mexico Press.

Earle, T. K. 1980. A Model of Subsistence Change. In *Modeling Change in Prehistoric Subsistence Economies*, edited by T. K. Earle and A. L. Christenson, pp. 1–29. New York: Academic Press.

Ellis, F. H. 1970. Irrigation and Water Works in the Rio Grande. Paper presented at the 1970 Pecos Conference, Santa Fe.

Ellis, F. H., and A. E. Dodge. 1983–1987. The Early Water Works of Three Jemez Valley Pueblos: Jemez, Zia, Santa Ana. In Papers of the Jemez, Santa Ana and Zia Pueblo Waters Rights Case, 1988. Unpublished MS, Cerro Gordo Research Associates. Archives of the Laboratory of Anthropology, Museum of New Mexico, Santa Fe.

Fish, S. K. 1984. Agriculture and Subsistence Implications of the Salt-Gila Aqueduct Project Pollen Analysis. In *Environment and Subsistence*. Vol. 7, *Hohokam Archaeology along the Salt-Gila Aqueduct Arizona Project*, edited by S. K. Fish, P. R. Fish, and J. H. Madsen, pp. 73–87. Tucson: University of Arizona Press.

Fish, S. K., and P. R. Fish, eds. 1984. Prehistoric Agricultural Strategies in the Southwest. *Anthropological Research Papers* 33, Arizona State Tempe University.

Ford, R. I. 1968. An Ecological Analysis Involving the Population of San Juan Pueblo, New Mexico. Ph.D. dissertation, Department of Anthropology, University of Michigan.

———. 1972a. Barter, Gift or Violence: An Analysis of Tewa Intertribal Exchange. In Social Exchange and Interaction, edited by E. N. Wilmsen, pp. 21–45. *Anthropological Papers* 46. Ann Arbor: Museum of Anthropology, University of Michigan.

———. 1972b. An Ecological Perspective on the Eastern Pueblos. In *New Perspectives on the Pueblos*, edited by A. Ortiz, pp. 1–18. Albuquerque: University of New Mexico Press.

———. 1977. Evolutionary Ecology and the Evolution of Human Ecosystems: A Case Study from the Midwestern U.S.A. In *Explanation of Prehistoric Change*, edited by J. N. Hill, pp. 153–184. Albuquerque: University of New Mexico Press.

———. 1980. The Color of Survival. *Discovery*: 17–29.

———. 1985. Patterns of Prehistoric Food Production in North America. In Prehistoric Food Production in North America, edited by R. I. Ford, pp. 341–364. *Anthropological Papers* 75. Ann Arbor: Museum of Anthropology, University of Michigan.

———. 1987. The New Pueblo Economy. In When Cultures Meet: Remembering San Gabriel del Yunge Oweenge. Papers from the October 20, 1984, conference held at San Juan Pueblo, New Mexico, pp. 73–91. Santa Fe: Sunstone Press.

————. 1994. Corn is Our Mother. In *Corn and Culture in the Prehistoric New World*, edited by S. Johannessen and C. A. Hastorf, pp. 513–525. Boulder: Westview Press.

Ford, R. I., with K. F. Anschuetz. 1989. Hopi Uses of Water in the Little Colorado River Watershed. Unpublished MS, The Hopi Tribe, Kykotsmovi, Arizona.

Ford, R. I., and K. F. Anschuetz. 1995. Pesedeuinge Pueblo Pottery Identifications. J. A. Jeançon Collection, Colorado Springs Pioneers Museum. Unpublished MS, Museum of Anthropology, University of Michigan, Ann Arbor.

Forde, C. D. 1931. Hopi Agriculture and Land Ownership. *Journal of the Royal Anthropological Institute of Great Britain and London* 41 (4): 357–405.

Hack, J. T. 1942. The Changing Physical Environment of the Hopi Indians of Arizona. Reports of the Awatovi Expedition 1. *Papers of the Peabody Museum of American Archaeology and Ethnology* 35 (1). Cambridge: Peabody Museum.

Hall, E. T. 1959. *The Silent Language*. Garden City, NY: Doubleday.

————. 1969. *The Hidden Dimension*. Garden City, NY: Doubleday.

Hammond, G. P., and A. Rey. 1953. *Don Juan de Oñate: Colonizer of New Mexico*. 2 vols. Albuquerque: University of New Mexico Press.

————. 1966. *The Rediscovery of New Mexico, 1580–1594*. Albuquerque: University of New Mexico Press.

Harrington, J. P. 1916. The Ethnogeography of the Tewa Indians. *Twenty-Ninth Annual Report of the Bureau of American Ethnology for the Years 1907–1908*. pp. 29–636. Washington, DC: Government Printing Office.

Henna, Louis. 1999. Personal communication.

Hill, W. W. 1982. *An Ethnography of Santa Clara Pueblo, New Mexico*, edited and annotated by C. H. Lange. Albuquerque: University of New Mexico Press.

Hodge, F. W., ed. [1907] 1971. *Handbook of American Indians North of Mexico*, pt. 1. New York: Rowman and Littlefield.

Kirch, P. V. 1980. The Archaeological Study of Adaptation: Theoretical and Methodological Issues. In *Advances in Archaeological Method and Theory*, vol. 3, edited by M. B. Schiffer, pp. 101–156. New York: Academic Press.

Koshear, J. 1987. Hopi Agriculture: Environmental and Cultural Change. M.A. Thesis, Department of Geography, University of California at Berkeley.

Lange, C. H., Jr. 1959. *Cochiti: A New Mexico Pueblo, Past and Present*. Albuquerque: University of New Mexico Press.

Lightfoot, D. R. 1990. The Prehistoric Pebble-Mulched Fields of the Galisteo Anasazi: Agricultural Innovation and Adaptation to Environment. Ph.D. dissertation, Department of Geography, University of Colorado.

————. 1993. The Landscape Context of Anasazi Pebble-Mulched Fields in the Galisteo Basin, Northern New Mexico. *Geoarchaeology* 8:349–370.

Lightfoot, D. R., and F. W. Eddy 1995. The Construction and Configuration of Anasazi Pebble-Mulch Gardens in the Northern Rio Grande. *American Antiquity* 60:459–470.

Maxwell, T. D. 1997. A Survey of Portions of the El Rito and Ojo Caliente Drainages, Rio Arriba County, New Mexico. *Archaeology Notes* 160. Santa Fe: Office of Archaeological Studies, Museum of New Mexico.

Maxwell, T. D., and K. F. Anschuetz. 1992. The Southwestern Ethnographic Record and Prehistoric Agricultural Diversity. In *Gardens in Prehistory: The Archaeology of Settlement Agriculture in Greater Mesoamerica*, edited by T. W. Killion, pp. 35–68. Tuscaloosa: University of Alabama Press.

Minnis, P. E. 1985. *Social Adaptation to Food Stress: A Prehistoric Southwestern Example*. Chicago: University of Chicago Press.

Moore, J. L. 1990. Prehistoric Agriculture in the Lower Rio Chama Valley. Unpublished MS, Office of Archaeological Studies, Museum of New Mexico, Santa Fe.

————. 1992. Archaeological Testing at Three Sites West of Abiquiu, Rio Arriba County, New Mexico. *Archaeology Notes* 33. Santa Fe: Office of Archaeological Studies, Museum of New Mexico.

Muenchrath, D. A., and R. J. Salvador. 1995. Maize Productivity and AGROECOLOGY: Effects of Environment and Agricultural Practices on the Biology of Maize. In *Soil, Water, Biology, and Belief in Prehistoric and Traditional Southwestern Agriculture*, edited by H. W. Toll, pp. 303–333. Special Publication 2. Albuquerque: New Mexico Archaeological Council.

Nabhan, G. P. 1989. *Enduring Seeds, Native American Agriculture, and Wild Plant Conservation*. San Francisco: North Point Press.

Naranjo, T. 1995. Thoughts on Migration by Santa Clara Pueblo. *Journal of Anthropological Archaeology* 14:247–250.

————. 1998. Brief Ethnohistory of El Rito, New Mexico. In Pre-Columbian Pueblo Agricultural Plots (AR-03–02–02–0460 [LA114161]) within the Proposed Las Clinicas del Norte Special-Use Permit Parcel, El Rito Ranger District, Carson National Forest, Rio Arriba County, New Mexico, edited by K. F. Anschuetz, pp. 106–120. *Community and Cultural Landscape Contribution* 2. Santa Fe: Rio Grande Foundation for Communities and Cultural Landscapes.

Naranjo, T., and R. Swentzell. 1989. Healing Spaces in the Tewa Pueblo World. *American Indian Culture and Research Journal* 13:257–265.

Neely, J. A. 1995. Recent Findings Concerning Prehistoric Water-Control and Irrigation Features and Systems in West-Central New Mexico. In *Soil, Water, Biology, and Belief in Prehistoric and Traditional Southwestern Agriculture*, edited by H. W. Toll, pp. 239–262. Special Publication 2. Albuquerque: New Mexico Archaeological Council.

Ortiz, A. 1969. *The Tewa World: Space, Time, Being, and Becoming in a Pueblo Society*. Chicago: University of Chicago Press.

————. 1972. Ritual Drama and the Pueblo World View. In *New Perspectives on the Pueblos*, edited by A. Ortiz, pp. 135–161. Albuquerque: University of New Mexico Press.

————. 1979. San Juan Pueblo. In *Handbook of North American Indians*. Vol. 9, *Southwest*, edited by A. Ortiz, pp. 278–295. Washington, DC: Smithsonian Institution.

————. 1994. Some Cultural Meanings of Corn in Aboriginal North America. In *Corn and Culture in the Prehistoric New World*, edited by S. Johannessen and C. A. Hastorf, pp. 527–544. Boulder: Westview Press.

Page, G. B. 1940. Hopi Agricultural Notes. Unpublished MS, USDA Soil Conservation Service, Washington, DC.

Parsons, E. C. 1939. *Pueblo Indian Religion*. 2 vols. Chicago: University of Chicago Press.

Peckham, S. 1990. *From this Earth: The Ancient Art of Pueblo Pottery*. Santa Fe: Museum of New Mexico Press.

Periman, R. D. 1996. The Influence of Prehistoric Anasazi Cobble-Mulch Agricultural Features on Northern Rio Grande Landscapes. In *Desired Future Conditions for Southwestern Riparian Ecosystems: Bringing Interests and Concerns Together*.

Coordinated by D. W. Shaw and D. M. Finch, pp. 181–188. General Technical Report RM-GTR-272. Fort Collins, CO: Rocky Mountain Forest and Range Experiment Station, USDA Forest Service.

Ramenofsky, Ann F. 1998. Decoupling Archaeology and History: Northern New Mexico. Papers of the 1998 Chacmool Conference. Unpublished MS, the Archaeological Association of the University of Calgary.

Rappaport, R. A. 1979. Adaptive Structure and Its Disorders. In *Ecology, Meaning, and Religion*, edited by R. A. Rappaport, pp. 145–172. Berkeley: North Atlantic Books.

Ritchie, S. W., J. J. Hanaway, and G. O. Benson. 1992. *How a Corn Plant Develops*. Special Report 48. Ames: Cooperative Extension Service, Iowa State University.

Rosenberg, M. 1990. The Mother of Invention: Evolutionary Theory, Territoriality, and the Origins of Agriculture. *American Anthropologist* 92:399–415.

Sanchez, C., and G. Cajete, eds. 1997. *Growing the Memories: Native American Farming*. Pojoaque Pueblo, NM: Pojoaque Pueblo Poeh Cultural Center.

Santa Clara Pueblo Cultural Preservation Program. 1995. *Agriculture at Santa Clara Pueblo*. Santa Clara Pueblo, NM: Santa Clara Pueblo Cultural Preservation Program.

Schroeder, A. H. 1979. Pueblos Abandoned in Historic Times. In *Handbook of North American Indians*. Vol. 9, *Southwest*, edited by A. Ortiz, pp. 236–254. Washington, DC: Smithsonian Institution, Washington.

Shaw, R. H. 1988. Climate Requirement. In *Corn and Corn Improvement*, 3rd edition, edited by G. F. Sprague and J. W. Dudley, eds pp. 609–638. Agronomy Monograph 18. Madison, WI: American Society of Agronomy.

Smith, S. J. 1998. AR-03–02–02–0460 (LA111461) Pollen Analysis. In Pre-Columbian Pueblo Agricultural Plots (AR-03–02–02–0460 [LA114161]) within the Proposed Las Clinicas del Norte Special-Use Permit Parcel, El Rito Ranger District, Carson National Forest, Rio Arriba County, New Mexico, edited by K. F. Anschuetz, pp. 73–84. *Community and Cultural Landscape Contribution* 2. Santa Fe: Rio Grande Foundation for Communities and Cultural Landscapes.

Stephen, A. M. 1936. *Hopi Journal of Alexander M. Stephen*, edited by E. C. Parsons, 2 vols. *Contributions to Anthropology*. New York: Columbia University Press.

Stevenson, M. (Coxe). 1894. The Sia. In *11th Annual Report of the Bureau of American Ethnology for the Years 1889–1890*, pp. 3–157. Washington, DC: Government Printing Office.

Stewart, G. R. 1940. Conservation in Pueblo Agriculture II. Present-Day Flood Water Irrigation. *The Scientific Monthly* 51:329–340.

Stewart, G. R., and M. Donnelly. 1943. Soil and Water Economy in the Pueblo Southwest: I. Field Studies at Mesa Verde and Northern Arizona, and II. Evaluation of Primitive Methods of Conservation. *The Scientific Monthly* 66 (January): 31–44 and 66 (February): 134–144.

Stone, G. D. 1993. Agricultural Abandonment: A Comparative Study in Historical Ecology. In *Abandonment of Settlements and Regions: Ethnoarchaeological and Archaeological Approaches*, edited by C. M. Cameron and S. A. Tomka, pp. 74–81. Cambridge: Cambridge University Press.

Titiev, M. 1938. Dates of Planting at Oraibi. *Museum Notes*. 11 (5). Flagstaff: Museum of Northern Arizona.

————. 1944. Old Orabi: A Study of the Hopi Indians of Third Mesa. *Papers of the Peabody Museum of American Archaeology and Ethnology* 22 (1). Cambridge: Harvard University.

Tivy, J. 1990. *Agricultural Ecology*. New York: Longman Scientific and Technical, with John Wiley and Sons, New York.

Toll, H. W., ed. 1995. *Soil, Water, Biology, and Belief in Prehistoric and Traditional Southwestern Agriculture*. Special Publication, 2. Albuquerque: New Mexico Archaeological Council.

Trigger, B. G. 1991. Distinguished Lecture in Archeology: Constraint and Freedom—A New Synthesis for Archeological Explanation. *American Anthropologist* 93:5511–5569.

Tylor, E. B. 1871. *Primitive Culture: Researches into the Development of Mythology, Philosophy, Religion, Language, Art and Custom*. London: John Murray.

Vivian, R. G. 1974. Conservation and Diversion: Water Control Systems in the Anasazi Southwest. In Irrigation's Impact on Society, edited by T. E. Downing, and M. Gibson, pp. 95–112. *Anthropological Papers* 25. Tucson: University of Arizona Press.

Ware, J. A., and M. Mensel. 1992. The Ojo Caliente Project: Archaeological Test Excavations and a Data Recovery Plan for Cultural Resources along US 285, Rio Arriba County, New Mexico. *Archaeology Notes* 99. Santa Fe: Office of Archaeological Studies, Museum of New Mexico.

Watts, M. 1980. Coping with the Market: Uncertainty and Food Security Among Hausa Peasants. In *Coping with Uncertainty in Food Supply*, edited by I. de Garine and G. A. Harrison, pp. 260–289. Oxford: Clarendon.

White, C. S. 1986. Analyses of Prehistoric Agricultural Soils. Unpublished MS, Office of Archaeological Studies, Museum of New Mexico, Santa Fe.

White, C. S., D. R. Dreesen, and S. R. Loftin. 1998. Water Conservation Through an Anasazi Gardening Technique. *New Mexico Journal of Science* 38 (November): 251–278.

White, C. S., S. R. Loftin, and R. Aguilar. 1995. Ecology of Cobble Mulch Gardens: Structures for Modification of Soil Moisture Dynamics. Unpublished MS, Department of Biology, University of New Mexico, Albuquerque.

White, L. A. 1949. *The Science of Culture*. New York: Grove Press.

Whiteley, P. M. 1988. *Deliberate Acts: Changing Hopi Culture Through the Oraibi Split*. Tucson: University of Arizona Press.

Whiting, A. F. 1939. Ethnobotany of the Hopi. *Bulletin* 15. Flagstaff: Northern Arizona Society of Science and Art, Museum of Northern Arizona.

Wills, W. H. 1988. *Early Prehistoric Agriculture in the American Southwest*. Santa Fe: School of American Research Press.

Winship, G. P., trans. and ed. [1904] 1990. *The Journey of Coronado, 1540–1542*. Golden, CO: Fulcrum Publishing.

II

VIEWS FROM THE PUEBLOS AND BEYOND

4

Native Seeds/SEARCH and a Tohono O'odham Perspective

Angelo Joaquin, Jr.

Editor's Note: Mr. Joaquin refers to the Tohono O'odham's rich mythology in his autobiographical information. I would like to expand on that mythology because it is tied into the sacredness of both the land and water for the native peoples. I draw from two excellent sources on the Tohono O'odham, namely Dean and Lucille Saxton's *Legend and Lore of the Papago and Pima Indians* and "Rain: Native Expressions from the Southwest," a traveling exhibit organized by the Heard Museum and directed by curator Ann Marshall.

In the myth, "Rain Goes Away" (Saxton and Saxton 1973: 317–340), Hummingbird goes to bring back Wind and Rain and is told that the people drove them away. Wind said that if "they really want us, they'll sing for us for four nights. When they finish the ceremony, we'll come and rejoice with them for a while. Then, we'll come here to our home again." Hummingbird returned with the news and the medicine men met to figure out what to do. Coyote gave the oration that was designed to summon back Wind and Rain: "Drink what we have prepared, my relatives, and be revived, be elated—begin from the east side to draw the east closer. A beautifully shining ancient house stands there in the east, wrapped in white clouds. Start there and be kind to us, mixed within, speaking softly within, lightning moving very zigzag, roaring beautifully, pattering rain moving along. Although the earth is wide, the clouds are braced across it and will come, though far away. . . . He then greets those on the east by their relationship to him, then those on the west, south, and north in turn. All greet the orator by his relationship to them. He tells of the four kinds of clouds that surround the ancient houses of the east, west, south, and north. Then, one of the baskets of wine is brought out. The first man sitting on the east

drinks some and sings the first song. The basket is then taken to the west
side and the first man drinks some and sings the song. . . ." The basket is
then taken to the south and the north, and again, the wine is drunk and the
song is sung four times.

The Rain Ceremony or wine feast, according to Marshall (1999) is a gift
to the people from Elder Brother, I'itoi. The ceremony begins with the ritual
of "pulling down the clouds" or the harvesting of the saguaro cacti fruit
(Marshall 1999). The harvest and processing of the fruit may take several
weeks. The public portion of the ritual includes the drinking and regurgi-
tation of the wine. Wine is the medium through which the people pray for
water. The saturation of the people with wine is akin to the saturation of
the earth with water.

I am a member of the Tohono O'odham Nation of southern Arizona. The Tohono O'odham (Desert People) live on the second largest Indian reservation in
the United States. It is located about 40 miles west of Tucson. I also serve as
the Executive Director of Native Seeds/SEARCH, a non-profit conservation organization which was founded in 1983.

I grew up in Florence, Arizona, which is located about midway between
Tucson and Phoenix. Today, the village outside the town limits is a 44-acre
satellite Tohono O'odham reservation. My father was a musician playing the
O'odham social dance music, *waila* (from the Spanish word for dance *baile*).
My brothers and sisters accompanied his band as it traveled to perform at all-
night Saint's Day feasts, weddings, and other celebrations throughout the Tohono O'odham Nation. I, therefore, had visited all 56 villages on the main
reservation at least once by the time I was 10 years old. During the summers,
my family would visit for two-week periods with my grandparents and extended
family members on the reservation.

Native Seeds/SEARCH (NS/S), located in the ancestral homeland of the Tohono O'odham, works to conserve traditional crops, seeds, and farming methods
that have sustained native peoples throughout southwestern United States and
northern Mexico. It promotes the use of these ancient crops and their wild
relatives by gathering, safeguarding and distributing their seeds, while sharing
benefits with traditional communities. We also work to preserve knowledge
about their uses. Through research, training and community education, NS/S
works to protect biodiversity and to celebrate cultural diversity. The nonprofit
organization strives to return benefits to the communities located in the area
consisting of Arizona, New Mexico, and northern Mexico. It also works to
conserve genetic diversity as well as to celebrate the cultural diversity of the
region.

The organization was formed in 1983 after O'odham elders commented on
the lack of traditional seeds including *hu:n* (60-day corn), *bawi* (tepary beans)
and *ha:l* (squash) and other O'odham crops. Two eventual cofounders of NS/S,
Mahina Drees and Gary Nabhan, began collecting seeds from isolated regions
of the reservation where these crops were still being raised and distributed them

to other O'odham farmers and gardeners. From each farmer they received a collection of all the seeds that the farmer was growing. Today, the NS/S seed-bank contains just over 1,900 collections of seed from the entire area referred to as the Greater Southwest. This region is roughly delineated as the area from Las Vegas, Nevada, east to Las Vegas, New Mexico, and from Durango, Colorado, south to the state of Durango in Mexico.

NS/S uses conventional freezers to store the seeds. This method allows for a storage time of about 10 years before the seeds begin to lose viability. A 60-acre farm was purchased in December of 1997 to rejuvenate the collections by allowing a grow-out of a greater number of seeds.

The organization currently offers free membership to Native Americans living in the Greater Southwest and a reduced membership rate to Native Americans residing outside of the region. Free seeds, in limited quantities, are offered to Greater Southwest Native American residents and at half-price to those residing outside the region. One does not need to be a member of NS/S to receive free seeds.

Another NS/S project is the Cultural Memory Bank which is a database for the acquisitions in the seed bank and pertinent cultural information about the seeds. The premise of the project is that a young O'odham will be able to insert a CD-ROM disk into a computer and type in the O'odham, scientific, or common name of a crop. On the screen will appear a photo of the crop with text describing the plant. One will be able to hear in the O'odham language, information on planting, harvesting, preparing for meals, planting songs and other associated information on the plant.

We have been dealing with intellectual property rights that loosely translated mean the protection of ideas. Seeds are ideas because someone at one time decided that a particular plant had unique characteristics and then gathered seeds which were planted and replanted many times to strengthen those characteristics. Traditional farmers then passed the seeds and the information on for generations—without the aid of books, microfiche or computers. A native farmer's techniques are not much different from those of a scientist who also manipulates the genes in a seed. While the scientist might hold up a seed and be proud of his work in producing a "capsule of genetic information," a traditional farmer will hold up a seed and be proud that he has created a "piece of life." When one considers the associated information passed down with this piece of life, including songs, prayers and ceremonies, one understands the significance of the seed to the people.

The Desert Foods for Diabetes project, another NS/S effort, provides culturally relevant information about diabetes and how eating traditional foods will help regulate blood sugar. In addition, the project looks at how traditional activities can encourage elevated activity levels. The materials include videotapes, pamphlets, and a cookbook developed from a cultural perspective with regard to the Desert People's traditions, beliefs, and values.

Diabetes rates are rising among indigenous groups throughout the world as these groups switch from their traditional diets to a western diet that offers hamburgers, french fries, and other fast food. These foods are high in fat and low in fiber. Foods from the plants of the desert, in the case of the O'odham, are high in fiber and low in fat. These desert plants have substances that help the plant stay moist in an arid environment. These same substances—pectins, mucilage, and gums—slow the introduction of sugar into the blood, because of the lengthy time it takes to break them down in the digestive system. The extra absorption time gives the pancreas time to produce the insulin needed to work with the sugar.

An important accomplishment of the Diabetes Project occurred in 1966 when Indian Health Service (IHS) staff from the hospital in Sells (the capital of the Tohono O'odham Nation) contacted NS/S to collaborate on a project to re-introduce traditional food into the hospital's menu. Apparently a hospital intern had remarked that a heart attack was imminent if he kept eating the food served by the cafeteria. The same fare was being served to O'odham patients with diabetes, high blood pressure, and other illnesses. The first step was to acquaint the doctors, nurses, and hospital cafeteria staff to the foods and the reason for the importance of including the dishes in the menu. We worked with the nutrition staff and came up with four dishes: a posole dish, a nopalito and red chile dish, *pe:lkan cucuma:t* (whole wheat tortillas), and a bean bread. All were accepted by the medical staff and the patients. IHS reports that the foods are commented upon favorably by patients when they are served.

Other projects of NS/S include the Proyecto de Recursos Tarahuma or our Sierra Madre Project. One of the challenges to the Tarahumara, or Rarámuri as they call themselves, is the soil erosion resulting from logging operations in their homeland. In many villages, bare-faced rock is evident due to the lack of plants to anchor the soil. A project to build trincheras, low stone walls, to capture the runoff is already showing good results after only one rainy season. Community members of the village I visited in September 1998 had constructed more than 100 trincheras ranging from 18 inches high and three feet across to nearly five feet high and 20 feet across. Seedlings, raised in a greenhouse as part of the project, were planted in the corners to anchor the newly captured soil. Small fences were constructed to protect the young trees from the hundreds of cattle and goats roaming the countryside. In another community near Creel, NS/S is helping gardeners expand the variety of crops grown for food by providing fencing materials and pipe to deliver water to the gardens. One gentleman is growing Thompson seedless grapes in addition to vegetables and doesn't have to worry about the domesticated animals eating them.

The Tohono O'odham live in the Sonoran Desert of southern Arizona. The average rainfall is 12 inches per year and there is virtually no surface water on the 2.8 million-acre reservation. This reservation represents approximately one-third of our traditional lands. Originally, O'odham lived in an area that extended beyond the present day reservation about 60 miles into the Mexican state of Sonora.

The Tohono O'odham are tied to the land. In this day and age of high mobility, indigenous groups stay put because of several factors. One very important reason is that our Creation Story tells how the *tohono*, or desert, was made for the O'odham (People). We are taught that everything needed to rejuvenate our physical, mental, and spiritual health is provided to us by the creators.

Our sacred mountain of Baboquivari Peak is where I'itoi (Elder Brother) lives and watches over the O'odham today. We make pilgrimages, at least four during our lifetimes, to pay respect to I'itoi and to give thanks for the support we receive from him in our lives. I'itoi is a spiritual being and creator. He can change forms and transform himself. That is why one can't harm animals—we never know if the animal is really I'itoi.

Our ceremonies are largely for the calling for rain and giving thanks for rain. We hold a wine ceremony with fermented saguaro cactus fruit juice to call for the summer rain or the desert "monsoon" season. This rainy season begins in July and ends in August.

Recently, a nonprofit O'odham group helped reinstate a wine ceremony in a small village on the reservation. The group also is helping an elder farmer plant and harvest a flood water field. We are hopeful that other parts of the reservation will soon be able to farm in the traditional manner once again.

O'odham believe that saguaros were once people. Young children are told that is why one must never throw rocks at, jab sharp sticks into, or shoot at saguaros.

One tradition that helped define when a boy became a man was the run to collect salt from the Gulf of California. Boys would run over a hundred miles from the present day reservation location to an area near Puerto Penasco in Mexico. Elder men would travel ahead of the group, setting up camps for the boys to eat and rest overnight.

There are about 22,000 registered tribal members of the Tohono O'odham Nation. Approximately 14,000 of these O'odham live on the reservation. Another 5,000 or so O'odham are not registered tribal members while about 4,000 more O'odham reside in Mexico.

Many challenges face the O'odham as we enter the new millennium. One of the most crucial is the survival of the O'odham language. Although close to 50 percent of the people currently speak the language, the number of the O'odham below the age of 30 who speak the language fluently is dropping.

Another challenge is the conservation of natural resources including the materials used for basket making. Harvesting methods taught by the O'odham *Himdag* or "Way of Life" require people to take only what they need when collecting. Plant materials used for baskets include devils claw, bear grass, yucca and banana yucca root. If these plants are over-harvested, the materials may not be available for future generations of basket weavers. The current resurgent interest in basket weaving has put pressure on these raw materials: in 20 to 30 years there will be twice as many weavers as there are today. The tribe might look into declaring harvesting areas as conservation reserves to protect the plants.

Some years ago, NS/S, along with the Arizona-Sonoran Desert Museum and others, sponsored a conference called "Losing Species, Losing Language, Losing Culture." The premise is that the loss of a species may result in the loss of the O'odham word for that plant as well as the potential loss of other cultural information pertinent to the species including songs, prayers, and ceremonies specific to the species.

Another challenge is to produce written materials in the O'odham language. It has only been a couple of decades since the O'odham language was written with its own orthography. In fact, two orthographies are now in place with a dictionary. A committee of O'odham is currently working on a new dictionary which will use the orthography officially adopted by the Tohono O'odham Nation.

The loss of ability to farm in the traditional way by flood water or *ak chin* (mouth of wash) has serious cultural implications for O'odham farmers living in traditional farming areas where these methods can no longer be used. Native farmers supplemented what foods could be gathered in the desert allowing for the survival of the Tohono O'odham. In addition to corn, beans and squash, O'odham raised crops introduced by the Spanish including melons. Overgrazing of the land—both before and after the reservation was formed—has resulted in the loss of underbrush. These plants would slow the flow of water from the mountain areas to the lowlands where farming villages were located.

To combat the threat of flooding, U.S. government agencies constructed dams and other water diversion devices. Consequently, no flood water is available for O'odham farmers wishing to use the water to grow crops in the traditional manner. Traditional farming is associated with the cultural uniqueness of the current distinct group of people living in this area. As traditional practices disappear, so too may disappear an important part of Tohono O'odham culture.

Development and use of water resources are hot issues in Arizona. The Tohono O'odham Nation filed a lawsuit in 1976 against the city of Tucson and the copper mines and farming businesses in the area. Today, Tucson is still the largest U.S. city that relies solely on ground water. The Central Arizona Project, an almost 400-mile aqueduct completed in 1992 which brings water from the Colorado River in the northwest corner of the state to Tucson, has proved largely ineffective because of the quality and cost of the water. Currently, the city of Tucson is deciding whether to use the water or to allow it to soak into the ground to recharge the aquifers in the area.

In summary, Native Seeds/SEARCH and the Tohono O'odham have similar missions with regard to the future. The role of NS/S is to conserve seeds, knowledge of farming methods, and other cultural knowledge including the use of traditional foods to combat the devastating effect of diabetes on the O'odham. The Tohono O'odham are striving to ensure that cultural knowledge, traditions, and the O'odham language will be available for the future generations of the

Desert People. A collaborative effort on the part of both groups will enhance the possibility of successfully accomplishing both missions.

REFERENCES

Marshall, Ann. 1999. "Rain: Native Expressions from the American Southwest." Exhibit organized by the Heard Museum, Phoenix, Arizona. Ann Marshall, Exhibit Curator.

Saxton, Dean and Lucille Saxton. 1973. *O'othham Hoho'ok A'agitha. Legends and Lore of the Papago and Pima Indians.* Tucson: The University of Arizona Press.

5

The Akimel O'othom: Pima People

Nathan Allen

Editor's Note: Nathan Allen passed away before the publication of this book. He had given me an unpublished report about the Gila River Indians. The report offered a lot of historical background that is important to understanding them. I have therefore included the following abstract from that report.

The Gila River Pima are one of the peoples known by the early Spanish as the Pimas Altos (Upper Pimas), who lived in Pimeria Alta, an area encompassing southwestern Arizona and northern Sonora, Mexico. The Pimas Altos share a Piman language of the Uto-Aztecan language family with the Pima Bajo (Lower Pima), who lived in lower Sonora.

All Pimas Altos call themselves "o'odham," or "we the people." The Pimas Altos consist of three major groups. Gila River Pima call themselves the "Akimel O'odham," or River People, which reflects the importance of the river in their lives. They were formerly known as One Villagers, and are the Pima of the Gila River Indian Community. The second group is the "Tohono O'odham," or Desert People. Until recently, they were known as Papago ("bean eater" in Spanish, considered a derogatory term), and were known previously as Two Villagers. They presently occupy the Tohono O'odham Reservation and traditional lands stretching south of the Arizona border with Mexico.

The third group is the "Hia-Ced O'odham" or Sand People, who were also known as the Sand Papago or No Villagers. They were said by the federal government in 1937 to have died out from disease and conflict early in the twentieth century.

In September of 1996, a 20-acre portion of the requested 103,680 acres of traditional lands south of Ajo was returned by the Bureau of Land Management to the Hia-Ced O'odham Alliance, a non-profit corporation representing the approximately 1,400 Hia-Ced O'odham that are living today but have no formal tribal recognition and no reservation. In 1984, they were allowed to enroll as members of the Tohono

O'odham without separate tribal status or reservation lands, and many Hia-Ced O'odham live on the Tohono O'odham Reservation today.

Midway through the Hispanic period, sometime between 1740–1780, the Maricopa, a Yuman-speaking tribe that lived along the Colorado River, united with the Gila River Pima for mutual protection against enemy attack. In 1823 the Confederation made an alliance by treaty with Mexico.

The first Americans to enter the Gila River Valley were fur trappers looking for beaver in 1825. The U.S. Army first officially contacted the Pima-Maricopa Confederation in 1846, during the first year of the Mexican-American War. Despite the Confederation's existing alliance with Mexico, American Brigadier General Stephen Kearny made an alliance with Confederation leader Juan Antonio Llunas and traded with the Confederation for food and grain on the way to fight in Mexico. The 1848 Treaty of Guadalupe Hidalgo ended the Mexican-American War and relocated the border between the U.S. and Mexico to the Gila River, making the Gila River Pima and Maricopa the northernmost citizens of Mexico.

By 1849, the California Gold Rush was on and increasing numbers of Americans traveled the Southern Wagon Road that passed through the Gila River Valley enroute to the California goldfields. By this time, the Pima were raising poultry in addition to horses, mules and cattle, and were growing great quantities of cotton, maize and wheat. Confederation exports included woven cotton sheets and Pima baskets in addition to produce. Trade with friendly Pima and Maricopa enabled 49'ers who underestimated their food needs to reach California.

In 1853, the Gila River Pima and Maricopa lands were now within the redrawn U.S. borders when the Gadsden Purchase incorporated southern Arizona into U.S. territory. A new federal agency, the Department of the Interior, was to supervise relations with Native Americans and carry out government programs and policies through its Bureau of Indian Affairs [BIA]. The tribes also had to deal with the Department of War, which was in charge of all U.S. military forces and operations.

The first land area to be designated as the Gila Reservation was surveyed in 1859. The reservation was laid out on a 4 mile by 25 mile east west strip bisected by the Gila River (64,000 acres).

While aggressive military campaigns [abetting Union soldiers in the Civil War] occupied Confederation leaders, [non-Indian] settlers upstream of the reservation founded the town of Florence and initiated a vast canal-building project. By the end of the Civil War, upstream farmers were diverting so much water from the Gila River that the Confederation entered a long period of economic depression and increasing dependence on the Federal government, particularly the BIA.

As Gila River water was diverted upstream, both the Pima and the Maricopa expanded croplands and pastures in areas irrigated by the Salt River. Following reports that a large number of settlers were heading to the Salt River Valley from Utah, in January of 1879 President Rutherford B. Hayes signed an Executive Order to halt sales of land on the north bank of the Gila River to the junction with the Salt River. Although this order protected the Confederation's water rights in the Salt River Valley, as guaranteed by the 1848 Treaty of Guadalupe Hidalgo, it proved to be only a temporary measure.

An 1879 territorial court decision, Kelsey v. McAteer, became the basic legal principle for water rights to surface-fllowing water in Arizona. The decision held that anyone's right to use surface-flowing water for irrigation or other "beneficial uses" in Arizona was derived from and depended upon "prior appropriation." The first person to "beneficially" use water from a stream established a right to continue to do so; latecomers could gain only "junior" or wet year rights. Unfortunately, the Pima-Maricopa "prior appropriation" rights were not protected or enforced by the federal government as the settlers took increasing amounts of water to irrigate their farms upstream. In 1888 the Florence-Casa Grande Canal Company purchased a huge dragline to excavate a main canal from the river to Picacho Reservoir and on southward to the Casa Grande railway station, without federal opposition.

For decades the federal government did little to improve the desperate plight of the Confederation. The U.S. Geological Survey was not concerned with the Indians' plight, but with conservation issues such as flood control and irrigation for development of arid lands. In the early 1900s, dams were constructed on the Gila River near San Carlos and on the Salt River at the Theodore Roosevelt Dam. If the system worked as the engineers claimed, the Pima and Maricopa farmers would benefit. However, they never received an adequate supply of water to restore their agricultural lands to production.

In 1917 the federal government gave control of the Salt River Project to a group of non-Indian landowners, making the Maricopa's legal rights to irrigation water almost meaningless. A more equitable distribution of Gila River water was planned in the 1924 San Carlos Act, which authorized construction of Coolidge Dam and creation of the San Carlos Irrigation Project. For the first ten years [of the project] there was never enough water to fill the reservoir. In 1949 . . . the Gila River Indian Community [GRIC] . . . filed suit regarding GRIC water rights and other issues before the Indian Claims Commission. The U.S. Court of Claims held that the 1924 San Carlos Act did not require the Pima and Maricopa to pay for the irrigation district operation and that the U.S. was to pay back, with interest, all of the fees collected since 1936. Although this brought financial gain, without fees the Coolidge Dam generators ceased operation in 1983. (Gila River Indian Community 1996)

In 1990 the Pima Irrigation Project was initiated, with 146,000 acres currently planned for agricultural production. In addition, water will be used for recreational facilities, wetland and riparian development, and municipal and industrial facilities. Construction for this project began in 1998 and will continue until 2003 (Gila River Indian Community, Pima-Maricopa Irrigation Project brochure).

Mr. Allen uses *O'othom* and not O'odham, *Huhukam* and not Hohokam when writing his history to reflect his "way of spelling certain words in our language."

In the deserts of south central Arizona, along the banks of the Gila River, live a people who are not very well known. The Pima, as they are called today, have lived within these deserts for well over a thousand years. Their ancestry begins in prehistoric times when an earlier people lived and farmed the Gila River Valley. The prehistoric Huhukam, as they are called by modern archaeologists, are the ancestors of the present day Pima.

According to scientific dating, the Huhukam thrived and prospered along the Gila River from the time of Christ to around 1450 A.D., long before the arrival of the Europeans. Their extensive canal system was the key to a very long existence. In addition, they had the ability to live in harmony with the desert. The whole desert, which seems so lifeless, was the salvation of the Huhukam and today's O'othom. It is here, we are at home. Both the Huhukam and O'othom used the water to irrigate crops of corn, beans, and squash. Desert plants like saguaro fruit, cholla buds, mesquite beans, various types of greens and edible roots along the river were also an excellent source of food. Game animals, abundant along the river, supplied fresh meat and fish.

> Perhaps this was the best of times, but who is to know today. I often look to the past for answers to my questions of today in an attempt to understand myself.

In 1934, Harold S. Gladwin undertook the first major excavation of a Huhukam site in the Gila River valley by Gila Pueblo out of Globe Arizona. The work was continued in 1964 by Emil W. Haury and the University of Arizona. From these excavations a long kept secret began to unfold from under the salt brush and gentle mounds of earth. The site gave the archaeological community a glimpse of the Huhukam by revealing evidence of a prehistoric people who thrived and prospered here. It must be understood that this was not the only village of the ancient people; there were many ancient Huhukam villages all along the Gila and Salt rivers. These are the prehistoric people from whom we have descended.

However, even though there are those in the scientific community who doubt our ancestry, archaeologists continue to seek *the* site which will validate our claim. They are looking for a site with physical evidence of a major transition from Huhukam to O'othom. In our minds we do not need to validate this transition. We believe it to be true, our legends and songs tell us this. Legends of the "cruel and bitter man who saluted the sun each day out of the holes in Civan Vahki (Casa Grande)," a legend first recorded in 1775 by Father Font. Astronomical alignments in the big house, which were finally proven scientifically in the 1970's, reflect the legend of I'itoi (the drinker), our Creator, who once resided there. Another legend tells of a Civan (a priestly person) who had in his possession the wind but lost it in battle and the eventual loss of his power over the wind god. There are songs of the Civan Vahki and the powers it held inside, and we have heard of the drink which enabled you to sing many beautiful songs. We have songs of other big houses and visits to them by a traveler who dreamt the songs of each house and sacred place. However, it is difficult to find respect for oral history in an age of written history. Nevertheless, I see a rich and valid belief system, still in place after three centuries of European contact.

> Before my father began to tell me legends and the related songs of our people, he would always say, "Before the 'bearded ones' came, this is the way it was."

When the Spanish arrived with Father Kino in 1694, they found a people living and thriving along the banks of the Gila River. We had crops of corn, beans, and squash in abundance, exactly like the archaeological evidence at the Huhukam village sites. Our aboriginal lands extended far beyond our present day boundaries: to the east as far as the Pinal mountains, north, far beyond the Salt River basin; west, as far as the great bend of the Gila River.

In 1694 the new arrivals first saw the massive building we call "Civan Vahki" but was given the name "Casa Grande" by the Spanish who were the first to arrive in our lands. The Casa Grande had been abandoned for more than 200 years by then. This period of time is what still puzzles the archaeological community. Are the Akimel O'othom the true descendants of the ancient Huhukam culture? We don't have to question this; we believe it to be so! The massive caliche structure was built around the mid-fourteenth century and the Huhukam culture came to an end, so the archaeologists say, around 1450 A.D. By the late 1600s Father Kino and the Spanish had arrived in our land and encountered the O'othom.

I was employed as a National Park Service Ranger at Casa Grande Ruins National Monument for 10 years and this is what Civan Vahki, the Casa Grande, says to me.

> For over 650 years I have withstood the forces of nature.
> I served the people well.
> Within my chambers the voices of the old ones still linger.
> I have kept the secrets of the old ones from the beginning.
> I am crumbling with increasing age.
> I will remain silent as the darkness of night.
> I will remain a mystery to all who come to see me.
> I will keep the secrets of the old ones
> Until you stop to listen.
> If they would only stop.
> Close their eyes and listen.
> I would then share the secrets of the old ones.
> Can you feel their presence?
> The old ones,
> They still come into my soul and ponder the heavens.

With the discovery of gold in California we saw the coming of the American settlers, the 49ers, into our lands. The settlers needed supplies and protection, and so they established military posts along the Gila River. The O'othom provided food, water, and protection to these new arrivals. The end result was that a number of the gold seekers stayed in the upper Gila River Valley. As their settlements grew, they begin to divert more and more water out of the Gila River upstream. Consequently, our supply downstream begin to dwindle. We had less water for our crops, and the people begin to suffer. Crops failed, and the natural vegetation along the river begin to disappear, natural springs and marsh areas eroded into memories. It is told the old ones would talk of days spent along the river and the giant cottonwood trees and willows they rested under after a day in the fields under the blazing sun.

During better times, the O'othom worked together to maintain a canal system similar to the Huhukam system in prehistoric times. Working together for the benefit of all, each village perhaps was responsible for a certain segment of canal as well as the laterals to their fields. Important decisions involving water and village matters were discussed and settled under the shade of a *Vatho*, a ramada in Spanish. Life was much less hectic perhaps then, but the water situation begin to worsen. The people began to voice their concerns about the water problems to the Superintendent at the Pima Agency in Sacaton, a government office. They were assured the problems would be taken care of by the government in Washington D.C.

In an attempt to supplement lost crops, the O'othom began to harvest mesquite wood for sale to the railroad lines and local merchants in the nearby towns and the huge mesquite bosques began to be depleted. Horse drawn wagons loaded with firewood for sale to buy food or needed supplies, trudging down the dusty trails, was a scene long before my time.

I was told of these rough times by my father who was actually there.

In the early 1920s the U.S. Government came up with a plan to solve the water problem of the O'othom. They proposed building an irrigation system to deliver water to the O'othom farmers. This was the beginning of the United States Indian Irrigation Service (USIIS). The lands were cleared by mule teams with blades called a *Fresno*. Canals were dug and head gates of concrete were constructed. Diversion dams were built across the Gila River at what is now Olberg and east of the village of Santa Cruz. The plan was to build an irrigation system all across the reservation from east to west. However, the system was never completed because the government ran out of money and the people in District 6 and 7, on the west end of our reservation, never received their fair share of surface water. This uncompleted project involved the Maricopa People in District 7 who had left their homelands along the Colorado and had come to live among the O'othom in historic times. District 6, where the villages of Gila Crossing, St. Johns, and Chichino are still located, also never got any surface irrigation water. The earthen canal systems have served the O'othom for over 70 years now and are in great need of rehabilitation. During the 1920's when the USIIS canal system was being built, the non-Indian farmers in the nearby areas were also battling for their fair share of water.

The battle which is still being fought in the judicial system today.

As part of the reclamation projects of the late 1920s and early 1930s, a dam was to be constructed across the Gila River in a canyon upstream. This was to solve all the water problems of both the Indian and non-Indian farmers. Waters of the Gila would be stored behind the multidomed structure for usage in times of drought and would also supply hydroelectric power. Great plan! The dam was started in 1926 and completed in 1929 and dedicated by Calvin Coolidge in 1930. Thus it was christened the Coolidge Dam. To my knowledge the reservoir behind it has only been full twice in its lifetime to this day. When the project was completed, without accomplishing either goal, it was placed under the U.S. Bureau of Indian Affairs for operation and maintenance. Under the new Department of the Interior it became the San Carlos Irrigation Project, a project which provided me with employment for 15 years. The location of Coolidge Dam is within the boundaries of the San Carlos Apache Indian Reservation which may explain the name of the project.

To me, these were just band-aid efforts to solve a major water problem.

By the time I was old enough to understand the waterworks, I also learned you just don't take water when you want it. There was a government appointed water master the people called a "whiz" (why he had that name, I will never know). Since the U.S. Government was charged with the operation and maintenance of the water delivery system, he was the man to see. He was the person you placed your order with for water to irrigate your crops. I still remember the days my brother and I spent in the field irrigating our father's barley.

There were not many of the O'othom farming during the time I was growing up because farming had become very expensive. The days of the horse drawn farm equipment were long gone, fond memories in the minds of the elders of our community. Perhaps this will give you a clue as to my feelings.

GRANDFATHER

He sits there, his head slightly bowed.
Dreaming perhaps. Dreaming of other days.
> *Joy and laughter?*
> *Youth and trying times?*
> *Days spent along the Akimel with friends?*
> *Hunts that put food on the table of his family?*
> *Dances of his people?*
> *Toiling in the fields?*
> *Heat, cold, wind and rain?*

His skin is deeply burned from the blazing sun, signs of a long and hard
life.
He now sits quietly, often encircled by the wide eyes of his
grandchildren.
He sings the songs of the "Old Ones" to them. He tells them the legends
that were handed down to him by his grandfather. He is hoping they will
be remembered and told to those who will follow.
Grandfather's silver hair streams down about his head.
He sits and dreams of other days.

The horses were sold during hard times to make ends meet. Most of the people had jobs off the reservation, mostly farm laborers because this was the only skill they knew. The purchasing of fuel powered farm machinery was next to impossible. Most lending agencies would not even talk with you if you were from the reservation. There was nothing to put up for collateral, no cattle, no horses, and no land because it was held in trust by the federal government, nothing at all. Even though the people had jobs, they usually only made minimum wage—no nice houses, very few new vehicles, and so forth. Our lifestyle was very different, and we lived well below standard, but the people were satisfied. We are a proud people who come together in a time of need. Whether it be family, village or tribal, we work together. If a house in the village burned to the ground, the family and villagers would rebuild it in a matter of days: men would construct the frame and apply the mud and dirt roof, women prepared the noon meal with what was donated. The only payment the people expected was the delicious food they shared and the visiting during work. They led a very simple but happy existence.

For most of my young life this was how it was. When I reached high school age, my father made a decision. He decided that I should go to one of the many boarding schools operated by the federal government at the time for Indian children, although I wanted to stay in the public school system at Casa Grande, Arizona. At this time in my life, my father and I were alone at home. I had lost my mother to cancer three years earlier which was the reason for his decision. At Phoenix Indian High School we were given the training skills needed to find gainful employment. In retrospect I realize we were not prepared for college. We were not offered an entry level education into college, just vocational training for the boys in trades such as welding, auto mechanics, and electrical repair. I took up welding and was a certified welder for more than 20 years.

Following four years of school at Phoenix Indian and one year of welding training in California, I returned to the reservation. I found it totally different. The water situation had worsened, and the giant cottonwoods and mesquites along the earthen canals (where I hunted doves, whitewing, and quail as a youth) had been ripped out. A water conservation measure, I was told. The land seemed so barren and lifeless. There were fewer O'othom farmers than when I had gone away to school. Large-scale Anglo farmers with modern machinery and financing capabilities were here leasing the lands once farmed by the landowners. Frequently they had a tribal member as the middle man. It was easier for a tribal member to obtain a lease than a nontribal member. Somehow this just didn't seem like home. However, we had to move on. Although we were an agrarian people, we had to look for other means of revenue.

In the 1970s the government came in to solve our problems again, this time with free money through revenue sharing programs. The tribe was given an amount of federal monies to divide evenly among the seven political districts according to population. These funds were to be utilized to provided social oriented services to the community members who could not afford them. Each district would create line items according to their priorities, such as, the elderly, community projects, recreation, service center operations, and so forth. Fine, but the people began to totally depend on these funds which was a bad idea in my point of view. Again, this was a short term solution to the many problems facing a people who were first and foremost farmers and just wanted their water back!

Although the O'othom have faced all these problems for more than 100 years, they did not fade into the mists of time. The people managed to continue their existence and retain their proud heritage. The loss of traditional ceremonies and rituals related to the river and its environment is perhaps the greatest loss of all in addition to the water. However our roots are here along the Akimel (river). People look for their roots, for where they came from and for what purpose they are here. We do not have to.

At the time of this writing, the Gila River Indian Community has begun construction of a water delivery system to irrigate 146,330 acres. The Pima Maricopa Irrigation project is a federally funded project under the Bureau of Reclamation. It was established in 1990 and was operated by the Bureau of Reclamation until 1995. The current Pima-Maricopa Irrigation Project is in the hands of the community now through Self-Governance. It will take 20 years to complete and will continue to be funded by the Bureau of Reclamation. This project is part of the Central Arizona Project which is bringing Colorado River water to central Arizona. It is a project of monumental proportions and every Indian Nation is watching the Gila River Indian Community and their efforts to regain an argricultural lifestyle. The Gila River Indian Community is determined to complete the main delivery system to bring their water back onto their lands to reestablish an agricultural base. It will involve a pipeline varying in diameter and an open channel through the community. The main stem will total 86 miles of pipeline and an open channel delivery system when completed. In the eastern communities, districts 1 through 5, the project will rehabilitate the old earthen canals which were constructed more than 70 years ago. The San Carlos Irrigation Project currently provides Gila River water, pumped water, and water from other sources. When the Pima Maricopa Irrigation project is completed, it will deliver Gila River water, settlement water (water which will be returned to the tribe following court settlements), pump water, and Colorado River water. We will be returning to our roots.

One Day

We are *Akimel O'othom*, people of the River Gila.
Just as our crops come from Mother Earth.
We, *Akimel O'othom*, come from Mother Earth
Jevid Makai, earth doctor, brought us forth.
Since then,
We have farmed the valleys.
Our crops have flourished from the waters of the *Akimel*.
Today
The songs and legends of the *Old Ones* can no longer be heard,
The waters of the *Akimel* no longer flow,
But they still linger in our hearts and minds,
And in our hands and land.

We, *Akimel O'othom*, long for the sweet music of flowing water.
One day, we, *Akimel O'othom*, will hear the sweet music of flowing
   water . . .

REFERENCES

Gila River Indian Community. n.d. Pima-Maricopa Irrigation Project brochure. Sacaton,
   Arizona: Pima-Maricopa Irrigation Project, Office of Public Involvement.
————. Gila River Indian Community. 1996. Unpublished report of the Gila River Indian
   Reservation.

6

Hopi and Zuni Cultural Landscapes: Implications of History and Scale for Cultural Resources Management

T. J. Ferguson and Roger Anyon

INTRODUCTION

The cultural landscapes of the Hopi and Zuni Indian tribes in the southwestern United States incorporate vast geographical areas and considerable time depth. For more than a millennium, the Hopi and Zuni people, and their ancestors, migrated throughout the Southwest, ultimately arriving at the Pueblo villages they continue to occupy. The cultural landscapes established during their ancient migrations have continuing historical and religious significance to the Hopi and Zuni people. During the historic period, these cultural landscapes became embedded within larger political territories established by Spain, Mexico, and the United States. Today the ancestral landscapes of the Hopi and Zuni are incorporated into the states of Arizona, New Mexico, Colorado, and Utah.

Historical events during the last 150 years have transformed the legal status of lands that were once the sole domain of tribal ancestors. The Hopi and Zuni Indian Reservations were established in the late nineteenth century by Executive Order, after much of the aboriginal land of the two tribes had been taken without payment to make it part of the public domain of the United States. The creation of the Hopi and Zuni Indian reservations encouraged additional appropriation of tribal land by state governments, private individuals, and businesses. The political processes that extinguished native land tenure left the Hopi and Zuni tribes in control of only a small fraction of their ancestral cultural landscapes. The rest of these cultural landscapes have become fragmented in a patchwork of land ownership subject to a variety of legal and regulatory constraints. A mosaic of federal, state, and private land divides managerial responsibilities between numerous agencies, many of which administer regulatory policy in a manner that alienates the Hopi and Zuni people from significant portions of their cultural landscapes. In response to this situation, the Hopi and Zuni tribes are using the legal framework established by the National Historic Preservation Act (NHPA)[1] and the Native American Graves Protection and Repatriation Act (NAGPRA)[2] to expand their control over ancestral lands through increased participation in managerial decision making.

This chapter examines the nature and extent of Hopi and Zuni cultural landscapes, identifying themes central to the management of these landscapes as cultural resources. For the Hopi and Zuni tribes, large cultural landscapes constitute the basis for consultation with federal and state agencies regarding historic preservation and repatriation. The focus of federal and state agencies, however, is on smaller parcels of land that are managed for their property or resource values rather than their cultural value as ancestral Puebloan landscapes. The fundamental disparity between tribal concepts of landscape and administrative concepts of land leads to misconceptions that make effective land management more difficult. This chapter takes a step towards resolving this managerial conundrum by explaining how the Hopi and Zuni tribes use cultural landscapes to define ethnicity and preserve the cultural well-being of their people. We trust that federal and state officials who grasp the meaning and importance of Native American cultural landscapes will be in a better position to manage these lands as cultural resources.

HOPI AND ZUNI: GEOGRAPHIC AND ETHNOGRAPHIC CONTEXTS

The Hopi and Zuni Indian Reservations are located on the Colorado Plateau, a physiographic province consisting of nearly horizontal sedimentary rock cut by deep canyons, interspersed with large basins and intrusive igneous features (Cordell 1997: 35). The primary drainage system is the Colorado River and its tributaries, including the Little Colorado River. The Hopi and Zuni Reservations are located along tributaries of the Little Colorado River. The Hopi Reservation is located in northeast Arizona, while the Zuni Reservation is located in west-central New Mexico and east-central Arizona (Map 6.1).

The Hopi Indian Reservation was established in 1882 as a rectangular block of land about 3,905 square miles in size (Jones 1950; James 1974: 100–101). The original Hopi reservation was subjected to encroachment by the neighboring Navajo tribe and in 1974, after a long period of litigation, was partitioned between the two tribes (Ferguson and Lomaomvaya 1999: 23). In 1992, as a result of related litigation, a tract of land surrounding the Hopi settlement at Munqapi on the Navajo Indian Reservation was transferred from the Navajo Nation to the Hopi Tribe. Today the trust lands of the Hopi Indian Reservation thus consist of two noncontiguous parcels of land in northeast Arizona. The larger parcel, encompassing about 2,410 square miles, includes three villages on First Mesa

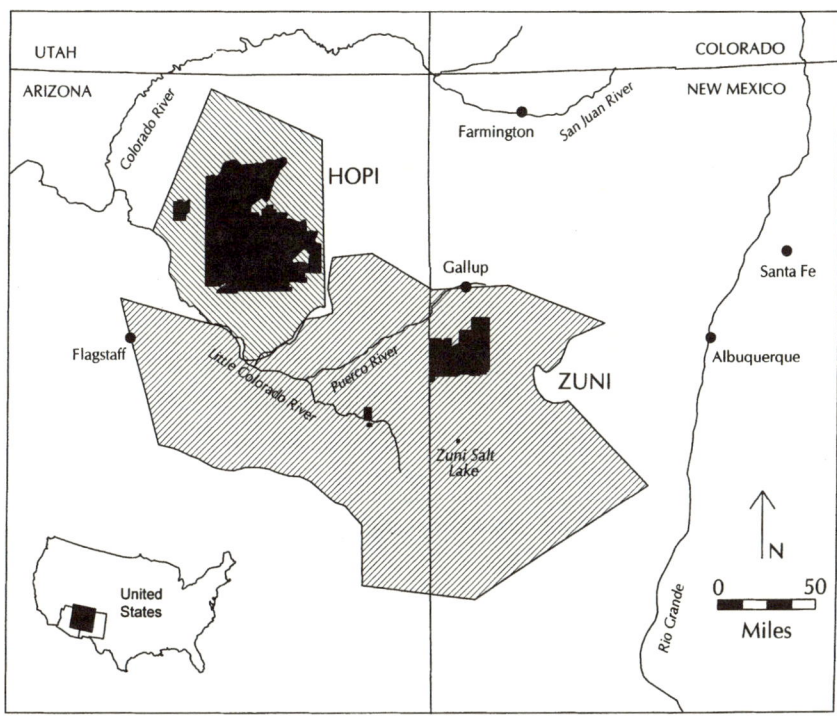

Map 6.1 The Hopi and Zuni Indian Reservations are depicted in solid black. Aboriginal lands as determined judicially are represented by hatched lines.

(Walpi, Sitsomovi, and Tewa), three villages on Second Mesa (Songoopavi, Supawlavi, and Musagnuvi), and four villages on Third Mesa (Orayvi, Hot'vela, Paaqavi, and Kiqötsmovi). The smaller parcel, encompassing 100 square miles, contains the Upper and Lower Munqapi villages, which are located about 40 miles northwest of Orayvi. Using funds provided from the settlement of land claims with the Navajo Nation, the Hopi Tribe recently acquired several ranches in the Little Colorado River Valley, but these have not yet been entered into trust status.

Hopi society is integrated by a social and religious organization based on traditional and ceremonial knowledge known as *navoti* and *wiimi. Navoti* is a historical knowledge derived from experiences handed down by ancestors to their descendants, including clan migration histories. *Wiimi* encompasses the ceremonial traditions, ritual objects, and songs that were brought to Hopi by migrating clans. Matrilineal clans, organized into phratries, are the cornerstone of Hopi social organization (Eggan 1950: 61–89).[3] The exact number of Hopi clans is hard to determine because anthropologists have confused clans with their *wu'ya*, or totems. Some clans have more than one totem, so the number of clans is exaggerated in the published literature. According to the Hopi Cultural Preservation Office, there are currently about 34 Hopi clans. Some Hopi clans that existed in the past are now extinct, but their knowledge and ceremonial functions continue to be represented in the *navoti* and *wiimi* of other clans in their phratries. Hopi ceremonial organization is complex and includes rituals associated with the *Katsina* belief system and 14 men's and women's religious societies (Eggan 1950: 89; Whiteley 1988: 59). The annual ceremonial cycle is divided into two parts, with a *Katsina* season lasting about seven and a half months and the remainder of the year being devoted to ceremonies conducted by the men's and women's religious societies. Hopi religious ceremonies are synchronized with agricultural seasons (Ferguson and Lomaomvaya 1999: 27–28; Washburn 1995: 30–34). Each Hopi ceremony is controlled by a clan (Eggan 1950: 90), but the ceremonies controlled by a particular clan vary among villages (Connelly 1979: 548; Frigout 1979: 575). The population of the Hopi Tribe is currently about 10,500.

The Zuni Indian Reservation was established in 1877 and expanded several times in the nineteenth and twentieth centuries (Ferguson and Hart 1985: 92–99). Today, the Zuni reservation consists of three noncontiguous parcels of land. The main parcel, centered on Zuni Pueblo, encompasses about 640 square miles. An area slightly less than one square mile surrounds the Zuni Salt Lake, located 42 miles south of Zuni Pueblo in New Mexico. The third parcel of the Zuni reservation, located in Arizona about 55 miles southwest of Zuni Pueblo, encompasses about 17 square miles surrounding the sacred area of *Kolhu/wala: wa*. Like the Hopi, the Zuni have used funds from the settlement of land claims to recently purchase land off their reservation. Most Zuni people currently reside in Zuni Pueblo and Blackrock on the main body of the Zuni Indian Reservation.

Zuni society and religion are organized in a complex system that integrates Zuni kin and clan through ceremonial activities (Kroeber 1917: 148–165). The Zuni socioreligious system is comprised of four interlocking components, including 14 matrilineal clans, six kiva groups, 12 curing societies, and the Rain and Bow Priesthoods (Ladd 1979: 482–485). Clans and kiva groups are organized in the Katchina (*Koko*) Society. Kinship structures the social relations that bind the Zuni people together as a tribal entity (Eggan 1950: 177–198). An annual ceremonial cycle follows the agricultural seasons, and the *Koko* appear throughout the year (Washburn 1995: 34–37). The population of the Zuni Tribe is currently about 10,000.

Although Hopi and Zuni share many cultural elements and are both classified by anthropologists as Western Pueblo (Eggan 1950: 1–3), they speak unrelated languages. Hopi is a member of Uto-Aztecan language family, a large group of languages spoken between Central America and the northern United States (Hill et al. 1998: xv). A small group of Tewa people from the Rio Grande Valley in New Mexico migrated to the Hopi at the end of seventeenth century (Stanislawski 1979: 587). After joining the Hopi Tribe, these Hopi-Tewa learned Hopi but also retained their own language. Today the Hopi-Tewa of Tewa Village thus speak both the Hopi and Tewa languages. Few Hopis, however, speak Tewa. Zuni is a linguistic isolate unrelated to any other language in the Southwest. The distinct languages spoken by Hopi and Zuni are indicative of their unique and separate tribal histories. Today, virtually all Hopi and Zuni are multilingual, speaking English as well as their native language.

CULTURAL LANDSCAPES AS MEMORY AND PROCESS

Conceptually, cultural landscapes encompass both land itself and how land is perceived by individuals given their particular cultural values and beliefs. Cultural landscapes are fashioned by cultural groups from a natural landscape. As Sauer (1963: 343) states, "culture is the agent, the natural area is the medium, the cultural landscape is the result." Cultural landscapes have complexity and power as a result of their creation by people through experience and encounters with the world. Landscapes are contextualized because people understand them in light of specific events and historical conditions (Bender 1993: 2).

There are fundamental differences between European and non-European concepts of landscapes. In this regard, Küchler (1993: 85–86) contrasts European landscapes *of* memory and non-European landscapes *as* memory. According to Küchler, Europeans envision landscapes as surfaces inscribed with named places and landmarks, a view that is closely related to the European tradition of making maps to *represent* memory. Non-European cultural landscapes, however, *are* memory. They are a template in the process of constructing and transmitting tradition that is an essential part of how memories are formed. The land itself is as important as the human activities that occurred on the land and marked it in the past, because it is through the land that the past takes form.

Native Americans conceptualize cultural landscapes in verbal discourse that has historical and moral dimensions. The place names and stories associated with landscapes serve as metaphors that both influence how people view themselves and affect patterns of social action (Ferguson 1999: 4.8). Cultural landscapes are storied landscapes. Young (1987: 4–9) notes how Puebloan people use landscape features as metonyms of narrative, evoking the image of named places, the values associated with them, and the stories embodied in them. Places and landscapes have the power to symbolize and recall the ancient past, thus projecting the ancient past into the contemporary world.

Cultural landscapes help situate people in historical time and space. In so doing, they provide a spatial conception of history. The places where Hopi and Zuni ancestors lived during their migrations mark the direction they traveled across the land to fulfill their destiny. When Hopi and Zuni people visit ancestral sites, the history of their migrations is called to mind. In some instances, the very form of the land itself was shaped during events believed to have occurred in the past, especially events surrounding the actions of spiritual beings. In this case, the land itself is part of the memory of the past, and it forms part of the conceptual framework of historical knowledge. Religious pilgrimages to shrines embedded in the landscape constitute an active reenactment of Hopi and Zuni traditional history. The ability to identify places in oral narratives with actual geographic locations is a form of historical validation. Past and present coexist, and ancient stories are one with current existence (Young 1987: 4–7; Schaafsma 1997: 13).

Young (1987: 2) observes that the Hopi and Zuni "regard the land as a living being and themselves as part of this living being" because, according to traditional history, the Puebloan people were born from the womb of Mother Earth. The Hopi and Zuni consequently treat the land as a relative and have a responsibility to care for the land and act as stewards. The people are part of the landscape in the Puebloan perspective, not apart from it (Silko 1986: 84).

Cultural landscapes are created and maintained by cultures that instill values, beliefs, and historical memory in the people belonging to a community. Cultural landscapes can consequently be sustained for long periods without physical use. Even after a long absence, people have the cultural processes of memory and history to renew the links with places that may have been forgotten, irregularly visited, or occupied by other groups (Ferguson 1999: 4.9; Morphy 1995).

Perceiving and talking about landscapes is thus a way for Native Americans to "do" history and share the past with others and, in so doing, to construct social identity (Basso 1996: 7). This provides Native Americans with an alternative approach to history that is qualitatively different from the academic forms of documentary history commonly embraced by scholars. Landscape history and documentary history have complementary value; one is not necessarily better than the other. They are simply alternative ways of knowing the past and making use of that knowledge in the present.

Differences in how landscapes are conceptualized are related to differences in how they are depicted, communicated, and used. As Basso (1996: 43) observes, Native Americans have "maps in the mind." These stand in marked contrast to the depictions of landscapes by scientifically trained archaeologists and land managers, who view landscapes as maps with inscribed and interpreted meanings, for instance, the maps in this chapter (Ferguson 1999: 4.7). Whereas Hopi and Zuni people want to conserve landscapes for cultural use in perpetuating history, federal and state land managers generally emphasize the implementation of policies for the productive use of the land entailing human modification of it.

Cultural landscapes have a political dimension because control of the underlying land is an instrument of political power (Mitchell 1994: 1–2). As a cultural medium, landscape naturalizes social constructions, representing the cultural world as if it were simply given and inevitable. Cultural landscapes are a "high tension" concept because they operate at the juncture of history, politics, social relations and cultural perceptions (Bender 1993: 3). Today, with the land fragmented and divided among numerous private and public owners, the Hopi and

Zuni find themselves alienated from large portions of their cultural landscapes. Federal and state regulations provide the tribes with some opportunities to consult about management, but the divergent tribal and non-Indian conceptualization of cultural landscapes creates social stress and uncertainty in discussions about how land should be managed.

ANCESTRAL MIGRATIONS AND CULTURAL LANDSCAPES

The ancestral migrations of the Hopi and Zuni took place over many centuries, involving travel across a vast geographic area. The Hopi and Zuni tribes have different migration traditions but their ancestors traveled over much of the same area, leaving similar marks on the landscape. These marks include ancestral villages, human burials, ceremonial structures, shrines, petroglyphs, artifact scatters, trails, and other material remains. These archaeological features serve as physical markers constituting a significant part of the cultural landscapes of the two tribes.

There are many published accounts describing Hopi clan migration traditions (Anyon 1999a, 1999b; Courlander 1987; Curtis 1922; Ferguson 1998a; Ferguson and Lomaomvaya 1999; Fewkes 1900; Mindeleff 1891; Stephen 1929; Voth 1905; Yava 1978). Each Hopi clan maintains its own traditions, emphasizing its own history and contribution to Hopi culture, so there are multiple Hopi histories rather than a single, unified account. Some Hopi clans associate the beginnings of their migrations with *Sipapuni*, located near the Grand Canyon (Ferguson 1998a: 77–92). Other clans recount that their migrations began at *Yayniwpu*, a place in Meso-America (Ferguson and Lomaomvaya 1999: 73–114; Washburn 1995: 21). A common thread in the traditions of the Hopi clans that migrated from the south is their sojourn in *Palatkwapi* ("Red Walled City" or "Red Land of the South"), described variously as both a geographical location and as an epoch or era (Anyon 1999b: 28–29; Ferguson and Lomaomvaya 1999: 76–78).

Many Hopi clans have members in more than one contemporary village. The clan members in each village preserve the history that relates how their ancestors came to reside at that particular place. Hopi clan narratives relate migration routes and past events that are exceedingly complex and varied. For example, many of the clans that migrated from the south followed different routes to *Palatkwapi*, and when they continued their migration they took different routes to the Hopi Mesas. Migrating clans did not always take direct routes to Hopi lands, as the migration traditions of the Young Corn Clan from Munqapi demonstrate (Map 6.2). Migration routes were often circuitous, with clans sometimes returning to places where they had previously lived. Clans would separate into smaller groups, later regroup, and along the way join with and diverge from the migrations of other clans. This separation, regrouping, and coalescing of clans is an integral feature of clan migration traditions of the Hopi. As a result of the temporal and geographic complexity of clan migrations, clans arrived at Hopi

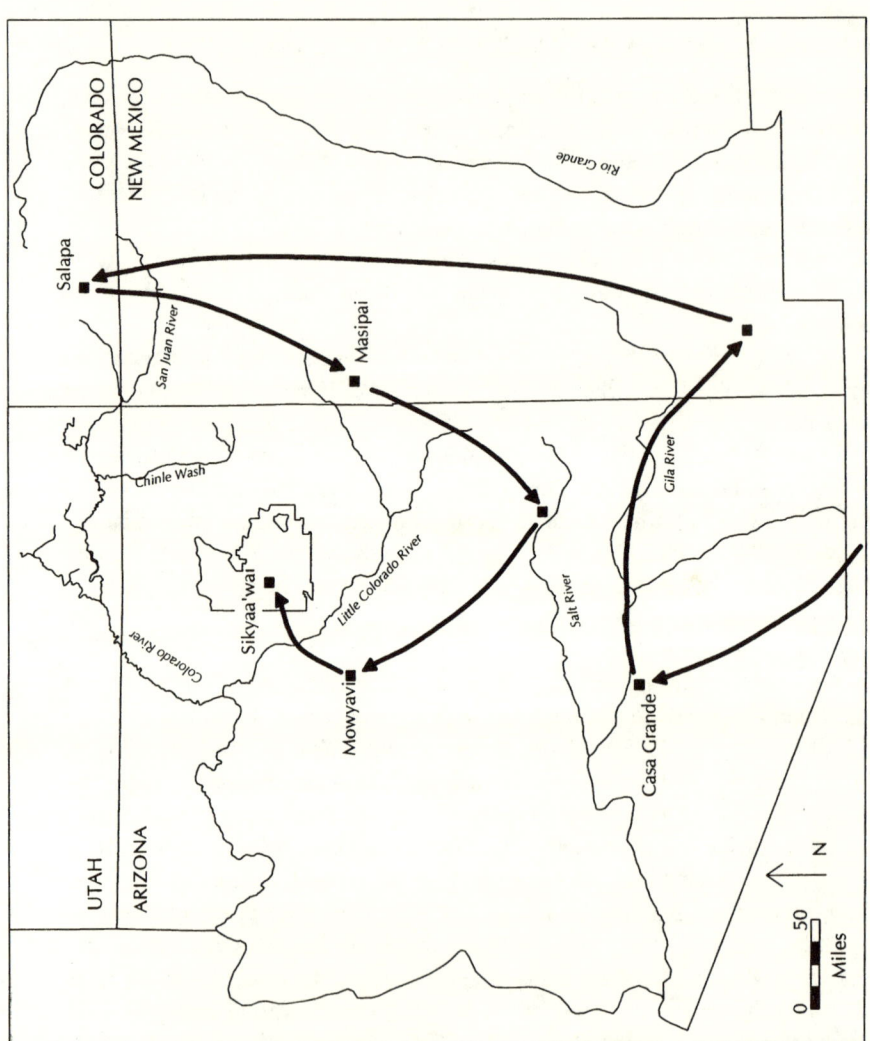

Map 6.2 Schematic depiction of the migration route of the Young Corn Clan of Munqapi

villages from different directions and at different times (Anyon 1999a: 30; Ferguson 1998b: 78–82).

Zuni traditional history is largely embedded in ritual narratives maintained by religious societies rather than clans. Zuni migration traditions begin at the place of tribal emergence, called *Chimik'yana'kya deya,* located in the Grand Canyon (Ferguson and Hart 1985: 20–23). *Chimik'yanakona penane,* the knowledge of tribal origin and migrations, is generally known by all Zuni but its esoteric details are only truly understood by members of the religious societies. After leaving *Chimik'yana'kya deya,* the Zuni people traveled together into the Little Colorado River valley, where they divided into four groups that took different migration paths. One group traveled southward to the Land of Everlasting Sunshine, never to return. The remaining groups separated and took different routes to the center place of the Zuni. One group traveled directly into the Zuni River valley, where they encountered another people, overcame them in an epic battle, and incorporated them into the Zuni tribe. This group was the first to arrive at *Halona:Itiwana* (the Middle Place or Zuni Pueblo). Another group traveled northward, through *Ki'wihtsi Bitsulliya* (Chaco Canyon), then eastward to *Shipa: bulima* in the northern Rio Grande valley of New Mexico, before heading westward to join their relatives in the Zuni lands. The third group traveled southward through the Mogollon highlands of New Mexico, before returning northward to Zuni lands (Ferguson and Hart 1985: 20). Many of the places where the Zuni ancestors traveled are named, commemorating connections with historical events and supernatural beings. Places along the migration routes remain sacred to the Zuni People.

Hopi and Zuni migration traditions encompass similar geographical areas and time frames. Consequently, Hopi and Zuni people regard many of the same places as ancestral, and the cultural landscapes of the two tribes have a substantial overlap. The correspondence of cultural landscapes is due in part to historical relationships between the two tribes. Fred Eggan (1950: 201), for example, suggests that the similarities between subclan groupings of the Zuni and phratries of the Hopi have a historical basis. Some clans migrated through the Southwest, leaving members in different pueblos. The Tansy Mustard Clan, for instance, left its home in the Chama area of northern New Mexico, and traveled westward to the pueblos of Santo Domingo, Laguna, Acoma, Zuni, and Hopi (Blair and Blair 1999: 5–6; Ferguson 1998b: 656; Stephen 1936: 944–945, 1085–1086). Today, the Tansy Mustard Clan has members residing at both the Hopi and Zuni pueblos. The history shared by some clans of the Hopi and Zuni provides linkages between the cultural landscapes of the two tribes.

Hopi and Zuni migration traditions are a key element for identifying each tribe's cultural landscape. These landscapes, as conceptualized by the Hopi and Zuni, encompass the total area where their ancestors lived, died, and were buried. The Hopi consider these ancestral places to be markers or "footprints" on the landscape that provide physical evidence of clan migrations (Ferguson et al. 1995a: 12; Nequatewa 1967: 34). The Zuni also view these places as markers that their ancestors left during the migrations to *Halona:Itiwana*. The Hopi and Zuni use ancestral sites as monuments on the land to demonstrate the veracity of historical traditions and instruct young tribal members in cultural teachings. In Hopi and Zuni thought, these ancestral places are imbued with life. The life forces embedded in cultural landscapes have spiritual power that connects the past, present, and future through ongoing cultural and religious activities (Anyon 1996: 46; Anyon and Ferguson 1985: 914–915; Jenkins et al. 1996: 36). The ancestral cultural landscapes of the Zuni and Hopi tribes are thus an integral part of their contemporary religions and cultures.

CULTURAL LANDSCAPES IN RELATION TO ABORIGINAL AREAS AND RESERVATIONS

There is an important distinction between cultural landscapes and aboriginal areas as defined by Indian land claims. Hopi and Zuni cultural landscapes extend far beyond their aboriginal areas. The tendency for federal and state land managers to reduce cultural landscapes to aboriginal areas conflates history and leads to misunderstanding of claims pursuant to historic preservation and repatriation. Maps of aboriginal areas can serve as useful guides for consultation (Akins 1993), but the historical context of aboriginal lands must be fully understood in order to interpret what they mean.

Aboriginal lands were defined through adjudication with the United States, the purpose of which was to compensate tribes for lands taken without payment. Hopi and Zuni land claims were thus confined to the lands used and occupied by the tribes at the time the United States assumed sovereignty over the Southwest in 1848. Furthermore, the evidentiary standard used to establish aboriginal title in Indian land claims was exclusive use and occupancy (Kaplan 1985: 73–74; Rosenthal 1985: 51–52). Areas that were jointly used by two or more tribes and areas that were occupied in the ancient past were thus excluded from aboriginal lands as judicially determined. As a result of the legal parameters of land claims, the definition of aboriginal land excluded many areas that are vital parts of the cultural landscapes of the Hopi and Zuni.

The Hopi Tribe filed its land claim in 1951 as Docket 196 of the Indian Claims Commission, which rendered its final judgment in 1970 (Indian Claims Commission 1974). The area established as Hopi aboriginal land by the Indian Claims Commission was much smaller than the area that had been claimed by the Hopi Tribe (Map 6.1). The Hopi Tribe's claim extended northward to the Colorado River, and eastward along the Little Colorado River to about the place where the Zuni Indian Reservation is now located in Arizona. Neither the Hopi Tribe's claim, nor the judicially determined aboriginal area, includes the entirety of *Hopitutukswa*, the historic heartland of the Hopi people (Page and Page 1982: 219), much less the entire Hopi cultural landscape.

The Zuni Tribe did not file a land claim before the expiration of the Indian Claims Commission. In 1978, however, Congress enacted legislation that authorized the Zuni to file a land claim in the United States Claims Court (Hart 1995; Boyden 1995: 224). This legislation also returned ownership of the sacred Zuni Salt Lake to the Zuni Tribe. The Zuni claimed an aboriginal area about 23,837 square miles in size (Map 6.1), and in 1987, the United States Claims Court upheld this claim, establishing this as the Zuni aboriginal area (Yanello 1995). The court found that more than 97 percent of the Zuni aboriginal area had been taken from the tribe, leaving it with a small land base on the Zuni Indian Reservation (Ferguson 1989: 96). As large as the Zuni aboriginal area is when compared to that of Hopi, it does not encompass all of the historically documented Zuni land use sites, much less the Zuni cultural landscape incorporating ancient settlements and migration routes (Ferguson and Hart 1985: 20; Ferguson 1995: 104).

Placed in historical context, the Hopi and Zuni aboriginal areas only represent the land the courts found to be exclusively used and occupied by the tribes in the mid-nineteenth century. Both the Hopi and the Zuni have many shrines and cultural sites located far beyond the boundaries of their aboriginal lands. Aboriginal lands may thus be used as a guide to define the historical core of the cultural landscapes of the Hopi and Zuni tribes, but they are only a pale reflection of the total areas incorporated in ancestral landscapes as defined by migrations and land use. This can be seen graphically by comparing the 232 land use sites identified by Zuni leaders during litigation research with the aboriginal land claim (Map 6.3). Zuni land use sites outside of their aboriginal land include shrines, ancestral sites, and hunting and collecting areas (Ferguson 1995: 107–112). These outlying sites are part of the cultural landscape of the Zuni people even though they are beyond the area the court found that Zuni people exclusively used and occupied in 1848.

Another example is provided by the popular depiction of *Hopitutskwa* (Hopi Land), which is often described as an area demarcated by a series of shrines that constitute places along a pilgrimage route (Map 6.4). In this conception, *Hopitutskwa* represents the landscape of Hopi destiny that repeatedly appears in clan migration legends and ritual practices (Page and Page 1982: 217–222; Whiteley 1989: 55–56). As Peter Whiteley (1989: 50) notes, however, "any notion that [Hopi]*tutskwa* includes the widest extent of habitual Hopi usage of the environment, let alone Hopi knowledge of geographic limits, either prehistorically, historically, or at present, is simply not credible." According to some Hopi, it is more appropriate to view the series of shrines ringing *Hopitutskwa* not as a boundary per se, but as a *homvi'ikya*. A *homvi'ikya* is a Hopi phrase connoting a route used in the offering of a sacred prayer meal (Jenkins et al. 1994: 7). The *homvi'ikya* shrines are visited regularly and are used "to pay homage to a greater domain of stewardship" that entails a larger area of Hopi land. In this view, the shrines are a symbolic representation of Hopi land, and *Hopitutskwa* as conventionally mapped is metaphorically viewed as the "plaza" for the larger "village" of the Hopi cultural landscape (Jenkins et al. 1994: 7–8).

The contemporary Hopi and Zuni reservations cover only a small portion of

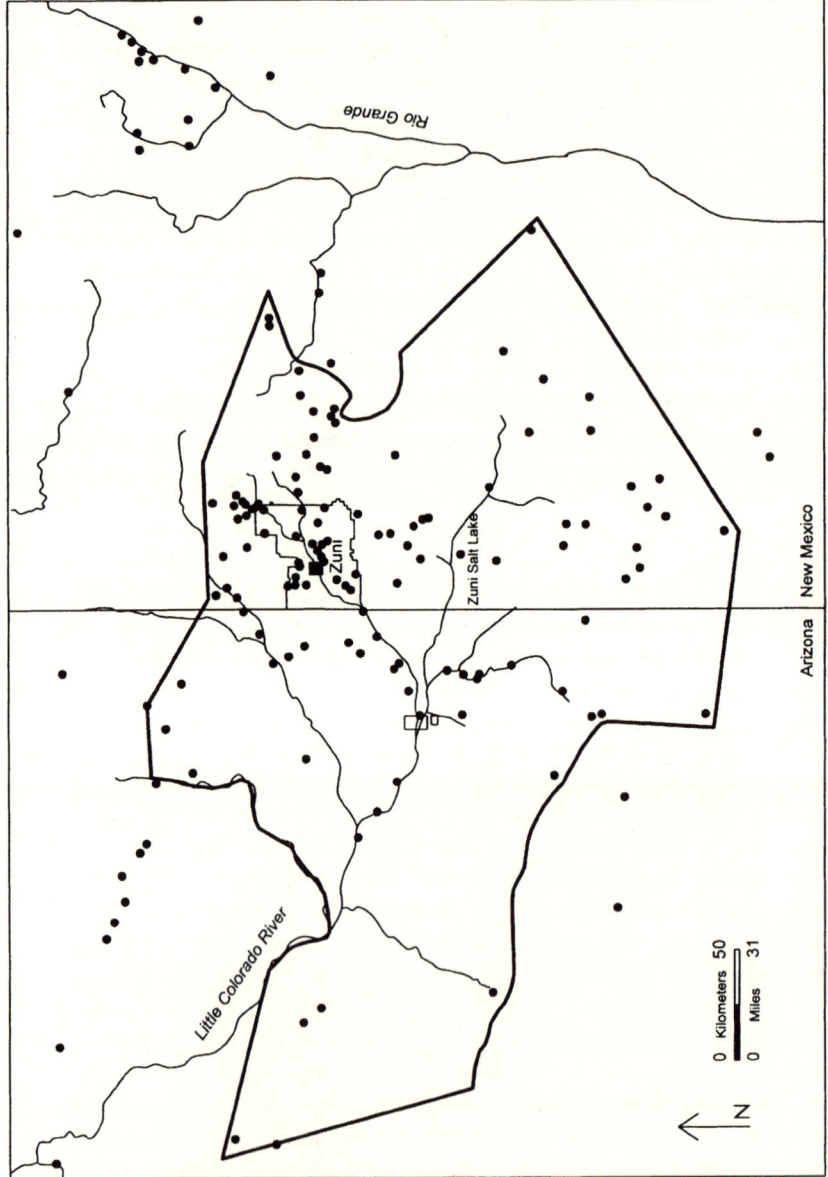

Map 6.3 Zuni land use sites (including agriculture, grazing, hunting, plant collection, and religious sites) are depicted by dots and shown in relation to the boundary of the Zuni aboriginal area. Land use sites outside the aboriginal area are part of the Zuni cultural landscape.

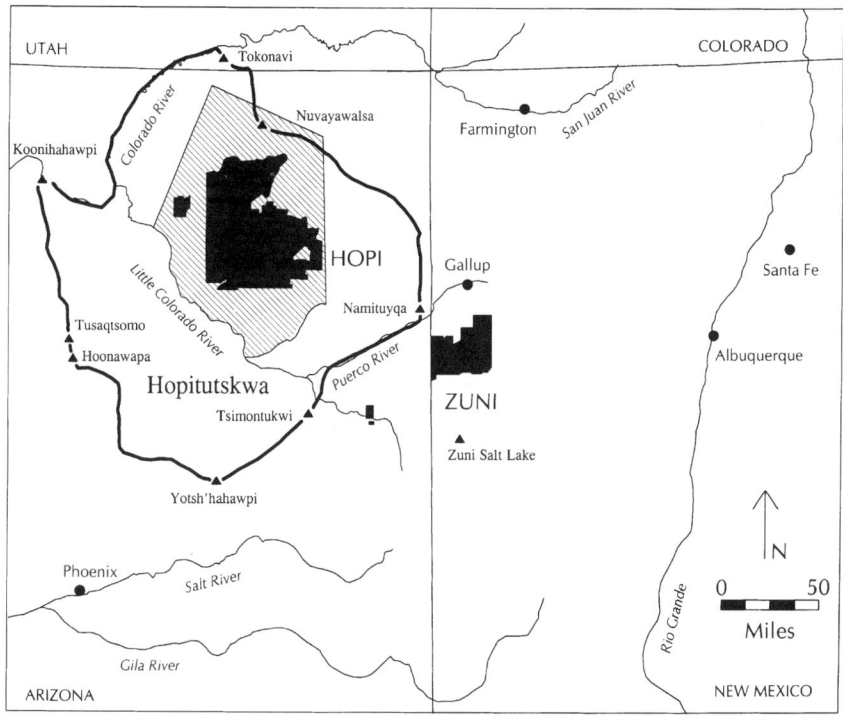

Map 6.4 *Hopitutskwa* as conventionally mapped, with shrines ringing its perimeter

the historically defined cultural landscapes of the two tribes. These reservations are the product of the Indian policy of the United States, which resulted in alienating tribes from all but the very minimum amount of land they needed to survive. The Hopi and Zuni reservations are today the lands over which the tribes have jurisdiction, and they thus represent the small portion of the cultural landscapes over which the tribes retain a substantial amount of control. While the reservations and aboriginal areas of the Hopi and Zuni comprise cultural heartlands, they do not represent the entire cultural landscapes of the tribes.

THE IMPLICATIONS OF CULTURAL LANDSCAPES FOR CULTURAL RESOURCES MANAGEMENT

Hopi and Zuni cultural landscapes, including but not limited to the core ab-original lands, have profound significance for tribal members. These cultural landscapes are used by Hopi and Zuni elders in teaching young tribal members about their history and cultural heritage. The named places and ancestral sites within the cultural landscapes are monuments that are used in personal verification of tribal traditions. Particular places on the land are understood by placing them in the frame of reference defined by the entire cultural landscape.

The geographic scale and temporal depth of Hopi and Zuni cultural landscapes is often misunderstood by cultural resource managers in federal and state agencies. Federal and state managers place different cultural values on Hopi and Zuni ancestral sites, and this creates a number of challenges for both tribal members and government officials. Tribal members feel an emotional and spiritual connection to their ancestors who inhabited their cultural landscapes. Federal and state officials, however, are bound by the National Historic Preservation Act to treat cultural resources as properties, commodifying them in the process.

Historic properties must be defined in relation to describable boundaries, and bounding cultural landscapes is problematic for most Hopi and Zuni cultural advisors because all boundaries have to be contextualized in time, as well as space. There is not a single boundary for a cultural landscape but multiple boundaries to describe the migrations of different clans, the locations of various shrines used by particular religious groups, and the area of ancestral villages at different times in the past. Both the Hopi and Zuni tribes are reluctant to inscribe a line on a map and make a final declaration that this is the geographical limit of their historical interest. In concert with ongoing archaeological and ethnographic research, the Hopi and Zuni tribes are refining the definition of their cultural landscapes based on the new documentation of ancestral use.

Aboriginal lands are referenced in both the NHPA and NAGPRA. The regulations promulgated to implement the NHPA, for instance, advise that "Federal agencies should be aware that frequently historic properties of religious and cultural significance are located on ancestral, aboriginal or ceded lands of Indian tribes . . . and should consider that when complying with the procedures. . . ." (36 CRF 800.2(c)(3)(iv)).[4] Accurate maps of cultural landscapes and ancestral lands are still being developed by the Hopi and Zuni tribes and are not widely available. Maps of aboriginal lands, however, are readily available because these are part of the public record of land claims litigation. However, all too often, maps of aboriginal lands convey different messages to land managers than they do to tribes.

The different ways in which aboriginal lands are viewed are based in part on the conceptual differences between landscapes of memory (maps) versus landscapes as memory (phenomenological experience). These differences also reflect the different geographic perspectives of the tribes and land managers. The Hopi and Zuni look out from their reservations at large expanses of land that were once the domain of their ancestors, from which they have been alienated by historic land ownership patterns. Land managers, on the other hand, focus on the relatively small parcels of land for which they have responsibilities, and, in many cases, view the Hopi and Zuni tribes as distant political entities far removed from the lands in question. When these lands are beyond the aboriginal lands of the tribes, the land managers often see this as a justification for not consulting the tribes about cultural resources.

Archaeological discourse about abandonment also influences how federal and state land managers view landscapes. Legally, the term "abandonment" means "complete and final giving up of property or rights with no intention of reclaiming them and to no particular person" (Oran 1983: 3). When archaeological sites and geographical areas are characterized as having been abandoned, the conscious or unconscious implication is that descendent communities no longer have any legal or cultural interest in these places. To the Hopi and Zuni, the notion that they have abandoned the ancestral sites that anchor their cultural landscapes is incomprehensible. Ancestral villages, burials, shrines, trails, and other cultural resources are still used by the Hopi and Zuni in active religious activities and as heuristic devices in the instruction of young tribal members. Hopi and Zuni ceremonies provide a spiritual connection between contemporary tribal members and their ancestors who still inhabit ancient villages (Ferguson 1998: 277; Anyon and Ferguson 1995: 914). Religious shrines and trails that have been blessed in ancient use continue to have cultural importance for the Hopi and Zuni. These landscape features retain their cultural and spiritual significance for all time.

Scientifically trained cultural resource managers commonly perceive places that have been abandoned as being nothing more than concentrations of inanimate material culture, whose value is their potential to provide information about the past. Archaeological artifacts and sites are thus the target of their interest. Cultural resources management based on scientific values thus tends to focus on the "cultural islands" (i.e., archaeological sites), paying less attention to the "ocean" of the cultural landscape. In contrast, the Hopi and Zuni perceive archaeological resources to embody vital life forces, and they see the entire cultural landscape as both the focus of interest, and the means by which individual resources are assigned meaning.

There is one other major difference in the ways that land managers and tribal people view southwestern landscapes. Hopi and Zuni view their cultural landscapes in terms of their ancestors, the real people who lived in the past from whom they are descended (Dongoske et al. 1997). Land managers, in contrast, tend to view landscapes in terms of archaeological cultures, abstract concepts based on patterns of material culture. Because Hopi and Zuni are Pueblo cultures, many land managers think of Hopi and Zuni ancestors only in terms of ancestral Pueblo archaeological cultures (e.g., Anasazi and Mogollon). The historical relationship the Hopi and Zuni believe they have with the people who participated in other archaeological cultures (e.g., the Hohokam) is less evident to land managers.

The narratives of Hopi and Zuni migrations, reified by ancestral sites embedded in cultural landscapes, provide insight into the mechanisms of cultural transmission and ethnogenesis that are significantly different than conventional archaeological views of the past. As Hopi and Zuni undertake their own ethnoarchaeological studies (*sensu*, Fewkes 1900: 579), the meaning of their cultural landscapes for archaeological culture history is gradually becoming more evident (Ferguson and Lomaomvaya 1999).

The implementation of NAGPRA is proving to be a vector of positive change in how cultural landscapes are viewed in the Southwest. Repatriation under NAGPRA is based in part on determinations of cultural affiliation, defined as "a relationship of shared group identity which can be reasonably traced historically or prehistorically between members of a present-day Indian tribe . . . and an identifiable earlier group" (43 CFR 10.2(e)). NAGPRA recognizes that tribes have legal claims of ownership and control of human remains, funerary objects, sacred objects, and objects of cultural patrimony; and this challenges the conventional archaeological notions of abandonment. As Hopi and Zuni claims under NAGPRA are found to be valid, it is becoming increasingly clear that archaeological sites, and the cultural landscapes they are part of, were never abandoned. They continue to play an ongoing cultural role in the life of the tribes.

Cultural affiliation studies undertaken to implement NAGPRA provide a dramatic view of Hopi and Zuni cultural landscapes that is substantially different from the view provided by archaeological culture history or maps of aboriginal lands. While some cultural affiliation studies are predicated on archaeological views of the past, with a concomitant reliance on geography (e.g., Doyel 1997; Wozniak 1996), other studies are forging new ground by integrating ethnographic and historical perspectives into the interpretation of archaeological data (e.g., Zedeño and Stoffle 1995). Barbara Mills and T. J. Ferguson (1999) analyze the results of 21 determinations of cultural affiliation published in notices in the Federal Register or documented in cultural affiliation studies. The distribution of human remains and cultural items that have been determined to be culturally affiliated with the Hopi (Map 6.5) and the Zuni (Map 6.6) documents these tribes have a shared history with people who lived throughout much of the Southwest. Determinations of cultural affiliation in the Southwest are corroborating the claims made by the Hopi and Zuni tribes (Hopi Tribe 1994; Pueblo of Zuni 1995). The cultural landscapes implicated in these determinations of cultural affiliation are being revealed in ongoing research and have yet to be widely assimilated into archaeological views of the past. In time, however, the studies being done for NAGPRA will have a far-reaching effect on how everyone views the ancient past in the Southwest and its relation to contemporary peoples.

CONCLUSION

The NHPA mandates that federal agencies undertake extensive consultation with tribes concerning the effects of undertakings on historic properties located on ancestral and aboriginal lands that are located outside of Indian reservations and that this consultation be coordinated with similar mandates required by NAGPRA, the American Indian Religious Freedom Act, the Archaeological Re-

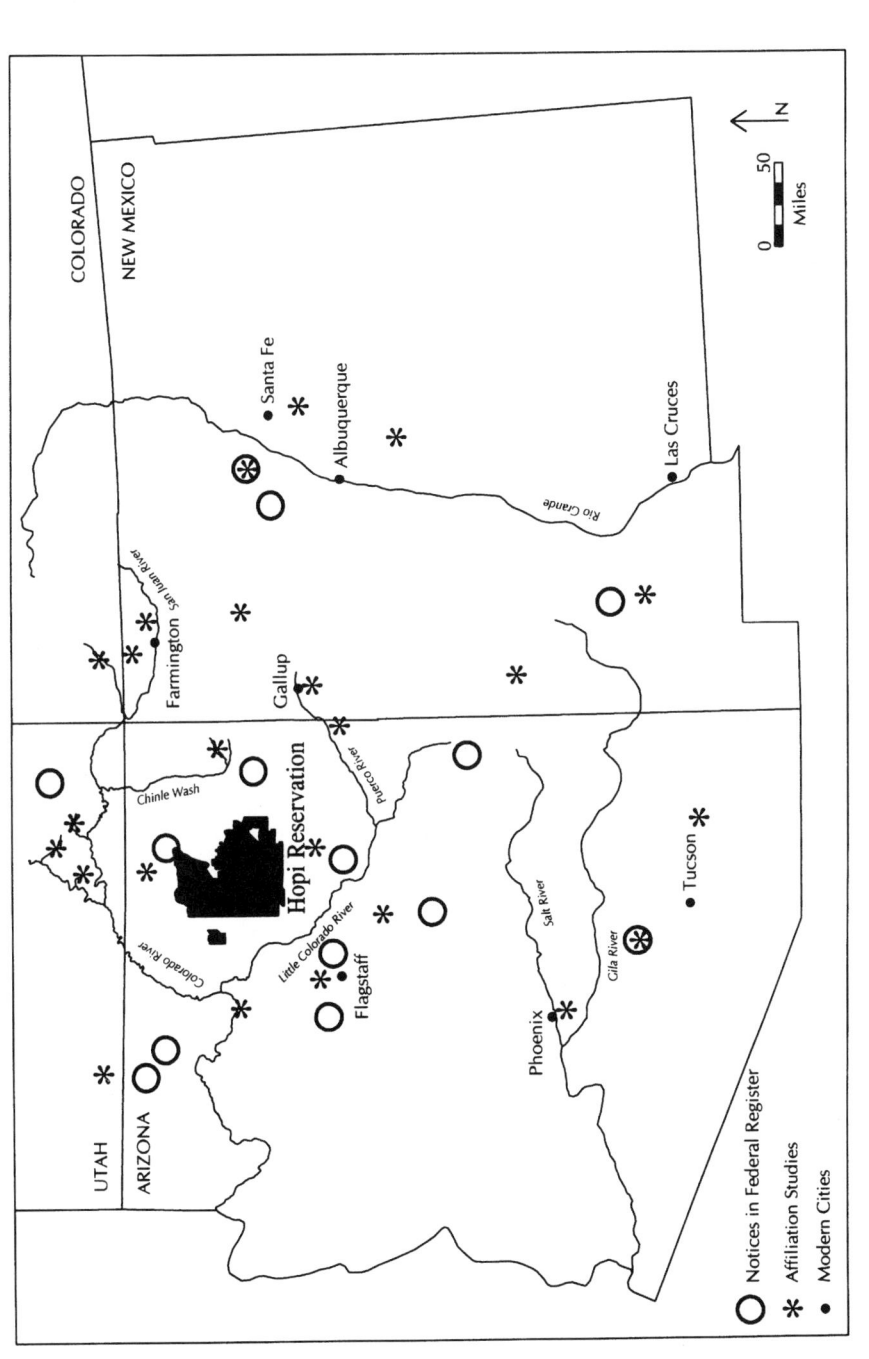

Map 6.5 Sites and areas with remains determined to be culturally affiliated with the Hopi Tribe

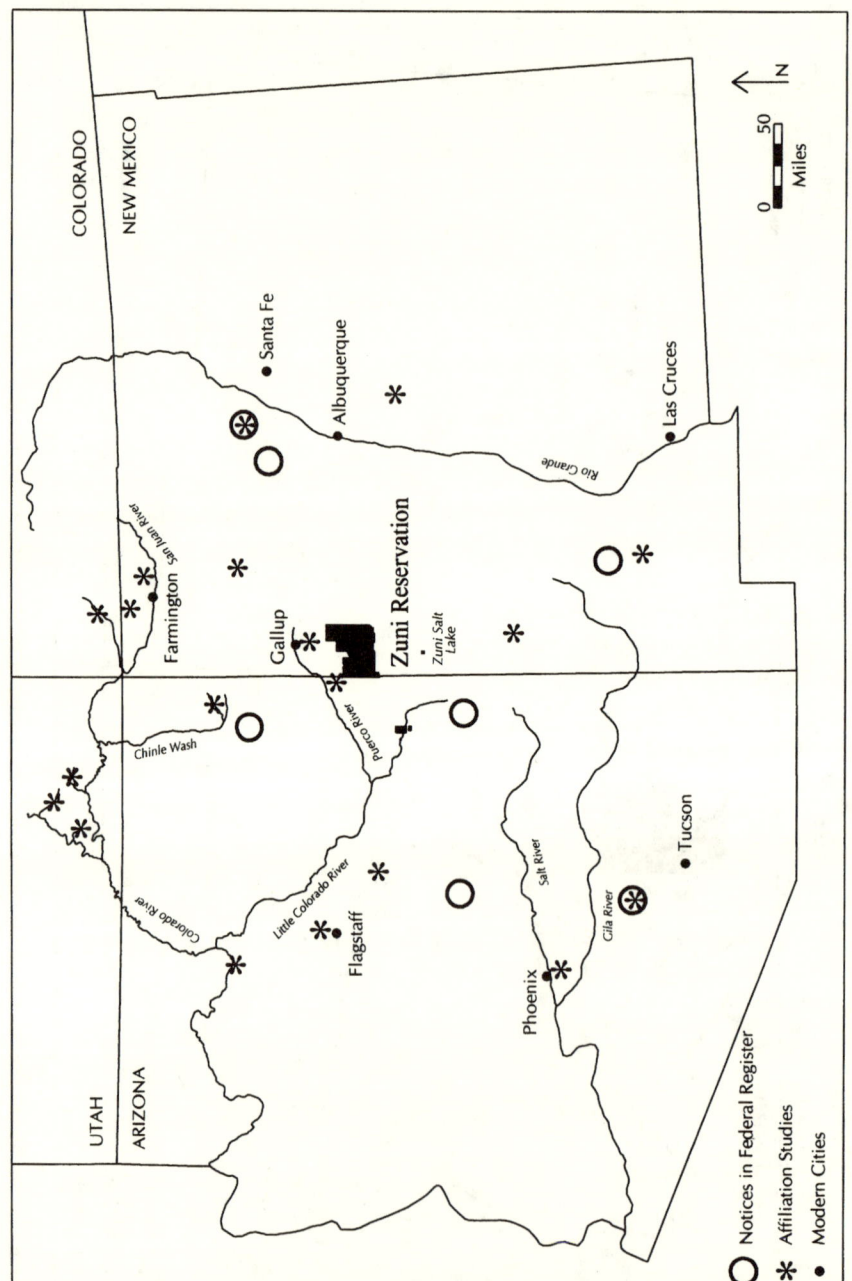

Map 6.6 Sites and areas with remains determined to be culturally affiliated with the Pueblo of Zuni

sources Protection Act, and the National Environmental Policy Act. The Hopi and Zuni tribes have embraced consultation with the federal government as a means to participate in the decision-making process concerning cultural landscapes.

Treating some types of cultural resources, especially shrines and religious areas, as historic properties for purposes of the NHPA is problematic because it reduces spiritual values to property concerns. In the absence of any other effective means to manage religious sites off of their reservations, however, both the Hopi and Zuni tribes have taken appropriately aggressive actions to make sure tribal values are considered in the management of the historic sites that constitute cultural landscapes (Anyon 1996; Dongoske et al. 1994; Jenkins et al. 1996; Mills and Ferguson 1998).

At present, there is still a marked divergence in how cultural landscapes are conceptualized by archaeologists, land managers, and tribal peoples. The implication of this divergence is more than philosophical; it has a direct effect on when the tribes are afforded a chance to consult on land management and the persuasiveness of their involvement when they do. A narrowly conceived interpretation of cultural landscapes diminishes the legitimate interests of the Hopi and Zuni tribes in how their cultural landscapes are managed. Without adequately considering the historical context of aboriginal lands as determined judicially, however, many federal and state land managers view maps of aboriginal lands as the maximum area of tribal concern for cultural resources. The Hopi and Zuni take an opposite view and maintain their aboriginal lands are the minimum area of concern for cultural resources.

Thankfully, the way cultural landscapes are viewed in the Southwest has begun to change, and there is an increasing congruence between the views of tribal people, land managers, and scholars. Much of this change can be traced to the implementation of NAGPRA. The ongoing work of the Hopi and Zuni tribes in defining their cultural landscapes promises to have a crucial effect on the management and preservation of these landscapes as cultural resources. This, in turn, will influence on how the Hopi and Zuni past is investigated and portrayed by scholars.

NOTES

We appreciate the assistance of Leigh J. Kuwanwisiwma of the Hopi Cultural Preservation Office, Barbara Mills of the University of Arizona, and Kurt Anschuetz of the Rio Grande Foundation in the preparation of this chapter. They gave us access to many of the reports and maps used in the preparation of this chapter and provided useful comments. We also thank the Hopi Cultural Resources Advisory Task Team and the Zuni Cultural Resources Advisory Team for their insights about cultural landscapes, which they shared with us during several years of collaborative field work.

1. The National Historic Preservation Act (NHPA) requires federal agencies to take into account the effects of their undertakings on historic properties, including places of

traditional cultural significance to tribes. This law provides many opportunities for tribes to consult with federal agencies regarding historic properties or lands within and outside their reservations.

2. The Native American Graves Protection and Repatriation Act (NAGPRA) was passed to protect Native American graves and mandate the repatriation of human remains and cultural patrimony. The law and accompanying regulations establish a process for determining the rights of lineal descendants, Indian tribes, and Native Hawaiian organizations to human remains, funerary objects, sacred objects, and objects of cultural patrimony with which they are culturally affiliated. Under NAGPRA, many of these items are returned to Native Americans. NAGPRA requires that museums provide information about their collections to Native Americans and establishes tribal control or ownership of culturally affiliated cultural items found on federal lands after passage of the act in 1990.

3. Hopi social organization is based on kinship. The primary social groups include households, clans and phratries. Households are often composed of extended families, and they comprise the basic economic unit. Hopi clans consist of larger groups of people descended from a common ancestor. With the Hopi, a person belongs to the clan of their mother, so clans are matrilineal. Phratries are groups of closely related clans that share religious and social obligations. Anthropologists think the social organization of the Hopi is complex because the close social bonds of kin and clan structure all social interaction and ceremonial activities.

4. CFR refers to the Code of Federal Regulations. Regulations are often promulgated by federal agencies to clarify the law and formally set out the procedures by which it will be implemented. The National Historic Preservation Act has regulations written by the President's Advisory Council on Historic Preservation and the National Park Service. The Native American Graves Protection and Repatriation Act has regulations written by the National Park Service.

REFERENCES

Akins, Nancy J. 1993. Traditional Use Areas in New Mexico. Archaeology Notes 141. Santa Fe: Office of Archaeological Studies, Museum of New Mexico,

Anyon, Roger. 1996. Zuni Protection of Cultural Resources and Religious Freedom. *Cultural Survival Quarterly* 19(4): 46–49.

————. 1999a. *Migrations in the North: Hopi Reconnaissance for the Rocky Mountain Expansion Loop Pipeline.* Kykotsmovi, AZ: Hopi Cultural Preservation Office.

————. 1999b. *Migrations in the South: Hopi Reconnaissance in the Barry M. Goldwater Range.* Kykotsmovi, AZ: Hopi Cultural Preservation Office.

Anyon, Roger, and T. J. Ferguson. 1995. Cultural Resources Management at the Pueblo of Zuni, New Mexico, USA. *Antiquity* 266:913–930.

Basso, Keith H. 1996. *Wisdom Sits in Places: Landscape and Language Among the Western Apache.* Albuquerque: University of New Mexico Press.

Bender, Barbara. 1993. Introduction, Landscape—Meaning and Action. In *Landscape Politics and Perspectives*, edited by Barbara Bender, pp. 1–17. Oxford: Berg.

Blair, Mary Ellen, and Laurence Blair. 1999. *The Legacy of a Master Potter, Nampeyo and Her Descendants.* Tucson: Treasure Chest Books.

Boyden, Stephen G. 1995. The Zuni Claims Cases. In *Zuni and the Courts: A Struggle for Sovereign Land Rights*, edited by E. Richard Hart, pp. 223–230. Lawrence, KS: University Press of Kansas.

Code of Federal Regulations. 36 CFR 800. 2(c)(3)(iv).

———. 43 CFR 10. 2(e).

Connelly, John C. 1979. Hopi Social Organization. In *Handbook of the North American Indians*, vol. 9, edited by Alfonso Ortiz, pp. 539–553. Washington, DC: Smithsonian Institution.

Cordell, Linda S. 1997. *Archaeology of the Southwest*. San Diego: Academic Press.

Courlander, Harold. 1987. *The Fourth World of the Hopi, The Epic Story of the Hopi Indians as Preserved in their Legends and Traditions*. Albuquerque: University of New Mexico Press.

Curtis, Edward S. 1922. *The North American Indian*. Vol. 12. Norwood, MA: The Plimpton Press.

Dongoske, Kurt E., Leigh Jenkins, and T. J. Ferguson. 1994. Issues Relating to the Use and Preservation of Hopi Sacred Sites. *Historic Preservation Forum* 8(2): 12–14.

Dongoske, Kurt E., Michael Yeatts, Roger Anyon, and T. J. Ferguson. 1997. Archaeological Cultures and Cultural Affiliation: Hopi and Zuni Perspectives in the American Southwest. *American Antiquity* 62(4): 600–608.

Doyel, David E. 1997. Cultural Affiliation Statement, Upper Gila River Valley, Arizona. Unpublished MS. Tempe, AZ: Archaeological Consulting Services Ltd.

Eggan, Fred. 1950. *Social Organization of the Western Pueblos*. Chicago: University of Chicago Press.

Ferguson T. J. 1989. The Impact of Federal Policy on Zuni Land Use. In *Seasons of the Kachina*, edited by Lowell John Bean, pp. 85–131. Hayward, CA: Ballena Press/ California State University.

———. 1995. An Anthropological Perspective on Zuni Land Use. In *Zuni and the Courts: A Struggle for Sovereign Land Rights*, edited by E. Richard Hart, pp. 103–120. Lawrence, KS: University Press of Kansas.

———. 1998a. *Öngtupqa niqw Pisisvayu (Salt Canyon and the Colorado River): The Hopi People and the Grand Canyon*. Kykotsmovi, AZ: Hopi Cultural Preservation Office.

———. 1998b. Hopi Footprints in the Jeddito Valley: Interpretation of Ethnohistory and Archaeology. In *Ethnohistorical Interpretation and Archaeological Data Recovery Along Navajo Route 9101, Jeddito Road, Navajo County, Arizona*. Vol. 1, pp. 639–680. Zuni Cultural Resource Enterprise Report 562. Zuni, NM: Zuni Cultural Resource Enterprise.

———. 1999. Western Pueblos and the Petroglyph National Monument: A Preliminary Assessment of the Cultural Landscapes of Acoma, Laguna, Zuni, and Hopi. In *That Place People Talk About: Petroglyph National Monument*, edited by Kurt F. Anschuetz, T. J. Ferguson, Harris Frances, Klara B. Kelley, and Cherie L. Scheick, pp. 4.1 to 4.29. Santa Fe: Rio Grande Foundation.

Ferguson, T. J., Kurt Dongoske, Mike Yeatts, and Leigh Jenkins. 1995a. Hopi Oral Tradition and Archaeology. Pt. 1: The Consultation Process. *Society for American Archaeology Bulletin* 13(3): 10–13.

Ferguson, T. J. and E. Richard Hart. 1985. *A Zuni Atlas*. Norman: University of Oklahoma Press.

Ferguson, T. J., and Micah Lomaomvaya. 1999. *Hoopoq'yaqam niqw Wukoskyavi (Those*

Who Went to the Northeast and Tonto Basin): Hopi-Salado Cultural Affiliation Study. Kykotsmovi, AZ: Hopi Cultural Preservation Office.

Fewkes, Jesse Walter. 1900. Tusayan Migration Traditions. In *Nineteenth Annual Report of the Bureau of American Ethnology for the Years 1897–1898*. Pt. 2, pp. 573–634. Washington: Government Printing Office.

Frigout, Arlette. 1979. Hopi Ceremonial Organization. In *Handbook of the North American Indians*, vol. 9, edited by Alfonso Ortiz, pp. 564–576. Washington: Smithsonian Institution.

Hart, E. Richard, ed. 1995. *Zuni and the Courts: A Struggle for Sovereign Land Rights*. Lawrence, KS: University Press of Kansas.

Hill, Kenneth C., Emory Sekaquaptewa, and Mary E. Black, eds. 1998. *Hopi Dictionary Hopìikwa Lavàytutuveni: A Hopi-English Dictionary of the Third Mesa Dialect*. Tucson: University of Arizona Press.

Hopi Tribe. 1994. *Hopi Tribal Council Resolution H-70–94*, May 23, 1994. Kykotsmovi, AZ: Hopi Tribe.

Indian Claims Commission. 1974. Commission Findings on the Hopi Indians. In *Hopi Indians*, pp. 387–424. New York: Garland Publishing.

James, Harry C. 1974. *Pages from Hopi History*. Tucson: University of Arizona Press.

Jenkins, Leigh, Kurt E. Dongoske, and T. J. Ferguson. 1996. Managing Hopi Sacred Sites to Protect Religious Freedom. *Cultural Survival Quarterly* 19(4): 36–39.

Jenkins, Leigh, T. J. Ferguson, and Kurt E. Dongoske. 1994. A Reexamination of the Concept of *Hopitutsqwa*. Paper presented at the Annual Meeting of the American Society for Ethnohistory, Tempe, AZ, November 11.

Jones, Volney H. 1950. The Establishment of the Hopi Reservation, and Some Later Developments Concerning Hopi Lands. *Plateau* 23(2): 17–25.

Kaplan, Michael J. 1985. Issues in Land Claims, Aboriginal Title. In *Irredeemable America, The Indians' Estate and Land Claims*, edited by Imre Sutton, pp. 71–86. Albuquerque: University of New Mexico Press.

Kroeber, A. L. 1917. Zuni Kin and Clan. *Anthropological Papers of the American Museum of Natural History* 18(2): 39–205.

Küchler, Susanne. 1993. Landscape as Memory: The Mapping of Process and its Representation in a Melanesian Society. In *Landscape Politics and Perspectives*, edited by Barbara Bender, pp. 85–106. Oxford: Berg.

Ladd, Edmund. 1979. Zuni Social and Political Organization. In *Handbook of the North American Indians*, vol. 9, edited by Alfonso Ortiz, pp. 482–491. Washington: Smithsonian Institution.

McKeown, C. Timothy. 1999. Preservation on the Reservation [Revisited]. *Common Ground*, Fall 1999, 10–13.

Mills, Barbara J., and T. J. Ferguson. 1998. Preservation and Research of Sacred Sites by the Zuni Indian Tribe of New Mexico. *Human Organization* 57(1): 30–42.

———. 1999. Cultural Affiliation of Western Pueblos: Theory and Practice. Affiliation Conference on Ancestral Peoples of the Four Corners Region. Vol. 2: Transcripts and Papers, February 20–21, 1998, pp. 147–161. Fort Lewis College, Durango, Colorado.

Mindeleff, Victor. 1891. A Study of Pueblo Architecture in Tusayan and Cibola. In *8th Annual Report of the Bureau of American Ethnology for the Years 1886–1887*, pp. 13–653. Washington: Government Printing Office.

Mitchell, W. J. T. 1994. Introduction. In *Landscape and Power*, edited by W. J. T. Mitchell, pp. 1–4. Chicago: University of Chicago Press.

Morphy, Howard. 1995. Landscape and the Reproduction of the Ancestral Past. In *The Anthropology of Landscape, Perspectives on Place and Space*, edited by Eric Hirsch and Michael O'Hanlon, pp. 184–209. Oxford: Clarendon Press.

Nequatewa, Edmund. 1967. *The Truth of a Hopi*. Flagstaff: Museum of Northern Arizona.

Oran, Daniel. 1983. *Oran's Dictionary of the Law*. St. Paul, MN: West Publishing Company.

Page, Jake. 1982. Inside the Sacred Hopi Homeland. *National Geographic* 162(5): 606–629.

Page, Jake, and Susanne Page. 1982. *Hopi*. New York: Harry N. Abrams.

Pueblo of Zuni. 1995. Pueblo of Zuni Statement of Cultural Affiliation with Prehistoric and Historic Cultures, July 11, 1995. Zuni, NM: Pueblo of Zuni.

Rosenthal, Harvey D. 1985. Indian Claims and the American Conscience, A Brief History of the Indian Claims Commission. In *Irredeemable America, The Indians' Estate and Land Claims*, edited by Imre Sutton, pp. 35–70. Albuquerque: University of New Mexico Press.

Sauer, Carl. 1963. The Morphology of Landscape. In *Land and Life: A Selection of the Writings of Carl Sauer*. Berkeley: University of California Press.

Schaafsma, Polly. 1997. Rock Art, World Views, and Contemporary Issues. In *Rock Art As Visual Ecology*, edited by Paul Faulstich, pp. 7–20. Flagstaff: American Rock Art Research Association.

Silko, Leslie Marmon. 1986. Landscape, History, and Pueblo Imagination. In *Anteaus*, edited by D. Halpern, pp. 83–94. New York: Ecco Press.

Stanislawski, Michael B. 1979. Hopi-Tewa. In *Handbook of the North American Indians*, vol. 9, edited by Alfonso Ortiz, pp. 587–602. Washington: Smithsonian Institution.

Stephen, Alexander M. 1929. Hopi Tales. *Journal of American Folk-Lore* 42: 2–72.

———. 1936. *Hopi Journal of Alexander M. Stephen*, pts. 1 and 2, edited by Elsie Clews Parsons. Columbia University Contributions to Anthropology 23. New York: Columbia University Press.

Voth, H. R. 1905. *The Traditions of the Hopi*. Field Columbian Museum Publication 96, Anthropological Series, vol. 8. Chicago: Field Museum of Natural History.

Washburn, Dorothy K. 1995. *Living In Balance: The Universe of the Hopi, Zuni, Navajo, and Apache*. Philadelphia: The University Museum University of Pennsylvania.

Whiteley, Peter M. 1988. *Deliberate Acts: Changing Hopi Culture Through the Oraibi Split*. Tucson: University of Arizona Press.

———. 1989. Hopitutskwa: An Historical and Cultural Interpretation of the Hopi Traditional Land Claim. MS at Laboratory of Anthropology, Museum of Indian Arts and Culture, Santa Fe.

Wozniak, Frank E., ed. 1996. *Cultural Affiliations, Prehistoric Cultural Affiliations of Southwestern Indian Tribes*. Albuquerque, NM: United States Department of Agriculture, United States Forest Service, Southwestern Region.

Yanello, Judith Ann. 1995. Appendix A: Findings of the United States Claims Commission Docket 161–79L, Aboriginal Area. In *Zuni and the Courts: A Struggle for Sovereign Land Rights*, edited by E. Richard Hart, pp. 241–282. Lawrence, KS: University Press of Kansas.

Yava, Albert. 1978. *Big Falling Snow, a Tewa-Hopi Indian's Life and Times and the History and Traditions of his People*. New York: Crown.

Young, Jane M. 1987. Toward an Understanding of "Place" for Southwestern Indians. *New Mexico Folklore Record* 16: 1–13.

Zedeño, M. Nieves, and Richard W. Stoffle. 1995. Casa Grande Ruins National Monument, Foundations for Cultural Affiliation. Prepared for the Western Archaeological and Conservation Center, National Park Service. Tucson, AZ: University of Arizona, Bureau of Applied Research in Anthropology.

III

THE MELTING POT: WATER, LAND, AND CONFLICT IN HISTORICAL PERSPECTIVE

7

Traditional Use in a Changing Landscape

Frances Levine

INTRODUCTION

Northern New Mexico, that area between Albuquerque and Taos, contains some of the oldest cultural landscapes in North America. It is a region of uncommon physical beauty as well as startling contrasts of ancient and modern cultures. The regional landscape records both the persistence of traditional ways of life and the onslaught of change. Spectacular ancestral archaeological sites survive within the confines of contemporary Pueblo Indian and Hispanic communities. Along the northern Rio Grande and its tributaries, the principal river system of northern New Mexico, ancient cultures continue to exist near bunkers of the Los Alamos National Laboratory where the first atomic bomb was developed and close to casinos built recently in several Pueblo Indian communities. Centuries-old adobe houses, constructed of earthen bricks baked only by the long months of sun and heat, stand next to prefabricated trailer houses, the only affordable housing left for many whose families have been native to this land for centuries.

It is not only the physical and built environments that impress visitors to the region. The cuisine of the area is famous for its blending of indigenous ingredients, foods introduced in the sixteenth century by the Spanish, Mexican, and Mexican-Indian colonists and augmented by the Anglo-American traditions brought to the region in the nineteenth century. The cuisine serves well as a metaphor for the larger social processes of blending that are the defining characteristics of the Northern Rio Grande cultures. Anthropologists, geographers, and historians study the complex regional history to record the persistence of traditional cultures despite centuries of conquest and political change (Carlson 1990; Jackson 1994; Kutsche 1979; Riley 1994; Rodriguez 1987, 1990). Northern New Mexico is alternately described as a region where traditional cultures are endangered by development or as a refuge region where older cultural forms persist. It is a region in which social tensions are palpable and change is often a threat to older cultural practices. We must ask: can the traditional cultures of northern New Mexico persist in the face of the increasing acculturative pressures of the twenty-first century?

Pueblo Indian communities, Spanish and Mexican land grant communities, vast tracts of federal land, and rapidly expanding Sunbelt communities demarcate the land holdings and in many ways separate the region into competing interests. Productive land and water resources are scarce in this semi-arid region, and they are the currency which is the subject of increasing competition. The value of land is being redefined throughout the region as the traditional basis of the economy has shifted away from agriculture, largely small-scale crop farming and livestock production, to a base of light manufacturing, tourism, and retirement homes. Throughout northern New Mexico there is a palpable sense of loss that recurs in the popular press and scholarly writing, as well as in the oral traditions of the Hispanic and Pueblo Indian communities. The losses include the loss of indigenous languages and regional variants of the Spanish language, the loss of *ejido* or common lands on which traditional communities gathered subsistence resources and building materials—for centuries in many cases, and the loss of cooperative relations among the Hispanic and Pueblo Indian communities. Within that palpable sense of loss, however, centuries-old customs persist, reflecting an adherence to traditional ways of life.

No contemporary issue is as symbolic of the struggle between traditional and modern lifeways as the water rights adjudications currently underway in much of New Mexico. I have served as an expert witness in water rights adjudications throughout New Mexico since 1982. Water rights adjudications are legal proceedings in which the rights of *acequia* or irrigation ditches, deep water wells, other uses of surface and ground waters are legally defined. My involvement has been primarily that of an ethnohistorian assisting community *acequia* associations[1] or the State of New Mexico in documenting the priority dates that establish the antiquity of water rights, or in documenting the customs that community *acequias* have used to share available water. Many of the issues that are addressed directly or indirectly in water rights adjudication lawsuits are related to the tensions between sustaining traditional ways of life and meeting the needs and demands of a rapidly expanding urban population in the region. Below I examine the process of adjudications and the question of how communities sustain the customs of traditional land use in the face of imposing pressures for change.

BACKGROUND TO WATER RIGHTS ADJUDICATIONS IN NEW MEXICO

The community *acequias* of northern New Mexico serve some of the oldest European settlements in the United States. Some of the communities served by these *acequias* date back to the earliest years of Spanish settlement in the late sixteenth and early seventeenth centuries. The Pueblo Indian communities have lived along the Rio Grande and its tributaries since at least the mid-fourteenth century. In recent years, water rights adjudications have heightened concerns in these communities over scarce land and water resources (Levine 1990; Rivera 1998). Theoretically, Pueblo Indian communities and the centuries-old Hispanic communities of the region would seem to have little to fear in the process of determining water rights. New Mexico is a prior appropriation state, meaning that rights are determined in part by seniority in years when water is scarce.

Traditional water right practices have evolved since at least the seventeenth century or colonial period to balance competing uses of the limited water supplies of New Mexico.[2] Since 1907, the New Mexico surface water code has governed the appropriation of water rights. A ground water code, adopted in 1931 and based on the doctrine of prior appropriation, similarly governs how wells and other ground water sources can be used. The surface water code, contained in Chapter 72 of New Mexico Statutes Annotated, seeks to confirm the validity of all surface rights which existed prior to its establishment, to regulate how new uses of available water are determined. Beneficial water uses made prior to 1907 must be adjudicated by a court to be recognized by the State Engineer Office (SEO), the state water resource management agency. Water rights adjudication suits are similar to quiet title suits. Adjudications establish the amount of water that a title holder can use, the place of use and the priority of use relative to other users of the same sources. Water uses made after 1907 must be permitted by the SEO before any appropriation is made. New Mexico water law is based on three principles:

1. All surface and ground water belongs to the public and is subject to appropriation for beneficial use; an appropriator does not own the water, only the right to divert it.

2. Beneficial use is the basis, the measure, and the limit of the right to use water for agricultural, domestic, recreational, municipal, and industrial uses.

3. Priority of appropriation gives the better right, so that first in time equals first in right.

New Mexico, unlike some other western states, does not distinguish among the beneficial uses of water. Agricultural and stock water are given no greater protection than industrial and recreational development. This has led to some intense intracommunity conflicts in which irrigation ditch users sell water rights to nontraditional users.[3] In essence, the limited amount of water in the state is controlled by those whose vested rights are recognized by the courts or by permits.

Priorities among water users are only implemented in times of water shortages. Then, those with the earliest dates take the water first, other users following in succession according to their dates of appropriation. The State Engineer may conduct priority administration based on a priority call by a senior user or on his own initiative when shortages are likely due to drought. Priority administration is similar to the way in which community *acequias* regulate their own members in times of shortage. An important difference is that in the traditional division of water, shortages are usually shared by all of the ditch users (called *parciantes* in Spanish), and the water is allocated upon factors other than priority date. Each community makes the rules of distribution based on the collective perceptions of the uses that are most important to the community. Gardens, orchards, or livestock might then be given the water before meadow lands or other uses, for example. Community *acequia* commissions might make these rules on an annual basis or might be governed by a formalized set of bylaws. In a priority system it is possible that those with more recent dates may get no water at all, since the most senior rights can take their full allotment before any water is released to holders of junior rights. In addition to establishing priority dates, the adjudication process establishes the right of a party to appropriate a fixed quantity of water for a specific purpose.

Water rights adjudications usually proceed in two phases. The technical phase consists of a hydrographic survey, usually performed by the State Engineer Office, to identify, map, and report the status of water use in a particular stream system or a ground water basin. In this phase, anthropologists and historians have worked with the hydrographic survey staff, and increasingly directly with communities, to date the time of construction of community ditch systems and to determine the patterns of community use that are the basis for determining the priority of appropriation of water in a stream system.

On the basis of this research, each water user is sent an offer of judgment by the State Engineer Office. That offer is a legal document defining the amount and purpose of a water right, the ownership of that right, the place of use and point of diversion or source of the water, and the priority date. The water user can sign the offer or can object to the determination of any element of the offer.

The second phase is the legal process of the adjudication or the court's final determination of the quantity of water each user has a right to divert and use for a specific beneficial purpose. During this phase, historians have been called as expert witnesses in northern New Mexico cases to address water rights and water uses of Pueblo and Hispanic communities under prior Spanish and Mexican law. Anthropological and archaeological testimony has been used in adjudications to explain aboriginal American Indian farming practices and customary Hispanic water use strategies.

There are at least three classes of participants or parties in water rights adjudications. The State of New Mexico, through the State Engineer Office, participates in the process as the stakeholder of all the water in the state. Communities often see the State Engineer as withholding or denying water through adjudications. The State Engineer, on the other hand, maintains that the office is mandated by statute to perform an independent analysis of claims and available water supply and to ensure that adjudications proceed on a correct factual and legal basis. The United States Attorney, within the Justice Department, participates in suits as the protector of federal rights, including those of American Indian tribes, the National Park Service, the Forest Service, and other federal agencies. In addition, American Indian tribes usually have their own attorneys. Individuals and groups of water users, such as mutual domestic water systems and associations of community ditches, participate to protect their interests in the water they use. The State Engineer Office is usually the plaintiff, bringing suit against non-Indian defendants or against the United States as trustee for Indians. In some cases, such as the Jemez River adjudication and the suit to establish water rights on the rivers of the Taos area, the United States and the Pueblos have joined the State as plaintiffs against all other users. As a result of the alignment of the parties, public perception seems to be that the only issues involved in adjudications are the definition of American Indian rights versus those of non-Indians. In fact this is only one of the many interethnic and intracommunity conflicts that accompany water rights adjudications.

Priority is one of seven elements of water rights determined by the hydrographic survey prepared for each adjudication by the State Engineer Office.[4] The interpretation of historical evidence is a fundamental part of assigning priority dates. The process of assigning priority dates is not, however, an exact science. Daniel Tyler (1986: 16) discusses the diverse sources that can be used effectively to make informed inferences about priority dates. He states

Ditch dating is an interesting kind of detective work involving research in a variety of archival materials. Archaeology, oral tradition, and geology may prove as significant to the researcher as written records. In fact, the historian would be well advised to resist the temptation to focus on a single document as evidence of an acequia's first use.... A better approach involves the creation of reasonable probability scenarios.

Tyler's multiple source approach recognizes that oral traditions have their place in the determination of priority dates. Local perspectives are crucial to understanding the conditions that may modify the strict application of priorities and are important in the historical reasoning applied to an analysis of the documents as well. Ditches and field systems were often among the first features built by early settlers in new communities, and yet they may not be recorded in documents for a number of reasons. Determinations of priority dates based solely on documents may fail to investigate community traditions of water sharing and may fail to establish the many social and historical reasons why relevant documents may not exist. Until the mid-nineteenth century, when American law was imposed on New Mexico, water was managed by customary law and guided by the exigencies of the subsistence economy. There was no legal requirement that a water use be formally recorded. Title documents may not have been publicly filed and might not include reference to an *acequia* unless it was important in a boundary call. Unless there was a dispute over water, as recorded in a number of cases (Baxter 1997; Ebright 1994; Rivera 1998), there were few proceedings that would have produced documentary evidence of a ditch. The use of water might be inferred, however, based on the presence of a settlement.

The way in which evidence is presented and arguments are structured to establish priorities focuses attention on priority as the most salient issue to be established in the case. In fact, there are many other issues in the adjudications that affect traditional use. Priority was only one of many legal and social factors weighed when rights were established under Spanish and Mexican law (Ebright 1994: 73–83; Meyer 1984: 145–167). Michael Meyer (1984: 145–167) discusses seven factors that were weighed in many instances of land and water disputes throughout the Spanish Borderlands. The elements were (1) just title, (2) prior use, (3) need, (4) injury to third parties, (5) intent, (6) legal right, (7) equity and common good. These factors, while by no means absolute or exhaustive, illustrate the pragmatic blend of written law and local custom by which rights were recognized and disputes were resolved under Spanish and Mexican law. These factors were weighed in the traditional *repartimientos* or water partitions that were made during the colonial period to distribute available water equitably among parties whose rights were being determined. *Repartimientos* did not seek simply to establish ultimate ownership of water; they established rights of use and, in some extant cases, apportioned water among competing interests.[5] The above seven factors and the process of *repartimiento* underscore the importance of communal accessibility to limited natural resources in a subsistence economy. Many of these elements remain central to water use customs in northern New Mexico communities.

Through the adjudication process water rights are prioritized, quantified, and privatized as property rights. The privatization of rights changes a fundamental principle of traditional water use in which water is a shared resource and carries with it obligations for shared labor and wise-use responsibilities. Traditional water use does not assume that that use is a fixed individual property right. Use rights are maintained only as long as the *parciantes* perform their communal obligations and exercise responsible water use. Recent adjudications of water rights among the community *acequias* in Taos, El Rito, and the lower Rio Chama communities have broadened the consideration of issues before the courts in attempts to protect not only the priority among community *acequias* but traditional means of sharing water as well.[6] Local customs of water sharing and distribution and the traditional understanding of land use and settlement practices in a particular community are, perhaps, among the most important issues that traditional users seek to protect. Local customs can be considered by the courts when these practices have bearing on the definition of rights. The possibility for including these considerations is found in a state statute, which recognizes "such other conditions as may be necessary to define the right and its priority" (Sec. 72-4-19, NMSA, 1978).

For many contemporary community *acequias*, the strict application of the priority system anticipated by the adjudication process is a threat to the practices of water distribution and water sharing by which community *acequias* have functioned for generations. The switch to a priority system represents a loss of local control over resource allocations, and is detrimental to the social fabric of community (Brown and Ingram 1987; Jacobs 1978; Levine 1990; Levine and Vigil 1997). In adjudicating water rights, New Mexico courts have the flexibility to incorporate customary water use agreements to ensure that the traditions of the local communities are preserved in the final decree (Crossland 1990a, 1990b).

TRADITIONAL USES, LOCAL CUSTOMS, AND THE
RESOLUTION OF CONTEMPORARY ISSUES

As anthropologists we are often more in touch with local customs and traditional uses of natural resources than are the policy makers whose decisions have long-term consequences for indigenous peoples and traditional communities. Anthropologists and historians are qualified by training and knowledge of local community concerns to work toward brokered solutions or more radical changes that incorporate community knowledge and concerns about natural resources into the long-term goals of many land management and regulatory agencies.[7] Water right adjudications are just such an issue, one in which I think historians and anthropologists have made lasting contributions toward making local perspectives heard by the courts and regulatory agencies.

Adjudications are contentious and fractious in the already fragile social environment of northern New Mexico. The cases have a social cost that often fails to be considered by the courts (Levine 1990; Levine and Vigil 1997; Rivera 1998). More importantly, the field studies and testimony in adjudications often reveal traditional uses and local customs that can be incorporated into the resolution process. "La Agua es Vida; Let's Share It" is a slogan seen on bumper stickers, campaign buttons, and walls in the Pojoaque Valley north of Santa Fe. The indirect reference is to a water rights adjudication properly known as *State of New Mexico ex. rel. Reynolds vs. R. Lee Aamodt, et. al.* [U.S. District Court Case No. 6639]. The *Aamodt* case was filed by the State Engineer Office in April 1966 to adjudicate the water rights of more than 2,500 claimants and 28 community ditches along the four rivers (Rio Nambe, Rio Tesuque, the Rio en Medio, and Rio Chupadero) that comprise the Rio Pojoaque stream system.[8] These streams serve the non-Indian settlements of Nambe, Pojoaque, Jacona, Cuyumunge, Tesuque, Rio En Medio, and Chupadero. These villages are still populated primarily by Hispanic people, although there has been a progressive growth in the Anglo-American population of this area within the last generation.

Water rights for the Tewa-speaking pueblos of San Ildefonso, Pojoaque, Nambe, and Tesuque are also being adjudicated in the *Aamodt* case.

Since its filing, the impact of the Rio Pojoaque adjudication has reached far beyond the communities of northern New Mexico. The sentiment behind the slogan seems to be that the water rights adjudication process has threatened or has destroyed the accommodations that have been established among Pueblo, Hispanic, and Anglo-American communities in the valley by centuries of sharing water and reallocating it among themselves according to fluctuating supply.[9]

Water sharing is a long-standing custom in many villages in northern New Mexico where water is chronically short and where subsistence agriculture was the dominant economy until quite recently (Baxter 1997; Crawford 1988, 1990; Hutchins 1928; Lovato 1974, 1975; Meyer 1984; Reich 1994: 871; Rivera 1998; Quintana 1990). Each village seems to have its own specific system, one that is adjusted and finely tuned at various points in time to meet changing community needs.[10] In most northern New Mexico villages, as well as in traditional cultures throughout the world, water is shared by allocating the amount of time in hours per day and days per week in which each user can divert the water to his fields or uses (Rivera 1998: 31; Wolf 1998). *Parciantes*, those who use *acequia* water, share shortages by using the available water for the benefit of the most people. Aaron Wolf (1998: 4) notes that allocating water by time, rather than by a fixed volumetric measure, shares not only the available water, but the risk as well. If water is appropriated by priority alone, the risk is laid entirely on the junior users in a "zero-sum" paradigm. Secondly, when water is allocated by time, decision-making and responsible use are recognized at the most local level.

I do not mean to imply that water sharing always worked, or that communities and individuals did not have conflicts over water. Malcolm Ebright (1994), John Baxter (1997) and David Reichard (1996) have analyzed numerous important eighteenth- and nineteenth-century cases found in New Mexico archives. These cases show not only the various causes of water rights conflicts, but also some of the steps that individuals and communities took to have courts in the past recognize local customs as binding agreements. What is important here is that communities in New Mexico have been dealing with issues of access to scarce land and water resources for many centuries. The historical case studies and local laws are not merely legal, historical, and anthropological curiosities. The analysis of these cases expands our understanding of how people traditionally allocate scarce resources, and they give us important guidance in the analysis of how traditional uses and local customs persist to this day in the villages of northern New Mexico.

Oral traditions, family history, and genealogy have their place in water rights adjudications. These sources are a means of incorporating local perspectives on water resources management. Oral traditions often suggest lines of argument that might not have been considered. Oral history may explain some of the customs and water-use practices that are unique to the community and which may modify the strict interpretation of priority. Marianne Stoller (1983) cautioned that oral testimony is a special type of oral history, one that may violate community standards about who has the right to speak about issues. Yet she recognized that oral testimony could also have value as testimony about the actual traditional uses that a person observed and practiced in his lifetime.

Among the Hispanic and Pueblo communities of northern New Mexico, oral history and oral traditions have a different value than they might have in the dominant culture of the United States. Charles Briggs (1987) discusses the special circumstances that lend credibility to oral history and oral traditions in northern New Mexico communities and discusses the place of these oral forms in litigation. Orally transmitted knowledge is often treated by trial judges and attorneys as a mere curiosity lacking in historical validity. Such views, which often inaccurately privilege the written word as an unbiased view of the past, permeate the literature of Spanish and Mexican land grant scholarship and legal writings in New Mexico and Colorado, according to Briggs (1987: 217). To the contrary, oral testimony is a rich source of reliable historical information when its uses, methodology and contexts are understood. Oral interviews require preparation that can be as rigorous as other field-based data collection methods. More importantly, it must be recognized that a formal interview is not a natural setting for talking about the past. The content of the interview must be treated within the context of the community history, family history, and the experiences of the community members who are interviewed. Oral history, focusing on family experiences and genealogy, is commonly used in more recent scholarship and legal land rights work in New Mexico and Southern Colorado (Briggs and Van Ness 1987; Stoller 1983)

Several authors, for example Jan Vansina (1984: 102) and Briggs (1987: 220), distinguish between oral history and oral traditions. Oral history is the systematic recording of an individual's recollections of past events and eras. In a more restrictive sense, oral history refers specifically to those events in which the speaker was a participant. Oral traditions, on the other hand, are the unwritten knowledge, the legends and other materials transmitted from generation to generation. Oral traditions speak directly to the core values that a community holds. They are those instructive recollections that are used to teach the values and ideals of the culture to which the speakers belong. Oral interviews often contain elements of family history, oral history based on personal experiences, and the instructive oral traditions of community history. Oral history and oral traditions are a rich source of information on local understandings that are crucial in land and water rights issues.

The question of whether the combination of oral traditions, documentary evidence, and family history, which define local understandings of traditional use, has a place in the determination of water rights now rests before the court in several key cases. A particularly sensitive case in which the value of local perspectives is being weighed by the court concerns water rights on the lower Rio Chama.[11] The adjudication began in 1959 when a survey of water uses in the area between El Vado Dam and Española, New Mexico, was completed by the State Engineer Office. A partial final decree was entered in the case in 1971 establishing priority dates for 20 *acequias*. For many of the *parciantes* on the community *acequias*, the dates offered were in marked contrast to what they understood to be the history and antiquity of their communities.

Community members believe that three of the *acequias* assigned priority dates in the 1720s were actually part of the acequia system established at the first Spanish colony of San Gabriel in the late sixteenth and early seventeenth century. During the early spring of 1996 I was hired by the Rio de Chama *Acequias* Association to assist in the preparation for the defense of priority dates and the documentation of local customs that the Association was offering to a Special Master hearing the Rio Chama adjudication. Through genealogical research and oral history interviews I was able to trace some of the families living along these three ditches to families that were known to have occupied the lower Chama Valley in the seventeenth and eighteenth centuries. Historian Dr. Stanley Hordes argued on behalf of the *acequia* association that documents from the seventeenth and eighteenth century supported the communities' beliefs that the *acequias* were part of the sixteenth- and seventeenth-century occupation of the lower Rio Chama. Dr. John Baxter, expert witness for the State of New Mexico, argued that the Oñate colony at San Gabriel was abandoned by 1610, and that the *acequias* in question were part of an eighteenth-century reoccupation of the area also found in the documentary records. The case was argued before a Special Master in August 1996, but no final decision had been issued by the court as of the winter of 1999.

My research was undertaken in part to answer a question posed to the *acequia* commissioners by the court's Special Master. If she were willing to recognize these three *acequias* as the first ditches on the Río Chama, why was it so important that they have a seventeenth-century priority date? Interviews conducted with commissioners, *parciantes*, and local genealogical researchers revealed the deep emotional, historical, and genealogical bonds of the people to the lands and settlements in the Chamita area served by the lower Rio Chama ditches. Community members spoke proudly about the depth of their ancestral connections to the land and to the people who settled the lower Chama Valley during the colonial period. Many of the people were familiar with professional historical and archaeological documentation of colonial settlement in the area, which established the antiquity of Spanish settlement of the San Juan Pueblo area (Agoyo 1987; Lent and Goodman 1992).

The earliest anthropological and historical studies in the Chamita area occurred more than 100 years ago in an attempt to locate the site of the Oñate colony. Occasional excavations at the site performed since the 1930s by state and federal agencies have confirmed that Chamita is the location of the Oñate settlement (Agoyo 1987; Levine 1997; Lent and Goodman 1992). The studies that have been performed in the study area over the last century have not gone unnoticed by local people. Many people grew up hearing stories from their ancestors about the antiquity of Spanish settlement in the area. Many knew of the court challenges to their land titles, and knew of the victories and losses. Through popular histories, promotional materials, lawsuits and scholarly study, the lower Rio Chama communities have been able to trace their roots to the earliest Spanish settlement.

The interviews I conducted in the study area revealed that community members identify strongly with a cultural heritage that connects them to their ancestors and to the struggles that their ancestors faced in settling the region. Finally, community members expressed the concern that to lose the recognition of their long history through the assignment of historically incorrect priority dates would deepen the erosion of rights that Hispanic people have faced since American conquest.

The slow pace of adjudications toward final decrees and closure of these protracted hearings and legal motions is contributing to social strains within communities and between Pueblo and Hispanic communities (Quintana 1990). I have come to suspect that the delays are tactical, even if they are not intentionally malicious. Delay allows market factors to contribute to a reassignment of rights, and has allowed a profitable market for paper water rights. Those with money to buy water rights often have greater resources to protect the older rights. These interests may buy up rights that still need to be perfected through the court hearings. Real estate developers, major corporations, and large landholders are able to sustain a legal fight longer than the *parciantes* in the traditional communities can. Family farms or small agricultural enterprises often cannot sustain themselves because of changes in the regional economy. To contribute limited resources to a protracted legal battle is beyond the means of most *acequia* associations, even when state funds are made available for legal services and technical support.[12]

Courts must be made to understand how local communities define their resource base and how they allocate rights of access. Lawyers and judges must be aware of the scale of value that local communities apply in defending their historical and traditional claims to land, water and natural resources. For many *parciantes*, the viability of the agricultural land uses and the availability of a water supply to feed the *acequia* system are affirmations of their heritage. For *acequia* commissioners, sustaining a way of life by keeping the ditch systems and the agricultural lands in production is a critical issue. Many commissioners express concern that to lose their early water rights would relegate the *acequias* to the status of artifacts or vestiges of a way of life. Sustaining the farm economy of the region is of paramount importance. Throughout northern New Mexico there are strong fears that water will be moved out of the agricultural communities and into the urban areas—that water rights will be severed from lands that have been farmed by Pueblo, Hispanic and Anglo-American families for generations, and moved to the urban areas of the state. This, it is feared, will ultimately destroy the communities.

In many ways the *acequia* is a metaphor for the shared traditions and shared values of rural life, and especially among the Hispanic communities of northern New Mexico. To be a *parciante*, a *mayordomo*, or a *comisionado* is to accept a place in the life of the community and a set of responsibilities to the land, to the people, and to the very fabric of community life. The adjudication process, while quantifying and defining the basis of individual water rights, further erodes the communal basis of the traditional communities in northern New Mexico.

The local perspective of the *acequias* has a contribution to make to regional and national issues. The water sharing agreements recorded in northern New Mexico legal cases are similar to agreements found throughout the world. Rivera (1998: xii–xiii) and Wolf (1998) note that increasingly, public policy administrators are turning to indigenous peoples and local perspectives in drafting resource management agendas. Stanley Crawford (1991) pleads urgently that we recognize the contribution of *acequias* before they are lost, and with them the lessons of communal responsibility for the land. The *acequias* contribute richly to the diverse social and physical landscape that makes the northern Rio Grande a diverse bioregion of the United States. They distribute water to make a broader riparian zone and provide habitat for birds and trees that might not exist without these sustaining waterways. *Acequia* associations have served for more than four centuries as local land managers, and there is much to be gained from implementing in modern land uses the shared perspectives of traditional resource use. Perhaps more answers for sustaining diverse cultural landscapes in the future may be provided by reexamining our heritage of customs and traditions. As we move forward into the twenty-first century, it is time to look back to the *repartimiento* process to find a way to balance the old and the new, the traditional and the innovative.

NOTES

1. Community *acequias* are among the oldest forms of local self-government in the Southwest. These irrigation ditches are supply ditches that feed the smaller systems of field ditches that serve individual farms and gardens. Each community *acequia* has a commission that makes the by-laws setting forth the conditions and obligations by which water is distributed to individual users. The commissioners set the assessments that pay for labor and equipment needed to maintain the ditch, and they serve often as a business decision-making group and to resolve local disputes over the use and rights of access to water in the ditch. *Comisionados* or commissioners are elected annually or biannually in some communities. The *mayordomo* is the ditch master, the person who releases the water from dams or turns the water into the community ditches. In most communities the commission oversees and directs the *mayordomo*. Stanley Crawford (1988) describes beautifully and evocatively his tenure as *mayordomo* of a ditch in the community of Dixon, New Mexico. José Rivera (1998) examines the bylaws and the workings of *acequia* commissions throughout Northern New Mexico.

2. Michael Meyer, a historian who testified in the Aamodt adjudication, traces the legal history of water rights acquisition, use and litigation in his synthesis *Water in the Hispanic Southwest* (Tucson: University of Arizona Press, 1984). Meyer is also the author

of "The Living Legacy of Hispanic Groundwater Law in the Contemporary Southwest," *Journal of the Southwest* 31(3) (Autumn 1989): 287–299. Slightly different perspectives on some of the points researched and discussed in more detail by Meyer are found by William B. Taylor, "Land and Water Rights in the Viceroyalty of New Spain," *New Mexico Historical Review* 50 (July 1975): 189–212; and by Richard E. Greenleaf, "Land and Water in Mexico and New Mexico, 1700–1821," *New Mexico Historical Review* 47 (April 1972): 85–112. Ira G. Clark, *Water in New Mexico; A History of Its Management and Use* (Albuquerque: University of New Mexico Press, 1987) provides a comprehensive overview of water resource management under territorial and state statutes.

3. Sylvia Rodriguez discusses the effects of water marketing in Taos County in "Land, Water, and Ethnic Identity," in Charles L. Briggs and John Van Ness's edited edition of *Land, Water and Culture: New Perspectives on Hispanic Land Grants* (Albuquerque: University of New Mexico Press, 1987). One situation described by Rodriguez was the basis of John Nichol's caricature, *The Milagro Beanfield War* (New York: Holt, Rinehart and Winston, 1974). An important New Mexico case involving water right transfers is *Ensenada Land and Water Association, et al vs. Howard M. Sleeper and Hayden and Elaine Gaylor vs. Steve Reynolds*, Nos. 8782 and 8830, Consolidated. The district court overturned the State Engineer's decision involving a transfer, finding that the transfer was contrary to the public welfare. The court held that the new use, intended for a ski area and recreational development, would be detrimental to traditional uses. The court of appeals reversed the district court on the grounds that the State Engineer did not have to consider public welfare. Since the *Sleeper* decision, New Mexico has amended state law to permit the consideration of public welfare in water right transfers.

4. The elements of a water right include (1) the name of the owner of the right, (2) the amount of water, (3) the period and place of use, (4) the purpose for which the water may be used, (5) the source of the water, (6) the point of diversion, and (7) the priority date.

5. Rivera (1998: 230) defines the *repartimiento de aguas* as a partition or division of water between ditches that share the same stream or among *parciantes* who use the same ditch. *Repartimientos* were also entered into between the Hispanic and Pueblo communities Meyer (1984: 160) briefly discusses the *Repartimiento* of 1823 that concerns the waters entitled to Taos Pueblo and the community of Arroyo Seco. Although Taos Pueblo was referred to in the document as the total owner, *dueno despotico*, of the water in question, settlers of Arroyo Seco were allocated a proportional share of available water. The meaning of the Spanish terms and the overall effect of the *Repartimiento* of 1823 continues to be argued by attorneys and historical experts.

6. The Taos adjudication involves adjudication of the water rights that Taos Pueblo and the non-Indian communities have along the Rio Pueblo de Taos and the Rio Hondo stream systems. The case involves the water rights of more than 4,000 defendants. The case is referred to as the *State of New Mexico ex. rel. Reynolds vs. Abeyta, and State of New Mexico ex. rel. Reynolds vs. Arellano*, U.S. District Court Cases, Nos. CIV-7896-SC and CIV 7939-SC. The El Rito and Rio Chama cases involve the adjudication of water rights along the main stem and tributaries of the Rio Chama. The water rights of more than 2,500 defendants are at issue in this case. The legal reference is *State of New Mexico ex. rel. Reynolds vs. Aragon*, U.S. District Court Cases, No.794.

7. Charles L. Briggs and John R. Van Ness (1987), Sylvia Rodriguez (1990) and Quintana (1990) present summaries of several land and water rights cases in northern New Mexico and southern Colorado in which anthropologists and historians have been

influential. Rodriguez (1990) critiques the role that applied anthropologists have played in some land and water cases. She admonishes applied anthropologists not to accept the "inevitable" domination and loss that brokered solutions offer, in her view. She urges applied anthropologists to work for change that truly empowers local community choices. She reminds us that applied research is often partisan research. She does not deal as directly with the dilemma of differing goals and values within the communities nor with the possibility that a solution adequate to one community or group may be seen as detrimental by other communities or groups within the same community. Two recent programs in New Mexico provide some important case studies. Neither project involved anthropologists, but both used focus groups, community summits, and some land-use mapping models to gain local input into land and resource management decisions. Both of these projects were administered by Western Network, a mediation, facilitation, and training organization that has worked throughout the Southwest mediating natural re-source issues. A water forum sponsored by the Thaw Charitable Trust in 1995 brought together water users, and county, city, and state officials to frame the issues relating to the availability of water and planned urban growth in Santa Fe. Two reports were issued, one by the Thaw Charitable Trust, *Water and Growth in the Santa Fe Area; Framing the Issues* (June 1995), and a report of the working groups and recommendations was also prepared by Western Network (July 1995). Western Network has also worked with communities that border the Cibola National Forest in central New Mexico to gain an understanding of their concerns for the management of access and use of forest products.

8. For a discussion of the importance of the Aamodt adjudication to issues of Pueblo Indian water rights, see Charles T. DuMars, Marilyn O'Leary, and Albert E. Utton, *Pueblo Indian Water Rights; Struggle for a Precious Resource* (Tucson: University of Arizona Press, 1984).

9. Community control and community traditions among rural Hispanic and Anglo-American communities are lost when water and other resource management decisions are made by state and federal agencies, conclude F. Lee Brown and Helen Ingram, "The Community Value of Water: Implications for the Rural Poor in the Southwest," *Journal of the Southwest* 29(2) (Summer, 1987): 179–202 and Sue-Ellen Jacobs, " 'Top-Down Planning'; Analysis of Obstacles to Community Development in an Economically Poor Region of the Southwestern United States," *Human Organization* 37(3) (Fall, 1978): 246–256.

10. A number of nineteenth-century local rules for the operation of *acequias* are con-tained in two historical compilations: *Laws of the Territory of New Mexico with Joint Resolutions Passed by the Legislative Assembly at the Session of 1863–1864* (Albuquer-que: Hezekiah S. Johnson) and *Local and Special Laws of New Mexico in Accordance with an Act of the Legislature, Approved April 3, 1884* (Santa Fe: New Mexican Printing Company). The latter text contains reprints of some of the materials found in the 1864 compilation as well. An analysis of the customs used by local communities is long overdue. Rivera (1998) includes the bylaws and minutes of many *acequias*. An ethnohis-torical analysis of existing local rules, ordinances, and laws would be useful for partic-ipants in water use discussions throughout New Mexico.

11. Fred Vigil, the Executive Director of the Rio Chama *Acequias* Association, and I wrote a paper on this case. I presented the paper at the Annual Conference of the Western Social Science Association in Albuquerque in April 1997 (Levine and Vigil 1997).

12. In an attempt to defray the terrific burden of adjudication costs, *acequia* associ-ations lobbied the New Mexico state legislature to create funding to assist local com-

munities. The Acequia and Community Ditch Fund Act of 1988 supports technical studies such as historical research, hydrographic studies, and engineering studies for acequia associations. Rivera (1998: 156, 199–200) sees this fund as exactly the type of direct assistance that *acequias* need to be sustained in the face of changing land uses and regional economic pressures.

REFERENCES

Agoyo, Herman, et al. 1987. *When Cultures Meet: Remembering San Gabriel del Yunge Oweenge*. Santa Fe: Sunstone Press.

Baxter, John O. 1997. *Dividing New Mexico's Waters, 1700–1912*. Albuquerque: University of New Mexico Press.

Briggs, Charles L. 1986. *Learning How to Ask; A sociolinguistic appraisal of the role of the interview in social science research*. Cambridge: Cambridge University Press.

———. 1987. Getting Both Sides of the Story: Oral History in Land Grant Research and Litigation. In *Land, Water, and Culture: New Perspectives on Hispanic Land Grants*, edited by Charles L. Briggs and John R. Van Ness, pp. 217–268. New Mexico Land Grant Series. Albuquerque: University of New Mexico Press.

Briggs, Charles L., and John R. Van Ness, ed. 1987. *Land, Water, and Culture: New Perspectives on Hispanic Land Grants*. New Mexico Land Grant Series. Albuquerque: University of New Mexico Press.

Brown, F. Lee, and Helen M. Ingram. 1987. The Community Value of Water: Implications for the Rural Poor in the Southwest. *Journal of the Southwest* 29(2): 179–202.

Carlson, Alvar W. 1990. *The Spanish American Homeland; Four Centuries in New Mexico's Rio Arriba*. Baltimore: The Johns Hopkins University Press.

Crawford, Stanley. 1988. *Mayordomo; Chronicle of an Acequia in Northern New Mexico*. Albuquerque: University of New Mexico Press.

———. 1990. Dancing for Water. *Journal of the Southwest* 32(3): 265–267.

———. 1991. An Open Letter to the State Engineer. *The Farm Connection* 2:(4): 1–4 (June 1991).

Crossland, C. B. 1990a. Water Rights Adjudication in Northern New Mexico: Culture History Meets State Law. *New Mexico Natural Resources Law Reporter* 41–44.

———. 1990b. Acequia Rights in Law and Tradition. *Journal of the Southwest* 32(3): 278–287.

Ebright, Malcolm. 1994. *Land Grants and Law Suits in Northern New Mexico*. Albuquerque: University of New Mexico Press.

Hordes, Stanley M. 1994. Irrigation at the Confluence of the Rio Grande and Rio Chama: The Acequias de Chamita, Salazar and Hernández, 1600–1680. Ms. prepared for the Río de Chama Acequias Association.

Hutchins, Wells A. 1928. The Community Acequia: Its Origins and Development. *Southwestern Historical Quarterly* 31: 261–184.

Jackson, John Brinkerhoff. 1994. *A Sense of Place, A Sense of Time*. New Haven: Yale University Press.

Jacobs, Sue-Ellen. 1978. 'Top-Down Planning': Analysis of Obstacles to Community

Development in an Economically Poor Region of the Southwestern United States. *Human Organization* 37(3): 246–256.

Kutsche, Paul, ed. 1979. *The Survival of Spanish American Villages*. The Colorado College Studies No. 15. Colorado Springs: Colorado College.

Laws of the Territory of New Mexico. 1864. *Laws of the Territory of New Mexico with Joint Resolutions Passed by the Legislative Assembly at the Session of 1863–1864*. Albuquerque: Hezekiah S. Johnson.

Lent, Stephen C., and Linda J. Goodman. 1992. Archaeological Testing and a Brief Ethnohistory of San Gabriel de Yunque Owinge, San Juan Pueblo, New Mexico. Archaeology Notes 102, Office of Archaeological Studies, Museum of New Mexico, Santa Fe.

Levine, Frances. 1990. Dividing the Water; the Impact of Water Rights Adjudications on New Mexican Communities. *Journal of the Southwest* 32: 268–277.

Levine, Frances, and Fred Vigil. 1997. Making a Place for Tradition in Land and Water Use Conflicts. Paper presented at the Annual Meeting of the Western States Social Sciences Association, Albuquerque, New Mexico, April 1997.

Local and Special Laws of New Mexico. 1885. *Local and Special Laws of New Mexico in Accordance with an Act of the Legislature, Approved April 3, 1884*. Santa Fe: New Mexican Printing Company.

Lovato, Phil. 1974. *Las Acequias del Norte*. Technical Report No. 1. Four Corners Regional Commission, New Mexico State Planning Office, Taos, New Mexico.

———. 1975. *Las Acequias del Norte*. Technical Report No. 2. Four Corners Regional Commission, New Mexico State Planning Office, Taos, New Mexico.

Meyer, Michael C. 1984. *Water in the Hispanic Southwest; A Social and Legal History, 1550–1850*. Tucson: University of Arizona Press.

Quintana, Frances Leon. 1990. Land, Water, and Pueblo-Hispanic Relations in Northern New Mexico. *Journal of the Southwest* 32(3): 288–299.

Reich, Peter L. 1994. Mission Revival Jurisprudence: State Courts and Hispanic Water Law Since 1850. *Washington Law Review* 69: 869–925.

Reichard, David A. 1996. The Politics of Village Water Disputes in Northern New Mexico, 1882–1905. *Western Legal History* 9(1) 9–33.

Riley, Michael. 1994. Constituting the Southwest; Contesting the Southwest; Re-Inventing the Southwest. *Journal of the Southwest* 36(3) 221–241.

Rivera, José A. 1998. *Acequia Culture; Water, Land & Community in the Southwest*. Albuquerque: University of New Mexico Press.

Rodriguez, Sylvia. 1987. Land, Water, and Ethnic Identity in Taos. In *Land, Water, and Culture: New Perspectives on Hispanic Land Grants*, edited by Charles L. Briggs and John R. Van Ness, pp. 313–403. New Mexico Land Grant Series. Albuquerque: University of New Mexico.

———. 1990. Applied Research on Land and Water in New Mexico: A Critique. *Journal of the Southwest* 32(3): 300–315.

Stoller, Marianne. 1983. Legal Testimony as Oral History. Paper presented at the Annual Meeting of the American Society for Ethnohistory, Albuquerque, New Mexico, November 1983.

Tyler, Daniel. 1986. Dating the Caño Ditch: Detective Work in the Pojoaque Valley. *New Mexico Historical Review* 61(1): 14–25.

Vansina, Jan. 1984. Oral Tradition and Historical Methodology. In *Oral History: An*

Interdisciplinary Anthology, edited by David K. Dunaway and Willa K. Baum, pp. 102–106. Nashville: American Association for State and Local History.

Wolf, Aaron T. 1998. Indigenous Approaches to Water Conflict Resolution and Implications for International Waters. Ms. on file., U.S. Institute of Peace and Department of Geography, University of Alabama, Tuscaloosa.

8

Myth and History of a Southwestern Land Grant: Baca Location No. 4 and Luis María Cabeza de Baca

Marianne L. Stoller

INTRODUCTION

For some while, scholars have found the study of the Spanish and Mexican periods' land grants one of the most productive avenues for understanding the social and cultural dynamics of settlement and interethnic relations in Mexico and the American Southwest (Chevalier, 1963; Lamar, 1966; Leonard, 1970; Westphall, 1983; Briggs and Van Ness, 1989). The legacy of these grants continues to affect the lives of contemporary citizens of these areas since they deal with commodities of primordial importance to all: land and water. In many parts of the American Southwest the ownership of the lands and waters most coveted by and suitable for human occupation derive from Spanish Colonial (1540–1821) and Republic of Mexico (1821–1848) administrations.

The Treaty of Guadalupe Hidalgo in 1848 ended the Mexican-American War and incorporated the area now known as the American Southwest into the United States. By provision of that Treaty, the property of Mexico's former citizens was to be protected for them. However, the process set up by the United States for adjudication of property rights in the Territory of New Mexico (which then included southern Colorado and Arizona) to determine the validity of titles was variable, ambiguous, ambivalent, and, in short, imperfect (see Briggs and Van Ness, 1989; and Ebright, 1994: 37–54). The result has been seemingly unending frustrations and fantasies, opportunities turned into injustices, corruptions, exploitations, elaborations, and almost perpetual litigation by the area's citizens over property rights, be they Native Americans, Hispanics, or Anglos.

The present study examines the history of one such grant, that known as Baca

Location No. 4, using the documentary records of the three national administrations and their courts. Since this grant is continuing to produce history, mixed
with myth, personal interviews and current newspaper and media accounts are
also used as well as the research and interpretations of other scholars.

MYTH AND HISTORY

Along a potholed Saguache County road between the small towns of Moffat
and Crestone in the northeastern corner of the San Luis Valley of south central
Colorado stands a gateway proclaiming the entrance to the "Luis María Baca
Grant" (Map 8.1; Photograph 8.1). The rustic gate, worked in wrought iron in
the Spanish style, is a symbol of what Carey McWilliams (1968: 35) called the
"fantasy heritage" of the Hispanic Southwest: the romanticizing of a past that
obliterates the hard reality of the present. More recently, David Weber, the most
outstanding historian today of the Hispanic Southwest, has devoted a book of
essays to the interrelationship of myth and history in this area noting,

History contains mythic elements, and myth contains historical elements. To suppose
otherwise is to place too great a faith in our ability to reconstruct the past through *logos*,
and too little imagination to seek the truths inherent in *mythos*. (Weber 1988: ix)

I use the word myth here not in the sense that some phenomena are illusory,
delusory, or necessarily false, but to mean a way of thinking that incorporates
seemingly chaotic bits of human history, ponders profound, fantastic, or contradictory human dilemmas, and attempts to construct meaning from them. In the
process of making sense, myths bring a certain order out of chaos and provide
guidance for subsequent ways of thinking, understanding and acting. They may
indeed contain false or misleading information. History, as *logos*, may illuminate
or attempt to correct these. Where myth works with chaos, history tries to bring
order: relying, as it does, on the concreteness of records, of tangible events of
the past recorded by real people, it assumes (1) a temporal linearity in the
sequence of events, and (2) a set of cause and effect relationships. It tries to
provide explanations of phenomena of the past clothed in an aura of factuality,
but like myth, it is open to interpretations and reinterpretations dependent upon,
again, constructing meaning for its audience.

What is mythic about the gateway? Luis María Cabeza de Baca never had a
grant there, indeed probably never walked on that landscape and certainly never
knew that he owned any of it. Yet events decades after his death gave his heirs
the ownership of 100,000 acres there in his name and the *mythos* of this land
being an old Spanish land grant became firmly established. Owners of the land
in the 1970s attempted to develop a resort and sell recreational and retirement
homesites on it. A widely circulated undated promotional pamphlet entitled "The
Story of the *Baca Grande*" provides the following "history" of it:

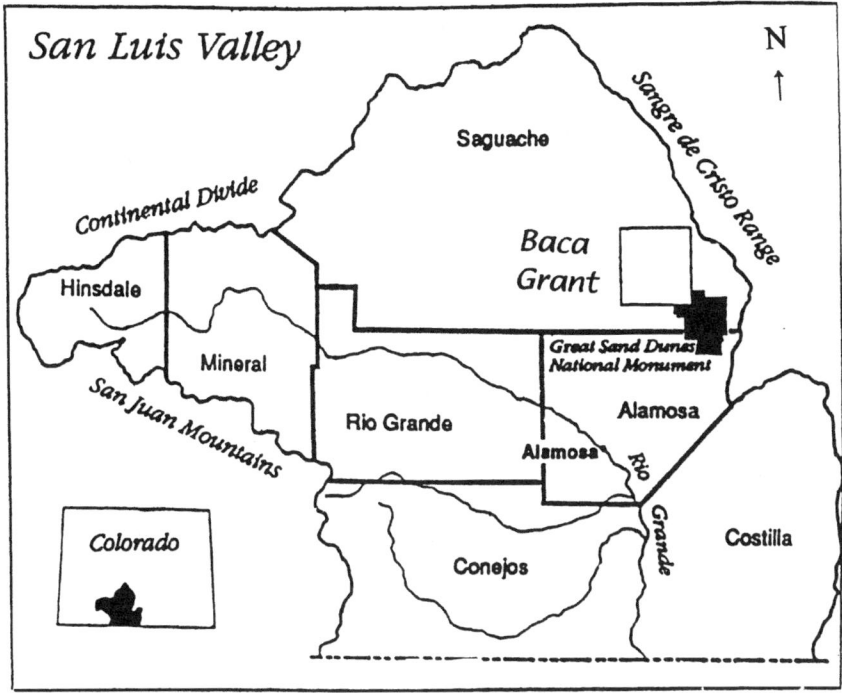

Map 8.1 Colorado map

In 1823, King Ferdinand VII of Spain wished to show his appreciation to his loyal subject Luis María Cabeza de Vaca and made a royal land grant of 500,000 acres in New Mexico to Vaca for himself, his 17 sons and the 600 head of horses and mules that he owned.

The Vaca [anglicized to Baca] family can be traced back many centuries in Spanish history to 1235 when the Spaniards were victorious over the Moors in battle, led by a man using the head of a cow as a symbol. Thereafter the family of this man was given the title "cabeza de vaca" meaning "head of a cow." Luis María Cabeza de Baca and his family made their home on the Grant and lived peacefully until a band of roving Navajo Indians drove them from their ranch to a home in the village of Peña Blanca.

Ferdinand VII was indeed King of Spain in 1823 but Spain no longer had possession of the area: it was part of the Republic of Mexico. The grant was made in 1821, and it is unlikely that the King had ever heard of "his loyal subject." If he had, the news would not have been good since Luis María Cabeza de Baca was in trouble over mistreatment of the Pueblo Indians. Land grants were ordinarily made by the governors of the provinces in the Spanish New World. There is no evidence that Baca was a descendant of the Spanish hero in a battle against the Moors in 1235 (actually 1212), although he so claimed (Twitchell, 1914: 376), and he seems to have been the first Baca in New Mexico

Photo 8.1 Gateway to Baca Ranch. Photo by the author.

to add Cabeza de to his name. According to baptismal records (Archives of the Archdiocese of Santa Fe [AASF]), he ultimately had 12 sons (Twitchell [1914: 47–48] lists 13, but one died in infancy); and 10 daughters (Twitchell lists nine), not 17 sons, and not all had been born by 1821 (Figure 8.1) Either Baca was a very inattentive father or perhaps he was counting sons-in-law, too. There is no good evidence that he and his family lived on this grant which, anyway, is not Baca Location No. 4 (the promotional pamphlet does acknowledge this clearly). Finally, "Baca" is not an anglicized version of "Vaca." In the historical records of New Mexico "b" and "v" are used interchangeably in spelling many words. Baca is the more commonly used spelling today.

This pamphlet is a fine statement of the "fantasy heritage" and illustrates how history and myth can be mixed. With similar news stories and advertisements in such publications as *Forbes* and *People* magazines and the *Wall Street Journal*, the owners (AZL Resources, Inc.) in the 1970s had only moderate success in selling homesites at the base of the remote but ruggedly beautiful Crestone Range of the Sangre de Cristo Mountains. They soon went into bankruptcy and the grant was acquired by one of that company's stockholders, Maurice Strong, at a tax sale.

In 1986, an application to mine underground waters on the site was filed in District Court, Water Division 3, Alamosa, Colorado (Case No. 86CW46), on behalf of the American Water Development, Inc. (AWDI), the Baca Ranch Company and the Baca Corporation (then owners of the grant), by Maurice Strong (a Canadian entrepreneur and president of all three companies), and other officers. The applicants proposed to mine the underground aquifers for 200,000 acre feet of water annually for 100 years from 92 deep wells (2,500 feet) on the grant and 20 more on adjacent lands they had acquired (Colorado District Court, Division 3, Case No. 86CW46; Figure 8.1).

The applicants first claim to rights to the water was "based on Spanish and Mexican law as recognized and affirmed by the United States," these rights running with the title to the land grant. This claim was heard as a separate motion for summary judgement and argued on July 5, 1990. The district court ruled that day to dismiss the motion, based on the successful arguments of the opposing attorneys that the Baca Location No. 4 land grant derived title from the United States—because of the peculiar history of the grant—and not from Spain or Mexico (Colorado District Court, Case No. 86CW46).

What is that peculiar history? How and why were grants made? What are the laws concerning water? Was there a grant actually made by authority of the Spanish Colonial government? Does a land grant convey rights to underground waters? And who was Luis María Cabeza de Baca?

The first of these questions to be explored are those on land grants and water rights under Spain and Mexico.

SPANISH AND MEXICAN LAND GRANT PROCEDURES AND WATER ALLOCATIONS

The procedures for making grants of land, by which an area was brought into economic usefulness and thereby attractive to settlers, were developed by the Spanish Colonial government of New Mexico in the 18th century, based on Spain's laws and customs adapted to the New World by the Council of the Indies and codified in 1681 in the massive *Recopilación de las Leyes de los Reynos de las Indias* (Malcolm Ebright [1987:17] discusses the precedent customs and practices in Spain). Land grants were not only a means of enticing colonists to the Spanish empire's new lands, they also provided the means of subsistence for the colonists and established Spain's sovereignty over her expanding territories. The actual procedures for granting lands are described in White, et al. (1971:10–12); further discussed in Stoller (1985; 1998). Although they followed a regular pattern discernable from the archival evidence (Spanish Archives of New Mexico [SANM], Series 1, which contains the records of the U.S. Surveyors General [SG] frequently referred to in this chapter), they were based on custom as much as they were on written codifications.

Citizens desiring to obtain lands made a written petition to the governor of the province who had the right to distribute lands. A single individual or a group of individuals could apply. The petition declared the desired land vacant, described it in terms of natural (and sometimes social) boundaries, and stated the need for and intended uses of the land. The governor then forwarded the petition to the *alcalde* (local official) in the district adjacent to the petitioned land, di-

Figure 8.1
Ground water, Rio Grande basin, Colorado

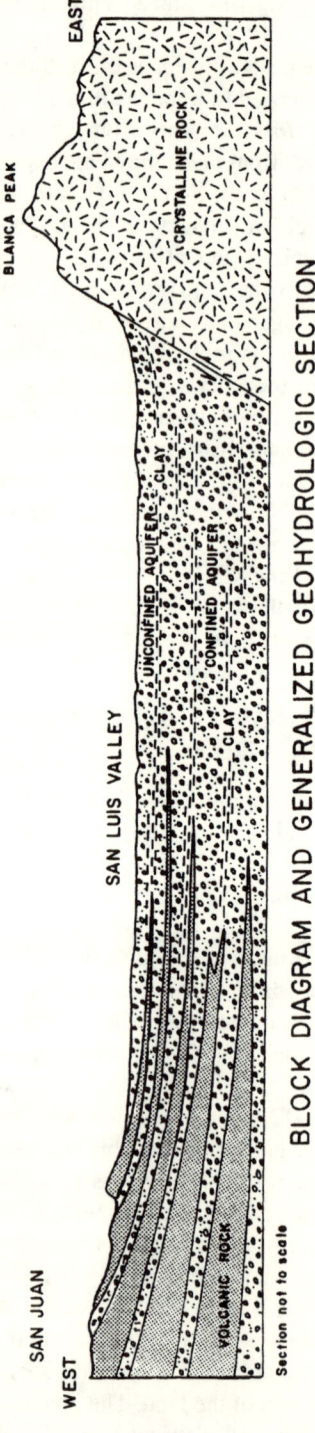

BLOCK DIAGRAM AND GENERALIZED GEOHYDROLOGIC SECTION

Source: Colorado Water Conservation Board and U.S. Department of Agriculture *Main Report,* IV–32, Figure IV–8

recting him to notify the Indians and Spanish settlers in the area and ascertain any adverse claims. The *alcalde's* report, signed by two witnesses, was submitted to the governor. If the land was indeed vacant with no conflicting claims, the grant was approved (approval was often written in the margin of the original petition and this constituted the title, a copy of which was given to the petitioners) and the *alcalde* was directed to place the petitioners in possession by pacing the boundaries of the land with them and performing a little ritual of throwing stones, pulling grass, and shouting, "Long live the King." The act of possession perfected the title. The successful petitioners usually had a defined period of time—commonly two to four years—to settle the land, or cause it to be settled, and brought into productive use. If the grant was to be inhabited and cultivated (as opposed to using the land for grazing only), the owners, or sometimes the *alcalde* himself, vested title to the settlers' individual homesites and cultivated lands after the period of time allotted for them to build homes, *acequias* (irrigation ditches), and so forth. If the grant was not occupied or brought into productive use, the grantees forfeited it, and it could be awarded to others.

The owners of a settlement grant usually selected the sites of *plazas* or towns. Such settlements were usually nucleated and followed fairly closely the Royal Ordinances of 1573 prescribed by Felipe Segundo, King of Spain, for the founding of new towns in the New World (see Nuttal 1921), although the settlers, wanting to be close to their fields and flocks, often had dispersed homesites as well (Simmons 1969). The initial settlers, who might or might not include the owners, could expand their holdings by additional donations from the owners or, more commonly, by purchase, and the owners sold remaining lands to later arriving settlers as well.

The lands surrounding a settlement and farming plots were called *ejido* lands. They were to be used in common, especially for grazing since raising livestock was a more important part of the local Spanish economy than farming. Such lands often included foothills and mountains which provided timber for construction purposes, fuel, wild game and fish, and wild plants used for dyes, medicine, etc., as well as summer pastures for domesticated animals. (Parenthetically, the *ejido* lands were the source of much land loss and economic disaster for Hispanic villagers under the United States, which declared them public domain and often denied usufruct rights to the inhabitants; these lands were then often exploited by Anglo newcomers who bought them or they were later incorporated in National Forests and other public lands [see Van Ness, 1980, for a succinct review of these problems]).

To what extent a grant of land also conveyed rights to its waters is a question with various answers, based not on a clear codification under Spanish law but to be inferred from the study of extant documents. Using this case study method, Michael Meyer and Daniel Tyler have done extensive research on water laws and customs under Spanish and Mexican administrations in the Southwest and northern Mexico (Meyer 1984; 1985; Tyler 1990, 1991). Others have argued the concept of implied consent, for instance, that a grant of land also conveyed rights to use at least its surface waters, springs, and water from shallow wells for domestic purposes, but never at the injury of a neighbor. However, as Meyer (1984: 87) notes, if water went with the land, why were there specific grants of water, and specifications in various grants about rights and usages? Meyer feels that the laws and customs were flexible, and decisions were based mostly on land use classifications (for farming, grazing, etc.). Tyler (1991) specifically investigated rights to underground waters under the same administrations. "Percolating waters," those from springs and wells, belonged to the land owner but were subject to various restrictions regarding public health and safety and the use rights of neighbors. To what extent the Spanish understood the presence of underground aquifers as the source of such waters is a moot question. Certainly they did not have the hydraulic technology in those centuries to exploit them.

In his study on the Myth of the Pueblo Rights Doctrine, Tyler (1990:45) summarizes studies of water law:

After reviewing extant Hispanic documents of New Mexico, the only supportable conclusion is that no municipal entity, Indian or non-Indian, had a right to enlarge its claim to water without consideration of the legitimate needs of other users, individuals, or communities. Equitable, or proportional when distribution was the objective, and although this might seem idealistic when viewed from today's perspective, both Spaniards and Mexicans developed a system of sharing which they hoped would function in avoidance of costly litigation. Absolute water rights were inconsistent with Spanish thinking and inappropriate to the New Mexican environment.

LUIS MARÍA CABEZA DE BACA: HIS BACKGROUND AND HIS LIFE

The next question to be considered is who was Luis María Cabeza de Baca? He has attained a somewhat mythical stature in New Mexico history: Ralph Twitchell (1914: 376) called him "one of the most notable men of his time" and Lynn Perrigo (1985: 21–23) included him in his book on historic leaders in New Mexico. Like Twitchell, Perrigo implies that he is a descendant of the explorer Alvar Nuñez Cabeza de Baca.

Luis María Cabeza de Baca's life does exemplify the Hispanic history of the Southwest, especially New Mexico, in many ways, providing information on family and social structure and interethnic relationships as well as on the manipulation of property. He was born in Santa Fe on October 26, 1754, the oldest of seven sons and three daughters of Juan Antonio Baca and María Romero (Chávez 1954: 152; see Figure 8.2). His grandfather, Antonio, who had married Monica de Chávez in 1726, is listed in the *Diligencias Matrimonios* (Chávez n.d.) at the time of his marriage as having *padres no conocido* or parents unknown. Twitchell (1914: 376) reported Luis María and his father Juan Antonio had come to New Mexico in the early part of the eighteenth(?) century and, as noted, were descendants of Alvar Nuñez Cabeza de Vaca. Not so, says Fray

Figure 8.2
Luis María Cabeza de Baca Genealogy

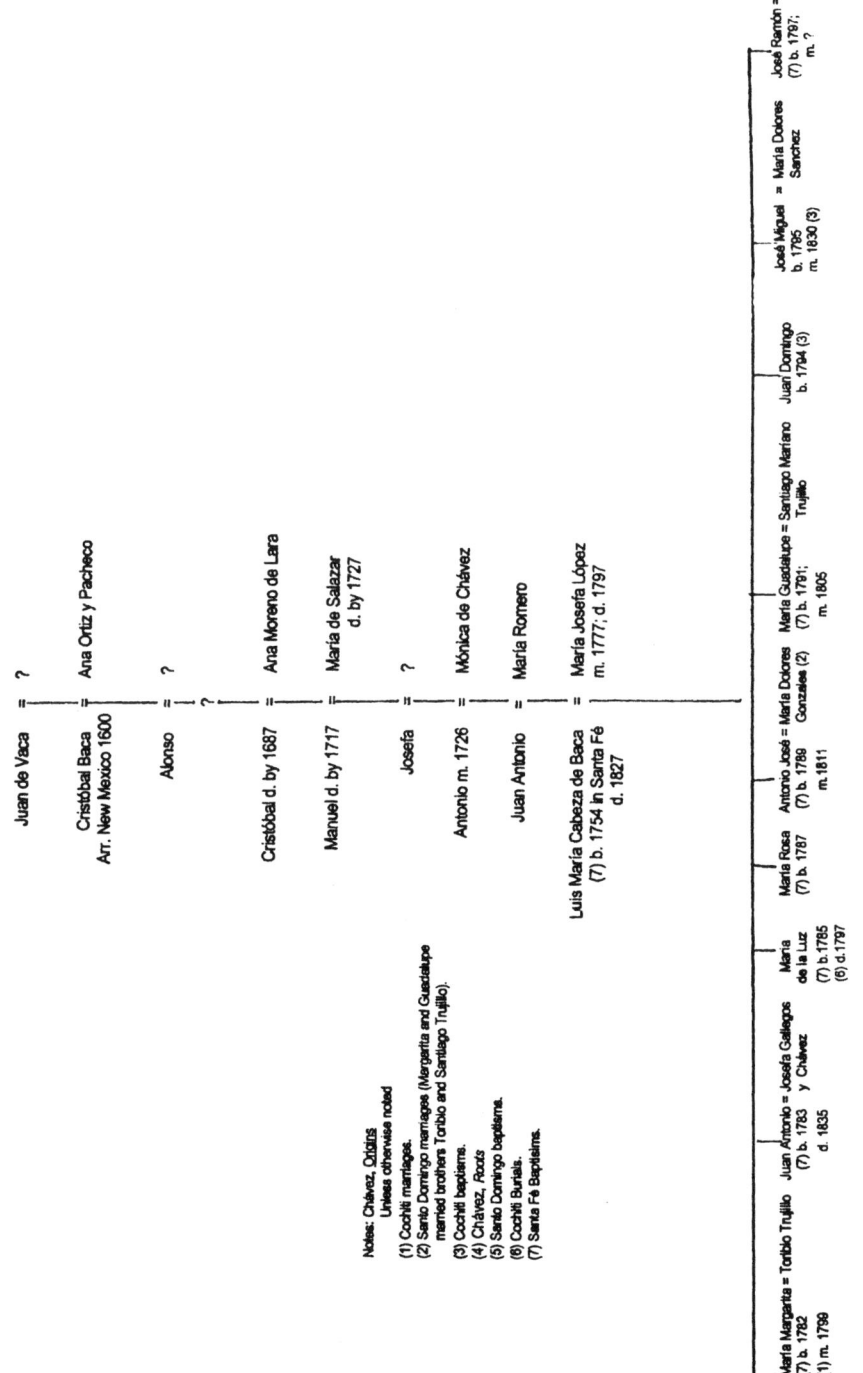

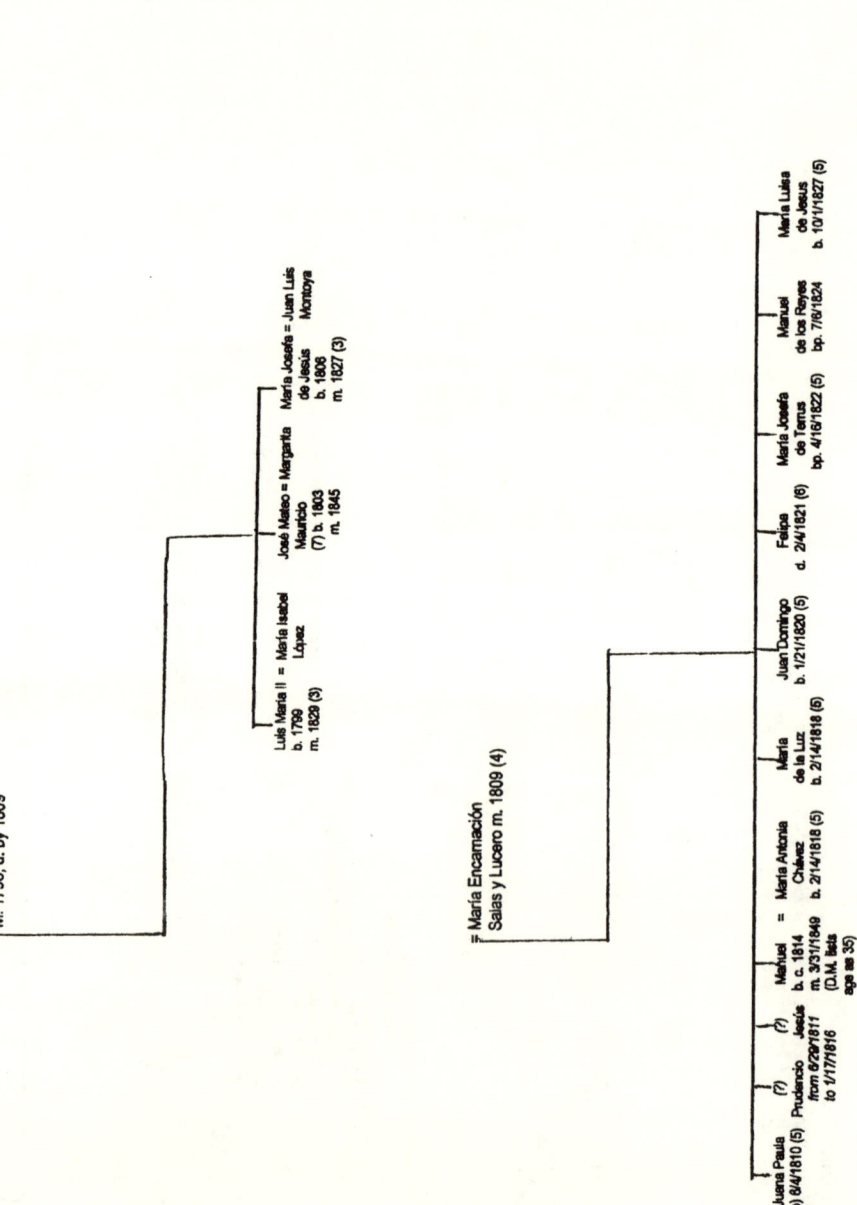

Angelico Chávez, they were all direct descendants of Cristóbal Baca, son of Juan de Vaca and Doña Ana Ortiz, both born in Mexico City, who brought three grown daughters and one small son, apparently Antonio, with them to New Mexico in 1600. They were among settlers recruited to reinforce the Oñate colony established in 1598 (Chávez 1954: 9, 152, 141).

Antonio Baca, Cristóbal and Ana Ortiz' son, was a ringleader in protests against Governor Rosas and his career earned him a beheading in Santa Fe in 1643 (Chávez 1954: 10). Another son, Alonso, apparently born to the couple in New Mexico, fathered another Cristóbal who was in New Mexico at the time of the Pueblo Revolt in 1680 but apparently dead in Guadalupe del Paso by 1687. Of this Cristóbal's three sons, José got in a fight with his brother-in-law who killed him in 1687, but his daughter, Juana, wife of Nicolas Ortiz III, returned to New Mexico. Cristóbal's son, Ignacio, a *Sargento Mayor* at the Guadalupe del Paso Presidio, died in 1689, but his widow, Juana de Anaya Almazan, returned to New Mexico in 1693 after the Reconquest where she, their two sons, and two of their five daughters were all killed in the Pueblo Revolt of 1696. Only Cristóbal's son Manuel, his wife, María de Salazar, and some of their eight children returned in 1693 to bring the Baca name and scatter it across time and space in New Mexico thenceforth (Chávez 1954:10–11).

Josefa, one of Manual Baca and Mara de Salazar's daughters, was the mother of Antonio Baca, Luis María's grandfather. When Josefa made her last will in 1746 she left her property to her six natural children of whom Antonio was the oldest (Chávez 1954: 144). Whether her children had various fathers, Indian fathers (whom the priests might not have recorded), or her son was just too scandalized by his mother's habit of having children out of wedlock, any of these may be the reason Antonio did not claim her as a parent when he married into the very prominent Chávez family. This may also be the reason why Luis María, who certainly had pretensions to high social status, invented a new name and story for himself and his descendants, who were Twitchell's informants. The historian and genealogist Fray Angelico Chávez, who shared more than a few relatives with Luis María including the lady of questionable virtue, points out that the name Cabeza de Vaca "was never once used by this New Mexico family for over two centuries" (Chávez 1954: 11) until Luis María adopted it. Several Vacas came to the New World in Cortes' time; either Diego de Vaca from León or Luis Vaca from Toledo were the likely fathers of Juan Vaca, the progenitor of the first Cristóbal and all succeeding Bacas (Chávez 1954: 11).

Listed as simply Luis Vaca, a soldier in the Santa Fe garrison when he married his first wife, María Josepha López, in 1777, and as Luis María Baca when he married his second, Ana María Sanchez, in 1798, he had attached "Cabeza de" by 1803 (Twitchell [1914: 47] has the first names of these wives confused). Thereafter the name appears regularly although his siblings did not use it and even immediate heirs sometimes used it and sometimes not (Chávez 1954: 152–153). Some contemporary descendants retain it in the form of C. de Baca.

When Manuel Baca and his family returned with Vargas in the Reconquest of 1693 they reoccupied father Cristóbal's old lands near Bernalillo (Map 8.2). From there Manuel's descendants spread out: from Tomé in the south to Santa Fe in the north and by the end of the eighteenth century to Laguna in the west and San Miguel del Vado in the east. The lineal line leading to Luis María, however, seems to have remained centered along the Rio Grande, especially in the vicinity of Santo Domingo and Cochití Pueblos by the mid-1700s.

As noted, Luis María was a soldier in Santa Fe and his first five children and his eighth were baptized there, but two sons, Juan Domingo, born in 1794, and José Miguel, born in 1795, were baptized at Cochití Pueblo. His name first appears in the church records of Cochití as a *padrino* (godparent) at a baptism in the latter part of 1790, and although his daughter, María Guadalupe, was baptized in Santa Fe in early 1791, it appears that he had moved his family to the area of Peña Blanca, between the Pueblos of Cochití and Santo Domingo sometime during 1790–1791. Except for José Ramón, baptized in Santa Fe the day his mother died there, all of Luis María's subsequent children, so far located, by his third wife were baptized in one or the other churches of those two pueblos. He had married María Encarnación Salas y Lucero in 1809. Research in the Books of Baptism of the Archives of the Archdiocese of Santa Fe by myself and student Jessica Betterly (1989) have found a total of 20 children by his three wives. The books are missing for the Cochití and Santo Domingo missions between 1814 and 1816 which may account for two sons, Prudencio and Jesús, named in the Surveyor General's file (SANM, Series 1, SG No. 20) who were not found in the extant records. In all, as noted, it appears that he had 22 children, but not the 17 male children (*"dies y siete hijos varones"*) he claimed in his land grant application.

Luis María, like his forebears, had a history of troubles with his Pueblo Indian neighbors, and therein lies the genesis, perhaps, of the land grant under scrutiny here. Post-Revolt returnee Manuel Baca and his sons were accused of mistreating the Indians of the Pueblos of Cochití, Santo Domingo, and San Felipe, and Manuel was deprived of the *Alcaldía* of Cochití in 1718. Son Antonio and his wife, Luis María's grandparents, were also so accused (Chávez 1954: 141; Cutter 1986: 68). Squabbles over lands with their Pueblo neighbors probably resulted from the Bacas' attempts to claim the *sobras* lands of these pueblos. *Sobras* were lands just outside the protected Pueblo league which might be used by them but could be applied for in grants by Spanish settlers, thus constricting Pueblo use and providing the possibility of accusations of encroachment (Jenkins 1988). The Pueblo Indians were primarily farmers, the Spanish settlers were ranchers, and many complaints resulted from unfenced livestock ravaging corn fields and breaking irrigation ditches. Grants, sales, and other land transfers between the Indians and Spanish further complicated relations.

In 1792, while in charge of a detachment of soldiers, Luis María was accused of mistreating the Indians of Cochití and Santo Domingo and using them to build a house, and so forth. He was arrested and marched to Chihuahua in chains, tried, convicted, and reprimanded (SANM, Series 2, Roll 13, frs.

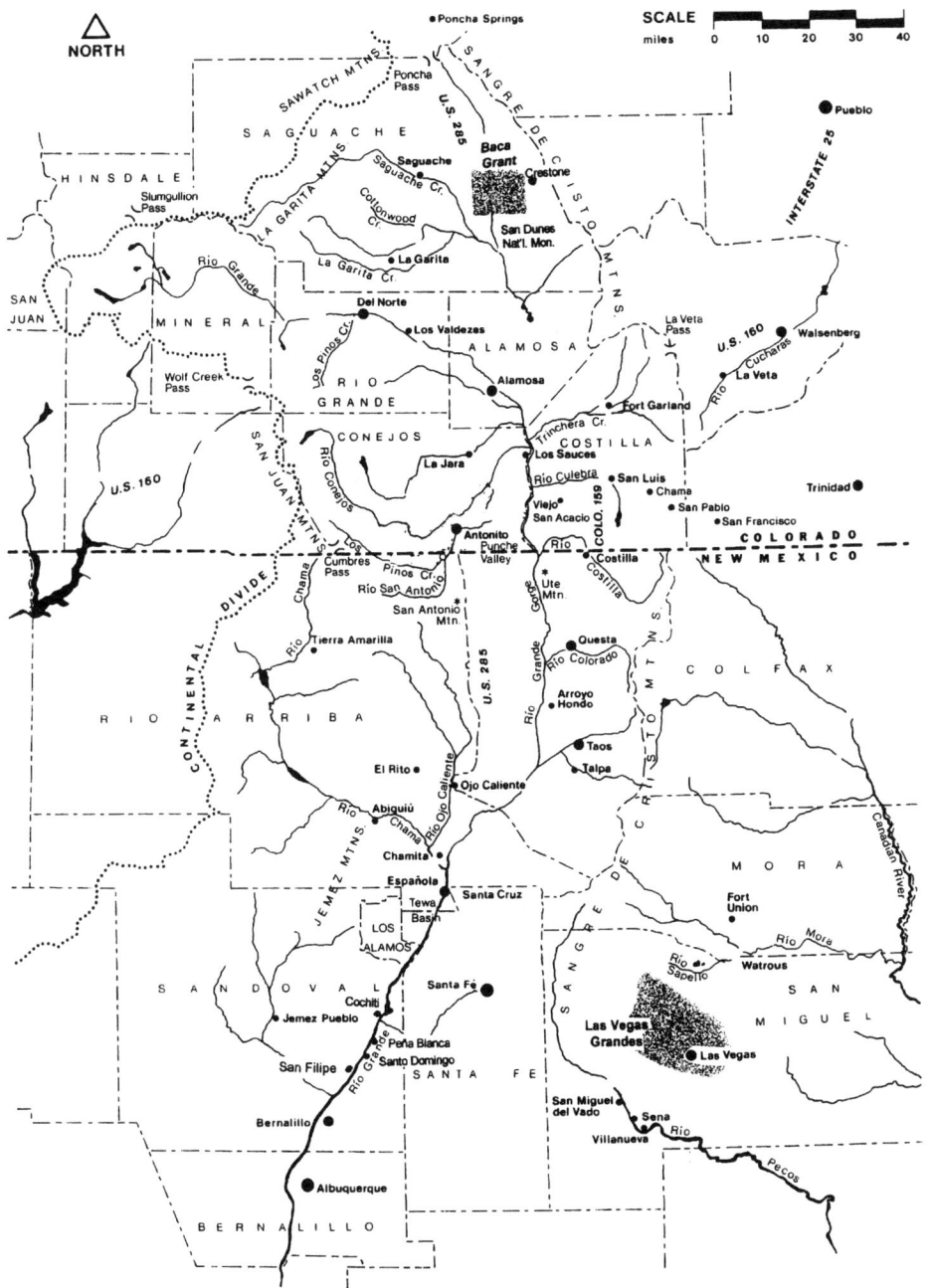

Map 8.2 Upper and middle Rio Grande basin, Colorado and New Mexico

25, 413, 419). This may have ended his army career and marked his move to Peña Blanca. Charles Cutter (1986: 88–92), in his excellent study of the office of *The Protector de Indios*, also recounts Luis María's problems with his Indian neighbors over land. In 1815, Cochití Pueblo disavowed a sale that some members of the pueblo had made to Luis María, claiming that "the transaction was the result of intimidation and fraud." He was accused of preempting 14 corn fields. At the same time, the Santo Domingo Pueblo Indians claimed some of the disputed land as a result of inaccurate measurement of their boundaries. Appealing through their *Protector*, Felipe Sandoval, the Indians convinced Governor Alberto Maynez to order Cabeza de Baca off the lands, leaving his houses and farmland to the pueblo. Baca did not leave, and a contingent of Cochití Indians carried their case south to a higher authority, the *Protector de Indios* in Durango (Mexico). Joaquin Reyes argued their case, citing the many Spanish laws enacted to protect the Indians and noting that Cabeza de Baca, besides the above transgressions on their lands, had used their water for his fields and had imprisoned them, put them in stocks, and whipped them when they had protested his actions.

Luis María hired a Durango attorney, Rafael Bracho, to defend him. Bracho argued against the special privileges enjoyed by the Indians under Spanish law, insisting that the Indians took advantage of their protection to cause harm to the Spanish settlers. The *Asesor* in Durango deferred judgment, pointing out that such appeals should be heard before the *Audiencia* of Guadalajara, under whose jurisdiction New Mexico was at that time. Somehow, however, the *expediente* (collection of depositions) of these proceedings wound up at the *Juzgado general de Indios* in Mexico City, followed by the persistent Cochití Indians who not only requested a legal representative to present their case against Cabeza de Baca in Guadalajara, but also asked for funds to finance their trip home. They were given both, and the tribunal in Guadalajara, on February 27, 1819, also found in their favor. Cabeza de Baca was ordered off the disputed tracts and assessed court costs. He apparently satisfied his debt with the payment of eight pack mules for the military company in Santa Fe (SANM, Series 2, Roll 22, fr. 400).

I have gone into some detail over Luis María's family and the above incident not only because it reveals something about his career and character, some of the myths he may have invented about himself, and the nature of interethnic relations between some Spanish settlers and their Indian neighbors, but also because I strongly suspect that these proceedings against him are closely connected to the land grant called Las Vegas Grandes he purportedly received from the Provincial *Diputación* of Durango in 1821. Baca Location No. 4 derives from the Las Vegas Grandes grant, so the circumstances surrounding the award of the latter grant, including how Spanish this "old Spanish land grant" is, become of considerable interest (Map 8.2.).

The question of the peculiar history of the background of Baca Location No. 4 will now be explored.

THE LAS VEGAS GRANDES GRANT

In the documents submitted to the Surveyor General of New Mexico (SANM 1, SG #20, Rolls 14 and 15 contain the information cited below unless otherwise indicated) for adjudication of the grant in 1854 is one signed by Luis María, addressed to no one, and dated "New Mexico, January 16th, 1821," the date that other documents claim the Las Vegas Grandes grant was made to him by the Durango *Diputación*. He asks on behalf of himself and those 17 male children for a "certain tract of land suitable for cultivation and pasturage, called the Vegas Grandes." He states, "being in the above condition" (i.e., with all those sons) and much confined, he suffers many injuries, and wants the land granted to him to cultivate the soil, pasture the animals he has, and live in "the quietude and repose I aspire to." The references to his confinement and suffering are apparently the result of his losses in the Cochití case. He goes on to say that the same grant was made to him in company with eight citizens of El Bado (San Miguel del Bado) on the 18th of February last, but since those persons take no interest in the grant, he is renewing his application to have the land donated to him and his children.

It was very unusual for the Governor and Deputation of one Province to make a grant in another (in fact, this is the only instance known to me), but authorities in Durango apparently approved the grant to Luis María providing that the others did indeed have other pasture lands and had erected no buildings.

Perhaps Luis María appealed in Durango, knowing that he was in disrepute in Santa Fe and unlikely to receive any favors from that government, and perhaps he had made some influential contacts there when defending himself in the Cochití case (my suspicion is shared by Ebright 1994: 175). Although the New Mexico Governor and Deputation approved the regrant, he apparently was not put in possession of the land, although it was so ordered on October 17, 1821, and again in 1823. In 1825, his eldest son, Juan Antonio, saying his father had lost the act of possession, again approached the New Mexico Deputation asking to have the Durango grant confirmed to his father and sons and to be placed in possession of the land by the *alcalde* of San Miguel del Bado (Mexican Archives of New Mexico, Proceedings, Book 2, folio 40). Towards the end of the same year, Luis María's sons Miguel and Mateo appeared before the *alcalde* of San Miguel del Bado yet again requesting to be put in possession, but that man claimed to be too ill to do so. On January 13, 1826, Luis María, signing himself "persecuted" appealed to Governor Narbona to be placed in possession and again the *alcalde* was ordered to do so. No act of possession, however, is present in any of the documents on this grant. Only depositions, attesting to Baca's use of the land to graze his stock of cattle, sheep, and horses, demonstrate his use of Las Vegas Grandes. According to these depositions (collected by the Surveyor General, SANM, Series 1, SG No. 20) the land was never cultivated nor had houses other than an *jacal* (rude shelter of chinked logs and brush) been built on it. One deponent consistently referred to Baca's possession as an *hijuela*, not a *merced* (land grant). *Hijuela*, as used in New Mexican documents, usually means a deed to a part or share of a tract of land (Ebright, 1994: 382; Westphall, 1987: 225). There were six people, more or less, when the (probably) Pawnee Indians took all the horses and mares (and the 3,000 sheep mentioned in one deposition?) and drove them off.

Luis María had served as *alcalde* of San Miguel del Bado in 1820 according to Ebright (1994: 175) and may well have started using the land then and aligned himself with some other residents there in petitioning for the first grant. Perhaps he disregarded his *compañeros* when applying for the regrant for himself and sons only. He must have incurred disfavor in that community for its local officials to stall and never actually place him in possession. If, as the one deponent claimed, Baca had an *hijuela*, a share, it would seem that others from San Miguel del Bado had shares, too. Perhaps they were unaware that Baca had claimed the whole in his second petition. The documentation on these grants made in Durango, especially the first, is scanty and somewhat confusing. Although other scholars (e.g. Ebright 1994, and Arellano and Vigil 1985) accept the record, Luis María's maneuverings border on the mythic. He seems to have taken advantage of the chaos between two administrations—Spain and Mexico—two provincial governors, and several people of San Miguel del Vado over whom he may have exercised some authority.

He died a violent death and was buried on May 21, 1827 (Photo 8.2). Accused of harboring contraband furs for American fur trappers and refusing to turn them over, he was shot by soldiers of his own country under Governor Narbona's orders (Weber 1968: 129; Cleland 1950: 219). Described in 1776 as a small man, five feet three inches tall, black hair and eyebrows, beardless with fair skin, and a scar above his right eyebrow (Lucero 1995: 244), Luis María had a career that encompassed much history and gave rise to perhaps even more myth.

BACA GRANT LOCATION NO. 4

The circumstances surrounding the Las Vegas Grandes grant are indeed peculiar but those surrounding its off-shoot, Baca Location No. 4, are even more so. They attest both to the political clout of the Cabeza de Baca family and their allies and to their acumen in taking advantage of political chaos during, first, the transition of sovereignty from Spain to the Republic of Mexico (1821–22) and, second, the transferal of what we call the Southwest to the United States by the Treaty of Guadalupe Hidalgo in 1848.

Baca Location No. 4 was derived, in a circuitous way, from the Las Vegas Grandes grant relinquished by him and his family apparently not long after Cabeza de Baca's death. Since it was not occupied and kept in use, another grant to the same lands was made by the Territorial Deputation of New Mexico in 1835 to a group of settlers (mostly from San Miguel del Bado) who subsequently established farms and ranches and founded the town of Las Vegas, New

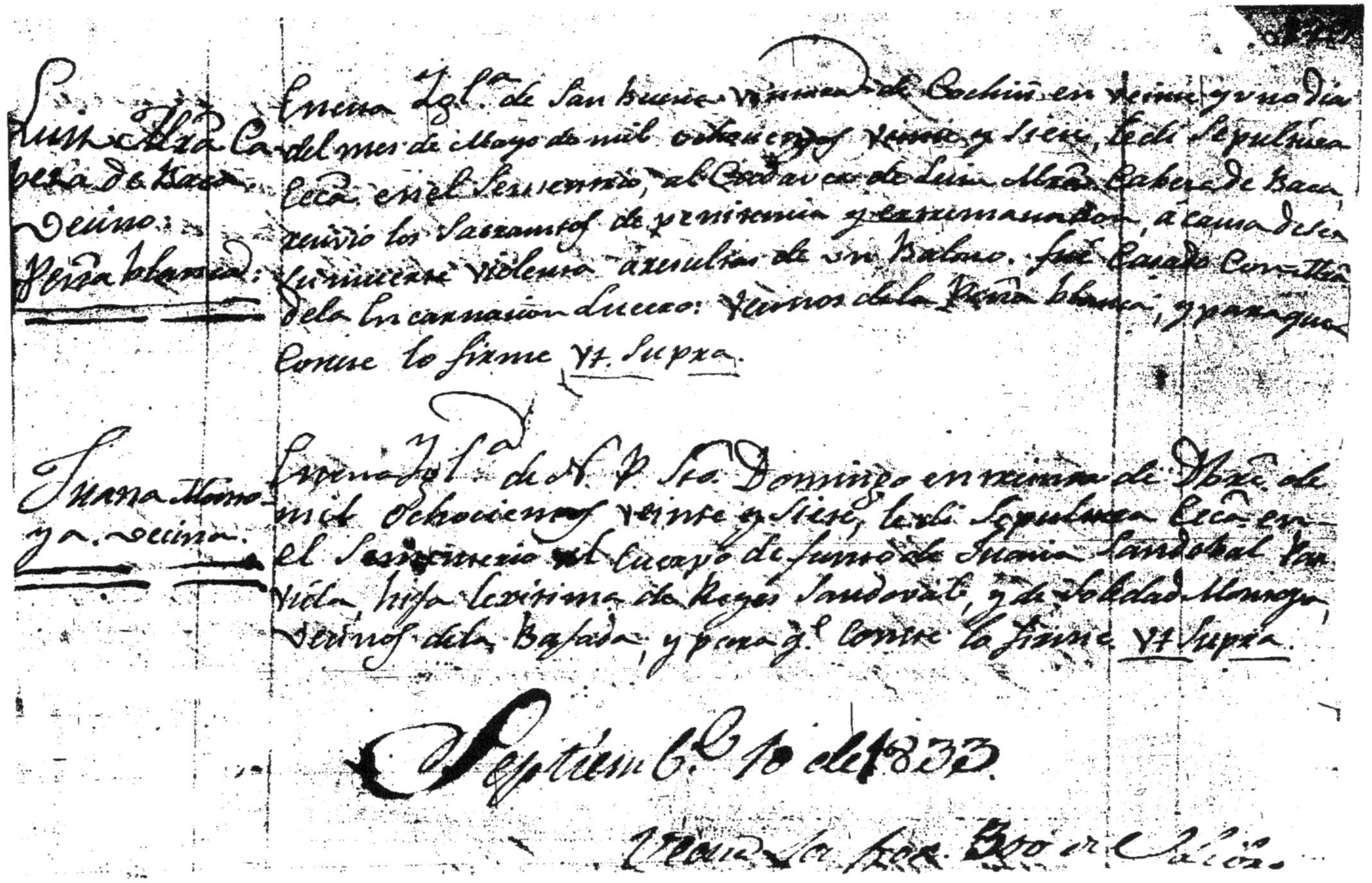

Photo 8.2 Record of Luis María Cabeza de Baca's burial

Mexico (SANM, Series 1, SG No. 20; Ebright 1994: 175–200; also see Arellano and Vigil 1985).

In 1854 the United States set up the Office of the Surveyor General of New Mexico whose duties included adjudicating land claims by the area's previous citizens of Spain and Mexico and recommending their confirmation or denial by the U.S. Congress (Ebright, 1994: 37–45). The first Surveyor General, William Pelham, did not know Spanish nor was he equipped with materials on Spanish and Mexican law. The most grievous part of this process, as Malcolm Ebright has written, was that "it lacked the essential element of all true adjudication—due process of law" (Ebright 1994: 39). The system was open to fraud and injustices, hence the long history of legal wrangling over many of the New Mexican land grants.

Heeding the Surveyor General's call to submit their claims, the Baca heirs as well as the second set of grantees presented their documents on Las Vegas Grandes to the Surveyor General, who, declining to decide which claim was the most valid, sent both on to the U.S. Congress in 1859 for confirmation. John S. Watts, the Bacas' lawyer, and formerly an associate justice of New Mexico's first Territorial Supreme Court, argued that it would be most unfortunate to dislodge the several hundred poor people then inhabiting the Las Vegas grant and magnanimously offered, on behalf of the Bacas, to accept other unappropriated lands of equal extent commensurate with the size of the Las Vegas Grandes after its outer boundaries had been surveyed (SANM, Series 1, SG No. 20, File 6). Feeling equally generous and not wanting to disrupt a thriving community, Congress awarded the Cabeza de Baca heirs five 100,000 acre "locations" or "floats" as they were then called, to be selected from the public domain, and confirmed the Las Vegas Grandes grant to the settlers on it (An Act to confirm . . . U.S. 12 Stat. 71 [1860]). It was stipulated that the Baca locations lands were to be uninhabited and nonmineral and selected from the public domain.

The Bacas were really only interested in the lands that became Baca Location No. 1—the lush pasture lands in the giant caldera known as the Valle Grande atop the Jemez Mountains, the purchase of which has been approved recently by the U.S. Congress and signed into law by the President (*Denver Post* 7/13/00). It adjoins Bandelier National Monument and Santa Fe National Forest. Thus, after 140 years, this land had been returned to the public domain.

Grateful to Watts for getting them 500,000 acres from the United States Congress, the Bacas sold to their lawyer in return for his services and the sum of three thousand dollars, three of these locations (there were five in all, one in Arizona, three in New Mexico, and one in Colorado). Location No. 4 had been selected by Watts' friend, ex-Territorial Governor of Colorado William Gilpin, and Watts promptly contracted with Gilpin in 1862 to buy it for 30 cents an acre (in fact, the contract between Gilpin and Watts predates the deed of the land in 1864 by the Bacas to Watts (SANM, Series 1, SG No. 20). Although the Territory of Colorado was not created until 1861, it was deemed legitimate to have the grant located there since the area was part of the Territory of New Mexico when Congress awarded the lands in 1860. However, Gilpin had bragged to the Commissioner of the General Land Office (forerunner of the U.S. Bureau of Land Management) about acquiring the location, which, he thought, contained rich minerals in the mountains. Commissioner Edwards warned the Surveyor General of Colorado that Gilpin's application could not be approved since Congress had directed that float lands were to be nonmineral (Records of the Surveyor General, Record Group No. 49, Entry 239, vol. 1, NAR). Despite Gilpin's protests, a new survey was made locating the grant out of the mountains; but in the meantime Gilpin had contracted to buy the Sangre de Cristo Grant in the southeastern part of the San Luis Valley whose boundaries he eventually parleyed into just short of one million acres (Brayer 1949, vol. 1, details this acquisition; the settlers use rights on common lands for this grant are still under litigation, see also see Stoller 1980, 1985, 1998).

Gilpin eventually sold Baca Location No. 4 in 1886 to George Adams for $350,000 who made it into a successful cattle ranch and whose successors sold it, in the early 1970s, to the Arizona Land and Cattle Company (the name later changed to AZL Resources, Inc.) of Phoenix, Arizona, an agribusiness conglomerate. As already noted, this company subdivided the foothills—the most attractive parts of the land—built a resort complete with a golf course, called it the Baca Grande, and proceeded to sell "parts of an old Spanish Land Grant" to vacationers and retirees. When sales faltered, the aforementioned Maurice Strong, bought it (Colorado District Court, Water Division 3, Case #86CW46; also Boychuk 1989; Knowlton 1980; Karnes 1970).

BACA LOCATION NO. 4 AND WATER LITIGATION

The grant lands of Baca Location No. 4 snuggle up to the western flanks of the Sangre de Cristo Mountains just north of Great Sand Dunes National Monument (Maps 8.1 and 8.2). The majority of the land is located on the San Luis Valley floor, is flat, and ranges in altitude from 7,000 to 8,000 feet. The climate is that of a high desert and the growing season is short. Lands of the Baca grant are sparsely vegetated and have been used mainly as range land. Lying in the rain shadow of the San Juan Mountains to the west, the valley receives less than eight inches of moisture annually. The small creeks rushing down from the precipitous 13,000 and 14,000 foot Crestone peaks above the Baca Grant fan out on the floor. Some water is channeled to irrigate hay meadows before forming swampy areas and small ponds and gradually disappearing into the sandy soil, contributing their water to the underground aquifers. This northern area of the San Luis Valley is considered a closed basin since none of its surface waters are tributary to the Rio Grande which begins in the San Juan Mountains to the northwest and flows south. The Rio Grande and its tributaries in the southern half of the valley provide water for irrigation of commercial crops, the most important of which are potatoes and malting barley. However, it is the waters in the underground aquifers of the closed basin (Figure 8.1) that have brought this grant and its claim to derive from Spanish Colonial administration into the *logos* of Colorado water court.

As previously noted, Strong and his associates formed a company called American Water Development, Inc. (AWDI) amd made an application in 1986 to the District Court, Water Division 3, to withdraw 200,000 feet of water annually from the aquifers underlying the grant (Colorado District Court Case No. 86CW46). They asserted an absolute right of ownership of the groundwater arising from the laws of Spain and Mexico, which awarded this grant. Hoping to quiet the alarm raised by local farmers and ranchers at the prospect of losing water from the aquifers, and promising to contribute to the economy of this chronically poor valley, the applicants proposed to use the water to bring 38,000 acres under cultivation, or, if not used for irrigation, for "municipal, domestic, industrial, commercial . . . and all other beneficial uses." Although the filing was subsequently modified to some extent, the claims for beneficial use were never made more specific. It soon became very clear that the applicants' intent was to transport this water out of the valley and sell it to the rapidly growing, ever thirsty cities of Denver and Colorado Springs along the Front Range of Colorado or ship it down the Rio Grande to equally thirsty New Mexico and Texas.

The management of AWDI, the major holding company, was entrusted to Dale Schaffer, former chairman of the Denver Water Board, which had just recently lost a proposal to place a large dam on the South Platte River (Two Forks Dam) to supply Denver and its suburbs with more water. Board members of AWDI included former governor of Colorado Richard Lamm and William Ruckelshaus, former director of the Environmental Protection Agency, the agency that stopped the Two Forks Dam.

Opposition to AWDI was filed in the district court by various federal, state, and local government agencies, conservancy and irrigation districts, and individual well owners in the San Luis Valley. Collectively known as the Joint Objectors, they taxed themselves heavily to fight AWDI, fearing that the loss of water would destroy their agricultural economy.

AWDI's rights to the Baca Grant's waters deriving from a Spanish land grant were denied by Water Court Judge Robert Ogborn in 1990 when the Joint Objectors' attorneys proved that the Baca Location No. 4 grant was made by the U.S. Congress and not a Spanish Colonial administration. The applicants' other claims to ownership of the underground water rested on their title to the land, no matter which government had awarded the grant. However, the determination that the grant was made by the U.S. Congress meant that their claim was subject to the water laws of Colorado.

Colorado water law is based on the Doctrine of Prior Appropriation, as is that of many Western states. The doctrine, as written in the State Constitution and interpreted by the Colorado courts, states that (1) water in its natural course is public property and not subject to private ownership; (2) a vested right to use the water may be acquired by appropriation and application to beneficial use;

(3) *the person first in time to use the water is first in right*; and (4) beneficial use is the basis, the measure, and the limit of the right (after Colorado Water Conservation Board and U.S. Department of Agriculture *Main Report*: III-6–7, my italics). In 1965 the Colorado General Assembly enacted a Ground Water Management Act, defining groundwater as all water not tributary to any natural stream. Such nontributary waters, if withdrawn, would not affect the rate of direction of flow of a surface stream within 100 years (Vranesh, 1989: 21).

AWDI's application for the water and the right to mine it from the aquifers under the land continued in court and went to full trial in October and November of 1991 before the same judge. The trial lasted five weeks and was a battle of computer models of the underground aquifers, especially the relationship of the unconfined acquifer (which all existing wells tap into and which, by definition, is considered a natural stream) and the confined aquifer (refer to Figure 8.1). AWDI, in its amended application, had proposed to mine the water from the confined aquifer, at a depth of c. 2,500 feet. This aquifer is estimated to hold two billion acre feet of water, although no one knows how much is actually there. An acre foot of water is enough to cover one acre of water one foot deep—326,000 gallons; an average American family of four uses about an acre foot of water a year.

It is estimated that the confined aquifer is recharged by waters from the upper margins of the closed basin at the rate of approximately one million feet a year, and, although this aquifer is not considered tributary to the Rio Grande in the sense that its waters visibly rise to flow on the surface in the valley, it is considered tributary by hydraulic connection to natural streams and springs. Contested by AWDI's models and experts, the models prepared by the State Engineer's Office for administrative purposes and presented by the Joint Objectors were persuasive, and Judge Ogborn ruled to deny the application, as noted earlier. Withdrawing water from the confined aquifer at the rate proposed by AWDI was clearly in excess of that allowed by law and would adversely affect natural stream flow and hence existing wells. In a separate hearing, the judge also awarded a little over three million dollars to the Joint Objectors for legal fees, expenses, and so forth (Colorado District Court, Water Division 3, Case No. 86CW46).

AWDI took the whole case on appeal to the Colorado Supreme Court, including the claim that title to the underground water ran with the land grant made by Spain (Colorado Supreme Court Case No. 92SA141). That court ruled on May 9, 1994, upholding in all respects the district water court's judgements, including the award of compensation to the Joint Objectors.

Not long after the supreme court's ruling, AWDI sold the Baca Grant to a new corporation, Stockman's Water Company, backed by California investors in Farallon Capital Management Inc. Gary Boyce, a long-time resident of the area, is the president of Stockman's Water, and he declared an intent to file an application to the district water court to mine 100,000 acres of water a year (*Denver Post* 8/30/98 and 12/30/98). His proposal had some differences from

AWDI's in that surface waters would be removed from agricultural production and used to restore wetlands and mined water would replace it, thus hoping to appease local farmers and ranchers, although they would have to pay the company for the replaced water. The excess mined water would then be sold to the highest bidder—again, presumably, the Front Range cities.

As yet, the application has not been submitted to the district water court. Boyce and Stockman's Water used a different strategy: they induced the Colorado State Legislature to place two ballot initiatives in the state elections in 1998. The first (#15) would have required metering all existing shallow wells (i.e., those tapping the unconfined aquifer) in the closed basin area (the claim was that farmers were wasting a lot of water), and the second (#16), under the guise of generating revenue for state schools, would require all members of the Rio Grande Water Conservation District to pay $40 per acre foot of well water from state land board lands.

The strategy of these two initiatives was perceived by conservancy district members as a way to bankrupt them so they could not mount a court fight when Stockman's Water submitted an application to the district water court. Both sides conducted an impressive media campaign over the initiatives, and Colorado's citizens soundly defeated them in the 1998 election. Most people outside the San Luis Valley felt they had no right to impose restrictions and fees on the people of that Valley and further feared that if the state metered water in one conservancy district, it would soon do so in others. The threats to wildlife, especially migratory bird sanctuaries which are on nearby state lands, and the stability of the Great Sand Dunes National Monument's unique ecosystem, were other persuasive arguments to conservation groups and environmentally conscious Coloradans (the Division of Wildlife could not afford to buy the water for those areas). After losing in the election, Stockman's Water Company has put the grant up for sale for a reported $30,000,000.

The latest development in issues surrounding the Baca Grant is that of incorporating the Baca lands and their waters, confined and unconfined, into the Great Sand Dunes National Monument (whose lands adjoin) and making the Sand Dunes into a National Park. Representative Scott McInnis, whose district includes the San Luis Valley, has introduced a bill into the House of Representatives in the U.S. Congress that would upgrade the Monument to a Park and expand the Monument's 38,000 acres to include the grant which would be purchased. The rationale for this expansion is the distinctive ecosystem, which includes seven species of insects and rodents found nowhere else in the world, that encompasses the Dunes. The other members—but for one—of the Colorado delegation to Congress have declared strong support for this bill, which Governor Bill Owens of Colorado and Secretary of the Interior Bruce Babbit also support. Senator Wayne Allard has introduced a similar bill in the Senate, supported by Colorado's senior Senator Ben Nighthorse Campbell.

Representative Joel Hefley from Colorado Springs is the sole opponent, calling it "a giant pile of sand" and not worthy of national park status. The problem is that Representative Hefley is a senior member of the House Parks and Public Lands subcommittee that considers park designations: hence he can, and so far has, blocked the bill from coming before the full House for a vote. In a recent article in *The Gazette*, Colorado Springs' newspaper, the following conversation is quoted:

McInnis said he's asked Hefley whether his opposition to the sand dunes plan had any-thing to do with an interest by Colorado Springs to get its hand on the water under the Baca Ranch.

He said "no," and I take him on his word for that, McInnis said. (Mary Boyle, *The Gazette* 4/9/00)

After the Colorado Legislature voted to support McInnis' park plan on April 26, Hefley protested that his opposition was not due to the bill impeding "the flow of water to Front Range cities" as had been claimed (*Denver Post* 4/29/00) and stated that he would like "to work with McInnis on a plan to keep water in the valley." He just thinks the Sand Dunes is not worthy of national park designation although the National Park Service does. A later editorial in the same newspaper challenged Hefley's rhetoric (*Denver Post* 5/24/00), but his opposition remained firm.

I, too, believe Representative Hefley when he says he has no interest in Stock-man's Water Co., but politicians incur debts to their supporters, and they have an obligation to protect the interests and future of their constituents. Representa-tive Hefley has served Congressional District 5 for eight terms and ran for reelection (unopposed) in 2000. Lynn Hefley, Congressman Hefley's wife, is a state representative whose district includes northern El Paso County, Douglas County, and the southern suburbs of Denver. She has not minced words about her desire to see the Baca's underground water made available to her Front Range constituency (Soraghan 2000). She, too, ran unopposed for reelection in 2000.

This current debate over the future of the Baca Location No. 4 land grant is not about partisan politics. McInnis, Allard, Nighthorse Campbell, Owens, and the Hefleys are all Republicans, and the Colorado State Legislature has a large Republican majority. It is about land and water, the most important elements in the history, and mythic history, of the Southwest.

Anthropological research on mythology has demonstrated the power of mythic thinking in order to resolve, in dialectic discourse, the oppositions and contra-dictions of human experience and the human historical imagination. The history of the claim that Baca Location No. 4 is an "old Spanish land grant" appears at this point to be an astounding example, in our own times, of the nature of mythic thinking. It has transformed an ambitious rogue, Luis María Cabeza de Baca, whose greatest claim to fame should be his reproductive success, into a hero, commemorated by a gateway. It incorporates a chaos of historical events, has set the stage for a legal dialectic, and brought a poignant power to the ever-present human problem in the Southwest: water in an arid land.

ADDENDUM

On November 22, 2000, President William J. Clinton signed House Bill No. 4095/52547 creating the Great Sand Dunes National Park. The Bill had already been passed by the Senate and the House passed it with one dissenting vote, that of Representative Joel Hefley. The Bill provided $8.5 million towards the acquisition of the adjacent Baca Grant and The Nature Conservancy will attempt to raise additional funds needed depending on negotiations with the owners.

NOTE

I am grateful for a grant (R077–0393–042) from the Colorado Endowment for the Humanities and for a Jackson Fellowship from the Hurlburt Center for Southwest Studies, The Colorado College, both of which provided for research time and travel on this project. The late Dr. Myra Ellen Jenkins assisted with translation of some documents, and archivists J. Richard Salazar, Al Regensberg, and Sandra Jaramillo of the New Mexico State Records Center and their staff helped locate documents, as did the staff at the National Archives-Denver Branch. The librarians at Adams State College provided access to their vertical files on the Baca Ranch. Judge Robert Ogborn, Colorado District Court, Water Division 3, and his staff kindly made the files on the water litigation cases available and discussed the cases with me. Court motions, briefs and decisions were also made available by Wendy H. Block, Esq., of Hill and Robbins, P. C., and by the State Attorney General's staff. Ralph Curtis, manager of the Bureau of Reclamation in Alamosa, Colorado, supplied more information and spent hours discussing water problems; Ronald Miller of the Soil Conservation Service, John Koshack of the Colorado Division of Wildlife, and Patricia Richmond of Crestone, Colorado, also provided information and insights. Catherine Lowis assisted with the maps and figures. I am grateful to all of these people and especially to Laurie Weinstein for her patience and support.

REFERENCES

Adams State College Library. Colorado Room, Baca File. Alamosa, CO.
An Act to confirm certain private land claims in the Territory of New Mexico. 1860. Chapter 167, U.S. 12 Stat. 71.
Archives of the Archdiocese of Santa Fe. Santa Fe: New Mexico State Records Center. Microfilm.
———. 1776–1829. Books of Baptism, Cochití.
———. N.d. Books of Baptism, Santo Domingo.
———. 1796–1814. Books of Baptism, Santa Fe.
———. 1776–1845. Books of Burial, Cochití, fr. 463.
———. 1800–1816. Books of Burial, Santa Fe.
Arellano, Anselmo F., and Julián Josué Vigil. 1985. *Las Vegas Grandes on the Gallinas 1835–1985*. Las Vegas: Editorial Telerana.
Betterly, Jessica. 1989. Intercultural and Interpersonal Relationships between the Indians of Santo Domingo and Cochití Pueblos and the Spanish Settlers in New Mexico

during the Spanish Colonial Period. Honors thesis, Dept. of Anthropology, The Colorado College, Colorado Springs, CO.

Boychuk, Rick. 1989. Money comes calling in a remote poor valley. *High Country News* (Paonia, CO) 21 (21) November 6.

Boyle, Mary. 2000. Hefley still blocks dunes park. *The Gazette* (Colorado Springs) July 6.

Brayer, H. O. 1949. William Blackmore: The Spanish-Mexican Land Grants of Colorado and New Mexico. 2 vols. Denver, CO.

Briggs, Charles, and John R. Van Ness, eds. 1989. *Land, Water and Culture in New Mexico.* Albuquerque: University of New Mexico Press.

Chávez, Fray Angelico. 1954. *Origins of New Mexico Families.* Santa Fe, NM: The Historical Society of New Mexico.

————. n.d. Roots of New Mexico Families. Manuscript copy in the New Mexico State Records Center, Santa Fe, NM.

Chevalier, Francois. 1963. *Land and Society in Colonial Mexico.* Berkeley, CA: University of California Press.

Cleland, Robert G. 1950. *This Reckless Breed of Men: The Trappers and Fur Traders of the Southwest.* New York, NY: Alfred A. Knopf.

Colorado District Court. Water Division 3, Case No. 86CW46. Alamosa, CO.

Colorado Supreme Court, Case No. 928A141. Denver, CO.

Colorado Water Conservation Board and United States Department of Agriculture. 1978. *Main Report. Water and Related Land Resources, Rio Grande Basin, Colorado.* Denver, CO.

Cutter, Charles R. 1986. *The Protector de Indios in Colonial New Mexico 1659–1821.* Albuquerque, NM: University of New Mexico Press.

Denver Post. August 30, 1998.

————. December 30, 1998.

————. April 29, 2000.

————. May 24, 2000.

————. June 24, 2000.

Ebright, Malcolm. 1987. New Mexico Land Grants: The Legal Background. In *Land, Water, and Culture,* edited by Charles L. Briggs and John R. Van Ness, pp. 15–64. Albuquerque, NM: University of New Mexico Press.

————. 1994. *Land Grants and Lawsuits in Northern New Mexico.* Albuquerque, NM: University of New Mexico Press.

The Gazette (Colorado Springs). April 9, 2000.

Jenkins, Myra Ellen. 1988. Personal communication.

Karnes, Thomas L. 1970. *William Gilpin Western Nationalist.* Austin, TX: University of Texas Press.

Knowlton, Clark S. 1980. The Town of Las Vegas Community Grant. In *Spanish and Mexican Land Grants in New Mexico and Colorado,* edited by John R. Van Ness and Christine M. Van Ness, pp. 12–21. Manhattan, KS: Sunflower University Press.

Lamar, Howard Roberts. 1966. *The Far Southwest 1846–1912.* New Haven, CT: Yale University Press.

Leonard, Olen. 1970. *The Role of the Land Grant.* Albuquerque, NM: Calvin Horn.

Lucero, Donald. 1995. *The Adobe Kingdom.* Pueblo, CO: El Escritorio.

McWilliams, Carey. 1968. *North from Mexico; the Spanish-speaking people of the United States.* New York: Greenwood Press.

Mexican Archives of New Mexico. *Proceedings*. Book 2, folio 40. New Mexico State Records Center, Santa Fe, NM.

Meyer, Michael C. 1984. *Water in the Hispanic Southwest: A Social and Legal History*. Tucson, AZ: University of Arizona Press.

———. 1985. The Legal Relationship of Land to Water in Northern Mexico and the Hispanic Southwest. *New Mexico Historical Review* 60: 61–79.

Nuttal, Zelia. 1921. Royal Ordinances Concerning the Laying out of New Towns. *Hispanic American Historical Review* 4: 743–753.

Perrigo, Lynn. 1985. *Historic Leaders in New Mexico*. Santa Fe, NM: Sunstone Press.

Records of the Surveyor General. Record Group No. 49, entry 237, vol.1. Denver, CO: National Archives, Denver Branch.

Simmons, Marc. 1969. Settlement Patterns and Village Plans in Colonial New Mexico. *Journal of the West* 8: 7–21.

Soraghan, Mike. 2000. Water worries bring dunes park supporters together. *Denver Post*, June 23.

Spanish Archives of New Mexico (SANM). Series 1 and 2. Santa Fe, NM: New Mexico State Records Center. Microfilm.

Stoller, Marianne L. 1980. Grants of Desperation, Lands of Speculation: Mexican Period Land Grants in Colorado. In *Spanish and Mexican Land Grants in New Mexico and Colorado*, edited by John R. Van Ness and Christine M. Van Ness, pp. 22–39. Manhattan, KS: Sunflower University Press.

———. 1985. Preliminary Manuscript on the Sangre de Cristo Grant. Expert Witness Testimony. Case No. 81CV5. Colorado District Court, Costilla County, CO.

———. 1998. *Report on the History and Claims for Usufruct Rights by the Residents of the Culebra River Villages on Portions of the Sangre de Cristo Land Grant*. Expert Witness Testimony. Case No. 81CV5. Colorado District Court, Costilla County, CO.

Twitchell, Ralph Emerson. 1914. *The Spanish Archives of New Mexico*. Vol. 1. Cedar Rapids, IA: The Torch Press.

Tyler, Daniel. 1990. *The Mythical Pueblo Rights Doctrine Water Administration in Hispanic New Mexico*. El Paso, TX: University of Texas at El Paso, Southwestern Studies Series No. 91.

———. 1991. Underground Water in Hispanic New Mexico: A Brief Analysis of Laws, Customs, and Disputes. *New Mexico Historical Review* 66: 287–301.

Van Ness, John R. 1980. Introduction. In *Spanish and Mexican Land Grants in New Mexico and Colorado*, edited by John R. Van Ness and Christine M. Van Ness, pp. 3–11. Manahattan, KS: Sunfower University Press.

Vranesh, George. 1989. *Primer—Colorado Water Law*. Westminster, CO: Front Range Community College.

Weber, David J. 1968. *The Taos Trappers*. Norman, OK: University of Oklahoma Press.

———. 1988. *Myth and History of the Hispanic Southwest: Essays by David J. Weber*. Albuquerque, NM: University of New Mexico Press.

Westphall, Victor. 1983. *Mercedes Reales*. Albuquerque, NM: University of New Mexico Press.

White, Koch, Kelley, and McCarthy, the New Mexico State Planning Office. 1971. Land Title Study. Santa Fe, NM: New Mexico State Planning Office.

9

Collaborative Conservation: Peace or Pacification? The View from Los Ojos

Maria Varela

Editor's Note: The 1990's saw deep divisiveness and conflict between some environmentalist groups and rural people who use the public lands in the West. In reaction, several communities attempted collaborative efforts to identify the commonalities between land dependent people and environmentalists. In those cases where environmentalists and public land users were similar in race, education and economic status, the collaborative effort had some successes. However the following essay indicates that these successes cannot be considered a template for all communities . . . in particular in the Southwest, where racism and poverty create an uneven playing field for people of color.

Sin Tierra No Hay Justicia: Sin Justicia No Hay Paz (Without land there is no justice: without justice there is no peace) graces a banner hung on the marbled walls of the New Mexico State Capitol Rotunda during the 1996 legislative session. In front of the banner, weavers arrange multicolored piles of wool, a spinning wheel and loom. There is a table of wild-crafted herbs, a corner where a drum maker works, and a display of micacious clay pottery. A woodcarver, oblivious to the throngs of politicians, lobbyists, and others attendant to the political process, remains absorbed in bringing a face out of gnarly wood. The materials used by these artisans originated in the national forests of northern New Mexico. *Poquiteros* (small-scale sheep and cattle growers), weavers, woodworkers, potters, and *curanderas* (healers) came together to make a gentle but powerful statement against environmental organizations seeking to close public lands to grazing and timber harvesting as well as to capturing ancestral village and tribal waters for instream flow.

The weavers, reluctant warriors in this latest struggle by villagers to retain centuries-old pastoral cultures, would prefer to be back in their workshop in the northern New Mexico village of Los Ojos, educating visitors through displays of beautifully woven rugs and tapestries. There, it is more comfortable to talk about how their enterprise, Tierra Wools, and its parent organization, Ganados Del Valle (a nonprofit with the mission of creating sustainable economies from cultural, agricultural, and natural resources), rescued the rare Churro sheep breed from near extinction and revitalized the centuries' old Rio Grande weaving tradition. But the weavers recognized that, in this continual struggle, artistic expression alone will not safeguard ancestral land and water rights.

Several hours south of Los Ojos, from pricey refurbished adobe and Victorian offices in Santa Fe, New Mexican environmentalists have fired off a nearly decade-long barrage of lawsuits, seeking domain over grazing and timber resources on public lands under the Endangered Species Act. To many northern New Mexicans of color, these barrages are the latest in a conquest that began in 1848 with the signing of the Treaty of Guadalupe Hidalgo and has not stopped since. The battlefield in this latest incarnation of conquest is in the courts and streets. In the fall of 1995 environmentalists shut down the Carson and Santa Fe National Forests to all timber harvesting (including fuelwood which villagers depended on for cooking and heating) because of the presence of spotted owl habitat. (The U.S. Forest Service spent almost two million dollars during the early 1990's attempting and failing to find the owls in either national forest.) Unable to afford legal council to respond to the injunction, villagers launched protests. Environmentalists were hung in effigy in October. Two months later, a candlelight prayer vigil was organized in Santa Fe, bringing out more than 400 people from northern and southern New Mexico. Unwittingly, the environmentalists' lawsuits had done what had never before been achieved in New Mexico's history: collaboration between Anglo ranchers and loggers from the south with the traditional Hispano *Poquiteros* and fuelwood harvesters from the north.

There is a long history that led up to the candlelight procession on that snowy December night. It began in the late 1890s, when U.S. and European resource barons clear-cut the bountiful forests that stretched almost uninterrupted from Santa Fe County north through Colorado, damaging the snow-holding capacity of upstream timber stands, leaving downstream agricultural villages to struggle with silt laden irrigation ditches and low or no water during dry years. Then in 1905, Theodore Roosevelt, ironically a hero of the conservation movement, commandeered the common lands of villages and pueblos (guaranteed by the Treaty of Guadalupe Hidalgo) into the Carson and Santa Fe National Forests.[1] After that, livestock barons purchased grazing allotments in the forests and sent truckloads of cattle from Texas, Oklahoma, and eastern Colorado, seeking the plentiful grasses that once sustained village and pueblo flocks and herds. Local families, still on a mixed barter and cash subsistence economy, found it difficult to compete with the livestock barons for these grazing allotments.

As bottomland villages were severed from upland grazing ranges, valley floor pastures became degraded and lost their capacity to sustain local communities. Before conquest, *Poquiteros* moved livestock from lowland to upland ranges and back again. As a result of this intensive but well-timed grazing system (with origins on the Iberian Peninsula), forage maintained its vigor and grew so high that elders recount how "we'd have to be up on horseback in order to find the lambs or calves."[2] Losing uplands grazing meant reducing herds and flocks to sizes that were not economically feasible. But because livestock were handed down from generation to generation, buffering families from hunger as well as symbolizing connections to ancestors (livestock were often used as dowry or gifts), many villagers clung tenaciously to their pastoral culture, which once fed family, village, and region while renewing the environment.

Those common lands not commandeered into the National Forest system were either seized for back taxes, stolen by Santa Fe-based land speculators or sold by village opportunists without consent from the rest of the residents. All of these acts broke the Treaty of Guadalupe Hidalgo, which promised that "property of every kind, now belonging to Mexicans . . . shall be inviolably respected . . . and all Mexicans shall enjoy . . . guarantees equally ample as if the same belonged to citizens of the United States."[3] As land eroded out of village and pueblo control, generations of knowledge about how to live on and with that land began to unravel. Although rarely recognized as such, this knowledge is primary environmental science. How to steward the grasses, the waters, the forests, and the soil in distinct ecosystems is a science steadily built over time through the process of trial and error. When the environmental science earned by these trials was trampled by outside forces and (in some cases) inside *oportunistas*, environmental degradation, poverty, and its bitter social fruits followed.

Five counties north of Santa Fe, in both New Mexico and Colorado, are designated by the U.S. Department of Agriculture as "Persistent Low Income Counties."[4] This means that since the census started tracking income levels in 1939, these counties have remained in the bottom quintile of all U.S. non-metro counties. Broken treaties and the industrialization of livestock production and timber harvesting over the last 150 years left villagers to eke out sustenance from several sources: sales of livestock, fuelwood, hay, flagstone, *vigas*, (posts), pinon nuts, and traditional arts and crafts. In the past, these revenues were supplemented by the most able-bodied in the family moving into the migrant farmworker stream, leaving the "ranch" to the elderly or to women with small children. Today, local villagers still take seasonal jobs or commute to urban centers, working low-paying, full-time jobs while maintaining the ranch back home. The goal is to insure a continuation of *la herencia*, or the handing down of family lands to the next generation, as well as to protect oneself from the deep poverty often experienced by those elders who have lost their land.

CONQUEST RECONSTRUCTED

Environmentalists, many of them new transplants to New Mexico, look at the ravages left by the industrialization of public lands and, perhaps to their credit, have decided to fix it. But it is unfathomable why environmentalists would not look to learn from the people who have lived for hundreds of years in agro-pastoral communities, which buffer public lands, as the first to be consulted and as peers in this effort. After all, Hispano villagers and Native Americans have life-long knowledge of these lands and have fought extractive industries and the U.S. Forest Service long before the modern environmental movement. By rendering people of color invisible, or vilifying them as violent or tools of livestock and lumber transnational corporations, many environmentalists have, in their historical and cultural illiteracy, assumed the cloak of conqueror.

Unexamined by environmentalists is the violence of poverty. Persistent poverty and economic dependency has resulted from a century and a half process where national and international capital forces sought to gain wealth and make more productive the seemingly idle or underutilized natural resources, land, and labor of western communities of color. As industrialists had their way with these resources, poverty and environmental degradation became a structural part of much of the rural West. It is not possible to repair the environment without repairing the inequities produced by this violent history.

THE NEW WEST AS A RE-COLONIZING STRATEGY

The single biggest threat to a sustainable environment are the so-called "New West economic growth strategies," rampant throughout the region. This latest colonizing wave comes on skis, golf carts, river rafts, and jeeps. Many environmentalists view recreation and tourism as "walking more gently on the land," a therapeutic antidote to mining, logging and grazing. Yet the growing tourism and recreation economy in the West has resulted in increased air and water pollution, degradation of scenic resources and loss of agricultural lands (and therefore wildlife habitat) to subdivisions and resorts. Proponents of a more environmentally beneficial economy generally dismiss grazing as economically unimportant to the West while ironically the demand for naturally grown meats and other natural agricultural products continues to increase annually. Others claim that tourism/recreational service jobs pay better, require more skills and higher educational levels, and have more potential for advancement. Unexamined is who benefits from the higher paying jobs and who gets the menial jobs. Virtually no published environmentalist has examined the impact of racism and economic inequity in a heavily tourist/recreational economy.

A case in point is the growth of the tourism/recreational economy in Taos County, New Mexico. In the 1950s, local people were told that expanding tourism would create jobs and improve incomes. Since the 1960s, gross revenues in Taos County have risen commensurably with the expansion of recreation and attendant retailing, restaurant, and service businesses. But even when economic activity doubles, as it did between 1980 and 1990, poverty statistics remain virtually unchanged. In 1980, the official poverty rate for Taos County was 25.7 percent. In 1990, it was 25.4 percent.

Clearly, the increased flow of revenues through the tourism/recreational economy of Taos had little effect on material poverty and has actually exacerbated ancillary poverty, including loss of ancestral lands and water, loss of resilience in family income-generating activities, increased taxes, and the erosion of community cohesion produced by growing racism and economic inequality. In the fall of 1999, a recent transplant to Taos published a feature article in the *Sunday New York Times* where she recounted incidents of perceived hostility towards her by young Hispano males which resulted in her decision to purchase a handgun for protection. She wistfully recounted her reasons for coming to this breathtakingly beautiful mountain valley from her previous urban residence and expressed anger at Taos' "dirty little secret" of hostile and violent locals.

RECONNECTING CULTURE, ECONOMICS AND THE ENVIRONMENT

In contrast to the neocolonialist economies and increasing social stratification in the New West are the efforts of those indigenous to the region who seek to build sustainable economies by reconnecting the best traditional cultural practices with modern production and marketing strategies. These groups focus on adding value to cultural, natural, and agricultural resources. Educational and cultural tourism are part of these economic development strategies because of the twin opportunities to educate mainstream America and create niche markets. These strategies strive to benefit those with limited economic status and educational levels and whose gender, race, and ethnicity have left them economically marginal. Such strategies require long-term, patient investment to underwrite human capacity building and meet the research and development needs of innovative, local enterprises.

Ganados del Valle, for example, spent seven years (1984–1991) supporting the technical assistance and training needs of Tierra Wools' weavers (operational costs were covered by sales). In 1992, Tierra Wools annual sales reached nearly $350,000, and in 1997 the business was spun off to its weaver-owners. Ganados went on to create four more enterprises from 1990 to 1996, which marketed naturally grown, local meat and produce, regional arts, crafts, and home decor items. Over 150 artisans and agriculturists in the region were assisted in bringing products to market; and 50 new jobs, many in management, were created locally. A work-based academic program was designed to professionalize the staff, nearly all of whom were women, most with a high school education. A small loan fund helped artisans and growers to be more productive, and a scholarship fund supports those wanting to complete their college degrees.

FROM CONFLICT TO COLLABORATION, AND
BACK AGAIN

Despite these accomplishments, the efforts of Ganados were constantly laced with conflict over use of resources. Whether protesting the transfer of agricultural water rights to a proposed ski resort, supporting local land owners in a title dispute with real estate developers, or supporting forest-dependent communities in a lawsuit against the Forest Service for discrimination in the allocation of timber and fuelwood sales, Ganados quickly discovered that one of the major barriers to a sustainable economy was control of natural resources.

The most difficult struggle for Ganados was access to summer grazing for members' flocks. Because the organization returned to the tradition of cooperative grazing (where flocks are pooled and flock owners share the costs of the shepherd), small-scale growers were able to bring their flock numbers up to an economically viable level. This put more pressure on Ganados to locate summer pastures for the growing flocks which was needed to supply the annually increasing demand of the weavers for high quality wool, especially from Churro stock (an ancient sheep breed "descended from the common sedentary sheep of southern Spain whose . . . heritage extended back to Roman times").[5]

In the mid-1980s, Ganados began discussions with New Mexico Game and Fish about the possibility of grazing one of the two state wildlife areas in the valley. Traditionally, Anglo cattle growers had grazed these areas. Ganados, in consultation with the local office of the U.S. Soil Conservation Service (SCS), offered the flock as an intensive grazing management tool to improve the quality and quantity of forage on the refuge, while eradicating what SCS identified as invasive shrubs and weeds, with little or no value for wildlife. After nearly two years of discussion, New Mexico Fish and Game settled the matter by convening a task force. Its first order of business was to put an indefinite moratorium on all grazing in wildlife areas.

In the summer of 1989, after a fruitless search for grazing lands for the cooperative flock, Ganados persuaded the Jicarilla Apache nation to let the sheep graze on its lands. However, several weeks into the summer, the tribe's attorney notified Ganados that the lease was suspended because of pending litigation with Game and Fish, which owned the wildlife area bordering the Apache nation's land. Bringing the flocks back to home pastures in July, before winter feed crops were fully grown and harvestable, would have forced growers to sell their flocks, including the Churro because they could not afford to buy winter feed. By this time, some growers were in their fourth year of a seven-year breed-back cycle required to return the Churro to its original characteristics. After a failed appeal to the Game and Fish for emergency grazing, Ganados growers, in an act of civil disobedience, moved their flocks in the night under a full moon to the adjacent wildlife area.

As soon as news of the "sheep in" hit the media, major New Mexico environmental and hunting organizations were quick to condemn (the wildlife areas are used primarily by Game and Fish for hunters of trophy elk). The shrillness of these attacks took Ganados by surprise as the organization had pursued environmental goals since inception: guard dogs, not poison were used for predator control, sustainable agricultural practices were encouraged with marketing incentives and inappropriate subdivisions were fought. Ganados leaders, as practicing environmentalists, assumed that card carrying environmentalists valued these efforts to protect land, water, wildlife, and local cultures.

Realizing that the strong coalition between hunters and environmentalists would be difficult to defuse, Ganados went to U.S. Senator Jeff Bingaman, considered the state's environmental legislator, to request assistance in convening a professionally mediated retreat. Twenty environmental leaders were invited to the table. Five agreed to come. Ganados found resources to pay the mediators and house the group for three days. Initially, these meetings seemed to defuse mutual hostilities. Ganados leaders learned to respect the dedication of the environmentalists. Environmentalists appeared genuinely moved when, after a lunch prepared by the weavers, the women made presentations on how important Tierra Wools and the members' flocks were to their lives. One weaver said sweetly and candidly "and if we had to put the sheep on the wildlife area again and go to jail, we would do it. It means that much to our families and our community."

Toward the end of the retreat, after sorting through commonalities and differences, the group resolved to go beyond just talking. Action around a mutually agreed-upon project would create genuine collaboration that could create lasting alliances. A land purchasing project in the Chama Valley was conceived, which would meet the environmentalists' desire to buffer development and protect wildlife habitat while meeting Ganados' need for grazing to continue its sustainable development strategy.

But instead of creating lasting alliances, this joint project eventually failed, revealing some core problems with collaborative approaches. Ganados learned that the environmentalists themselves are not united. Their different membership bases and corporate cultures often result in different approaches to environmental problems. Those who came to the table felt they had little influence over those who did not. Those who did not come to the table felt that they didn't need to. They could achieve their environmental goals through the courts and legislatures. Those who came to the table were unwilling to stand up to other environmentalists to ask them to reconsider their tactics. Their continued collaboration with Ganados opened them up to criticism from the nonparticipating groups. When those who worked for national organizations found themselves growing closer to Ganados' point of view, they often ended up at odds with their superiors and membership. One member of the group dropped out because his board would no longer underwrite his working on the joint land purchase project.

In the end, it was Ganados who really needed the joint land project in order to continue its sustainable development strategies. Those environmentalists who participated wanted to demonstrate that they and their organizations were not insensitive to the economic and cultural needs of New Mexico's communities of color. But this was a moral gesture, not a need. When parties in collaboration are not there because of equal needs, the effort depends on the charity of those wanting to make a moral gesture. Charity does not result in justice nor does it reverse the ravages of racism. Without economic justice and authentic cross-cultural learning, collaboration is an exercise in the pacification of rural populations.

CONCLUDING THOUGHTS

The so-called "New West" is neither new nor west. In reality, this region is only west for a few: It is the north for its Hispanic populations and central to the Native American populations who have occupied the region for at least two millennia. It is here in this region that mainstream Anglo-American culture comes to terms with the fact that it is a minority in the world. Managing that role in a mature fashion depends on learning how to negotiate with the diverse cultures and races in the region. Peace in the region (just as peace in the world) depends on all groups examining their ethnocentrism as well as making an authentic commitment to eradicate racism, prejudice, and poverty.

Beginning steps to peace include

1. acceptance of the fact that prejudice and racism towards and between native cultures is only hastening the destruction of indigenous cultures of the region.
2. acceptance of the fact that many treaties with Native Americans and the Treaty of Guadalupe Hidalgo, protecting the land, water, customs, and culture of Hispano and Native Americans continues to be violated. If the region's populations are expected to be law abiding, then all laws including treaties must be observed.

Without the recognitions of these two facts, followed by effective steps to re-mediate their realities, there will be no end to the hostilities. Without justice, there can not be peace.

Without promoting environmentally sound economic development, the West will continue to face even more rapid environmental degradation. The hard fought battles for the acequia systems, the stand-off between environmentalists and Ganados, and the enduring chronic poverty of a quarter of the population of Taos, New Mexico, even while its tourism and recreational economy continues to grow, all suggest that the answers to the future are complex, yet not unreachable. Ganados and other community-based organizations in the region continue to model a kind of economic development, which is inclusive and protects cultural resources and the environment. The challenge for these groups is a lack of appropriate long-term funding to underwrite research, development, technical assistance, and debt and equity investments necessary for successful business development.

Public monies are burdened with often-inappropriate guidelines. Private funders now want a return on their investment, requiring over the short-term certain outcomes and results that can sometimes take a half a generation to accomplish. The most successful development strategies have provided sufficient money, time, and technical assistance resources for people to test business development ideas that fit into—rather than are imposed upon—their culture and community.

NOTES

1. Sylvia Rodriquez, "Land, Water and Ethnic Identity," chapter 6 in *Land, Water and Culture. New Perspectives on Hispanic Land Grants*, ed. Charles L. Briggs and John R. Van Ness (Albuquerque: University of New Mexico Press, 1987).

2. Octaviano Ulibarri, Tierra Amarilla resident, conversations with author, 1986.

3. Treaty reprinted in *Foreigners in their Native Land: Historical Roots of the Mexican Americans*, ed. by David Weber (Albuquerque: University of New Mexico Press, 1973), 162–168.

4. Thomas F. Davis, *Persistent Low-Income Counties in Non-metro America*, RDRR-12 (U.S. Dept. of Agr. Econ. Res. Serv., May, 1979. Updated by Robert A. Hoppe in Jan. 1985).

5. John O. Baxter, *Las Carneradas: Sheep Trade in New Mexico 1700–1860* (Albuquerque: University of New Mexico Press, 1987), 20.

10

The Navajo and Hopi Land Dispute from Historic through Contemporary Times

David Brugge

BACKGROUND

The migration of peoples, resulting in one tribal or linguistic group replacing another, has been a recurring phenomenon in human affairs as far into the past as archeology, comparative studies, and history will permit us to see. Movements of this sort that have taken place within recorded history or human memory often result in continuing conflict over extended periods. Such has been the case in relations between the Navajos and the Hopis in northeastern Arizona, although neither history nor memory can give a clear view of their origins.

The modern Hopi Tribe can trace its cultural ancestry to the Kayenta Branch of the Anasazi and perhaps other related Anasazi peoples, the Sinagua, and certain Mogollon cultures of late prehistoric times, all of whom spring from an archaic cultural base. Thus, culturally they can claim a southwestern past on the order of several millennia (Cordell 1984).

The Hopi language is most closely related to the Numic languages of California, Nevada, and Utah and is, in fact, classed as a Shoshonean language. It is thought to have been spoken in the general area of the Hopi mesas as early as A.D. 500 and, if the Hopi speakers were the carriers of the Virgin Branch culture, perhaps as late as the twelfth century (Hale and Harris 1979: 175; Foster 1996).

It would appear that the Hopis encountered by the initial Spanish explorers were a people of mixed ancestry. As a sociopolitical entity, however, a fairly long occupancy in northeastern Arizona may be postulated, either on the basis of direct ancestry or as inclusive of peoples absorbed in essentially their entirety by an immigrant group. Archeological evidence shows strong cultural continuity from prehistory into the historic period in the vicinity of the modern Hopi mesas.

The Navajos speak an Apachean language, part of the Athabaskan family centered in Alaska and western Canada. They are generally regarded as a unitary cultural linguistic sociopolitical unit that arrived in the Southwest sometime between A.D. 1000 and 1525. That they adapted to their new homeland more thoroughly than their Apache cousins is usually attributed to the incorporation of Puebloan refugees from Spanish rule. The refugees were, at the very least, founders of a significant number of clans among the Navajos. That remnant Anasazi or even surviving Archaic peoples may have joined the immigrant Navajos has also been suggested. The preponderance of the evidence indicates a mixed ancestry for the Navajos as well as the Hopis (Brugge 1979; Brugge 1996: 265; Begay and Roberts 1996: 208; but see Hogan 1991 for a different view).

The circumstances under which the Navajos came to occupy a large territory at one time the home of Puebloan peoples are not known, although several theories have been advanced. The earliest supposition was that they were an enemy people who dispossessed the Pueblos by warfare. As the dating of southwestern ruins became more firmly based, the armed aggression hypothesis lost favor. Defensive Anasazi sites were found to occur ever further into the past. The discovery of abandonment of major areas, beginning about A.D. 1150 and culminating in the total vacating of the San Juan drainage by A.D. 1300, coupled with the lack of identifiable Apachean remains earlier than about A.D. 1500, led to the abandonment of the armed aggression hypothesis (Wilcox 1981: 213–17). Any post-1300 arrival would imply movement into country that was not effectively occupied by others.

Despite the fact that most Anasazi country ceased to be occupied by Puebloan peoples in prehistoric times, some modern Pueblo groups today assert a claim to the entire region on the basis of the Anasazi ruins. The historically documented peoples in the regions formerly occupied by the Anasazi include Navajos, various Apaches, Utes, Paiutes, and Havasupais. The Navajos resided in the greatest part of the former Anasazi territory. While there is some disagreement over just when the Navajos entered the most westerly of these lands, both archeological and historical evidence can be interpreted as placing them in most of the region by early historic times.

There can be no doubt that the Hopis and Navajos have been neighbors for centuries, the only question of consequence being how close Navajo lands came to the Hopi villages. There is good reason to believe that, like neighboring peoples elsewhere, relationships were variable, with good times and bad times. Selective memories can be drawn upon to emphasize friendship or enmity, as has been done in recent years by differing factions in the land dispute.

EARLY HISTORY

The earliest explicitly documented trouble over land occurred in 1819 toward the end of Spanish rule in New Mexico (1598–1821). After 1680, Spanish rule did not extend to the Hopis, and the New Mexicans had a limited knowledge of conditions that far to the west.[1] Navajos driven from their homes by a war with the Spanish colony had settled some five miles from the easternmost Hopi villages on First Mesa. Hopi leaders came to the Zuni Pueblo to request Spanish assistance, and the governor of New Mexico subsequently led a campaign that displaced these Navajos; he anticipated that by doing so he might bring the Hopis back under Spanish control. Again, early in the period of Mexican independence (1823), campaigners in the vicinity of Hopi encountered Navajos but found that while some Hopis were willing to guide the Mexicans against the Navajos, others tried to protect the Navajos. Similarly conflicting reports of Navajo-Hopi relationships continued to be written throughout the years of the Navajo wars until the Navajos went into exile as captives from 1863 to 1868 and again following their return in the latter year (Brugge 1994: 15–25).

When the United States government eventually began efforts to administer affairs among the Hopis, two of the problems with which its agents had to deal were a deep factionalism that existed among the Hopis and the relations between that tribe and the Navajos. The traditional Hopi intratribal antagonisms extend into the prehistoric past and have led to extreme violence and civil war on several occasions (Brew 1949: 31–32; Lomatuway'ma et al. 1993; Thomas 1932: 159; Titiev 1944). At an early date, the English terms coined for the factions were the "Friendlies," those who accepted government activities, and the "Hostiles," those who resisted them. Both factions bid claim to extensive lands, but with significant differences. The Friendlies wanted all of the land for themselves, for they were early converts to the federal economic programs based on establishing farms and ranches well away from the villages. The Hostiles were content to live in their old settlements and saw the Navajos as allies of sorts in fending off the bureaucracy. The Navajos, as long as they filled that role, were welcome to live on the outlying lands as a buffer between the Hopis and the whites. As a result, the Hopi factional split became entangled with relations with the Navajos as well as with the government (Brugge 1969).

One early federal objective was to establish boundaries among the various peoples. The Navajos already had a reservation, established first by the treaty of June 1, 1868, and expanded by two executive orders (Map 10.1). A basic requisite was that the Hopis also live on a reservation. When, in 1882, a dispute arose between an agent and his predecessor who had settled in one of the Hopi villages, the creation of a Hopi reservation was seen as urgent in order that the new agent might have legal authority to expel those whom he considered troublemakers. With no real study of the land use patterns of the Hopis or their neighbors, a tract of land defined by 110° to 111° of west longitude and 35°30' to 36°30' of north latitude was set aside by executive order for "the Moqui [Hopi], and such other Indians as the Secretary of the Interior may see fit to settle thereon" (Correll and Dehiya 1972: 13). While this established a boundary between Indians and non-Indians, it clearly did not resolve the question of intertribal boundaries.

Within little more than six years, the problem of land rights between Navajos

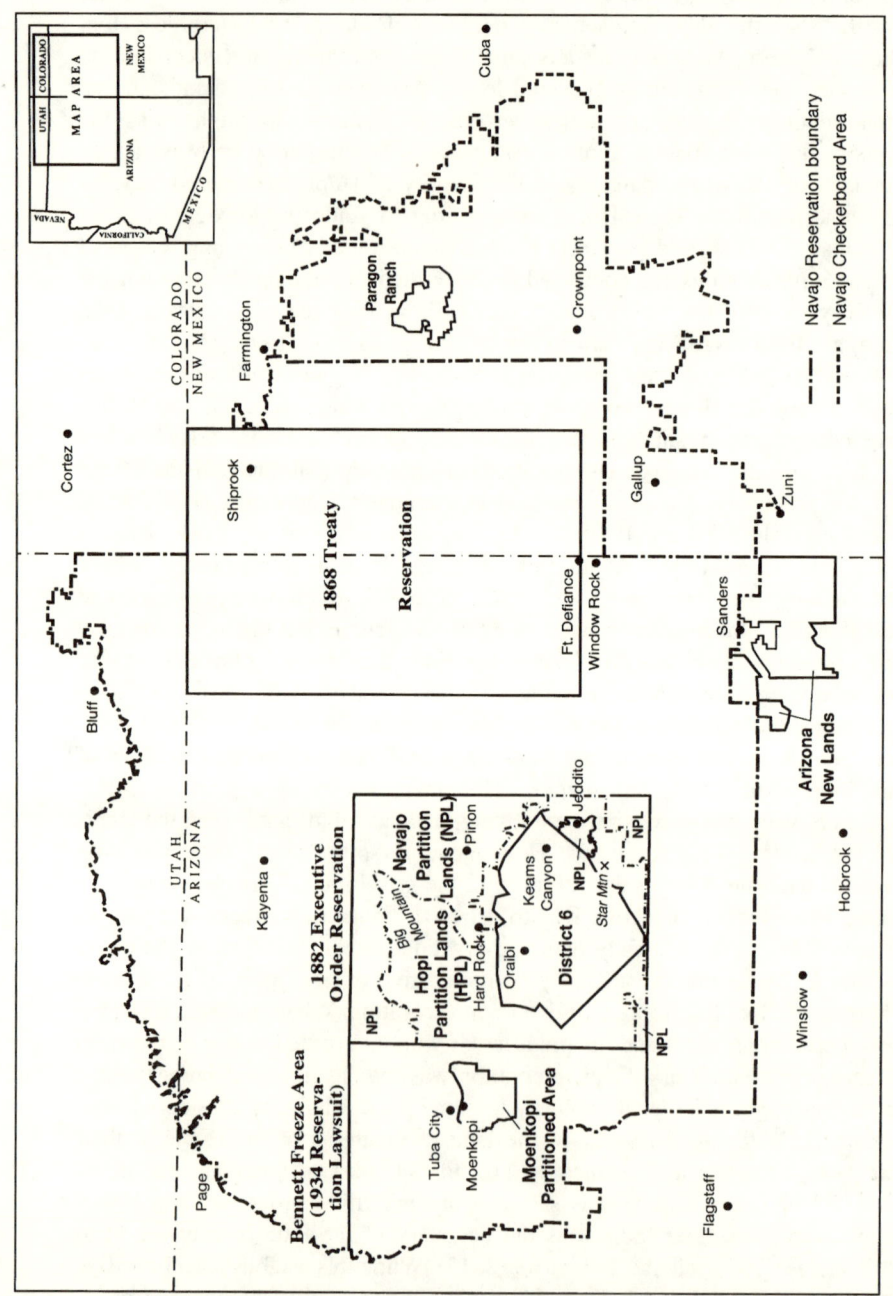

Map 10.1 Navajo and Hopi Reservation and Partition Lands

and Hopis required action when, in response to Hopi complaints, troops were sent to remove Navajos accused of trespassing. Arriving in winter weather, the army found Navajos in established homes and unprepared to be uprooted on short notice. The matter was resolved by ordering the Navajos to remain no less than 12 miles from the villages. This edict was but one of many divisions of land proposed over a period of more than half a century, from as early as 1876 into the 1930s. Finally, in 1936, as a result of the perceived need to control grazing, the Navajo and Hopi countries were divided into several grazing districts or "land management units." Grazing District 6 was designated for Hopi use within the 1882 executive order reservation (Map 10.1). A number of minor boundary adjustments were implemented, and in 1943 the division was given official sanction (Brugge 1994: 25–33).

District 6 did define rights to surface use of the lands by members of the two tribes to a large degree; most Navajos inside the district were ordered to move. A few people of each tribe continued to reside on the other tribe's side of the line, but their numbers were negligible. Trespass issues involving people living within their own tribal boundaries also arose. For example, sometimes unfenced sections of the line allowed free-ranging horses and cattle to cross unimpeded. Sometimes, too, droughts led herders to bring their flocks of sheep and goats to springs still flowing, even when a fence intervened. Other issues, such as rights to use schools and hospitals on each other's reservations, bootlegging and other violations of law on the respective Navajo and Hopi areas, and personal quarrels of various sorts, helped to keep tribal rivalries alive. To what extent any of these were associated with factions within the two tribes is unclear. A newly created Hopi Tribal Council was controlled entirely by the Friendlies; the Hostiles refused to even vote in tribal elections. What is clear is that all official Hopi tribal actions were exclusively done on the initiative of the more progressive faction.

HEALING VS. JONES

As long as conflicts over land involved only the Indians themselves, the powers that were in Washington found little reason to give a search for a more comprehensive solution very high priority (Ibid.: 33–36).

There were, however, other resources that non-Indians coveted and that some tribal leaders, hoping to relieve the chronic poverty of their people, felt should be developed. Coal deposits in the northern part of the 1882 executive order reservation were well known, and it was believed that if these were not soon leased for use in generating electricity, nuclear fuel would quickly make them valueless. Uranium was being mined not far beyond the reservation's boundaries, and oil was thought to exist beneath District 6 itself. The reservation was still in a limbo as far as tribal property rights were concerned. Neither tribe could sign leases for either exploration or exploitation with assurance to the energy companies that it had clear title to the resources (Kammer 1980: 43–44; Brugge 1994: 36–37; Benedek 1992: 132–33).

Both tribes had hired legal counsel in order to deal with the increasingly complex issues of law that they faced. In 1947, the Navajo Tribal Council made a selection from two competing applicants. They awarded a contract to Norman M. Littell, a Republican attorney from Washington, D.C., and rejected John S. Boyden, a Mormon lawyer who was highly placed both in his church's hierarchy and in the Democratic Party in Utah. After losing his bid to be the Navajos' attorney, Boyden manipulated the revival of a moribund Hopi Tribal Council and secured the contract to represent them (Kammer 1980: 122; Iverson 1981: 52–53; Benedek 1992: 134–37).

There can be little doubt that both attorneys anticipated substantial settlements in the suits filed on contingency, which included the land claims of the two tribes before the Indian Claims Commission and the dispute over the 1882 executive order reservation heard by a special three-judge court (Kammer 1980: 219–220).[2] Preparation for both kinds of cases entailed much the same kinds of evidence: information that was based on tradition, anthropology, and history. The Indian Claims Commission was authorized by Congress in 1946, prior to the retention of legal counsel by the two tribes, but the creation of the three-judge court did not come about until 1958 following efforts by Navajos and Hopis to convince Congress that litigation was the best way to resolve their conflict (Iverson 1981: 53; Brugge 1994: 37–39).

While the potential for economic gain for both the tribes and the attorneys is readily apparent, the role of outside interests is not clear at this stage of the developments. Stewart Udall, who was then a member of the House of Representatives from Arizona, in 1986 claimed a very naive view of Navajo-Hopi relations, one hardly in keeping with either his pioneer family background in Arizona or his subsequent position as Secretary of the Interior charged with overseeing Indian affairs. A University of Arizona study of the mineral resources of the Navajo and Hopi reservation lands may have stimulated interest in both the oil potential and the coal. It had identified extensive deposits of low-sulphur coal on Black Mesa and suggested strip-mining and use of the coal to power electric generators, a proposal prophetic of forces soon to influence the course of tribal affairs (Kiersch 1956: 51–53; Redhouse 1985: 10; Benedek 1992: 32, 36–37, 398).

Research by each tribe was already underway. The Museum of Northern Arizona, long closely involved with the Hopi Tribe, produced an archeological report by Dr. Harold S. Colton for presentation in court to demonstrate Hopi use and occupancy in prehistoric times. The Navajo Tribe had hired archeologists to do field investigations for both cases. Dr. Lyman Tyler at Brigham Young University did the Hopis' historical research while Dr. George Peter Hammond with the Bancroft Library of the University of California performed the same services for the Navajos. Federal government workers from the Bureau of Indian Affairs (BIA) employed in the administration of affairs of the two tribes would be called upon to testify on behalf of their respective tribes (Brugge 1994: 40, 73, 86).

The Hopi Tribe filed suit against the Navajos and initiated a legal action that became known as *Healing vs. Jones* after the chairmen of the two tribes at that time. In the midst of court hearings at Prescott in 1960, it became apparent that current use and occupation should be given as much attention as that of the past, and a large number of tribal members from within the area testified, supported again by presentations by BIA workers. A critical issue was the continuity of Navajo occupation. The Hopi attorney, in describing the Navajos in pejorative terms, characterized them as nomadic and pictured a continual stream of Navajos coming into the disputed area to deprive the Hopis of their rights. The Navajo testimony demonstrated long occupation by the same Navajo families within circumscribed use areas. The news accounts emphasized the mineral potential of the lands in dispute (Brugge 1994: 67–92).

Following the submission of proposed findings by attorneys on both sides and responses of each to the other's contentions, a decision was rendered almost two years later. The court concluded "that the Navajo Indians used and occupied part of the 1882 reservation, in Indian fashion, as their continuing and permanent area of residence from long prior to the creation of the reservation." It added that some 300 Navajos were legally settled there by action of the Secretary of the Interior from 1909 to 1911, while tribal settlement was accomplished by secretarial actions from 1931 to 1943. Navajo occupation beyond the District 6 lines was essentially exclusive (Hamley et al.: 335–36, 46–62, 75).

The key section of the decision evaded making a division of the reservation, however, on the basis of limitations in the congressional act establishing the court. The court gave exclusive ownership of District 6 to the Hopi Tribe, but declared that the rest of the land was held with "joint, undivided and equal rights and interests" by both tribes (Ibid.: 228). It may be that the judges felt that their reasoning protected the surface use of the Navajos while allowing both tribes to share in the mineral wealth that was expected to be opened to development by the case. Unfortunately, this was not to be.

The three-judge court had functioned at the district court level, but in the interest of expediency, the Act of 1958 provided that any appeal should be made directly to the Supreme Court. Both sides elected to take that option. On June 3, 1962, the Supreme Court declined to hear their appeals, thereby affirming the lower court's decision as the law of the land (Brugge 1994: 104).

POST-LITIGATION NEGOTIATIONS

Resolving the practical application of the decision was now up to the two tribes, but under the auspices of the BIA and ultimately, of course, the Department of the Interior. It was the Bureau that took the initiative, having the obligation to administer the joint-interest area under the terms of the decision. The full implications of the decision in legal terms were not well understood, and a high priority was to obtain such agreement as might be possible as to the law's meaning from the attorneys on the two sides. With this in mind, several meetings were held, at least two in Washington and a final one in Scottsdale, Arizona, in August, 1962. These sessions reached consensus on very few points. The tribes agreed to cooperate in leasing for development of subsurface resources, but were far apart on the issue of surface rights. Until the surface rights were determined, the federal government placed a freeze on any developments except those having the approval of both tribes. This put a stop to any permitted activities on the joint-interest lands except those associated with mineral extraction. The Hopis insisted on partition and were strongly supported by the BIA. The commissioner promised to draft legislation to authorize this solution. The Navajos were very much opposed to any solution that required the dispossession of any of their people. Boyden threatened to hold up mineral leasing if the Navajos should not agree to vacate their homes, saying that he was relying on the political support of the mining interests. The ultimate decision was that the two tribes should appoint committees to negotiate with each other (Brugge 1994: 105–09).

The initial negotiations arrived at a stalemate within a few months. A feud between Secretary of the Interior Udall and Littell then led to a court battle over Udall's authority to terminate Littell's contract as tribal attorney for the Navajos. In addition, both tribes became immersed in turmoil between opposing factions. A bill to authorize partition failed in Congress while mineral leasing for oil exploration and strip-mining of coal proceeded at the expense of some hard bargaining. The Hopis evicted some Navajos living inside District 6 and later served eviction notices on others who refused to move; new issues were now added to the dispute. Littell, searching for a bargaining chip in order to support the people threatened with eviction, brought up the issue of the Hopis living at Moenkopi (west of the executive order reservation), and Boyden demanded that the rights of the Hopis there be recognized by the Navajos. There seemed to be an implication in BIA statements that such recognition might be a basis for a land exchange. In 1966, Commissioner of Indian Affairs Robert L. Bennett signed an order placing all of the Navajo reservation lands directly west of the 1882 reservation under a freeze on "exploration, mining, rights-of-way, traders or other use or occupancy authorized by permit, lease or license" without the consent of the Hopi Tribe. Various explanations were made as to the reason for this action, but the real purpose seems to have been to force the Navajos to negotiate on this issue (Ibid.: 105–46; Carroll 1992b: 50).

Udall won his case against Littell in February 1967, and Littell resigned in that same month. This resignation left tribal legal affairs under the interim charge of one of his assistant attorneys, William G. Lavell, until Chairman Raymond Nakai could contract with another permanent general counsel, which he eventually did, hiring his personal attorney, Harold Mott (Brugge 1994: 111, 147, 169; Iverson 1981: 88–89).

Bennett appointed Wayne Pratt as his special representative to report on Navajo and Hopi affairs and to explain the BIA position, apparently in hopes of gaining Navajo acceptance of partition. In time, Pratt learned to appreciate the Navajo dilemma, however, and he ceased to propagandize for Navajo removal.

He even advocated unsuccessfully for aid for the Navajos being evicted from District 6. He soon disappeared from the scene, his influence undermined by more powerful forces (Brugge 1994: 148–68).

Negotiations between the two tribes resumed the month after the approval of Mott's contract, largely as a result of prodding by Bennett who personally chaired the next three meetings and steered the discussions into the problem of the Moenkopi question. These negotiations led to more field research and competing Navajo and Hopi proposals for a boundary in that area, but no linkage to the resolution of the conflicts engendered by the *Healing vs. Jones* decision. An attempt by the Hopi conservative faction to participate in the meetings was rejected at the insistence of the Hopi Council representatives. Just as the meetings appeared to be making progress toward resolving the Moenkopi issues, a failure of Bennett to attend one session brought about another collapse of negotiations, but there is reason to think that some on the Hopi team wanted to prevent any agreement (Ibid.: 169–95).

A POLITICAL "SOLUTION"

As the negotiations wound down and the dispute degenerated into visits to Washington by tribal delegations, Nakai and Mott were replaced in 1970 by Peter MacDonald as tribal chairman and George P. Vlassis as general counsel under a contract with the Phoenix law firm of Brown, Vlassis and Bain. About the same time, Arizona congressional representative Sam Steiger began efforts to pass a partition bill in Congress. His first bill was introduced too late in the 1970 session for any chance of passage, but it prepared the way for another in 1971. Others followed, and a lengthy series of bills by different authors was subject to heavy lobbying by both tribes. The Hopis used the services of a mining and energy-related public relations firm in Salt Lake City to publicize intertribal conflicts stirred up by aggressive enforcement of trespass laws against Navajo stockraisers while forcing stock reduction through court action. Toward the end of 1974, a partition act was passed by both houses and signed into law by President Gerald Ford (Brugge 1994: 201–39; Kammer 1980: 91–137; Benedek 1992: 147–55).

The Relocation Act, as the partition law or Public Law 93–531 came to be known, provided for an equal division of the land, either by negotiation or court order. It called for the further reduction of livestock, additional legal actions by the tribes against each other, and relocation of those tribal members on lands not assigned to their tribe, under the administration of a three-member commission to be known as the Navajo and Hopi Indian Relocation Commission (NHIRC). Lastly, the Act provided guidance and financial assistance to relocatees in acquiring new homes and adjusting to their new locations. The Navajo Tribe was allowed to purchase 250,000 acres from the Bureau of Land Management which would be made a part of the Navajo Reservation. Expenditures under the act were not to exceed $31,500,000 (Kammer 1980: 129–30; NHIRC 1981: 280–91).

The negotiations authorized by the act began in 1975. Partition was accepted as the inevitable solution and discussions thereafter grappled with the boundaries to be drawn. When a six-month limit for the bargaining expired with no agreement, a federal mediator, William Simkin, felt that he still was able to recommend a division which he submitted to the *Healing vs. Jones* court. The Simkin boundary was challenged, however, and a final line was not decided upon until April of 1977 (Kammer 1980: 153–56; NHIRC 1981: 2) (Map 10.1).

A Hopi effort to unilaterally impound Navajo livestock on the Hopi Partitioned Lands (HPL) within a few weeks of the court's approval of the Simkin line came close to inciting violence and upsetting a BIA five-year program to reduce livestock to half the carrying capacity with Navajo acquiescence. Action from Washington was required to halt Hopi Chairman Abbott Sekaquaptewa's determination to confiscate all Navajo livestock immediately, but the Hopi opposition led to the punitive measure of revocation of an agreement to provide aid to families deprived of their livestock income (Kammer 1980: 156–59; Wood et al. 1982: 12–14).

RELOCATION

In the meantime, the relocation commissioners were appointed in July 1975 and an administrative staff was soon gaining familiarity with the work they were to do through meetings with Navajo chapters, the local unit of government among the Navajos. Actual relocations began shortly after the initial approval of the Simkin boundary; they were halted during the appeals and then resumed in August 1978. With final approval of the areas allocated to each tribe, the commission also began preparation of its *Report and Plan* for submission to Congress as required by the relocation act (Lewis et al. 1981: 1–2).

Until the *Report and Plan* was approved, relocation proceeded under the general terms set forth in the Relocation Act. Those relocating prior to the approval of the plan were rather euphemistically described as doing so "voluntarily," despite the fact that they had been repeatedly told by government representatives through the years that the law permitted them no alternatives. These voluntary relocations, accomplished with no systematic planning, provided a database of 38 families for a study under the direction of Thayer Scudder (1982) of the effects of relocation from the HPL in December 1978 and January 1979 under the auspices of the Navajo Tribe. Paired with this is a study of the stock removal program by John J. Wood, Walter M. Vannette and Michael J. Andrews (1982) performed under contract with the BIA and based on field work in 1977 and 1978. It was evident as a result of these investigations that the impacts on Navajo relocatees would be severe. Despite these and other early warnings, the commissioners' plan submitted in 1981 was superficial with regard to economic, social, and cultural issues that needed to be addressed

(Lewis et al. 1981; Brugge 1993).[3] Prior to the completion of the planning, however, relocation continued to be actively and energetically carried out.

An important precursor to resettlement, the provision of the lands authorized for the purpose, initially 250,000 acres but later increased to 400,000 acres, was delayed until 1986 by political opposition and bureaucratic hurdles.[4] This meant that a great many Navajo families had been relocated to off-reservation urban centers or to small homesites in Navajo communities outside the HPL with no opportunity to select a location where they might still carry on a traditional ranching way of life. Development of the Newlands, as this addition to the Navajo Reservation has been named (Map 10.1), has lagged well into the 1990s (Kammer 1980: 138–52; Benedek 1992: 101; Brugge 1993: 8; Warburton et al. 1993).

The Navajos faced numerous problems with relocation. Their livestock was reduced, and there was a freeze on economic development that was extended to the building and repair of housing. Many Navajos left their lands in search of shelter and security. Many of these refugees financed their own moves as well as they were able, despite the fact that they were entitled to the assistance guaranteed them by law. However, the limited budgets given to the commission by Congress have long delayed any succor for most of the Navajos who moved to escape harassment (Brugge 1993).

The drawing of the partition line did lead to the end of the freeze on development for the Navajos in the Navajo Partitioned Lands (NPL), but they were finding themselves hosts to many of those displaced on the other side of the boundary. The stress and conflicts arising from resettlement among those outside the NPL, both for relocatees and host communities, were further evidence of the lack of foresight in planning by the commission (Tamir 1991 and 1993; Joe 1998 and n.d.).

Even more dramatic evidence of inadequate planning appeared in the increasing loss of new homes by traditional Navajos relocated to off-reservation cities. Adults with little or no formal education or even facility in English and accustomed to hogan life frequently found themselves in debt and were often induced by loan sharks to mortgage their houses, which were ultimately lost to foreclosures. The creditors then sometimes sold the properties back to the relocation commission for resettling other families (Brugge 1985; Tamir 1986).

RESISTANCE

Navajo resistance developed quite quickly. The most effective organizations were the Sovereign Dine Nation and the Big Mountain Legal Defense/Offense Committee (BMLDOC), both located in the Big Mountain area on Black Mesa. They solicited volunteer help, acquired legal representation, and publicized widely the plight of those affected. The courts regularly turned down their lawsuits. The presence of unconventional young whites and of members of the American Indian Movement (AIM) among their supporters was used to subject the resisters to ridicule in northern Arizona, but they persisted nonetheless. The Sioux Sun Dance was introduced at Big Mountain through AIM as a means to bolster younger people's hopes. Elderly Navajo women, however, provided most of the leadership (Benedek 1992).

On the southeast corner of the HPL, resistance was focused on Star Mountain—a major sacred place in Navajo religion. Several singers (native religious leaders) were prominent in opposing the loss of lands and homes there, but they lacked the kind of drama of the Big Mountain area. Consequently, there has been far less public awareness of events in that direction.

There were also more mainstream groups that opposed relocation, such as Clergy and Laity Concerned (CALC), a Christian organization with nationwide membership. As the congressional deadline of July 7, 1986, approached, by which time all relocation was to have been completed, members of this group visited Big Mountain as witness participants at a Sun Dance. The non-Indians included a diverse array of outsiders, visitors from Europe, Black Muslims, and reporters expecting to cover a story of massive dispossession, perhaps by the military, on the day following the ceremony. The federal government delayed hasty action, however, thereby avoiding any dramatic mass forced removal that might become a major media event. (Ibid.; Kemper and Thomas 1986; Whitson and Roberge 1986; Schoepfle et al. 1986; Kammer 1986).

MANYBEADS VS. UNITED STATES

The most successful attempt to stem the evictions came about in a lawsuit filed in 1988, entitled *Manybeads vs. United States*. This lawsuit is based on an assertion that the right of relocatees to practice their religion was violated. It was a last desperate measure, yet initially even that attempt seemed destined to fail completely. An appeal led to a court order in 1991 for new negotiations under the guidance of a mediator. In an agreement reached after prolonged bargaining among representatives of the Hopi Tribe, the Navajo Nation,[5] and the federal government, the Hopi Tribe, in exchange for $15,000,000 from the Navajos and $50,000,000 from the United States would permit a limited number of Navajo families 75 year leases based on inherited life estate provisions.[6] Lessees would receive three-acre homesites plus 10 acres of farmland and a grazing permit that would be adjusted to the current carrying capacity. A major concern of the resisters has been that they would be subject to Hopi tribal jurisdiction, but would lack any representation and have no formally recognized way of appeal to protect their interests (Weinberg 1997; Norstog 1996: 54; Big Mountain Dine 1996; Kelley and Francis 1994).

As of this writing, 369 Navajos representing a claimed 84 of 97 homesites have signed leases, although the figures are challenged by some. Twenty of those who signed leases have since decided to accept relocation rather than remain under Hopi jurisdiction. There appears to be hope among federal officials that, "If the older folks go, most of the younger kids disperse also. Once that anchor is gone. . . ." (Taylor in Young 1998). While there is still resistance, the number of resisters is dwindling and the strategy seems to be to attempt to reduce that number to so few people that eviction will no longer seem a big issue to the media and the public. There also remains, however, the large reservoir of Navajo refugees who are entitled to new homes and other relocation benefits. As of the end of October 1998 there were still 366 Navajo families and one Hopi family certified as eligible who had not received relocation benefits. In theory, at least, it would seem that the almost 1,500 Navajo individuals in these families would retain their right to live on the HPL if they so chose until they should receive these benefits (Young 1998; Office of Navajo and Hopi Indian Relocation [ONHIR] 1998).

THE MOENKOPI CASE

As mentioned above, the course of the 1882 reservation dispute did not directly involve the lands to the west. Navajo tribal personnel had begun research on the history and use of the Bennett Freeze area in hopes that a land exchange might be possible (Map 10.1). Data on current occupation and several proposed early boundaries were gathered. The status of the Hopi occupancy was conditioned by the Arizona Boundary Bill of 1934, which seemed to provide a different legal basis from that governing the *Healing vs. Jones* area. The Moenkopi lands failed to have potential for a compromise because the Hopi council and its attorneys tried to use the Hopi settlement as a basis for a claim to a half interest in all lands within the exterior boundaries of the Navajo Reservation in Arizona, excluding only the 1882 executive order reservation and the Arizona portion of the original treaty reservation. As a result, the Bennett Freeze remained in force even after the partition of the joint-interest area (Brugge 1994: 145–80).

In 1974, Congress had authorized a separate lawsuit between the two tribes to settle this new conflict. The Hopi Tribe initiated legal proceedings in the matter against the Navajo Tribe in the same year. The freeze on development remained in effect throughout the prolonged delay of the lawsuit. Consequently, Navajo residents were threatened with persecution for such simple acts as repairing a broken window or a leaky roof or even merely repainting a house. In 1980, two small areas around Moenkopi and Tuba City were declared "administrative units" not subject to the freeze, primarily to permit the federal government to carry out its own projects in education and medical care.[7] This allowed some private Navajo construction at Tuba City as well as a federal housing project, but brought no relief for Navajos living on the range (Fenzl et al. 1990: 14; Fenzl et al. 1993; Carroll 1992a: 2–3, 9 n. 7, 52–56; Yazzie 1993).

There was early skirmishing in the courts, with motions filed as early as 1977, a district court ruling in 1978, an appeal, and a court of appeals decision. Both tribes conducted extensive research in support of their respective claims. A trial was held between October 17, 1989, and February 8, 1990, in order to determine which areas the Hopis held exclusively and which were jointly used in 1934. Judge Earl H. Carroll issued a decision on April 27, 1992, defining the criteria that would confirm Hopi title, describing lands used exclusively in 1934 by Hopis which were to be awarded to the Hopi Tribe, and describing other lands used jointly by both peoples (Fenzl et al. 1990: 6; Carroll 1992a).

Phase 2 of the trial was heard in court from July 7 to July 21, 1992, following a tour by helicopter and on the ground of the disputed area on June 27, 1992. The final decision, issued September 25, 1992, refined somewhat the boundaries of the areas delineated in the first decision and drew a line around all the lands ruled to be Hopi after partitioning the jointly used area (Carroll 1992b).

The most important consideration in drawing the boundary was "avoiding the relocation of individuals" (Carroll 1992b: 58). Insofar as possible, "the disruption of grazing areas and other use patterns" (Carroll 1992b: 58) was also avoided. The division gave the Hopi Tribe all of the exclusively Hopi area plus about a quarter of the joint-use area, where Hopi use was not as intensive as Navajo use in 1934, and inclusive of all areas currently "used in any significant way" by the Hopis in 1992 (Carroll 1992b: 58). Equitable division of water sources was also given consideration. The final criterion was to establish a well defined area that could be easily administered. The line divided both surface and subsurface rights (Ibid.: 58–61, 67–68).

The area awarded the Hopis was far less than their claim to half of most of the 1934 boundary reservation. The Hopis appealed the decision to the Supreme Court, which declined to consider the case (*Albuquerque Journal* 30 April 1996: C–3). As of this writing the case is again on appeal by the Hopis asserting their right to access to religious sites (U.S. 9th Circuit Court of Appeals 1995).

COMPARISON OF THE TWO CASES

It is instructive to compare the outcome of these two disputes, assuming that the Moenkopi case will remain essentially unchanged. There have been two major differences.

First is the fact that the 1882 case was unique at the time it took place, while the precedents and experiences of that case seem to have had an influence on the later case. Second is the fact that real and imagined mineral resources within the 1882 reservation brought outside interests into the picture, in some instances in ways yet to be elucidated, in others, in direct involvement that is quite evident.

The contending parties in the 1882 area had little in the way of precedents for guidance. Assumed legal issues and methods often were misjudged on both sides. Perhaps the greatest fallacy was the belief that the standards set for aboriginal title by the Indian Claims Commission would be applicable. Both the Navajos and the Hopis relied on data regarding prehistory and early history that were essentially irrelevant in court beyond a bid for sympathy. The legislation authorizing a judicial settlement was poorly worded, allowing the judges to evade a decision in what had become far too complex a matter for easy resolution, but which they, with undue optimism, believed the tribes would be able to settle themselves.

Following the decision, high officials in the Department of the Interior and the BIA asserted all too facilely that partition and relocation would be simple undertakings that could be carried out quickly, easily, and cheaply, something that their own staff knew, or at least should have known, to be untrue. Congress let politics and wishful thinking rule over common sense, perhaps influenced by outside interests, creating an agency that became immersed in a morass of requirements for which it was unprepared and underfunded. All the while, for over a third of a century, many Navajo families suffered heavy bureaucratic impositions that stifled their economy, disrupted their families and communities, hindered the education of their children, and adversely impacted their physical and mental health, pressures that continue even today to a greater or lesser extent for many of them. The confrontation has aggravated relations between the two tribes in ways that will continue, for many years to come, to affect their interactions as neighbors, while it has had an even greater effect on relations with non-Indians and especially on how both Navajos and Hopis view the federal government.

The Moenkopi case was already deeply involved in actions taken in the maneuvering for advantage in the earlier case, in particular in terms of the Bennett Freeze. Neither Congress, the Department of the Interior, nor the courts seem to have comprehended the suffering imposed on the people living on the land as the issue with all deliberate delay wended its way toward a distant resolution. Congress did provide the courts with a mandate that allowed for a decisive judgement, however, perhaps because the unpleasant fact that the earlier case was still far from over must have been evident in 1974.[8] Even more significant, Judge Carroll, having found himself for years caught between insistent tribal litigants and the higher courts in the aftermath of the three-judge court, of which he had not been a member, brought with him to the new case a realization that greater wisdom was required in the new dispute. He must also have become aware that the demonizing of the losers, the clamor that they be punished for alleged transgressions of their ancestors, and the harassment directed at doing so had led to injustices that should not be perpetuated.

The influence of the mining and energy interests in the former case was obvious, but not exactly as controlling as many observers would like to believe. Their support for partition could not be hidden, but the full extent of their intrusion into the decisions made in Washington may never be known. There can be little doubt that it played a role in both the Department of the Interior and in Congress. Several key players in Washington later left the government for good positions with the Hopis' attorneys or with energy companies. Interlocking corporate relationships allowed ample opportunity for less conspicuous "carrots." One example is the fact that during the key period in which the relocation act was passed, Peabody Coal Company, which was mining coal on Black Mesa, was owned by Kennecott Copper Company (Whitson and Roberge

1986: 51; Sills 1986: 60–70). Nobody appears to have looked into what this parent company might have done to help steer the debate toward relocation.

It seems significant, however, that two probable expectations of those with mining interests did not materialize. First, efforts to demonstrate a correspondence of the HPL with the coal deposits actually show considerable divergence, and this is especially evident in the actual extent of the strip mines. Second, the removal of Navajos from the HPL has been remarkably slow, the major impediment being an unwillingness on the part of Congress to finance resettlement at a rate that would allow relocation to meet the deadlines that Congress itself set. Perhaps the mining and energy interests decided that further prodding was futile after learning how much of the coal they wanted to mine in the immediate future remained under the NPL. This idea, however, can be only speculation. It may also be that the strength of Navajo opposition to displacement suggested that a more gradual approach might be less likely to lead to violence. Certainly this dilatory eviction program has been a factor in the low level of violence.

In the more recent case, the fact that no people will be forced from their homes has not resulted in a media campaign to derogate Navajos or a movement in Congress to legislate a resettlement program that would overturn the judicial decision. Congress is clearly tired of the contentious process of evicting so many people and would like only to see the one effort concluded and no other begun. With no concerted drive to promote displacement of people, the government will not readily embark on a course that resulted ultimately in so much adverse press. No new vote seeker is likely to try to politicize such a cause as did Sam Stieger in the 1970s and no attorney will be able to arouse the press to the same degree of enthusiasm for removal. It appears that the Hopis, in their pejorative and punitive campaign against the Navajos, went too far, with a resultant backlash of sympathy for those they tried to paint as villains.

In one respect the two cases do have a similarity, although arrived at by somewhat different routes. The last resort of the Navajo resisters to relocation has been an appeal to their rights under the Constitution to practice their religion. This appeal was first expressed in the *Manybeads* litigation that led to the 75-year leases, an outcome seen as barely acceptable by most resisters. In 1996 as the drive for signatures on the leases got underway, an entirely new element arose.

A 96-year-old blind Navajo woman and her 61-year-old daughter reported a visitation by two Holy People, Navajo dieties, who warned the Navajos that they must continue to make offerings at the sacred places and to pray and to perform the traditional Blessingway ceremonies. The context, as the revelation was publicized, was in general terms of the drought then afflicting the region, but the women were resident within the HPL and the underlying message seems to have been, "Why can't we all just get along?"

The news brought thousands of Navajo pilgrims from the four directions to stand in line and offer corn pollen where footprints in the soil indicated that the Holy People had stood on the earth's surface. The Speaker of the Navajo Nation

Council initiated a day of prayer that has become an annual observance open to Navajo adherents of all faiths. Navajo officialdom has guided the revelation into an admonition to spirituality for all Navajos, but the original impetus was almost certainly a muffled protest of the oppression imposed by the dispute (Linthicum 1996: A1, A6; Blackgoat 1996: B3; Brenner 1996: 1–2; Smithson 1996: A1–A2).

More recent assertions of religious claims were made before Abdelfattah Amor, a United Nations Special Rapporteur on Religious Intolerance, on Black Mesa in February 1998. Resisters to relocation testified to their situation along with Navajos impacted by the Peabody coal mines and traditional Hopis complaining of BIA and Hopi Tribal desecration of shrines (Bautista 1998; Shebala 1998).

Although Hopi tribal officials have taken a deprecating view of Navajo religious concerns, they have resorted to raising similar objections in their appeal of Judge Carrol's decision in the Moenkopi case, a matter that is still under review. It is ironic, certainly, that the Hopi Tribal Council, after disparaging Navajo religion, now finds itself falling back on a very similar strategy, one based entirely on religious values.

CONCLUSION

The land disputes between the Hopi and Navajo have led to ethnic discord, adverse environmental impacts, dysfunction in both the national and tribal political systems, and to damaging the reputation of the United States internationally. These problems, as well as human suffering, cannot be easily calculated. Only if we recognize just how bad was the entire process can we learn to avoid similar calamities in the future so that lasting good can come out of these disputes. Above all, we must learn to regard with suspicion any cause based on the stereotyping of a people as evil.

APPENDIX: TIMELINE

ca AD 1300	Anasazi abandonment of the entire San Juan River drainage.
by 1450–1500	Navajos' ancestors established as hunters and farmers in the San Juan watershed.
1540	Spain made formal claim to a vast region including the lands of the Pueblos and the Apacheans.
1598	Settlement of first Spanish colony in New Mexico.
1629	Missions established among the Hopis.
1680	The Pueblo Revolt drove out the Spanish settlers and missionaries.
1692–96	Reconquest of New Mexico.

1700	Return of Catholic priests to Awatovi led to destruction of that town by the other Hopi villages.
1819	Hopi ask Spanish aid to drive away Navajo settlers.
1821	Mexican independence.
1846–1847	War between the United States and Mexico.
1848	Treaty of Guadalupe Hidalgo cedes lands of Navajos and Hopis to the United States.
1863–1868	Last Navajo war and exile at Fort Sumner.
1868	Final Navajo treaty of June 1 created Navajo Reservation in a small portion of their homeland.
1882	Creation of the Moqui Reservation by the Executive Order of December 12.
1886	First federal attempt to draw a boundary between the Hopis and Navajos.
1909–1911	Allotment program recognizing rights of individual Navajos to lands within the 1882 reservation.
1932–1943	Establishment of District 6 as an exclusive Hopi grazing unit surrounded by Navajo units.
1946	Indian Claims Commission authorized.
1958	Three-judge court established to hear Navajo-Hopi dispute over land in the 1882 reservation.
1960	*Healing vs. Jones* heard before the three-judge court in Prescott, Arizona.
1962	Decision in *Healing vs. Jones* created a Hopi Reservation of District 6 and declared the rest of the 1882 reservation to be jointly owned by both tribes.
1963	Supreme Court declined to hear appeals, making the decision in *Healing vs. Jones* final, followed by the Scottsdale Conference and a moratorium on development in the joint-interest area.
1966	Bennett Freeze extended the moratorium over the portion of the Navajo Reservation directly west of the 1882 reservation.
1967	Navajo attorney resigned following Supreme Court decision that the Secretary of the Interior has the authority to dismiss him.
1967–1973	Negotiations between Navajos and Hopis end in a stalemate.
1974	Public Law 93–531, the Relocation Act, becomes law. A lawsuit between the two tribes over lands outside the 1882 reservation authorized.

1975	Navajo and Hopi Indian Relocation Commission (NHIRC) appointed.
1977	Partition line of the 1882 reservation approved.
1981	NHIRCs *Report and Plan* submitted to Congress, initiating the five-year period for completion of relocation.
1986	Deadline for relocation extended.
1988	*Manybeads vs. United States* filed to assert religious rights of Navajos resisting relocation.
1989–1990	Court hearings on the Bennett Freeze suit before Judge Earl H. Carroll.
1991	Negotiations begun under court order in the *Manybeads* case.
1992	Division of the Bennett Freeze by Judge Carroll.
1996	Public Law 104–301 formalized the negotiated agreement in the *Manybeads* case allowing 75-year leases for resisters.
1998	United Nations hearings on religious freedom held on Black Mesa.

NOTES

I owe a debt of gratitude to more people, Indian and non-Indian, scholars and laymen, over a period of decades, than can be listed here. Because of this and in deference to the fact that some wish to remain anonymous, I can give credit only in general terms. So, to the many Navajos and other Indian people whom I have known as friends, colleagues, employees, or otherwise, to my fellow anthropologists and scholars in related fields with whom I have discussed or corresponded on these issues, to federal and tribal workers who have been associates, supervisors or supervisees, and even to certain members of the legal profession, I say thanks, gracias and ahéhee'. A great many of my own data and views derive from my participation in both disputes, perhaps most dramatically by having seen firsthand the change in the quality of life for the Navajos in the Bennett Freeze from 1968 to 1992.

1. As used herein, "New Mexicans" refers to those people living in the country under effective European or Euroamerican rule (an area at various times termed la Reina de Nueva Mexico, la provincia de Nueva Mexico, New Mexico Territory, or the State of New Mexico) who were predominantly Spaniards, Pueblo Indians, and various peoples of mixed ancestry in the early years of the colony but who came to include a substantial number of captives from the free tribes as time went by and, following the Mexican War, an increasing number of "Anglo" Americans of various racial and ethnic origins. Between 1598 and 1821, New Mexicans were Spanish subjects, from 1821–1846–48, Mexican citizens and since 1846–48, United States citizens or "wards" in the case of tribal peoples. Members of free tribes still living independently under their own tribal sovereignty are not included in this term until their tribes come under effective foreign rule, for the Navajos this might be 1848, the date of the first ratified treaty with the Unites States, or more certainly, 1868, the date of the final Navajo Treaty.

2. The Navajo land claims case, *The Navajo Tribe of Indians vs. The United States of America*, Docket 229 before the Indian Claims Commission and the Hopi land claim case, *The Hopi Tribe, et al, vs. The United States of America*, Docket 196 before the Indian Claims Commission, were claims for compensation for lands lost due to federal actions or failures to act, not for return of territory, filed under the Indian Claims Commission Act of August 12, 1946. Both were settled in favor of the tribes after extended court hearings, first on the issue of occupancy, then on the issue of evaluation of lands allowed by the commission.

3. These reports in their original form were made available to the NHIRC in 1979, that sponsored by the Navajo Tribe in March and the BIA report at least by February (Scudder et al. 1982: 4; Wood et al. 1982: v).

4. Congress stipulated that most of this land should be in Arizona and adjacent to the Navajo Reservation, but 35,000 acres were to be in New Mexico. The lands chosen in New Mexico were in the Paragon Ranch, where the Navajos hoped to lease coal mining to provide money for services to the relocatees the Congress failed to fund.

5. By 1991, the official name for the Navajos had been changed from "tribe" to "nation."

6. This money was used to purchase up to 50,000 acres that became Hopi trust (reservation) land.

7. Some minor adjustments were also made in 1980 to the exterior boundary of the freeze on the west. Technically the area became a statutory freeze rather than the administratively imposed Bennett Freeze, with a stricter definition of the conditions to be met. The San Juan Paiute Band was also recognized as having some rights within the freeze area (Fenzl et al. 1993).

8. It was apparent, at the very least, that partition and relocation would take several years for completion, but it was not foreseen that this process would still be underway a quarter of a century later. Certainly some of the more astute observers, having witnessed the bitter fight over the partition bill, would have had strong intimations of future complications.

REFERENCES

Bautista, Liberato C. 1998. A Counterinsurgency of a Different Kind. *Christian Social Action* 2 (1): 35–36.

Begay, Richard M. and Alexander Roberts. 1996. The Early Navajo Occupation of the Grand Canyon Region. In *The Archaeology of Navajo Origins*, edited by Ronald H. Towner, pp. 197–210. Salt Lake City, UT: University of Utah Press.

Benedek, Emily. 1992. *The Wind Won't Know Me: A History of the Navajo-Hopi Land Dispute*. New York: Alfred A. Knopf.

Big Mountain Dine. 1996. Big Mountain Dine to Senator McCain. *Fourth World Bulletin* 5 (1–2): 59.

Blackgoat, Roberta. 1996. Revelation Reinforces Resistance to Relocation. *Albuquerque Journal*, 9 June, B3.

Brenner, Malcolm. 1996. Reports of Navajo "Visitation" Inspire Spiritual Unity Week. *Gallup Independent*, 23 May, 1–2.

Brew, John Otis. 1949. The History of Awatovi. In *Franciscan Awatovi: The Excavation and Conjectural Reconstruction of a 17th Century Spanish Mission Establishment at a Hopi Indian Town in Northeastern Arizona.* Papers of the Peabody Museum of American Archaeology and Ethnology, vol. 36, edited by Ross Gordon Montgomery, Watson Smith, and John Otis Brew, pp. 1–43. Cambridge, MA: Peabody Museum.

Brugge, David M. 1969. Pueblo Factionalism and External Relations. *Ethnohistory* 16 (2): 191–200.

——. 1979. Navajo Prehistory and History to 1850. In *Handbook of North American Indians.* Vol. 10, *Southwest,* edited by Alfonso Ortiz, pp. 489–501. Washington, DC: Smithsonian Institution.

——. 1985. Directed Culture Change through Relocation in Navajo Historic Context. *COAS* 3 (1): 9–23.

——. 1993. The Relocation of Navajos from the Hopi Partitioned Lands in Relation to the World Bank Standards for Involuntary Resettlement. In *Papers from the Third, Fourth, and Sixth Navajo Studies Conferences,* edited by June-el Piper and compiled by Alexandra Roberts and Jenevieve Smith, pp. 7–15. Window Rock, AZ: Navajo Nation Historic Preservation Department.

——. 1994. *The Navajo-Hopi Land Disputes: An American Tragedy.* Albuquerque, NM: University of New Mexico Press.

——. 1996. Navajo Archaeology: A Promising Past. In *The Archaeology of Navajo Origins,* edited by Ronald H. Towner, pp. 255–271. Salt Lake City, UT: University of Utah Press.

Carroll, Earl H. 1992a. *CIV 74–842 PCT EHC, Findings of Fact and Conclusions of Law re: Hopi Claims.* Phoenix: U.S. District Court for the District of Arizona.

——. 1992b. *CIV 74–842 PCT EHC, Findings of Fact and Conclusions of Law and Judgment re: Partition of the 1934 Reservation.* Phoenix: U.S. District Court for the District of Arizona.

Cordell, Linda S. 1984. *Prehistory of the Southwest.* San Diego, CA: Academic Press, Inc.

Correll, J. Lee, and Alfred Dehiya. 1972. *The Anatomy of the Navajo Indian Reservation: How it Grew.* Window Rock, AZ: The Navajo Nation.

Fenzl, Terry E., Craig W. Soland, and John W. Rogers. 1990. *Navajo Tribe's Responses to Hopi Tribe's Proposed Findings of Fact and Conclusions of Law.* Phoenix, AZ: Brown & Bain, P.A.

——. 1993. *Appellee's Response Brief, United States Court of Appeals, Ninth Circuit, No. 93–15109.* Phoenix, AZ: Brown & Bain, P.A.

Foster, Michael K. 1996. Language and the Culture History of North America. In *Handbook of North American Indians.* Vol. 17, *Languages,* edited by Ives Goddard, pp. 64–110. Washington, DC: Smithsonian Institution.

Hale, Kenneth, and David Harris. 1979. Historical Linguistics and Archaeology. In *Handbook of North American Indians.* Vol. 10, *Southwest,* edited by Alfonso Ortiz, pp. 170–177. Washington, DC: Smithsonian Institution.

Hamley, Frederic G., Leon R. Yankwich, and James A. Walsh. 1962. In the *United States District Court for the District of Arizona, No. Civil 579 Prescott, Opinion of the Court, Appendix to Opinion—Chronological Account of Hopi-Navajo Controversy, Findings of Fact, and Conclusions of Law, Judgement.* San Francisco, CA: Pernau-Walsh Printing Co.

Hogan, Patrick. 1991. Navajo-Pueblo Interaction during the Governador Phase: A Reassessment of the Evidence. In *Rethinking Navajo Pueblitos,* edited by LouAnn

200   Native Peoples of the Southwest

Jacobson and Stephen L. Fosberg, pp. 1–27. Farmington, NM: U.S. Bureau of
Land Management.

Iverson, Peter. 1981. *The Navajo Nation*. Westport, CT: Greenwood Press.

Joe, Jennie R. 1998. The Impact of Relocation on Hardrock Chapter. In *Dine Bikeyah:
Paper in Honor of David M. Brugge*, edited by Meliha S. Duran and David T.
Kirkpatrick, pp. 129–141. N.P. : The Archaeological Society of New Mexico,
no. 24.

———. n.d. *1980–1995: The Impact of Forced Relocation on the Community of Hardrock*. Window Rock, AZ: Navajo-Hopi Land Commission, Navajo Nation.

Kammer, Jerry. 1980. *The Second Long Walk: The Navajo-Hopi Land Dispute*. Albuquerque: University of New Mexico Press.

———. 1986. The Navajos, the Hopis, and the U.S. Press. *Columbia Journalism Review*,
July/August, 41–44.

Kelley, Klara Bonsack and Harris Francis. 1994. *Navajo Sacred Places*. Bloomington
and Indianapolis: Indiana University Press.

Kemper, Vicki, and Diane Thomas. 1986. The Battle for Big Mountain: Navajo and Hopi
Peoples Resist Relocation. *Sojourners*, August-September, 8–9.

Kiersch, George A. 1956. *Mineral Resources: Navajo-Hopi Indian Reservations,
Arizona-Utah*. Vol. 1, *Metalliferous Minerals and Mineral Fuels: Geology, Evaluation, and Uses and a Section on the General Geology*. Tucson, AZ: University
of Arizona Press.

Lewis, Roger K., Hawley Atkinson, and Sandra L. Massetto. 1981. *Report and Plan*.
Flagstaff, AZ: Navajo and Hopi Relocation Commission.

Linthicum, Leslie. 1996 Navajo Hogan Houses Hope. *Albuquerque Journal*, 30 May, A1
and A6.

Lomatuway'ma, Michael, Lorena Lomatuway'ma, and Sidney Naminghaa, Jr. 1993. *Hopi
Ruin Legends: Kiqötutuwutsi*. Flagstaff, AZ: Northern Arizona University.

NHIRC (Navajo and Hopi Indian Relocation Commission). 1981. *Report and Plan*. Flagstaff, AZ: NHIRC.

Norstog, John. 1996. Update on the Navajo-Hopi "Land Dispute." *Fourth World Bulletin*,
5 (1–2): 54–58.

ONHIR (Office of Navajo and Hopi Indian Relocation). 1998. Relocation Program Status
for Oct. 1998. Flagstaff, AZ: ONHIR.

Redhouse, John. 1985. *Geopolitics of the Navajo Hopi Land Dispute*. Albuquerque, NM:
Redhouse/Wright Publications.

Schoepfle, G. Mark, Rose T. Morgan, and Peggy Francis Scott. 1986. It Used to Be
Home. *Technology Review* 89 (5): 52–55, 78.

Scudder, Thayer, et al. 1982. *No Place to Go: Effects of Compulsory Relocation on
Navajos*. Philadelphia, PA: Institute for the Study of Human Issues.

Shebala, Marley. 1998. UN Rep Hears Pleas of People. *Navajo Times*, 5 Feb, A-1 and
A-3.

Sills, Marc. 1986. Relocation Reconsidered: Competing Explanations of the Navajo-Hopi
Land Settlement Act of 1974. *The Journal of Ethnic Studies* 14 (3): 53–83.

Smithson, Shelley. 1996. Leader Urges Navajos to Pray. *Farmington Daily Times*. 17
June, A1–A2.

Tamir, Orit. 1986. *Some Consequences of Compulsory Relocation on Navajo Socioeconomy*. Master's thesis, Department of Anthropology, Arizona State University,
Tempe, AZ.

———. 1991. Relocation of Navajo from Hopi Partitioned Land in Pinon. *Human Organization* 50 (2): 173–178.

———. 1993. A Local Drama in a Historical Context: Relocation from HPL in Pinon. In *Papers from the Third, fourth, and Sixth Navajo Studies Conferences*, edited by June-el Piper and compiled by Alexandra Roberts and Jenevieve Smith, pp. 17–25. Window Rock, AZ: Navajo Nation Historic Preservation Department.

Thomas, Alfred Barnaby. 1932. *Forgotten Frontiers: A Study of the Spanish Indian Policy of Don Juan Bautista de Anza, Governor of New Mexico, 1777–1787.* Norman: University of Oklahoma Press.

Titiev, Mischa. 1994. *Old Oraibi: A Study of the Hopi Indians of Third Mesa.* Papers of the Peabody Museum of American Archaeology and Ethnology, vol. 2, no. 1. Cambridge, MA: Peabody Museum.

United States Court of Appeals, Ninth Circuit. 1995. *Masayesva v. Zah. 65 Federal Reporter*, 3d Series, pp. 1445–1461.

Warburton Miranda, G. Lennis Berlin, and David Ortiz. 1993. *Sanders Rural Community Indirect Impacts: A Study of Long-term Effects on Cultural Resources in the Sanders Rural Community, Arizona.* Navajo Nation Archaeology Department and Northern Arizona University, Flagstaff, AZ.

Weinberg, Bill. 1997. Requiem for Big Mountain. *Native Americas* 14 (3): 30–39.

Whitson, Hollis, and Martha Roberge. 1986. Moving Those Indians into the Twentieth Century. *Technology Review* 89 (5): 46–51, 56–57.

Wilcox, David R. 1981. The Entry of Athapaskans Into the American Southwest: The Problem Today. In *The Protohistoric Period in the North American Southwest, AD 1450–1700*, edited by David R. Wilcox and W. Bruce Masse, pp. 213–256. Arizona State University Anthropological Research Papers, no. 243, Tempe, AZ.

Wood, John J., Walter M. Vannette, and Michael J. Andrews. 1982. *"Sheep is Life": An Assessment of Livestock Reduction in the Former Navajo-Hopi Joint Use Area.* Northern Arizona Anthropological Paper no. 1, Flagstaff, AZ.

Yazzie, Herb. 1993. Supplemental Statement of Herb Yazzie, Attorney General of the Navajo Nation, to the Subcommittee on Interior Appropriations, United States Senate, with Appendices A-L. Manuscript in possession of author.

Young, Wendy R. 1998. First Year of "Agreement" Passes. *Navajo Times*, 21 May.

11

"The Matter Was Never Resolved": The Casta System in Colonial New Mexico, 1693–1823

Adrian Bustamante

Several descriptive and demographic studies have been published on the Spanish colonial *casta* system,[1] although an analysis of how the system functioned in a frontier province like New Mexico has not been done. To fill that gap, this essay examines the implementation in New Mexico of the legal plan to keep elements of a polyethnic society clearly identified and stratified so that the mixed progeny of Spaniards, Indians, and blacks could be kept in socially subordinate positions [Table 11.1].

That this boundary-maintaining mechanism did not work as the Spanish civil and ecclesiastical authorities intended is not surprising because colonial society possessed a mitigating element, acculturation, that worked against the system's efficiency. Spain required every individual in the society to acculturate, i.e., speak the Spanish language, obey the same laws, adhere to Catholic beliefs, fight the same enemies, and exhibit other culturally standardizing behavior. As a consequence the real or ascribed cultural characteristics of each group (casta) were not sufficiently stable to persist in the close inter-ethnic contact that occurred on the frontier. As in other areas of New Spain, ethnic boundaries in New Mexico became blurred, causing the system to become muddled and largely ineffective. In fact, as will be seen, ecclesiastics and other officials had trouble in using the casta-categorizing nomenclature that gradually evolved. A second goal of this study is to supply a glimpse of the polyethnic origins of the group today known as the Hispanos of New Mexico.

For the purposes of this study, examination of the casta system and the concomitant development of the Hispanos as an ethnic group in northern New Mexico has to begin in the post-1693 colonial period. Although Juan de Oñate

Table 11.1
Ethnic mixture of castas

---

1. Español × India = Mestizo (NM)
2. Español × Mestiza = Castiza (NM)
3. Español × Castiza = Torna a Español
4. Español × Negra = Mulato (NM)
5. Español × Mulato = Morisco
6. Morisco × Español = Albino
7. Albino × Español = Tornatrás
8. Mulato × India = Calpamulato
9. Negro × India = Lobo (NM)
10. Lobo × India = Cambija
11. Calpamulato × India = Jivaro
12. Indio × Cambija = Sambahiga
13. Mulato × Mestiza = Cuarteron
14. Cuarteron × Mestiza = Coyote [According to census reports, in New Mexico the term coyote included the mixture of Mestizo × Indio and that of Spanish × Indian.]
15. Coyote × Morisca = Albarazado
16. Albarazado × Saltatras = Tente en el Aire
17. Mestizo × India = Cholo
18. India × Mulato = Chino (NM)
19. Española × China = Cuarteron de China
20. Negro × India = Sambo de Indio
21. Negro × Mulato = Zambio
22. Genízaro – Cambujo × China = Genízaro en Mexico [In New Mexico, the term genízaro had a somewhat different meaning.]

Source: Composite list from Nicolás León, *Las Castas del Mexico Colonial o Nueva España* (Mexico: Talleres Graficos del Museo Nacional de Arqueologia, Historia, y Etnografía, 1924).

and his colonists had settled New Mexico in 1598, the Native American revolt of 1680 caused the colonists to flee to the area of El Paso del Norte, near present Cuidad Juárez. For these first eighty-two years of colonization, no extant census furnishes an ethnic breakdown of the New Mexico population, even though Fray Alonso Benavides, in his optimistic report of 1630, described the population of New Mexico as made up of Spaniards, *mestizos*, and Indians and supplied population figures for some ethnic groups.[2] In addition, France V. Scholes, the authority on seventeenth-century New Mexico, notes evidence that eighty-to-ninety percent of the early colonial population was native born and that the castas practiced exogamy (i.e., marrying outside one's group) during this period.[3] Scholes adds that "it is impossible to estimate the proportion of Spaniards, creoles and *castes*, during this period."[4] Documents mention individuals as being *mestizo* or *mulato*, but because of insufficient demographic statistics, it is difficult to speak precisely about the colonial society's ethnic makeup. Such statistical information disappeared during the 1680 revolt when the Pueblos and Apaches destroyed all of the Spanish documents left in New Mexico, severely limiting knowledge of the 1598 to 1692 period.

When Diego de Vargas reconquered the area in 1693, a new historical era began for New Mexico's Hispano population. Only a few of the families living in New Mexico during pre-revolt days returned. Others, probably disheartened by the harshness of frontier life or by the memories of the massacre of their loved ones, chose not to return. As Fray Angélico Chávez has noted, the return of New Mexico to Spanish control after 1693 "was really a new and distinct colonization of New Mexico."[5]

Of the 187 new colonists in 1693, 45 were swarthy or of swarthy color, i.e., *trigüeno or color trigüeno*;[6] thus 24 percent were either castas or perhaps dark-skinned Spaniards. Looking at this group by families, 27 of the 67 families, or 40 percent, may have been castas.[7]

The 1695 muster roll, resulting from de Vargas' sending Juan Paez Hurtado to Mexico to recruit additional settlers for the colony, is even more helpful in determining the ethnicity of other new arrivals. The muster roll reveals that of the 141 persons who signed up 30 percent were classified *español*, 39 percent were *mestizo*, 11 percent were *coyote*, 11 percent were *mulato*, 2 percent were *lobos*, and 1.5 percent were *castizo*. Of the twenty-four married couples, ten were exogamous unions between castas, including four españoles who married outside of group.[8] At this very early date, then, the casta system was firmly reestablished in New Mexico.

Church records, baptismal, marriage, and burial registers for the first half of the eighteenth century, also reveal that the friars made no great effort to record the specific casta to which an individual belonged. For example, the church baptismal files for Nambé pueblo (one of the earliest existing records) from 1707 to 1727 give only the tribe or pueblo residency of the *indio* baptisms, e.g., *del pueblo de Pojoaque; de la nación Panana*; or *de la nación Apache*. For the colonizers the term español appears, but no other classification is given.[9] The same holds true for the baptismal records of Pecos between 1725 and 1744.[10] Marriage records for Santa Fe beginning in 1728 also reveal a lack of consistent classification for the castas. The Indians of the various pueblos and those belonging to the surrounding plains tribes are identified, but very few of the *gente de razón* (castas) are listed by the specific casta to which they belonged. The few castas clearly classified in the church records illustrate that the colonial population of New Mexico practiced exogamy.

An example of this exogamic practice is given in the following marriage entries. On October 5, 1734, in Santa Fe, it was recorded that "Estevan de Estrada [mulato servant of vicar Don Joseph de Bustamante]" married "Juana Mata de Espinoza, *India* a free widow . . .";[11] on May 6, 1741, Juan de la Vega, *collote* (coyote) married Margarita de Bustamante whose casta was not given.[12] After 1750 the casta of the bride and groom were listed more frequently, but many persons were still not ethnically categorized. Since most friars were also responsible for villages surrounding their missions, they conscientiously included the name of the village in which the persons were *vecinos* (residents), and thus the classification was used more frequently than terms for varied castas. Listing the village in which the individual resided was useful to the friars in identifying persons properly and in distinguishing between individuals with the same name. For example, Juan Pino (de Truchas) could readily be differentiated from Juan Pino (de Pecos). In addition, the Spanish government used physical descriptions to identify individuals, e.g., Juan José Domínguez, of ruddy complexion, with a full dark beard, and a scar over his left eye. The casta designation could have also been used to supply this proper identification.

Since so many settlers were not identified by casta category, they were probably members of the more acceptable castas such as mestizo. This assumption can be made because, given the importance placed on being español, families who claimed that category would have made certain that the friars noted their status in their records. Some friars, however, seem not to have cared to add the casta designation. They differentiated only when listing Indians. They probably did so because they wanted to demonstrate to their religious superiors in Mexico that the Indians were indeed being converted and receiving the sacraments, thus revealing successful missionizing activity. Moreover, perhaps taking for granted that villagers knew the family, the friars did not bother with designating the casta—unless it was español or indio.

During the last quarter of the eighteenth century, mention of the castas in records become more frequent. Possibly this happened because of the *Concilio IV Provincial Mexicano* (1771), which decreed that all parishioners must be classified according to their family status, i.e., single, married, or widowed and also according to their casta *"españoles, indios, negros, mulatos and other mixtures ..."*[13] This law applied to all official business conducted with the church, including baptismal, confirmation, marriage, and burial registers. One reason for the issuance of this decree may have been that anyone aspiring to the priesthood had to give evidence of being puro español.

Still, demographic statistics for this period continued to give only the broad categories. Nor did churchmen making official visits to northern New Mexico and citing its population statistics break down the population into castas. Bishop Pedro Tamarón y Romeral, whose canonical visit occurred in 1760, for example, states that the "villa of Santa Fe had 379 families of citizens of Spanish and mixed blood ..."[14] The only casta he identifies is the *genízaros* when he mentions Abiquiú and other villages where genízaro Indian families lived.[15]

In 1776 the Mexican superiors of Friar Francisco Atanasio Domínguez assigned him the task of making a canonical visit to all the churches and missions of New Mexico. From this visit came the most detailed and extant description of these edifices and of general aspects of New Mexican society of that period. In his instructions Fray Francisco was to distinguish among "españoles, de razón, and indios."[16] Domínguez did not precisely carry out his orders, for in giving the population of the Villa of Santa Fe, he distinguished only between

Spanish families and genízaro families. In reporting the census figures for the satellite villages of Santa Fe—Quemado, Cieneguilla, and Rio de Tesuque—he provided a breakdown only by family, including the number of individuals in each unit.[17]

In describing the citizens of Santa Cruz de la Canada, Friar Domínguez mentioned that a majority *could be taken for Spaniards,* suggesting that the castas considered themselves to be "Spanish" or were "whitened" enough to be classified as such. That Domínguez was conscious of the status of the persons whom he considered to be castas is clear in his description of the vecinos of the village of Las Trampas, whom he describes as *"gente baja,"* i.e., people of low class.[18] The 1790 census confirms that castas predominantly inhabited Trampas[19] and thus in Domínguez' eyes merited such opprobrium.

Friar Domínguez' report is thus helpful in understanding that some castas were probably passing themselves off for Spaniards (commonly done in the frontier provinces of New Spain), apparently hoping to improve their upward social mobility. This revelation, however, is not helpful in determining the demographic composition of each casta. The report also clearly illustrates the patronizing attitude of some españoles towards the castas.

Next, in September 1800, friars and secular priests making out the report required by the Junta del Gobierno del Real Consulado de Guadalajara also combined españoles and gente de razón,[20] although they were not consistent in their nomenclature. For instance, Friar Vergara, reporting on Sandia pueblo, distinguished only between indios and españoles, while Friar Merino reporting for Pecos used "indios and españoles y gentes de otras clases."[21] Father José Bibian de Ortega, secular curate of Santa Fe, noted that the Villa of Santa Fe had "three thousand sixty nine inhabitants of all classes." Here genízaros, as newly acculturated Indians descended from *"varias naciones,"* were seemingly being considered Catholic neophytes and indios, and thus not constituting a legal casta category.[22]

Although census-takers for the civil government during the first half of the eighteenth century also made little effort to classify society by casta, a few of the friars did note in the census of 1750 the ethnicity of a portion of the population. In fact, the census offers indisputable evidence that the society consisted of españoles and castas and that the two groups were mixing ethnically.[23] The census-takers did not specify, however, the ethnicity of the residents for most of the villages. Indian pueblos such as Taos, where Tanos and Apaches were listed as living among the Taos, constitute an exception. In some areas, such as the village complex of Nuestra Senora de la Soledad del Rio del Norte Arriba, genízaro families were also singled out. Fifteen genízaro families were enumerated and may well have been the vecinos of Abiquiú.

The most revealing section concerning the casta system in New Mexico is that enumerating Albuquerque. Here Fray José Yrigoyen included the casta designation of a majority of the adults. An analysis of marriage partners that Albuquerque males chose, for whom Fray Yrigoyen gives a casta or español

Figure 11.1
Casta mate choice in Albuquerque (Source: 1750 census)

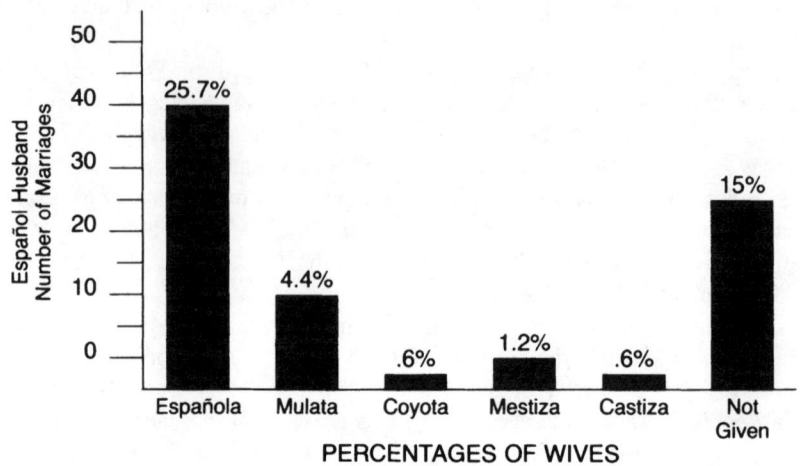

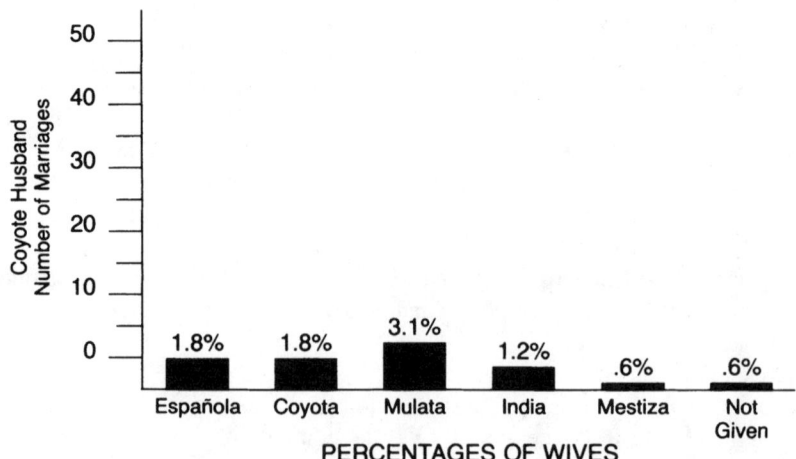

designation clarifies a good deal [Figures 11.1 and 11.2]. First, the trend among españoles was towards endogamy, although they did not strictly adhere to this practice. Second, after españolas, español males preferred *mulatas* (and *mulatos* preferred *españolas*). These two combinations make up 10 percent of the sampling. Third, indios vecinos preferred indias. Fourth, other castas mentioned in the census were fairly evenly represented in the figures. Also included in this section of the census, but not indicated in Figures 1 and 2, were the marriages of mestizos with coyota—one; lobo with china—two; and lobo with coyota—two. This small sampling from Fray Yrigoyen illustrates that on the frontiers of

Figure 11.2
Casta mate choice in Albuquerque (Source: 1750 census)

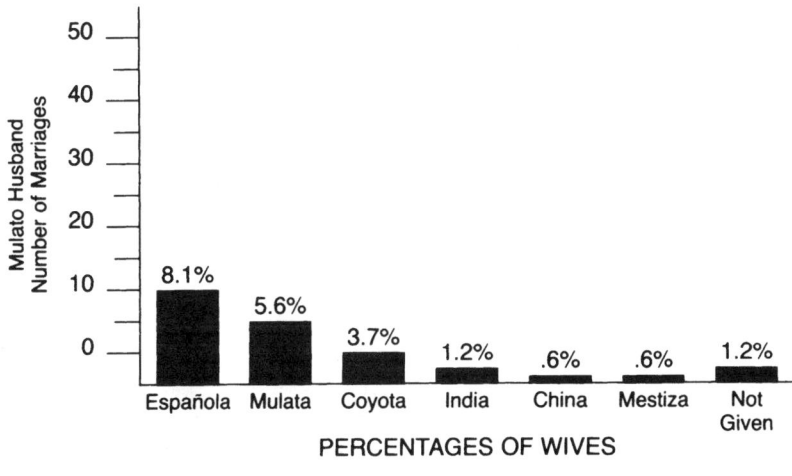

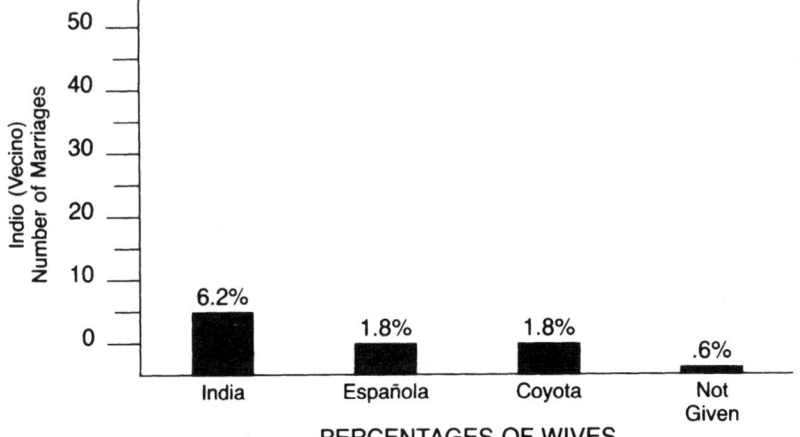

New Spain physical unions between whites, Indians, and blacks, begun in the Caribbean and Mexico, were continuing. Even more accurate statistics on castas are available in the 1790 census.

The 1790 census is the most complete, most useful one taken during the Spanish colonial period. This enumeration includes the names of husband and wife or head of household and occupation, and, more important for this study, the ethnicity of listed adults. Unfortunately, children's names are not given, with only their sex and age listed. In her exhaustive analysis of this census, Alicia Tjarks gives the following breakdown for some of the major areas of New

Mexico. (See Table [11.2] notice El Paso is eliminated from her table.)[24] My analysis of the jurisdiction of the Villa of Santa Fe, including its satellite villages, yields the statistics in Table 11.3.

These breakdowns clearly indicate that nomenclature used to describe castas depended on the individual census-taker. For example, the Santa Fe jurisdiction is the only area where the census-taker uses *color quebrado* (broken color), i.e., persons not pure Caucasian. Apparently the recorder thought it was impossible to determine precisely the casta of these individuals, or perhaps he was not troubled with his categories as long as he indicated that residents were not españoles or indios vecinos by using color quebrado. Although probably not a pejorative term, it did connote a status lower than español. Despite the imprecision of these reported ethnic categories (no more imprecise in New Mexico than in the other areas of New Spain[25]), one should attempt to understand what friars and officials meant when they used these various ethnic categories. Obviously, in the polyethnic society of the New World, español was considered the highest category of status. Consequently, one can assume that individuals strove to achieve that status. This category would include not only those who were genetically Spaniards but also those who claimed to be Spaniards by ascription. Self-ascribed Spaniards probably had to be considered among the upper class colonial society to be accepted as Spanish. It certainly follows that if influential Jews living in Spain could have their ethnic classification changed, influential members of castas in frontier colonies could also change classification.[26]

Clearly, direct immigration of Spaniards and other Europeans to New Mexico was very light during the eighteenth century.[27] Indeed, most of the colonists from Spain lived in Mexico for a while before migrating to New Mexico. Some married or cohabited with indios producing the mestizo casta.

The mestizo classification probably followed general usage in New Spain. It indicated that an individual's parents were español and indio, though by the late eighteenth century, mestizo had lost its specific one-half and one-half meaning and came to refer generally to racial mixtures. Since mestizo, next to español, was the most desirable status, the 1790 census reveals, not surprisingly, that 22 percent of New Mexico's population was classified mestizo. Those who could not become español probably settled for this next best ethnic identity available to them.

The next category was that of coyote. This classification seems to be an ascriptive ethnic category, i.e., a descriptive term used for persons by other groups as opposed to self-identifying (self-ascriptive) terms. Unfortunately, no clue exists in the Santa Fe Archdiocesan church or Spanish government records to indicate the origin of this term or its precise local meaning when employed to classify a group of people.

In his exhaustive study of the castas in colonial Mexico, Nicolás León asserts that coyote is a "*mexicanismo* derived from the *nahuatl coyotl (canis latrans Harlen)* or jackal. The hair is grayish yellow. White and Indian dominate this

Table 11.2
Español and *Casta* population in New Mexico 1790

	Spanish		Indian		Mestizo*		Mulato		Undetermined	
	No.	Percent	No.	Percent	No.	Percent	No.	Percent	No.	Percent
Albuquerque	2,079	46.64	621	14.46	1,703	38.24	7	0.15	23	0.51
Santa Fe, Tesuque, and Pecos	1,476	53.84	456	16.56	706	25.75	70	2.55	33	1.30
Santa Cruz, San Juan and Picuris**	2,525	58.57	590	13.68	1,113	25.81			83	1.94
TOTALS***	6,080	52.93	1,667	14.51	3,522	30.60	77	.67	139	1.21

*Tjarks includes *coyotes* and *color quebrado* in this category
**Note that the Taos area is not included.
***Totals were not included in Tjarks's table.

Table 11.3
Español and *Casta* population in Santa Fe 1790

Españoles		Indios and Vecinos		Mestizos		Coyotes		Color Quebrado		Genízaros		Mulatos		Undetermined	
No.	Percent	No.	Percent	No.	Percent	No.	Percent	No.	Percent	No.	Percent	No.	Percent	No.	Percent
1,719	57.10	113	3.75	225	7.40	20	.66	411	13.65	49	1.60	79	2.60	394	13.00

Source: Alicia V. Tjarks, *Demographic Structure of New Mexico,* 83.

casta. To José Alzate y Ramírez *coyote* is synonymous with *mestizo.*"[28] But the domination of both white and Indian blood is not readily clear in the ethnic mixtures León cites from other colonial works to explain the usage of coyote in Mexico.[29] These other works do bear out, however, that coyote usually referred to a person about one quarter Spanish and with some black heritage. Clearly, then, coyote was as imprecise as other terms used for the castas.

Judging all this evidence, the term coyote in New Mexico usually meant a mixture of Spaniard and Indian or black. In a parallel situation in 1785, Fray José Francisco López, reporting on the mission of San Antonio de Valero in Texas, referred to "*mulatos and mestizos* (who are called *coyotes* in this country)."[30] The widespread use of these terms may suggest that true mestizos wished to be distinguished from persons they considered less Spanish than themselves.

In New Mexico, Fray Antonio Barrera made an ambiguous statement about coyotes. When making his report to the Junta del Gobierno del Real Consulado de Guadalajara in 1801 he stated that among the Indians of San Felipe "live three families of Indians who are already *coyotes [entre ellos viven tres familias ya coyotes].*[31] Did he mean that these Indian families had mixed ethnically with the españoles and thus could be considered coyotes, or did he suggest that they had acculturated sufficiently to be considered coyotes? Probably he meant the former since as gente de razón they would have already been acculturated. Whatever his exact meaning, Fray Antonio implied that categorizing someone as coyote could be a step upwards on the social scale. This being the case, it is not surprising that the term became as acceptable as mestizo.

Later evidence suggests that coyote supplanted mestizo in New Mexico, as it did in Texas. For example, in his census report of 1860 for the Santa Fe area, Charles Blumner utilizes "M/IND" as the ethnic classification for an individual, then explains that "M/IND means mixed white and Indian, called by the Mexicans 'coyote.' "[32] Today, coyote is generally used for the offspring of Anglos and Hispanos or Mexican Americans, although, as previously noted, the inclusion of black blood is a possibility.

The smallest population in the 1790 census was the mulato casta. Blacks and the mulatos came to New Mexico very early in the colonial period, with Gaspar de Villagrá mentioning mulatos as a casta accompanying Oñate in 1598.[33] France V. Scholes also notes the existence of mulatos in New Mexico during the seventeenth century.[34]

In the eighteenth century, mulatos seem never to have exceeded 2.5 percent of a population of 15,045 non-Indians in the New Mexican districts, excluding El Paso.[35] This group includes only one lobo.[36] Those listed are free mulatos, including a very few servants. Although a small minority, the mulatos are highly "visible" in these documents. The most notable of the mulatos is Sebastián Rodríguez, who came to New Mexico as Diego de Vargas' drummer and town crier and seems to have started a large family in New Mexico.[37] Because of his occupation he was known as "*El Tambor.*"[38] Sebastián's son Esteban succeeded his father as drummer and town crier, and his brother Melchior helped to found Trampas.[39] Overall the 1790 census indicates that in seventy-six of the provinces eighty-six mulatos were living in the jurisdiction of Santa Fe, most of whom seemed to reside in the Barrio de Analco.[40] Other documents mention court proceedings against mulatos for livestock theft, assault, and hexing, thus suggesting that mulatos were a conspicuous part of society.

Although persons genetically Negroid were considered members of the lowest castas, mestizos, coyotes, or color quebrados may also have belonged to the same casta, but they had been able to "whiten" themselves through intermarriage or by misleading the census-takers. Such actions may have led Pedro Baptista Pino to report to the Spanish Cortes in 1811 that "in New Mexico there are no castas of people of African origin."[41] Possibly, too, he was an astute politician willing to tell the Cortes what it wanted to hear to obtain requested favors for New Mexico. This conclusion is based also on his attempt to picture the Pueblo Indians (those living in their own villages) in a positive light by arguing they were nearly indistinguishable from the Spaniards. All these documentary mentionings suggest that the mulatos contributed noticeably to the genetic make-up of New Mexican society.

Another noteworthy category was the indios vecinos. Although not considered a separate casta, these indios had been acculturated into Hispanic society, were distinguished from other indios through the term vecino, and were considered separate from genízaros. Early in the eighteenth century indios vecinos may have been Mexican Indians accompanying new colonists, but later in the same century they seem to have been former members of the surrounding nomadic tribes or natives no longer living in their pueblos.[42] The 1790 census lists 473 persons (4.2 percent of New Mexico's population) among this group. Making up the fourth largest population group, indios vecinos resided primarily in the jurisdiction of Santa Fe and San Juan pueblo. In addition to the 52 percent living in those two areas, others were spread throughout the colony.

At this point, the Village of San Miguel del Vado will be used to illustrate the sometimes confusing and inconsistent use of the casta by the friars during the late colonial period, a misuse that led to the demise of the system. The San Miguel del Vado land grant, located approximately forty miles from Santa Fe, was on the banks of the Pecos River, and issued by Governor Fernando de Chacón to a group of fifty-six petitioners on November 25, 1794.[43] Although San Miguel del Vado has long been considered a genízaro town, a close review of the baptismal records of San Miguel reveals that only ten of the forty-two original settlers identified were clearly genízaros.[44] In fact, between 1794 and 1817, when nearly all type of casta designation disappeared, only nineteen of the baptized children are identified as genízaros.

On the other hand, it seems españoles, whether valid or self-ascribed, were always identified, as were the indios. The great majority of individuals, however, are identified only as vecinos, sometimes as *vecino del Vado*, or just as vecino.

Vecino clearly identified those who were considered full members of the Hispano society, even though the term's exact meaning referred to a resident and citizen of a specified town.

Unfortunately, the four friars enumerating New Mexicans were inconsistent even among themselves in making ethnic classifications, as were most other friars in New Mexico. Although Fray Diego Martínez, who served at Pecos pueblo from 1800 to 1804 and who was also responsible for San Miguel del Vado, seems careful in identifying españoles, he used vecino (resident of San Miguel del Vado) for other persons. Serving the same parish from 1804 to 1810 and again from 1818–1825, Fray Francisco Bragado used only español, genízaro, and indio. During 1810, the last year of his residency as pastor, he began to use "del bado" [sic], but when he returned in 1818 he used genízaro for only one entry and did not specify either a casta category or vecino for the remainder of the baptismal entries.

Still another priest, Fray Juan Bruno Gonzalez, who served only one year from March 1810 to March 1811, distinguished between only the settlers of San Miguel and those of San José del Vado, the new satellite settlement up river from San Miguel. Only one ethnic entry is included in his records, *india de Pecos*. Of course, by this time entries for the Pecos pueblo were becoming fewer and fewer because Pecos, once the mightiest of all the pueblos, was in its final stages of collapse.[45]

The most inconsistent in his use of ethnic terms, however, was Fray Antonio García del Valle, who replaced Friar Gonzalez and served until 1818. He employed español, mestizo, indio, and, surprisingly enough *castiza* once, possibly one of the few times it was used in New Mexico. In his fourth entry, on March 14, 1811, Father García states that he baptized María Francisca Paula de Jesus, castiza, daughter of Santiago Aragon and María Matiana Salaz, mestizos. For the children of other mestizos, however, he uses mestizo. Since a castiza, according to casta lists, denotes the offspring of an español-mestizo union, Fray Antonio was not utilizing this categorization as it was normally employed in Mexico. Possibly the Aragones complained that their daughter should be classified as español because on July 9, 1807, Friar Bragado had previously baptized María's older sister and had listed her as española. To conjecture, perhaps the compromise was to classify María as castiza.

Another case of inconsistency concerned José Miguel Brito, one of the original San Miguel grantees. In 1808 Friar Bragado had listed Brito as a genízaro, but in 1811 to Friar del Valle mentions José as just a vecino. Later, in 1814, del Valle categorizes Brito as an *"Yndio"* [sic]. Of course, one does not know whether these categorizations depended on a colonist's being in or out of the good graces of the friar.

From 1812 on, Friar del Valle primarily uses "del Vado" in his entries. Still, when the priest came to entries for the Esparza and Tapia families, he sharpened his quill, used his best penmanship, and categorized these individuals españoles, noticeably employing the polite don and doña for the parents. This exceptional treatment indicated the high social status of these families.

By the latter half of the eighteenth and the early years of the nineteenth centuries, society was mixing genetically, and clear racial categories had become blurred on the frontier. Several incidents occurring at this time, however, leave no doubt about the second-class status of the castas.

For instance, in 1766 a Joseph Baca was recommended to serve as *teniente politico* because he "knows how to read and write and is recognized as a white man."[46] Two years later, Governor Pedro Lara Mendinueta, tired of receiving complaints from farmers regarding the theft of their produce, issued a decree that stated:

If a man or woman, boy or girl is found with stolen produce or in the act of stealing produce from someone's garden and if that person is of broken color, he or she shall receive twenty-five lashes at the pillory. *If the person is white* he or she shall [only] be tied to the same pillory with the shameful stolen produce hung around the neck.[47]

Obviously, a more severe punishment was meted out to the casta. Here, too, color quebrado stands for a catchall category for the castas. That the coyote was considered inferior to the español is demonstrated by a statement in 1819 concerning an altercation between a coyote and Manuel Vigil over irrigation water. Vigil felt that as an español and a soldier, judgment should be rendered in his favor because "a coyote is inferior to a Spaniard who is also a soldier."[48]

In short, colonists of the Spanish crown came into New Mexico as an ethnically diverse group, representing a genetic mixing begun in Mexico [see Photos 11.1 and 11.2]. Furthermore, in New Mexico, the genes of the Pueblos and the nomadic tribes added other ingredients. The term genízaro became useful in identifying those who were not ethnically casta, as did the term indio vecino. Español was the category of status, and some families, possessing status legitimately, attempted to protect it through the practice of endogamy. Españoles also protected their status by trying to make certain their position was noted in church transactions, probably to the amusement of the friars if the individual demonstrated color quebrado. However, since most colonists were members of the same culture, love and passion among members of the society would not be denied. The castas, and even some who were or called themselves españoles, practiced exogamy so that by the end of the Spanish period these interracial marriages and liaisons had formed a genetically homogeneous population from the three great trunks of humanity—the Caucasoid, the Mongoloid, and the Negroid races.[49]

In 1821 when Mexico won its independence from Spain, and the Plan of Iguala gave equality to all citizens and in effect eliminated the casta system, one might assume that any further references to the system would have been eliminated because casta connoted inferior citizenship. Surprisingly this was not the case in New Mexico. The census of 1823 divides the population into es-

Photo 11.1 Illustrations from Señor Don Pedro Alonso O'Crouley, *A Description of The Kingdom of New Spain*, trans. and ed. Seán Galvin (San Francisco: John Howell Books, 1972).

Photo 11.2 Illustrations from Señor Don Pedro Alonso O'Crouley, *A Description of The Kingdom of New Spain*, trans. and ed. Seán Galvin (San Francisco: John Howell Books, 1972).

pañoles eligible to exercise their rights as citizens and those not eligible. Other categories included indios, eligible to exercise their rights as citizens and those ineligible, and finally *pardos*, eligible to exercise their rights as citizens and those not eligible. Since social habits die slowly, especially in isolated frontiers, the mention of español and indio could be explained in that way. However, most surprising is the use of "pardo" to categorize a segment of the population.[50]

From a careful reading of the census one can infer that the term pardo (meaning literally gray) was a one-word substitute for the casta nomenclature in use during the colonial period.[51] The casta that pardo designated usually were people of black or part-black descent.[52] The term had also become more common in other parts of New Spain, and by the latter part of the eighteenth century it was replacing "negro" and "mulato" in official documents.[53] The terms had apparently not been used in New Mexico, however, until this period.[54] Why was it being used now? This question is difficult to answer, but some assumptions can be made.

On February 1, 1795, a *cedula* authorized pardo and *quinterones* to contract matrimony with whites, permitted them to hold public office, and allowed them to enter Holy Orders.[55] This fact, coupled with a bulletin issued by Generalissimo Augustín de Iturbide of Mexico that the present "organic law [Spanish Constitution of Cadiz 1812] should remain in force so far as it was in harmony with the independence of Mexico until her representatives adopted new institutions," may shed some light on the issue.[56] By 1822, when the census was being taken, Mexico still lacked a constitution; therefore the census-taker may have wanted to lift the status of *infame* (opprobrium) from the castas in New Mexico and thus may have chosen to use this term. On the other hand, one might argue that the census-taker was insulting the castas in New Mexico by intimating that they possessed black ethnic ancestry. This last argument is weakened, however, by the reference in the census to *derechos de cuidadanos* (rights of citizens). The cedula of 1795, as we have seen, granted certain rights to pardos, and the constitution of 1812 "left the door open to" persons of "African" ancestry to become citizens with derechos.[57] Thus, it would not have behooved the census-taker to insult the castas in this manner.

Here, then, was the last gasp of the casta system in New Mexico. During the Mexican period (1821–1846) the only categorizations utilized were indio and genízaro, categories technically not considered castas. In this era, the change to *mexicano* as the principal ethnic categorization must have been a momentous and positive transformation for those who had previously been identified as castas.

Considering this complex and convoluted ethnic history of New Mexico, is it surprising that doña Seferina Quintana of Pecos, age 90, could recently state, in what may have been the collective unconscious at work, "the matter was never resolved. Some say we are Spanish, others that we are Indians, and others that we are Mexicans."[58]

NOTES

Adrian Bustamante is Division Head of Arts and Sciences at Santa Fe Community College and has done extensive research on colonial New Mexico.

1. "Casta" will be used in this essay instead of the term "caste." Casta was utilized by the Spanish from the sixteenth century through the early part of the nineteenth century as a term denoting ethnic categorization, while the term caste connotes more of a categorization of class as when used to describe the traditional social system of India. For descriptive studies of the Casta system, see Nicolás León, *Las Castas del Mexico Colonial o Nueva España* (Mexico: Talleres Graficos del Museo Nacional de Arqueologia, Historia, y Etnografía, 1924). This is an early work, but most of the information is still current. L. N. McAlister, "Social Structure and Social Change in New Spain," *Hispanic American Historical Review* 43 (August 1963), 349–70. Peggy K. Liss, *Mexico Under Spain, 1521–1556: Society and the Origins of Nationality* (Chicago: University of Chicago Press, 1975). Magnus Mörner, ed., *Race and Class in Latin America* (New York: Columbia University Press, 1970), and Mörner, *Race Mixture in the History of Latin America* (Boston: Little, Brown and Co., 1967). For demographic studies of colonial New Mexico, see Janie Louise Aragon, "The People of Santa Fe in the 1790s," *Aztlan* 7 (Fall 1976), 391–417; Antonio José Rios-Bustamante, "New Mexico in the Eighteenth Century: Life, Labor and Trade in the Villa de San Felipe de Albuquerque, 1706–1790," *Aztlan* 7 (Fall 1976), 357–90; Alicia V. Tjarks, "Demographic, Ethnic, and Occupational Structure of New Mexico, 1790: The Census Report of 1790," *The Americas: The Academy of American Franciscan History* 35 (July 1978), 45–88; Oakah Jones, Jr., *Los Paisanos: Spanish Settlers of the Northern Frontier of New Spain* (Norman: University of Oklahoma Press, 1979).

2. Alonso de Benavides, *Benavides' Memorial of 1630*, trans., Peter P. Forrestal, ed. Cyprian J. Lynch (Washington, D.C.: Academy of American Franciscan History, 1954), 24.

3. France V. Scholes, "Civil Government and Society in New Mexico in the Seventeenth Century," *New Mexico Historical Review* 10 (April 1935), 97.

4. Ibid.

5. Angélico Chávez, *Origins of New Mexico Families in the Spanish Colonial Period in Two Parts: The Seventeenth (1598–1693) and the Eighteenth (1693–1821) Centuries* (Santa Fe: Historical Society of New Mexico, 1954), x–xi.

6. Ralph Emerson Twitchell, *The Spanish Archives of New Mexico* (2 vols., Glendale, California: Arthur H. Clark Co., 1914), 92–105.

7. Microfilm roll 2, Document No. 54-C, Spanish Archives of New Mexico, State Records Center and Archives, Santa Fe (hereafter SANM). For a discussion of this list, see: Brian Alexander Young, "The History of the Black in New Mexico From the Sixteenth Century Through the Nineteenth Century" (master's thesis, University of New Mexico, 1967).

8. Clevy Floyd Strout, "The Resettlement of Santa Fe, 1695: The Newly Found Muster Roll," *New Mexico Historical Review* 53 (July 1978), 261–70.

9. Baptismal Records, Reel 6, Archives of the Archdiocese of Santa Fe (hereafter AASF).

10. Ibid.

11. Ibid. Marriage Records, reel 31, frame 21, AASF. This entry is of interest because it illustrates that the secular clergy also kept slaves or *criados*. Author's translation.

12. Marriage Records, reel 31, frame 36, AASF.

13. León, *Las Castas*, 15–16. Author's translation.

14. Eleanor B. Adams, ed., *Bishop Tamarón's Visitation of New Mexico, 1760* (Albuquerque: Historical Society of New Mexico, 1954), 46.

15. Ibid., 64.

16. Legajo 10, Number 86, Biblioteca Nacional de México (hereafter BNM), Special Collections, Zimmerman Library, University of New Mexico, Albuquerque. For a translation of Domínguez' report, see Adams and Fray Angélico Chávez, ed. and trans., *The Missions of New Mexico, 1776: A Description by Fray Francisco Anastacio Domínguez with other Contemporary Documents* (Albuquerque: University of New Mexico Press, 1956).

17. Legajo 10, Number 86, BNM.

18. Ibid.

19. Reel 12, frame 500, SANM.

20. Varios Documentos, 1800 (Bundled documents dated 1800.) Archives of the Archdiocese of Durango, Mexico (hereafter AAD).

21. Ibid. Author's translation.

22. For a brief study of the *genízaro*, see Steven M. Horvath, Jr., "The Genízaro of Eighteenth-Century New Mexico: A Reexamination," *Discovery* (Santa Fe: School of American Research, 1977), 25–40.

23. Legajo 8, Number 81, BNM.

24. Tjarks, "Demographic Structure," 83. For a total of New Mexico's population in 1790, see Sherburne F. Cook and Woodrow Borah, *Essays in Population History: Mexico and the Caribbean* (2 vols., Berkeley: University of California Press, 1974), 214–15, 220–23.

25. Mörner, *Race Mixture*, 58.

26. For an example of an influential Jew changing his ethnic classification, see McAlister, "Social Structure," 353.

27. Tjarks, "Demographic Structure," 83.

28. León, *Las Castas*, 22.

29. León gives a long explanation of the term *coyote* that helps one understand how confusing casta nomenclature could be. On p. 40 he gives the genetic origin of a *coyote* as *mestizo* × *indio* = *coyote*. Since a mestizo should be one-half Spanish and one-half Indian, coyote is only one-quarter Spanish with Indian blood predominating. However, León also gives other sources indicating that a coyote could also have black blood. He cites the following examples: *mulato* × *mestizo* = *quarteron and quarteron* × *mestizo* = *coyote* (p. 39). The term quarteron comes from the one-quarter each of Indian and black that the quarteron possesses. The rest of his ethnic balance would be made up of 50 percent Spanish, which differs from the cases cited above. In this case the offspring coyote, from quarteron and mestizo, is ethnically half Spanish and one-eighth black and three-eighths Indian. León also gives the following combination: *barcino* × *mulato* = *coyote* (p. 56). A barcino comes from *mulato* × *albarazado*. Another survey in Hensley Woodbridge "Glossary of Names Used in Colonial Latin America for Crosses among Indians, Negroes and Whites," *Journal of the Washington Academy of Sciences* 38 (1948), 357, shows that none of the various mixtures used for the classification coyote ever had less than 25 percent Spanish blood with the range being 25 to 75 percent.

30. Fray José Francisco López, "Report and Account that the Father President of the Missions in the Province of Texas or New Philippines Sends to the Most Illustrious Señor Rafael Jose Verger" in Ernest Wallace and David Vigness, eds., *Documents of Texas History* (Austin: Steck, 1963), 29.

31. Varios Documentos, 1801, AAD.

32. 1860 Census of the United States of America, 6, dwelling 31, household 36. Microfilm copy, New Mexico State Records Center and Archives, Santa Fe.

33. Gilberto Espinosa and F. W. Hodge, trans., *History of New Mexico by Gaspar Pérez de Villagrá Alcala 1610* (Los Angeles: Quivira Society, 1933), 282–83.

34. France V. Scholes, "Troublous Times in New Mexico," *New Mexico Historical Review* 12 (April 1937), 140.

35. Tjarks, "Demographic Structure," 83.

36. Ibid.

37. Chávez, *Origins of New Mexico Families*, 270.

38. Twitchell, *Spanish Archives of New Mexico* 2, Number 77.

39. Chávez, *Origins of New Mexico Families*, 270.

40. Roll 21, frames 383–89, SANM.

41. Pedro Baptista Pino, *Exposición Sucinta y Sencilla de la Provincia del Nuevo Mejico*, in H. Bailey Carroll and J. Villasana Haggard, *Three New Mexico Chronicles* (Albuquerque: Quivira Society, 1942), 243.

42. Twitchell, *Spanish Archives of New Mexico* 1, Number 512, gives evidence that the *"indios mexicanos"* were considered a separate group during the early eighteenth century. In 1727 Don Salvador Montoya, Regidor de la Villa de Santa Fe, in his last will and testament says that a piece of land that he owned was bounded "on the west by the lands of the Mexicans." Author's translation.

43. Surveyor General of New Mexico Reports, file 49, report 119, State Records Center and Archives, Santa Fe.

44. Roll 6, frame 666, AASF.

45. John L. Kessell, *Kiva, Cross and Crown: The Pecos Indians and New Mexico 1540–1840* (Washington: National Park Service/U.S. Department of the Interior, 1979), 413–63.

46. Roll 9, frame 962, SANM. Author's emphasis and translation.

47. Roll 10, frame 402, SANM. Author's emphasis and translation.

48. Number 2846, SANM 2. Author's translation.

49. Tjarks, "Demographic Structure," 72.

50. Felipe Tena Ramírez, *Leyes Fundamentales de México, 1808–1956.* (Mexico: Editorial Porrúa, 1957), 115. The author wishes to thank Dr. Myra Ellen Jenkins for showing him that this term was still used in the 1823 census.

51. Roll 3, frames 217–18, Mexican Archives of New Mexico.

52. Cook and Borah, *Essays*, 2, 464.

53. McAlister, "Social Structure," 368.

54. A more thorough search of the Spanish Archives of New Mexico may reveal a few of these terms, but they would be highly exceptional.

55. McAlister, "Social Structure," 368.

56. William Spence Robertson, *Iturbide of Mexico* (Durham, North Carolina: Duke University Press, 1952), 96.

57. Ramírez, *Leyes*, 63.

58. Interview with doña Seferina Quintana, Pecos, 1977. Author's translation. The author wishes to thank the National Endowment for the Humanities for financial assistance in the preparation of this article.

12

Fiesta Time and Plaza Space: Resistance and Accommodation in a Tourist Town

Sylvia Rodríguez

This article describes the Taos, New Mexico, summer fiesta of Santiago and Santa Ana as a living ritual event and considers the voices of participants and opponents of the festival. My analysis shows how the fiesta enacts collective and individual identities while staging a moment of communitas. This invented tradition expresses resistance as well as accommodation to the conditions and structures of power within which the celebration takes place and constructs meaning.

Festivals telescope sociocultural processes in the making. As anthropologist Stanley Brandes puts it, "Each fiesta seems to yield its own body of specialized information about the relationships among political and social entities" within a particular setting (1988:178). Like other ritual genres, festivals "provide a home to and a stage for the exercise of power" (Stoeltje 1993:135), and may therefore be examined for what they can tell us about how power operates within any given setting. Beverly Stoeltje suggests that scholars of ritual are interested in the same two questions scholars of power are concerned with, regarding the outcome and locus of power. "We are searching," she says, "for outcomes when we search for meaning and transformation in ritual, and we are looking for the locus of power when we examine the means by which ritual achieves its effects" (1993:140). She also argues for a dual theoretical approach that combines hermeneutic with Marxist perspectives in order to address the cultural creativity of power as well as the inequality of social relations power functions to uphold (1993:140). The locus and outcome of power observable in a local community festival is one theoretical focus of the following ethnographic account.

Mikhail Bakhtin (1984) put forth a thesis about the subversive-regenerative nature of carnival that is not novel to anthropologists or folklorists but which he ingeniously explicates in terms of Rabelais's position in literature and language, as well with reference to power struggle in the ancient and modern worlds. Many analysts emphasize the conservative role of ritual behavior (Scott 1990) while others like Bakhtin focus on its subversive aspect, or following Victor Turner (1974), attempt to chart the processual dynamic between them. Roger Abrahams (1983) distinguishes between the containment exerted by ritual and the release occasioned by festival, while Brandes (1988) calls fiestas agents of social control, their paradoxical nature notwithstanding. Like other ritual genres, festival "is accessible to both reactionaries and revolutionaries for their various political purposes" (Stoeltje 1993:135). This dual or contradictory character of fiesta is a major source of its sheer experiential power.

In addition to a dual or fused Marxist or radical-hermeneutic framework, the study of festivals requires both diachronic and synchronic approaches in order to understand social relations and cultural politics through time. Historiography identifies process and traces it with reference to macro- and microcontextual factors. Ethnography records live behavior and spoken exegesis, in order to decode their meanings within specific historical and political contexts. These methods can be systematically applied to the scrutiny of particular and generic features of festival, which include parades and processions, contests and costumes, music, song and dance, food and drink, a dense crowd, and routinized calendric and ritual formats. In addition to these, it is important also to examine organization, structure, and process among those individuals who together make a festival happen. Stoeltje condenses all of these elements into a threefold model for theorizing power in the ritual genres which focuses on: (1) the evolution of form, (2) the performance of discourse, and (3) the organization of production.[1] Although my investigation of the Taos fiesta was not originally conceptualized in terms of Stoeltje's model, my findings can nevertheless be usefully organized in terms of the categories she has proposed.

This article represents the second in a series of articles of mine about what a summer fiesta reveals about social relations in the contemporary tourist town of Taos, New Mexico. Each article focuses on a distinct aspect of the festival: (1) its history; (2) an ethnographic analysis of its present form; (3) the "queen complex" at the heart of its symbolic meaning; (4) what its parades, marches, and processions reveal about political order; and (5) the workings, role, and status of the fiesta council. Each builds one aspect of a cumulative, overall analysis by pursuing a particular question or issue. Together, these articles or chapters carry out an analysis akin to the kind Stoeltje proposes, in that the first one deals specifically with the evolution of form, the second through fourth scrutinize discourse and performance, while the fifth examines the organization of production. Each piece, moreover, addresses issues of form, discourse, and production with respect to its particular subject matter.

My historical article (1997) documents the invention of the Taos fiesta and chronicles how one ethnic constituency (Hispanos) gradually took over fiesta while another (Anglos) withdrew from it. It points out that despite this slow ethnic switch, middle-class control over fiesta remains intact. The present article describes the fiesta as a ritual event that enacts collective and individual identities while achieving communitas through a mixture of resistant and accommodationist practices. My narrative incorporates the voices of participants as well as opponents of the festival to show how locals construct the meaning of fiesta in relation to perceived conditions and structures of power. Together, these first two articles appear to make a case for fiesta/carnival as resistant or oppositional practice.

But with a third article (forthcoming), on what the fiesta queen complex tells us about the intersection of gender and ethnic identity in Taos, the institutional, hegemonic role of fiesta swings into focus. There I ask why the queen must always be Hispana, and I consider the narratives of queens and other participants plus the discourse and practice surrounding her selection, public display, and personal comportment. The queen complex enacts what Roberto Da Matta (1984) argues for Brazilian carnival: a transformational inversion that merges the separate, dialectically related domains of the house/home and the street. Fiesta "domesticates" the plaza by bringing crowds of longtime familiars together to eat and party within its open, yet bounded, confines. It furthermore domesticates alienated, commodified space by installing a queen, the virgin who embodies an ethnic boundary through symbolic allusion to a moral code of endogamous holy matrimony—indeed the original theme in New Mexico interracial politics (see Gutiérrez 1991).[2] Every festival queen complex is hegemonic insofar as it models a heterosexual gender norm structured by class, nationality, and the state (see Cohen et al. 1996).

The queen's procession, the grand wedding march (*La Gran Marcha*) she leads at dances, and especially the historical parade she appears in, symbolically display interlocking relations, or systems, of power. This is the argument of my fourth article (in progress). In the parade, symbols of membership and division along the primary axes of difference—gender, ethnicity, class, nation, state— are driven into the home and into the self via the street. A parade is the public enactment par excellence, wherein state and national identities emblematically subsume all others (see Davis 1986). Changes over the years in parade order, composition, and route all register change in social, political, and cultural relations, and in the symbolic representation of self vis-à-vis community, the family, capital, and the nation-state. The fifth article will return to the point that while festival control has shifted from Anglos to Hispanos, the reins of fiesta remain firmly in the hands of the middle class. I ask why the middle class always controls fiesta, and I look at the makeup and workings of the fiesta council and the location and roles of its members in Taos society. Together, these five articles build toward a concluding theoretical article about the study and politics of ethnos, gender, class, and place in a tourist town.

A word must be said about voice and viewpoint in this study. The most important fact about my ethnographic approach to the Taos fiesta is that I am a native of Taos who grew up participating in the fiesta, sharing over the years in a range of local sentiments, memories, and perceptions about its character and the ways it changed. Like so many Taoseños, I remember walking or riding in the childrens' parade, of excitedly waiting to ride the antique merry-go-round known as Tío Vivo. I recall the thrill of water gun fights or sniping at unwary fiesta goers amidst the throng; of squandering my money at the booths on cotton candy and trinkets; of dressing up in fiesta skirts and cowboy outfits. My parents were a young interethnic married couple when the fiesta was born in the late 1930s, and both were enthusiastic early participants in its activities. Later on, my father, who ran a drugstore located on the plaza, complained about how hard it was to do business during the fiesta, to serve water to hundreds of thirsty celebrants who would use the bathroom and then go outside to buy their hamburgers at a festival booth instead of his soda fountain. The employees watched like hawks for shoplifters among the crowd that squeezed into the store during the inevitable afternoon rainstorm.

But by my middle teens I had grown indifferent and then disdainful toward the fiesta, and for years never bothered to go. Then, little by little, after living away from Taos for almost two decades, I began to attend again. Twice in the early 1980s I was involved in the big parade and worked in food booths to raise money for local causes. The float I rode on in 1985 seems especially revealing. It consisted of a sparsely decorated flatbed with canned music, and a dozen or more members of the Northern New Mexico Club, including myself. This organization consisted of about two hundred Taoseños and other northern New Mexicans living "in exile" in the urban wilderness of Los Angeles. A downpour began just as the parade started and persisted for an hour, drenching us all, trapped there, as we wended our way slowly from the courthouse toward town, around the plaza, and finally northward to the post office. A number of individuals on that float, including myself, have since moved back to New Mexico. About the only time I am sure to see them is at the fiesta.

In short, I am no detached observer of the fiesta, which I officially began to study in 1992, after casually participating in it over my lifetime. It seems as much a consequence of my ethnographic moment as my native positionality that I cannot tell whether I am studying the fiesta because I cannot stay away from it, or if I cannot stay away from it because I am studying it. In either case, the question here is based my own experience of the fiesta: like others, I am irresistibly drawn there. Once the fiesta is underway, if I am anywhere in the Taos area, it feels to me virtually impossible not to gravitate to the plaza. Many are likewise drawn, despite their resistance and grumbling.

My ambiguous native/insider/outsider/halfie/coyote,[3] gendered, middle-class positionality makes this inquiry experimental also insofar as it reflexively addresses the politics of ethnography with reference to the study of invented tradition. In a recent discussion of the troubled relations between scholars and those whose invented traditions they study, Charles Briggs seems to imply that "indigenous" scholars are more in the habit of inventing tradition than of deconstructing it (1996:461). Yet most indigenous scholars seem to be engaged in both operations simultaneously. Thus, like nationalist as well as "outsider" work, my deconstructive analysis of the Taos fiesta constructs the event as never before, by virtue of entextualizing and thus placing it "in the literature." The question of ethnographic authority is always problematic, as is the oversimple native/outsider binary (see Abu-Lughod 1991; Haraway 1988; Narayan 1993). Having said this much, I will defer further discussion of the politics of this ethnography to forthcoming articles.

The following ethnographic account describes the Taos summer fiesta as a ritual event with a precise temporal structure and spatial locale. I examine the site where the fiesta takes place, the town plaza, and describe the three-day event as it unfolds there during the 1990s. Next, I present a few opposing voices, pro and con, about the fiesta. These first-person narratives tell why people go and like or dislike the fiesta, and explain what it means to them. Finally, I analyze the overall fiesta text/script with reference to the inversions it orchestrates, as well as with respect to the eternal paradox of fiesta/carnival—its simultaneously hegemonic and subversive character.

LAS FIESTAS DE SANTIAGO Y SANTA ANA

Every year during the third week of July, the town of Taos celebrates its so-called traditional fiestas of Santiago and Santa Ana. This two-and-a-half-day festival is held on a weekend and is marked by several features. To begin with, the downtown plaza is closed off to automobile traffic and concession booths are set up all around on the street, along with Taos's antique merry-go-round, known as Tío Vivo. The celebration begins on the evening before the first day with a vespers mass at the Catholic church, followed by a procession and coronation of the fiesta queen. For the next two days, a constant stream of music and dance entertainers perform atop the gazebo platform near the center of the plaza. There is a children's parade on one day and an adult Historical-Hysterical parade on the next, and dance balls on at least two nights.[4] Thousands of locals crowd onto the plaza to watch the coronation and parades, enjoy the entertainment, sit, walk around, visit, eat, drink, and generally have a good time.

The Taos fiesta is smaller, less complex, and less spectacular than the Santa Fe fiesta, which has been studied by Ronald Grimes (1976, 1982) and others (Pierce 1985; Wilson 1997). But like its fancier counterpart to the south, the Taos fiesta is nonetheless of interest as a public cultural event that can be examined for insight into its larger sociocultural and political milieu. The fiesta offers a window onto the changing face of interethnic relations and cultural politics over six decades of an evolving tourism economy in Taos. The character and management of the fiesta at different points in time register social concerns, political climate, and the balance of local power particular to the moment in question. Rhetorical-symbolic, organizational, and spatial control over the fiesta, including its site on the Taos plaza, defines a field of contestation reflective of the larger context of sociopolitical struggle between ethnic groups, classes, intragroup factions, and cross-group sectors.

The late-July fiesta was invented around 1938 by a group of mostly Anglo boosters for the explicit purpose of attracting customers to the Taos plaza during the height of the tourist season. For the next two decades, Anglos ran the event and few Hispanos participated in its organization. But in the 1960s a gradual transition began toward Hispanic control and predominance such that today the organizers are high-status Hispanos and the fiesta itself is attended almost exclusively by Hispanos and Mexicanos from the greater Taos area. During this gradual transition, fiesta council rhetoric went from a romantic celebration of "tricultural harmony" to a self-conscious "preservation of Hispanic tradition." The Hispanization of the fiesta crystallized during a phase of resort development, when the plaza changed from a center of commerce for locals to a reconstructed and gentrified site geared exclusively to touristic consumption. Today, most residents tend to avoid the plaza. The fiesta is the only time during the year when local Hispanos, through sheer numbers, physically reoccupy and thus symbolically reclaim the public space that was once the center of their community but is now a kind of theme mall from which their daily social lives are effectively banished.

Most Taoseños over 40 nevertheless claim that the fiesta is no longer as good as it used to be, before it became so commercialized. In the 1950s and 1960s, the fiesta crowd was ethnically more "balanced" than it is today, meaning the proportion of Anglos and Hispanos was more equal, and more Taos Indians went. Today local Anglos disdain the event and rarely go, and none outside the civic clubs participate in any aspect of its organization. My observation of who has gone to the fiesta between the mid-1980s and the late 1990s indicates a light smattering of local Anglos and a rate of tourist attendance persistent but small in comparison to other seasonal festivals and events contrived to attract them. At best, only a handful of adults from Taos Pueblo go, fewer, it seems, every year.

The overwhelming proportion of people who go to the fiesta are local *raza* (colloquial term for *mexicanos*), most of whom range between the ages of 13 and 30, but they are always joined by substantial numbers of the middle-aged and elderly. Scores of *viejitos* (diminutive-affectionate term for the elderly) find a seat along the low wall or one of the benches inside the plaza. They sit there all day and listen to the music, survey the crowd, and visit with friends and relatives who drift by. Yet many no longer attend the fiesta. They say it is not what it used to be, that there is nothing worth going for. All there is to do, they point out, is walk around and around, or maybe sit down for a while. A typical refrain, repeated by those who go as well as those who do not, is that the fiesta *no tiene nada* (has nothing) or that *no hay nada* (there is nothing). As one woman, sitting nonetheless at a *fiestacita* dinner, put it, "*no me interesa* [doesn't interest me]." Indeed, nearly everyone disparages the fiesta. Critics typically comment on how it would be better, if only: the booths were not so tacky or run by outsiders, or the entertainment more traditional, or the parades bigger or more imaginative, and so on. One Taoseño, a good friend who never missed the fiesta himself, even scolded me for wasting my time on such a phony and trivial event.

So why, if the fiesta no tiene nada, do so many people go anyway, year after year? Some Taoseños who have moved away even schedule their trips home to coincide with the fiesta. In the following pages I will try to answer this question. My query seeks to illuminate why so many people, in spite of their perennial complaints, cannot manage to stay away. It aims to explain why the fiesta persists and what it means to those who celebrate it. After all, if the fiesta is really so worthless, why not just stop going and let it die out? Clearly, this did not happen in its almost 70-year history. On the contrary, over the decades the fiesta has not only survived its contrived, blatantly commercial beginnings, but has grown stronger and taken on effective meaning for a substantial portion of the local Hispano population. Any observer might conclude that the fiesta must fulfill some kind of collective need. Nor is this need economic, since the fiesta's value to local business has diminished as its popularity has grown.

THE TAOS PLAZA

Setha Low observes that the Iberian-Mesoamerican *zocalo* (public square) is "the most sacred and political of Mexican spaces" (1995:749). In Taos as elsewhere throughout Spanish America, the plaza "remains a contested terrain of cultural meaning, providing an example of how cultural meanings of the past are presented and represented in the built environment" (1995:759). My argument is that the Hispanization of the Taos fiesta was concurrent with the gentrification of the plaza, and that this was and is in fact a twin process. The fiesta is inextricably wed to the plaza and registers and responds to what has happened to it. It is a temporal event and creature of place. It stages a ritual interruption of the prevailing material and spatial reality. During fiesta the plaza becomes the transformed site of multiple social, symbolic, and political inversions. These center around the themes of dislocation, familial or ethnogendered identity, and the struggle between evanescent, nostalgic communitas on the one hand, and the powers of capital, the state, and even the church, on the other.

The Taos plaza is a thoroughly reconstructed, autoinscribed, postmodern tourist site. It is one of three major architectural structures in the area that are touristically "sanctified" in Dean MacCannell's sense (1976), the others being the endlessly photographed adobe Ranchos church and, of course, the even more famous multistoried north side of Taos Pueblo. The plaza has always been the epicenter of commerce and especially tourist activity in Taos, and its appearance and function have been shaped by the needs and dictates of tourism for over a century. But notwithstanding its gentrified, mall-like character, the plaza constitutes the historic and symbolic heart of town, and its murky origins are those of the town itself. Its exact age and original appearance are not known.

The present plaza acquired its modern, pseudo-adobe Pueblo-Revival appearance in the late 1930s, when the north, south, and west sides were rebuilt after a series of catastrophic fires. This period of reconstruction coincided with the town's incorporation and, significantly, the creation of the summer fiesta to promote tourism. Today the plaza area contains approximately 70 separate storefront businesses. In 1996 all but 25 of these were curio (including jewelry) shops. These "exceptions" included 11 art galleries, six T-shirt stores, six boutiques, three restaurants, a candy store, a photo store, a bank, a hotel, a bookstore, and an office. Interestingly, while the number of businesses has multiplied over the decades and their diversity dwindled, the number of properties and owners has remained fairly stable. In 1917, 15 parties owned buildings or property around the plaza, whereas 14 did in 1930, and 16 in 1996. Only three families continue to own plaza property since 1917, plus one other since 1930. The ethnic balance between Anglo and Hispanic owners has remained roughly equal. The plaza became a gentrified theme mall given over entirely to shops for tourists between 1960 and 1980. But as late as 1970 it still contained the courthouse and a variety of stores, and functioned as the business center for locals.

THE LIVING FIESTA

Until recently, the plaza was not roped off for booth construction until Friday afternoon or evening, and most concessions were set up and taken down at night. But by the early 1990s the setting-up phase expanded to an entire day, so that all of Friday is devoted to setting up. By sundown on Sunday the fiesta is over and the booths and merry-go-round are being taken down. Thus within the past decade, the entry phase into fiesta time and space has expanded to a full day and its exit phase has contracted to a couple of hours. The magic begins when the first strains of music blare over the loudspeaker on Friday afternoon.

The Queen's Coronation Mariachi Mass is held around six in the evening. The Friday mass rotates, theoretically, among the three neighboring parishes of Nuestra Senora de Guadalupe (in town), St. Francis (in Ranchos), and Holy Trinity (in Arroyo Seco). In fact, it seldom takes place in Taos because the town priest refuses to say mass for Santiago (July 24) or Santa Ana (July 25) on any other than their actual days, whereas his colleagues in the neighboring parishes are more willing to accommodate the fiesta council's insistence on Friday evening. This conflict between the town priest and the fiesta council will be returned to later.

The fiestas's religiosity is most apparent in the mass-coronation-procession complex that inaugurates the festivity. Mariachis accompany the procession and play for the mass. The Knights of Columbus attend in full regalia along with visiting officers of the Santa Fe fiesta council or even the Española or Las Vegas royal courts. Images of Santiago Matamoros, the patron saint of Spain, and Santa Ana, the Virgin Mary's mother, are displayed, and the royal entourage, joined by the mayor and other politicians, proceeds to the gazebo where the queen is introduced to the crowd and the opening ceremony takes place. The mariachis play for about an hour and later *bailes*, or dances, are held at local lounges. The queen, fiesta council, and mariachis make the rounds of these dances on Saturday night. They make a grand entry and lead the dancers in *La Marcha*. The queen and her court make appearances on the plaza throughout both days, on the bandstand, in both parades, and on the street. She is the premier ceremonial presence of the fiesta, its human and spiritual embodiment. She is guarded, watched, and treated like an honored guest wherever she goes. Indeed, the queen, who is and has always been Hispana, stands at the heart of the fiesta's meaning as a symbolic expression of personal, gendered, ethnic identity.

Live music and the merry-go-round—Tío Vivo—are the dual motors of fiesta time. Tío Vivo starts up around eight in the morning and runs continuously both days until evening, about two minutes per ride, with its own prerecorded music. Live music and dance continue for both days from 8:00 A.M. until night. The program of paid performers strive for a balance between Latin and other musics, local and outside talent, popular and "traditional" styles. Adults and older people come to the plaza to hear the music, children come to ride Tío Vivo, and everyone comes to eat, visit, and behold the queen.

The major daytime events during fiesta are the two parades, which include the "little," or children's, pet parade on Saturday morning, and the "big," or adult, Historical-Hysterical parade on Sunday afternoon. These days, the children's parade barely lasts ten minutes and seems over in the blink of an eye. Until 1990, both parades always went around the plaza. Today, only the children's parade even touches the plaza but no longer fully circles it. The big parade lasts about an hour and attracts a large crowd that lines its route through town. The order and content of the parade symbolically encode information about structure and power from micro- to macrosocial levels. This ceremonial march of individuals, horses, banners, and vehicles comprises a form of symbolic discourse which, like the queen complex, has perdured but changed over the decades, ripening like a fruit, waiting for some ethnographer to come along and decipher it. The big parade begins, ends, and is threaded throughout with representations of the local, state, and federal governments. It symbolically encapsulates New Mexico's interethnic political history and macrosocietal hegemonic order from gender to nation.

The fiesta crowd fluctuates in density and intensity throughout the two days. The crowd peaks right after the big parade on Sunday afternoon. Everyone flocks to the plaza to buy a cold drink, listen to the music, and take it all in during the fiesta's final and fullest hours. The fiesta reaches its high point at this stage, when the sidewalks, street, and the plaza are so crammed that one can but slowly swim through the crowd. Usually it is either sunny and hot or it rains, but in either case hundreds take shelter under the storefront portals. The crowd is typically very slow and very mellow. Three thousand people or more are squeezed into the plaza at this time. The prevailing mood seems easy, low-key and warm, even intimate. The crowd oozes along the portals and street and presses to a standstill at the center. It is virtually impossible to walk through the plaza without making physical contact with other bodies. People stand or sit facing the bandstand, some buoyed or lulled by the music, while children, caught up in more energetic pursuits, wriggle through the sea of bodies.

The fullness of the last hours is produced by the knowledge that soon it will all be over for another year. The council is so well organized that the cessation and cleanup of the fiesta occurs abruptly, starting promptly at 7:00 P.M. Around 6:30, the end of the fiesta is announced by the master of ceremonies. The mariachis play one last song, and then it is over. The end of the fiesta is stunning because it is so quick. It is doubtless the least-appreciated part of the entire proceedings, because it is inherently dysphoric, and most people leave soon after the music stops. A few children may linger, but a point comes before dark when there is virtually no one on the plaza who is not part of a small crew working diligently. By the fiesta's end, trash cans are overflowing and litter fills the street. It is all swept up and hauled away within two hours, while the booths, stage, and Tío Vivo are dismantled and removed. By 10:00 P.M. the plaza is open to traffic and back to normal. No one would ever guess how different it looked only hours before.

OTHER VOICES

During the 1994 fiesta, I conducted a small number of tape-recorded, on-the-street interviews. I asked people how they experience the fiesta, why they come, and if it has changed. The following are a few excerpts from longer texts elicited from several of these individuals, all of whom are native Hispanos.

Corine, in her fifties, grew up in town. She lived in Los Angeles for 15 years, came back in the late 1980s, and works as a waitress. All the years she was in California she came back to Taos for the last two weeks of July, and says she "never, never, never, never" misses the fiestas.

I love fiestas. I've always loved 'em. I can be in fiestas forever and ever. I just love it! 'Cause you get to see everybody that you haven't seen for a long, long time. I think it means where everybody gets together. And you get to see your friends. Family reunions. You get to eat your hamburgers, corn-on-the-cob. If I don't have a corn-on-the-cob and a hamburger for the fiestas to me it's not fiestas. And I love to go around the plaza. . . . Just get together with your friends and family. You see people you don't see anymore. Unless you go to Wal-Mart or Furrs, you don't get to see anybody. So you get to see everybody. That's what I like about fiestas.

She lists several ways in which fiestas have changed and ends on this note:

There's something else I would like to add to this. Before, the Indians would all get together and we'd all celebrate it with one thing here on the plaza. San Geronimo was celebrated at the pueblo, but Santa Ana and St. James was celebrated here in the plaza and Indians would participate in everything. And that is something else I would like to bring back. I really don't know why that changed, I'll never know. I guess I don't get involved too much with the fiesta council but that is one thing I would really like to find out. Why they don't participate like they did years before.

Esteban is a well-known man from Ranchos, in his late forties, who has lived in Taos most of his life. Every year he brings his family's popular Comanche dance troupe to perform for the fiesta and appear in the parade. Speaking in Spanish, he likens fiesta to Mexican radio stations, which years ago you could only get at night or for one hour a day on the local station. He continues (my translation):

But what I liked most about fiesta was the opportunity to get together with friends I've known for years and years. And to listen, and the reenactment, if not to say, to revive the culture . . . for me the fiesta has been a way to get together with friends and also slap the face of the stranger who came, the oppressor who came to oppress us, take away the base of our culture and steal the lands. [He] took away the economic base that was the lands, the forests. And gave us milk powder and food stamps and welfare, like they gave to the Indians, and then later they also wanted to take away the churches, and they took some *moradas* [lay chapter houses of the so-called Penitente brotherhood]; they took almost most of the saints, now they have them in museums. And so on. And now they are taking away our language, because the influx of English is so great that there are hardly any children, including my own, who know how to speak Spanish. Oh yes, they are *Chicanos de la raza*, but as soon as they say *la raza* they have to speak in English because they don't know Spanish, you see. But the fiesta gives a happiness, an energy, and it gives me the opportunity to bring the Comanches who dance, and to push some of the base of our culture.

Ana, a local schoolteacher in her forties, left Taos after high school but came back about ten years later to raise her sons. She recalls dressing up in fiesta skirts as a little girl and compares her memories with how it is now:

It wasn't as touristy, and if the tourists were there, they blended in, whereas a lot of the people who come in now don't blend in as well. And I guess the thing that stands out most was the Tío Vivo, because we always had to ride on that. Standing in the hot sun, and paying, I think it was a dime that we paid to get on it, and we always had to put our skirts over the horse, you know. It was just real neat back then. And nowadays we come, I guess, to see the entertainment, which is really something we didn't stick around for when we were little. Then we were just walking around. And now we sit down and listen like the old folks did back when we were small. I guess that's why I come back to see people that I grew up with and the familiar faces that come back. Sometimes it's a hassle, you say "I don't want to go," but once you're here it's nice. It's nice that we still have that and I hope it continues.

Asked if the fiestas have changed, she responds,

Yes, they have changed. I think that now a lot of people are selling things that we didn't
see back then. It is becoming very commercialized. And I think what's sad also is that
we don't have what we had back then was, for example, your dad's drugstore, and the
Walgreens and the familiar things around town. It almost feels like the plaza doesn't
belong to us anymore. And back then it did. I think that's why I feel sad about it. But
if we still keep on coming at least we're holding on to a little bit of culture and tradition
that we used to experience.

Rosemary, Ana's older sister, is also a schoolteacher. She links the theme of
feeling displaced with why she comes to the fiesta:

I keep coming back because I don't want to see what's happening take over. If we don't
teach our children what it's all about then they are going to establish their own and
that's not what fiestas are all about, I guess. Another thing I would like to see is the
three cultures more involved during fiestas than they are because the Indians come in,
and for sure the Spanish come in, but the white people just stay away. They want to live
in Taos, yet they don't want to mingle with them. Why is this? Are they a part of Taos
or not? Do we push them out because they don't want to blend in? What is happening?
I keep going back because it is just fun to see everybody again and eat, and eat, and eat
and eat. You just see people that move away, they come from all over, all over, that are
just scattered. It's nice to see the old people sitting around and enjoying *la resolana* [a
sheltered, sunny spot]. I just don't want it to ever stop.

CONTRARY VOICES

Merchants have grumbled for decades about the adverse effect of fiesta on
plaza business, apparent in my father's time but more extreme today for several
reasons. For one thing, the rows of booths block off the portals entirely. They
also cater to a completely different crowd than the stores, which was less the
case 25 years ago. The entertainment likewise draws locals rather than tourists.
Except for the few that sell food or liquor, plaza businesses are at best "under-
stimulated" by fiesta, and the T-shirt and souvenir shops get major competition.
Up to half of the merchants now close on Saturday, and perhaps two-thirds on
Sunday.

During the 1992 fiesta, I asked workers and managers in a number of plaza
stores what they thought of the event and how it affected business. Responses
ranged from open dislike of the fiesta to acknowledgment of its importance for
locals, but only one bartender said it helped business. Most reported either neu-
tral or negative impact on sales and mentioned the heightened danger of shop-
lifting. They routinely remove small items from the counters during fiesta. The
inconveniences they enumerated include being blocked off by booths and
crowds that spill food, track in mud, and ask for restrooms or a place to sit
down. One shop owner calls the fiesta a "security nightmare." She says that few

businesses can afford to close even one day a week, given the high rents on the plaza (she pays about $3,000 a month), and blames the town for failing to provide (permanent) public restrooms and for being generally indifferent to merchants' concerns. A few believe the fiesta should be relocated from the plaza to Kit Carson Park, which has more trees, grass, and open space.

The harshest business critique of the fiesta comes from the owner of seven businesses and one building on the plaza. His analysis is couched in stark economic terms. He points out that 80 percent of the booth vendors are from out of town. Collectively they must take in, he calculates, a minimum of between $30,000 and $50,000 during the three days of fiesta, yet the only money they spend in Taos is for their booth fee. They sleep in their campers, eat their own food, pay no taxes, and take their profits with them when they leave Sunday night. They impair the business opportunity of taxpaying local shop owners for three entire days during the peak tourist season of the year, yet they must pay no more than locals for booth space. He considers it "extortion" that the town charges plaza businesses the same fee to put up or to exclude booths in front of their own stores in order to compete with the itinerants. He disparages the fiesta as nothing more than "an open-air carnival," and claims that a "true fiesta," like the one in Old Town in Albuquerque, raises money for the church or the community itself.

This individual, interestingly enough, is a coyote (see note 3) whose Hispanic mother is a Taos native. He lives in Albuquerque but spent part of his boyhood in Taos. In the past, he has attempted to stop the construction of booths in front of his stores, complained to the town government, and tried to spur plaza merchants into greater activism. He has contemplated suing the town but finds the prospect too costly, and so contents himself with waiting for the catastrophe he predicts will one day occur, when the fiesta crowd will obstruct a timely crisis response. After years of frustrated effort, he says,

I finally decided, okay . . . we [he and other business owners] have got to start taking pictures of the fiesta to show the liability that the town is involved in 'cause if there is a major fire or injury or death the town is going to be liable for allowing the congestion that goes on there. . . . They have allowed the way the booths are set up, they have allowed the way the streets are blocked off, they have allowed the amount of people there. So the town of Taos is liable. So every taxpayer is liable for what could happen. Politicians in Taos aren't going to do much because of the vote. You know . . . you're getting predominantly Spanish people at the fiesta, they're predominantly who vote for the people who are in power, so that's why they're not going to rock the boat. Even though they know that they're sitting on a powder keg if something should happen, which could happen. They're not so much concerned with the businesses being affected, that doesn't bother them whatsoever.

The importation of vendors who hurt local merchants betrays, he believes, not merely governmental indifference to business interests, but actual hostility on the part of the fiesta council itself:

It shows, it's kind of telling the merchants of Taos, "Screw you, we don't need you, we don't like you, we're going to let someone in here and hurt your business." That's kind of the attitude of the fiesta council for allowing it.

This man further claims the fiesta is distasteful to tourists as well as irreligious and out of control:

And we have seen numerous tourists come and the minute they see what is going on, they turn right around and they leave town. They don't want to be involved in it what-soever. And I think it's got, why that is, is because of the carnival atmosphere where there is still alcohol involved. People are running around intoxicated to where they are using foul language. The problem is that it doesn't revolve around religion like the fiesta used to revolve around religion. You don't even see priests walking around the plaza. You don't see anybody with a religious figurehead being there. So what we have is actually an open-air carnival. With no restrictions whatsoever.

The other prominent figure whose public lack of sympathy for the fiesta has led to tense relations with the fiesta council is the town parish priest, who refuses to conduct a mass on Friday evening to inaugurate the fiesta. He will gladly perform mass on Sunday and on the actual saints' days, but not on Friday evening for the convenience of the council. This is why they must hold the queen's mass in more accommodating nearby parishes. In effect, this priest charges the fiesta council with profaning the liturgy for their own ends. He describes a situation out of control when he arrived in Taos in the early 1980s, involving public conduct he took measures to correct with the help of solicited directives from the archbishop of Santa Fe. Like the merchant quoted above, he starts out with the assumption of a more religious past, blames the booths, and expresses disgust at the "carnival atmosphere" the fiesta has degenerated to today:

I guess the church used to be a very big part of that [the town celebration of Santiago and Santa Ana], but in the early 1980s when I first came to Taos there was a big, I would say, misuse of the religious activities of the church, regarding the fiesta in relation to the use of the Eucharist and the use of a religious procession. At that time, the pastor back then was Father Smith, he came to the point where he did not even want to celebrate the mass because it was such a circus and the procession itself was even worse. Before the procession even got halfway through the plaza it would be consumed by all the people. Before, in the early days of the fiestas, the booths were not open until after mass. But in the early 1980s . . . the booths began to open . . . by twelve o'clock in the after-noon, 90 percent of them. And so I would say about eight years ago we had a talk with Archbishop Sánchez. . . . I met with him and we agreed that the situation was unaccept-able in regard to the use of religious practices simply because there was very little respect in terms of the procession, in terms of the Eucharist itself, the masses were not done right, . . . one time a group from Mexico, a mariachi group, youth group came, they just came and fit right in, they didn't even plan for them and we got to the point that priests from the outside were the only ones that would celebrate and after . . . they said they would not do it again because of the carnival atmosphere during the mass.

The fiesta council's expanding celebration of Santiago and Santa Ana, who are not even the parish's official patrons, became secular, the priest says, when it attached to a weekend instead of the true feast days. He is also quick to note that Taos Pueblo continues to celebrate, with its Corn Dances, the true feast days.

Needless to say, this priest's position does not please the fiesta council, who resent being forced out of their own parish in order to celebrate a mass for their own community fiesta. They are offended by the implication that their motives are anything other than genuinely religious. For them, it is a matter of accommodating to the needs of working people who must conform to the conventional five-day work week in order to earn a living. This marks a shift from agricultural time to industrial time. As one member put it, in the old days when people lived by farming, they could celebrate their saints' days in the middle of the week, but now in most cases it is impossible for regular wage earners to do this. The fact that they want to have a mass and procession on Friday evening attests not to crass opportunism, but rather to the depth of their religious sentiment and need. Some attribute the priest's attitude to the fact that he is Native American. But while his ethnicity may indeed dispose him more toward the Pueblos' feast day celebration, conflict between Catholic clergy and parishioners for control over local ritual expression is by no means unique to the Taos fiesta. It is a widespread and recurrent theme, as old as the history of New Mexico.

CONCLUSION

Themes that emerge from the fiesta as a text ring familiar to any reader of Bakhtin. They include struggle between "the people" and at least two of the three "political villains" of traditional society: the bourgeoisie, the empire, and the church (Clark and Holquist 1984:314). Fiesta-carnival involves reversal, much public eating, and the physical massing of many bodies pressed close together in the marketplace. With respect to the latter, Bakhtin writes,

The carnivalesque crowd in the marketplace or in the streets is not merely a crowd . . . but . . . outside of and contrary to all existing forms of the coercive socioeconomic and political organization, which is suspended for the time of festivity.

This festive organization of the crowd must be first of all concrete and sensual. Even the pressing throng, the physical contact of bodies, acquires a certain meaning. The individual feels that he is an indissoluble part of the collectivity, a member of the people's mass body. In this whole the individual body ceases to a certain extent to be itself; it is possible . . . to exchange bodies, to be renewed. . . . At the same time, the people become aware of their sensual, material bodily unity and community. [1984:255]

Reversal inheres in the occupation and use of the marketplace for three whole days of public merriment while plaza merchants languish. To the horror of the priest, the crowd even swallows the procession, defiling its official religiosity. But while the struggle between the fiesta and merchants or between the council and the church are perfectly clear, the struggle against empire seems less obvious. It may instead be that fiesta involves a certain alignment with empire or in this case with nation-state, spelled out above all in the parade.[5] Notwithstanding the impoverishment or tameness of modern and postmodern festival compared to Rabelaisian carnival, or of a small fiesta to Brazilian carnival, the same subversive, regenerative impulses toward communitas and reversal are present. Yet the hands of patriarchy, capital, and the state mold the entire event and leave their indelible imprint on all designations of identity. The suffusion of the queen complex with religiosity represents not merely a colonial legacy but an attempt, orchestrated by an emergent and insecure middle class, to sacralize an ethnic boundary.

A final question is not whether the fiesta's religiosity is genuine or spurious, but why people would fret about this at all. The fiesta's greatest moral vulnerability is its "authenticity," which is more or less synonymous with its religiosity. Whereas the fiesta's critics as well as most sympathizers believe its origin and past to be more religious than its degenerate present, in reality the event was invented for the explicit purpose of promoting business on the plaza. If anything, its religiosity has *increased* over the years, if this is to be measured by the accretion of Spanish Catholic imagery to fiesta doings. Although virtually everyone considers today's fiesta "more commercial," it has also grown, in an oddly covert manner, increasingly anti-tourist and anti-merchant. This transformation into the functional opposite of its original purpose occurred as the plaza became gentrified and the Anglo (or non-Hispanic white) proportion of the population went from six percent in 1970 to 28 percent in 1990.

The fiesta is a symbolic *and* literal occupation-seizure of the central public architectural space of Taos by thousands of members of a self-identified ethnic community. By simultaneously "handing over" the plaza to outside vendors, they are subjecting the downtown merchants to an experience of displacement and loss for the benefit of transients. In one sense, there is nothing subtle about what is going on here. But in another sense, what is going on seems extremely oblique, veiled, convoluted, and complex. No council member would ever voice so negative or deliberate a motive for the fiesta. On the contrary, for them it is a positive effort made in good faith for the benefit of the community and the promotion of "traditional cultural-religious values." It is significant that the fiesta council seeks always to enhance the religiosity, legitimacy, and moral import of the fiesta, through an elaboration of the mass, procession, hagiography, and queen complex as key features of the event.[6] The fiesta amounts to a profoundly conservative, even accommodationist, form of resistance. Its dramatic reclamation of the plaza affirms the reign of tourism by agreeing to interrupt it but once a year. It enacts collective and individual ethnic identities and stages a moment of communitas, by transforming the contested public space to which it intrinsically is bound. The power, genius, and irony of fiesta lie in the fact that it simultaneously undermines the status quo it reinforces.

NOTES

Earlier versions of this article were presented at the 1996 annual meetings of the American Studies Association and the American Anthropological Association. It was also presented at the University of New Mexico (Snead-Wertheim Lecture) and at the Conference on Holidays, Ritual, Festival, Celebration, and Public Display at Bowling Green State University in 1997. The research upon which this study is based has been funded over several years by grants from the Rockefeller Foundation, New Mexico Endowment for the Humanities, and the Center for Regional Studies; the College of Arts and Sciences; and the Snead-Wertheim Lectureship, all at the University of New Mexico.

1. In Stoeltje's model, ritual *form* refers to the discrete and repeated event in question, which exhibits the generic features she and other folklorists have identified, which themselves broadly conform to cross-culturally observable patterns that change and vary through time (see Stoeltje 1983). *Discourse*, as a key locus of power in Foucault's sense (1986).

includes not only the language of ritual performance itself, but the language used by the producers of it in texts they produce, such as the program, or in the texts they provide for newspapers and television. However, the discourse is also widely disseminated through the oral tradition which surrounds any ritual event, ancient or modern.... [Production] refers to the organization or forces, energies, and materials that constitute the actual production of the event.... Not only is it performance itself that generates power, but those who are generally behind the scenes making decisions about the way that form and performance will converge are exercising power over the performers. They control the access to the performance of ritual, whether it be sacred or secular, and they exercise a degree of control over form. [Stoeltje 1993:141, 143]

2. This refers to the structural features of New Mexico Spanish colonial society, in which Europeans subjugated Pueblo and other Indian peoples using force, discourse, and practices that enforced hierarchy and gender, boundary maintenance, and separation, all supported by notions of purity. This ideology was contradicted by the overwhelming fact of universal miscegenation, which the colonial apparatus attempted, ultimately in vain, to control. The postcolonial, fleetingly Mexican, legacy of Reconquest New Mexico was compounded in the 19th century by a new ethnoracial order imposed with Americanization. This history of successive conquest established the structures of inequality that still constitute the sociopolitical order of late-20th-century touristic, postnuclear New Mexico. Taos society registers this legacy in microcosmic form, while the town fiesta encodes the multiple local struggles which ensue from it.

3. In contemporary New Mexico, the term *coyote* represents a vestige of the colonial *casta* system, which categorized and ranked all possible ethnic types and combinations. Today the term refers to a "half-breed" mix, usually between Hispano-Mexicano and Anglo, but sometimes to Indian-Hispano or even, from the Hispano vantage, an Indian-Anglo hybrid.

4. The Historical-Hysterical parade is meant to incorporate both historical and satirical themes. It was originally inspired by the Santa Fe version, today known by the same name, which came into being in [the] 1920s as part of the "counter fiesta," as Chris

Wilson (1997) calls it. The Santa Fe fiesta was "revived" or invented in 1919 by a group of boosters much as the Taos fiesta came into being over two decades later, although the two histories show important contrasts as well as parallels. According to Wilson, the counter fiesta expressed a bohemian reaction against a more militaristic tone imposed by an earlier generation of Anglo orchestrators. It introduced the *Pasatiempo*, or "grand carnival," that included the Hysterical Pageant, a queen contest, and immolation of the giant effigy Zozobra (see Wilson 1997:208–224). The Taos fiesta, which never included anything quite like Zozobra, nevertheless came into being more or less modeled on the counter fiesta format.

5. In their discussion of festival as an enactment of modernity, Stoeltje and Bauman (1983) propose an interesting alternative to the tendency among scholars to view the symbolic presence of state and national governments in local parades as a manifestation of dominant, centralizing forces imposed from above and outside. The folkloristic perspective, they suggest, instead places emphasis on the viewpoint of the local festival community, which experiences itself as central and active rather than peripheral and acted upon within the larger national or global structure (1983:169–170). I suggest that both perspectives are important to understanding the tension between the local and the "imperial," which inheres in parade discourse and practice through time.

6. Recent manifestations of the fiesta council's ongoing campaign to sacralize fiesta include their commission in 1996 of a *bulto*, or statue, of Santiago, or Saint James the Apostle (his peaceful rather than his alternative martial embodiment as Matamoros, or Moor-killer, the patron saint of Spain) by a local *santero*, or woodcarver of saints' images. The bulto, which cost $2,000, is carved from a cedar trunk and stands over five feet tall. This official icon accompanies the council in their formal photographs and rides on their float in the parade. A companion bulto of Santa Ana with Mary was acquired in 1997, and a novena, or nine-day prayer recitation, was also observed for the first time by the queen's royal court.

REFERENCES

Abrahams, Roger. 1983. Shouting Match at the Border: The Folklore of Display Events. In *"And Other Neighborly Names": Social Process and Cultural Image in Texas Folklore*, eds. Richard Bauman and Américo Paredes, pp. 303–321. Austin: University of Texas Press.

Abu-Lughod, Lila. 1991. Writing Against Culture. In *Recapturing Anthropology*, ed. Richard Fox, pp. 137–162. Santa Fe, N.M.: School of American Research Press.

Bakhtin, Mikhail. 1984. *Rabelais and His World*. Bloomington: Indiana University Press.

Brandes, Stanley. 1988. *Power and Persuasion: Fiesta and Social Control in Rural Mexico*. Philadelphia: University of Pennsylvania Press.

Briggs, Charles. 1996. The Politics of Discursive Authority in Research on the "Invention of Tradition." *Cultural Anthropology* 11:435–469.

Clark, Katerina, and Michael Holquist, eds. 1984. *Mikhail Bakhtin*. Cambridge, Mass.: Harvard University Press.

Cohen, Colleen Ballerino, Richard Wilk, and Beverly Stoeltje, eds. 1996. *Beauty Queens on the Global Stage*. New York: Routledge.

Da Matta, Roberto. 1984. Carnival In Multiple Planes. In *Rite, Drama, Festival, Spec-*

tacle, ed. John MacAloon, pp. 209–240. Philadelphia: Institute for the Study of Human Issues, Inc.

Davis, Susan G. 1986. *Parades and Power: Street Theater in Nineteenth-Century Philadelphia*. Philadelphia: Temple University Press.

Foucault, Michel. 1986. Disciplinary Power and Subjection. In *Power*, ed. Stevens Lukes, pp. 229–242. Oxford, England: Basil Blackwell.

Grimes, Ronald. 1976. *Symbol and Conquest: Public Ritual and Drama in Santa Fe*. Ithaca, N.Y.: Cornell University Press.

———. 1982. The Lifeblood of Public Ritual: Fiestas and Public Exploration Projects. In *Celebration: Studies in Festivity and Ritual*, ed. Victor Turner, pp. 272–283. Washington, D.C.: Smithsonian Institution Press.

Gutiérrez, Ramon. 1991. *When Jesus Came the Corn Mothers Went Away*. Palo Alto, Calif.: Stanford University Press.

Haraway, Donna. 1988. Situated knowledges: The Science Question in Feminism and the Privilege of Partial Perspective. *Feminist Studies* 14:575–599.

Low, Setha, 1995. Indigenous Architecture and the Spanish American Plaza in Mesoamerica and the Caribbean. *American Anthropologist* 97:749–762.

MacCannell, Dean. 1976. *The Tourist: A New Theory of the Leisure Class*. New York: Schocken.

Narayan, Kirin. 1993. How Native Is a "Native" Anthropologist? *American Anthropologist* 95:671–686.

Pierce, Donna. 1985. *Vivan Las Fiestas!* Santa Fe: Museum of New Mexico Press.

Rodríguez, Sylvia. 1997. The Taos Fiesta: Invented Tradition and the Infrapolitics of Symbolic Reclamation. *Journal of the Southwest* 30:33–57.

Scott, James. 1990. *Domination and the Arts of Resistance*. New Haven, Conn.: Yale University Press.

Stoeltje, Beverly. 1983. Festival in America. In *Handbook of American Folklore*, ed. Richard M. Dorson, pp. 238–246. Bloomington: Indiana University Press.

———. 1993. Power and the Ritual Genres: American Rodeo. *Western Folklore* 52:135–156.

Stoeltje, Beverly, and Richard Bauman. 1989. Community Festival and the Enactment of Modernity. In *The Old Traditional Way of Life: Essays in Honor of W. E. Roberts*, ed. Robert E. Walls and George H. Shoemaker, pp. 159–171. Bloomington, Ind.: Trickster Press.

Turner, Victor. 1974. *Drama, Fields, and Metaphors: Symbolic Action in Human Society*. Ithaca, N.Y.: Cornell University Press.

Wilson, Chris. 1997. *The Myth of Santa Fe*. Albuquerque: University of New Mexico Press.

Appendix

NATIVE SEEDS/SEARCH

Native Seeds/SEARCH NS/S works to conserve the traditional crops, seeds, and farming methods that have sustained native peoples throughout the southwestern U.S. and northern Mexico. We promote the use of these ancient crops and their wild relatives by gathering, safeguarding, and distributing their seeds, while sharing benefits with traditional communities. We also work to preserve knowledge about their uses. Through research, training, and community education, NS/S works to protect biodiversity and to celebrate cultural diversity.

Native Seeds/SEARCH was founded in 1983 as a result of requests from Native Americans on the Tohono O'odham reservation near Tucson who wished to grow traditional crops but could not locate seeds. We are now a leader in the heirloom seed movement, with more than 1,800 collections in our seedband. We specialize in both domesticated varieties—such as corn, beans, squash, melons, gourds, chiles—and wild crops, including chiltepines, desert greens, and teosinte, the wild "mother of corn."

You can become involved in our efforts by joining Native Seeds/SEARCH. Members receive our quarterly newsletter, "The Seedhead News." Each issue contains gardening tips, recipes, previews of workshops and other special events, book reviews, and feature articles on Native American farmers and crops. Members receive a 10 percent discount on purchases and workshops and reduced admission to special events.

Visit our Web Site to learn more about NS/S and to join!

http://www.nativeseeds.org

email: nss@azstarnet.com

ARIZONA STATE MUSEUM

For 107 years, Arizona State Museum (ASM) has been an incomparable resource for exploration of the cultural heritage of the American Southwest and northern Mexico. Founded as a territorial museum by the state legislature in 1893, ASM was part of the original Territorial University, now University of Arizona. ASM is the oldest and largest anthropological museum in the region. It seeks to enrich the present and connect decisions for the future with an understanding of the past. ASM's rich holdings, leading research, innovative programs, and exhibits engage and educate lifelong learners of all ages and backgrounds. The museum brings to life the prehistoric and historic lifeways of indigenous peoples of the desert Southwest—from the very first mammoth hunters to the urban transformations reshaping the borderlands today. Research on ASM's collections has shaped the very foundation of our understanding of life in the unique and arid environment of this region.

ASM scholars are among the leaders in their field. They serve as the state's experts; their counsel is sought on subjects from archaeology to public policy issues. ASM was the first, and remains the only, anthropology museum in the region with a conservation lab. The museum houses a library of nearly 60,000 volumes on the Southwest. The museum archive houses the field notes, maps, and documents resulting from some of the most important excavations in the region. ASM's photographic collection holds more than 225,000 prints and negatives. ASM's Southwest Indian pottery collection of 20,000 whole-vessels reflecting almost every culture in the region is, perhaps, the most significant of its kind and is an official project of Save America's Treasures, a national initiative to celebrate and preserve our nation's cultural legacy. ASM holds permitting authority for all archaeology on public lands and is the repository for objects resulting from these projects.

The museum holds objects of material culture in trust for tribal communities throughout the region. ASM's American Indian Internship Program involves students directly with the collections providing valuable hands-on experience. Native artists are shown regularly in the contemporary gallery. Artists and craftsmen show and sell their work in the museum store, Native Goods, and annually at the museum's most popular event, the Southwest Indian Art Fair.

You can become a member of Arizona State Museum and learn more about the museum, its programs, exhibits, and special events. Membership begins at $5 for Junior Archaeologists (Under 10 years old!) going to $30/50 for individuals/families. Membership levels continue at $100, $250, $500, and $1,000, all with a range of benefits. Checks to UAF/ASM may be sent to Arizona State Museum Marketing Office, PO Box 210016, Tucson AZ 85721. For more information call 520–626–8381 or email darlene@al. arizona.edu. See more of the museum at our web site: www.statemuseum.arizona.edu.

Index

About the Contributors

NATHAN ALLEN was a member of the Akimel and Tohono O'odham tribes of Southern Arizona. He attended Central Arizona College and the University of Arizona. He served the O'odham on various tribal boards and committees. He was serving on the Governor's Archaeology Advisory Commission at the time of his death. Because he was brought up in a traditional way, he assisted other O'odham in their search for a place in both worlds. Mr. Allen was a published poet and writer. His works have been published in journals for Native American Studies across the country and in various magazines in the state of Arizona.

KURT F. ANSCHUETZ is an archaeologist and anthropologist. He serves as the Program Director of the Rio Grande Foundation for Communities and Cultural Landscapes in Santa Fe, New Mexico. Foundation projects include work with contemporary Pueblo people in the northern Rio Grande Valley in identifying, documenting, and interpreting the field work of their late pre-Columbian and early Historic period ancestors. Dr. Anschuetz also consults with the Bureau of Indian Affairs and the Department of Justice to prepare archaeological testimony for use in water adjudication cases on behalf of various Pueblo communities. Throughout both his Foundation and consulting work, Dr. Anschuetz has shared valuable insights with the Pueblo people about their traditional farming practices, and they have provided Dr. Anschuetz with opportunities to conduct research at archaeological field complexes that otherwise are not accessible to noncommunity members.

ROGER ANYON is employed by Pima County, Tucson, Arizona. During the past two decades he has worked on various cultural resources projects with a number of southwestern tribes, including the Zuni, Hopi, Taos, and Hualapai. Between 1985 and 1996, he was the Director of the Pueblo of Zuni Archaeology Program and Zuni Heritage and Historic Preservation Office. Mr. Anyon is presently a member of the Smithsonian Institution Native American Repatriation Review Committee. Between 1992 and 1995 he served on the Society for American Archaeology Executive Committee. He has participated in archaeological research projects in the southwestern United States, Italy, and England. He is author of a number of books and peer reviewed articles.

DAVID BRUGGE is a retired anthropologist living in Albuquerque, New Mexico. His principal employers have included the Unitarian Service Committee, the Navajo Nation, and the National Park Service. Major publications are *Navajos in the Catholic Church Records, 1694–1875; Navajo Bibliography with Subject Index* (with J. Lee Correll and Editha L. Watson); *A History of the Chaco Navajos; Tsegais: An Archeological Ethnohistory of the Chaco Region; Navajo Religion and Culture: Selected Views, Papers in Honor of Leland C. Wyman* (ed. with Charlotte J. Frisbie); and *The Navajo Hopi Land Dispute: An American Tragedy.*

ADRIAN BUSTAMANTE is Associate Professor of Southwest Studies at Ft. Lewis College, Durango, Colorado. He received his Ph.D. in American Studies from the University of New Mexico. The title of his dissertation is "Los Hispanos: Ethnicity and Social Change in New Mexico." His primary research interests are the cultures of the Southwest with a focus on the Spanish/Mexican culture.

T. J. FERGUSON works for Heritage Resources Management Consultants in Tucson, Arizona. He earned a Masters of Community and Regional Planning and a Ph.D. in Anthropology at the University of New Mexico. For the past 25 years, Dr. Ferguson has conducted research on southwestern archaeology, history, and land use, focusing on the western pueblos.

PAUL FISH is curator of Archaeology and Professor of Anthropology at the Arizona State Museum, University of Arizona. He received his Ph.D. in Anthropology from Arizona State University in 1976. His research interests include settlement patterns and emerging political complexity in southwestern United States, northern Mexico and coastal Brazil.

SUZANNE K. FISH is Associate Curator of Archaeology and Associate Professor of Anthropology at the University of Arizona. Her research interests include ethnobotany, traditional agriculture, political configurations of middle range societies, and southwestern United States and Mexico.

ANGELO JOAQUIN, JR. was formerly the Executive Director of Native Seeds/ SEARCH in Tucson, Arizona. He is also a member of the Tohono O'odham Indian Nation. He grew up in Florence, Arizona, and he credits his father for giving him the understanding, respect, and appreciation for his Indian ancestry early on in his life when he used to accompany his father on his trips throughout the reservation to play O'odham social dance music. Mr. Joaquin is dedicated to working with native growers. Seeds represent a connection to the past and Indian ethnicity as well as an important tool for conservation and the health and wellness of his people.

FRANCES LEVINE is the Division Head of Arts and Sciences at Santa Fe Community College in Santa Fe, New Mexico, where she teaches classes in New Mexico history and the ethnohistory of the Pueblo and Hispanic communities of the Southwest. She holds a doctorate in anthropology from Southern Methodist University. Her doctoral research examined historic settlement and land use on three Pecos River land grants in New Mexico. She has served as an expert witness in land and water use adjudications, testifying on behalf of the State of New Mexico and numerous *acequia* commissions. She has been a consultant to Pueblo communities on studies relating to traditional use lands.

SYLVIA RODRÍGUEZ is an associate professor in the Department of Anthropology at the University of New Mexico. Her research interests focus on interethnic relations in the United States-Mexico borderlands, particularly the Upper Rio Grande Valley of New Mexico. She has published articles on ethnic relations and tourism, land and water issues, and ritual expressions of identity. Her book, the *Matachines Dance: Ritual Symbolism and Interethnic Relations in the Upper Rio Grande Valley*, won the 1997 Chicago Folklore Prize.

MARIANNE L. STOLLER is Professor of Anthropology (retired) Colorado College. She has written extensively about Mexican land grants, water rights, and Pueblo-Hispanic-Anglo relationships. She is a past President of the American Society for Ethnohistory and her research combines the keen insights of history with the cross-cultural approach of anthropology.

MARIA VARELA is a rural planner and community organizer who, since 1963, has worked with African American, Mexican American and Native American rural communities committed to creating or recreating sustainable economies. In 1990, Varela was awarded a MacArthur Foundation Fellowship for her life's work including the founding of Ganados del Valle and Tierra Wools in the remote mountains of northern New Mexico. Ms. Varela is on the faculty at the Community and Regional Planning Department in the School of Architecture and Planning at the University of New Mexico. She is co-author of *Rural Environmental Planning for Sustainable Communities* published in 1992 by Island Press. In 1997–98 Varela was awarded the Hulbert Endowed Chair of the Southwestern Studies Department at Colorado College and continues there as adjunct professor. Currently Ms. Varela is the owner of The Rural Resources Group which works primarily with Western communities and tribal nations desiring to preserve cultures, environments, and family agriculture.

LAURIE WEINSTEIN is Professor of Anthropology at Western Connecticut State University. She has written numerous books, anthologies, and articles about Native Americans, particularly in New England, and women and the military. She directs the archaeology program at Western Connecticut State University where she also co-directs Women's Studies.